Chekhov Criticism

CHEKHOV CRITICISM

1880 Through 1986

by
Charles W. Meister

McFarland & Company, Inc., Publishers
Jefferson, North Carolina, and London

Frontispiece: Anton Chekhov in 1894

British Library Cataloguing-in-Publication data available.

Library of Congress Cataloguing-in-Publication Data

Meister, Charles W., 1917–
  Chekhov criticism, 1880 through 1986.

  Bibliography: p. 331.
  Includes index.
  1. Chekhov, Anton Pavlovich, 1860–1904–Criticism and
interpretation. 2. Chekhov, Anton Pavlovich, 1860–
1904–Plots. I. Title.
PG3458.M36 1988   891.72′3   88-42508

ISBN 0-89950-355-1 (lib. bdg.; 50# acid-free natural paper)

Printed in the United States of America.

McFarland Box 611 Jefferson NC 28640

This book is dedicated to
my daughter Marilyn and
my son Charles John

Table of Contents

Preface

Why another book on Anton Chekhov and his works? First, because the writings of Chekhov can serve admirably as a cultural bridge between the United States and the Soviet Union. While the world applauds the reduction in tension between the superpowers, the humane values of the humble Russian doctor are prized on both sides of the Iron Curtain. Chekhov fought for freedom, intelligence, justice, and kindness – precisely those qualities most needed in the modern world.

Furthermore, Chekhov is one of the great humanitarians in recent times. As a doctor, he treated peasants free of charge. He volunteered to serve during famines and cholera epidemics. He traveled laboriously across the continent to the penal colony at Sakhalin, with the intent of improving treatment of prisoners. He built schools at his own expense, and served without pay as a school inspector. He raised funds for medical clinics and libraries. Everywhere he lived he planted trees, saying that his goal was to make of Russia one big garden. Anti-Semitism was one of the targets of his talented pen. He always found time to help struggling authors with their manuscripts.

Modern drama is inconceivable without the plays of Chekhov. His technical innovations in theatrical art are the most profound contributions since Shakespeare. He introduced the concept of the centrifugal plot, one in which the focus of attention is not so much on the events and how they shape the lives of the characters as it is upon the world in which both players and spectators live, demonstrating the salient importance of small choices made in seemingly everyday life. Chekhov's plays, like life, have no heroes or villains, but simply people like us, with some good points and some bad. In language he introduced disconnected dialogue, in which people fail to respond meaningfully to each other's discourse, being lost in absorption with their own concerns. Chekhov's settings evoke such a strong sense of individual identity that many critics call the effect "atmospheric," meaning total rendition of the site and time.

In the field of fiction, Chekhov stands as the last great figure in the Golden Age of Russian literature that started with Pushkin. Although he did little in the genre of the novel, his short stories are universally ranked among the finest ever written. A realist, Chekhov nevertheless managed to evoke deep emotion by a careful handling of his characters and their values. He erases himself as narrator, and lets the story unfold in a natural sequence. Often his real plot is the "buried life" of a sensitive person too shy to achieve the recognition his character merits. His nature descriptions, though vivid, are organic to the overall effect. Many of his stories plead subtly for a more humane world.

What can this book contribute to Chekhov scholarship? Chekhov's dramatic technique was so innovative that at first it was badly misunderstood, as can be seen in the attacks by early critics. As perceptive readers clearly demonstrated the rich values of the new dramaturgy, Chekhov's plays came to be highly praised and soon they were influencing dramatists throughout the Western world. This study of the changing reaction to his plays shows on the one hand the radical change from opprobrium to approval, and on the other hand the evolution in critical taste towards drama during the twentieth century.

In short fiction, critics marveled at the profound effects Chekhov achieved with apparently simple language and plots. Various critics attempted to explain this paradox, as recorded in this book. Slowly a consensus evolved to account for Chekhov's fictional art. Most great short story writers of this century are familiar with Chekhov's tales, and many have praised his technique or tried to incorporate aspects of it into their own styles.

Because of the uniqueness of Chekhov's writing, critics played a crucial role in getting his work read, understood, and appreciated. This book tells the story of Chekhov's critical acceptance in England, Russia, and the United States, from the early days in 1880 through 1986. Also included are views of European and Asian critics.

There have been anthologies of Chekhov criticism, as well as critical books on Chekhov and his technique, but this is the first comprehensive historical summary of the highlights of Chekhov criticism.

A lifelong student of Russian culture, I wrote a Ph.D. dissertation at the University of Chicago in 1948 entitled *English and American Criticism of Chekhov.* Since that time there have been many more dissertations on Chekhov, many of which I have read. I have also done considerable recent research on Chekhov, partly for my *Chekhov Bibliography* (McFarland, 1985). I have written a number of critical articles and reviews on Chekhov for scholarly publications. I have also taught courses on Chekhov and Russian literature at several American universities.

No one work ever is truly exhaustive. Much of my research was in the *New York Times* and the *Times* (London) and their indexes. It is my sincere hope that not much crucial criticism of Chekhov has been missed.

As usual, I am indebted to my wife Eleanor, who has been my research colleague and the prime proofreader of this book.

1. Chekhov in World Literature

Human survival in the twenty-first century may well depend upon the ability of the two great superpowers to avoid a nuclear war. The potential, growing daily, exists for mankind to be exterminated unless peace can prevail between the United States and the Soviet Union. Humanists, whether secular or religious, must search for common ground, for bonds of unity between these nations.

Fortunately there looms in the field of literature the ever growing stature of a person admirably suited to be such a cultural bridge. The modest Russian physician Anton Chekhov, who wrote short stories and plays, is respected not only in Russia and America but in every quarter of the globe. After an initial period of perplexity, critics in every nation have grown to appreciate Chekhov's stories as among the greatest ever written, and his plays as important innovations in sophisticated dramatic technique. As his literary works became understood and admired, the esteem for Chekhov as a person has evolved similarly.

Crucial to the whole upsurgence of interest in Chekhov and his writings are the values revealed in his stories and plays. In a letter in 1889 he wrote that "my holy of holies is the human body, health, intelligence, talent, inspiration, love, and the most absolute freedom—freedom from violence and lying, whatever forms they may take."[1] Capable of serving as the framework of a universal ethos are Chekhov's values—freedom, honesty, human dignity, simplicity, sincerity, and the sanctity of human personality. Leo Tolstoy called Chekhov "an incomparable artist, an artist of life. And the worth of his creations consists of this—he is understood and accepted not only by every Russian but by all humanity."[2]

Vladimir Nabokov said that Chekhov enjoyed depicting the intelligentsia of his period. Even though they were ineffectual, Nobokov says, "the mere fact of such men, full of fervor, pureness of spirit and moral elevation, having lived and probably still living somewhere somehow in the Russia of today is a promise of better things to come for the world at large—for the most admirable law of Nature is the survival of the weakest. The person who prefers Dostoevsky or Gorky to Chekhov will never be able to grasp the essentials of Russian literature and Russian life, and, which is far more important, the essentials of universal literary art. I heartily recommend taking as often as possible Chekhov's books and dreaming through them as they are intended to be dreamed through."[3]

1

In accounting for Chekhov's rapid spread of fame to places like America, England, Germany, and Scandinavia, Marc Slonim said that Chekhov "transcends the limitations of his period. Like all great writers, Chekhov reveals the hidden springs of our action and gives us an original interpretation of human behavior."[4]

The Short Story Writer

Since Chekhov strove valiantly to avoid artificiality and insincerity, early critics deplored his lack of traditional plot structure. He often shuns orthodox beginnings and endings, choosing to focus on one quintessential action, when all that a character stands for is revealed. Life was his esthetic norm, and thus he uses real-life unity, probability, and structure or form. He avoids the "well-made" plot that moves towards a climax, since life too moves on invisible feet. His real plot is the "buried life" of one who is often too shy to star in a trumped-up melodrama.

Plot is de-emphasized at the expense of character. Chekhov had a deep, intuitive understanding of human nature. His characters are almost always interesting and are sometimes unusual. Finding no heroes or villains in life, he gives us none in his stories. But in a stroke we are instantly at home with his characters, for they live on our block. Chekhov shows deep compassion for his people, especially if they are underdogs or undervalued persons. The dramatic force of his stories generally grows out of his use of character contrasts.

Chekhov's stories are provocative. They impel the reader to think, or more often to feel, in a new and sometimes oblique direction. His general theme is human inhumanity to fellow humans. In his stories the "enemies" are hypocrisy and the misuse of power, and the "heroes" are gentleness, forgiveness, simplicity, understanding, and work.

Chekhov's language is simple and unadorned, but exceedingly accurate and precise. His language never violates the texture of his thought. Extreme accuracy and economy of diction give his stories a lyrical effect. His characters speak in natural dialogue. He rarely employs puns, symbols, or double entendres.

Chekhov's nature descriptions, like Turgenev's, are organic to his overall purpose. Some settings are so vivid as to evoke an atmospheric effect. Again, economy prevails, and there is no description for its own sake, as one might find in Scott.

Along with Maupassant, Chekhov deserves credit for helping contribute to the evolution of the form of the modern short story. In Chekhov's hands the genre gained status as a high achievement of literary art. "The perfection, the finish of his stories, their combination of simplicity and complexity, the graceful artistry of all his work, its economy of means enlivened by the lyrical movement of his style, all acted upon Russian literature as a new stimulant. 'After Chekhov it is impossible to write carelessly.' This was a slogan for many pre–Revolutionary writers. Chekhov initiated a new phase of realism. Between 1900 and 1917 not only Gorky and Korolenko but a large number of writers of the young generation, such as Leonid

Andreyev, Ivan Bunin, Alexander Kuprin, Boris Zaitsev, and others, joined what was then called the Chekhovian Trend."[5]

Following World War I Chekhov's reputation spread rapidly throughout the Western world. British writers of fiction influenced by him include Elizabeth Bowen, A.E. Coppard, E.M. Forster, James Joyce, Katherine Mansfield, Sean O'Faolain, and Virginia Woolf. A particular Chekhov disciple was Mansfield, who not only praised his work but emulated his style. Points of likeness between them include use of atmosphere, creation of daydreams to reveal a character's thoughts and feelings, themes depicting "the life of the soul," and a grimly realistic outlook often portraying the frustration of the characters.

American fiction writers showing an influence from Chekhov include Conrad Aiken, James T. Farrell, Ellen Glasgow, Ernest Hemingway, Flannery O'Connor, Dorothy Parker, Katherine Anne Porter, and Eudora Welty. Clarence Gohdes observed that Chekhov held a position in Russian literature corresponding to the combined contributions of Hawthorne and Poe in the American short story.[6] Calling Chekhov "the greatest short-story writer who ever lived," Farrell designated him "a part of the great tradition of world literature" without whose presence the world would have been spiritually poorer. Farrell recommended that young writers study Chekhov's stories, since he was "one of the greatest single literary influences" upon the form and the content of the short story in America, England, and Ireland.[7]

The Dramatist

In what was probably the greatest piece of criticism of Chekhov's drama ever penned, English dramatist George Calderon in 1912 accounted for the peculiar but penetrating effect of Chekhov's plays.[8] Chekhov, said Calderon, used centrifugal plots, in which attention is directed not inward, toward what happens to the characters, but "outward to the larger process of the world which those events illuminate." The emotions aroused are not so much hope and fear for the characters as "pity and amusement at the importance which they set on them, and consolation for their particular tragedies in the general comedy of life in which they are merged." Had they known this, generations of critics could have saved themselves much anguish bemoaning "lack of plot action" or "apathy" in the characters.

Chekhov observed, said Calderon, that people play varying roles in the different groups of which they are members. If a character seems inconsistent, therefore, he may be appearing in a new social group. Moreover, people are carried along by group emotions, which may be different from the private emotions of each group member. Chekhov developed a method of conveying group emotions through atmospheric effects.

Calderon noted that one of Chekhov's great innovations was disconnected dialogue—people seem not to be replying to one another. This lifelike dialogue provides a number of functions: it reveals character, it shows life's isolation and irony, it can be comic, and it helps create the atmosphere of group emotions. In addition, the stage may contain two or three small discussion circles at one time, and dialogue which seems disconnected may simply be faithfully interlacing strands from each circle.

The alert spectator, Calderon cautioned, should differentiate between action dialogue and atmosphere dialogue. In *The Sea Gull*, for example, the first two acts are primarily atmospheric, and the final two acts chiefly action oriented. In *The Cherry Orchard* action-lines and atmosphere-lines alternate repeatedly. Although at first this may be somewhat hard to follow, the result is to produce a much richer and deeper effect than is possible in traditional technique that ignores group emotions.

Chekhov's brand of tragicomedy is unique, Calderon felt. Though his characters generally suffer, they have a remote comedic point of view which enables them to experience their misfortune without malice.

Chekhov, said Calderon, saw evil in the modern world emerging not so much from a person's malicious intent but perversely, as an unintended byproduct of the interplay of seemingly innocent actions. Since life has no villains, neither do Chekhov's plays. But no modern heroes seem to be able to counteract life's perverse evil, and so Chekhov's drama lacks heroes too. The problem for the spectator is to dissociate himself from a hoary dramatic tradition which exaggerated good and bad in characters in order to make a point.

Calderon showed how Chekhov used seeming irrelevancies to build character, create atmosphere, provide humor, or show life's irony and indifference. He also discussed Chekhov's contrapuntal technique of playing characters' leitmotifs against each other. Release of exposition is natural and unobtrusive, as in life. This can easily be overlooked unless the spectator actively participates in the drama. By enormous restraint, emotions are suggested rather than elaborated upon, achieving an effect which can be called "spiritualized realism."

A great deal of the subsequent criticism of Chekhov's unconventional plays merely rediscovers, or amplifies upon, the seminal insights provided by Calderon.

The American critic Stark Young found similarities between the techniques of Chekhov and Shakespeare: "Very much as a dramatic poet like Shakespeare used poetic speech and every freedom of figure and imagery to establish the complete quality of the moment, Chekhov, without saying or doing anything that would not be quite possible in ordinary life, discovers and puts together separate remarks and reactions which, by the time the scene ends, have suddenly fused into a revelation of the very soul of that moment of life represented."[9]

Particularly as performed by the Moscow Art Theatre under the direction of Konstantin Stanislavsky, Chekhov's plays have become classics in the modern dramatic repertoire. Along with Henrik Ibsen and August Strindberg, Chekhov is one of the fathers of modern drama. His innovations in dramatic technique are the most important developments in the theater since Shakespeare. Even when the overall effect of one of his plays seems thin and somewhat unrewarding, the very dramatic methods employed chart the course for the technical achievements of future playwrights. Realism, naturalism, symbolism, The Theater of the Absurd, existentialist drama – all owe great indebtedness to the modest doctor from Taganrog.

The Humanitarian

A roll call of modern saints would have to include Gandhi, Albert Schweitzer, Thomas Dooley, Mother Teresa, Pope John XXIII – and Anton Chekhov.

By the age of 18, Chekhov was the chief support of his family. He put himself through medical school by writing stories after his studies were over. He was a charming host. One would never have known, judging by his horseplay and jokes, that he resented time that socializing took away from his writing and his medical practice.

The sick came to Melikhovo from miles away to be treated by Dr. Chekhov. He never billed the poor. When a cholera epidemic threatened, he organized a campaign of preventive medicine. He induced wealthy citizens to build clinics in each of the 25 villages for which he was responsible, and the epidemic was averted in his area. For two years he wrote very little, because of his work in fighting cholera. He led a campaign against famine. He got a number of wealthy landowners to buy the peasants' horses in the fall, feed them all winter, and then give them back to the peasants in the spring.

He spent a year inspecting the penal colony on Sakhalin Island. Each day he arose at sunup, interviewed convicts, and took copious notes. He visited every settlement on the island, and had cards on over 10,000 convicts. Upon his return he published a lengthy report which called for prison reforms. A more humane administration on Sakhalin Island resulted from his trip.

Chekhov was a good citizen. As jury foreman, he attended many court sessions. He gave reading instructions to peasants. He read manuscripts for budding writers, and recommended them to publishers. He got roads and bridges built and repaired. He instigated the installation of post offices and telegraph stations. He tried valiantly to rescue a financially doomed medical journal, *Annals of Surgery.*

In 1895 Chekhov was named school inspector in his district. He built three schools at his own expense, and worked unceasingly to raise the salaries and the respect given teachers. He drew up plans for each school, and supervised the construction. In his lifetime no one knew that Czar Nicholas II had bestowed a title of nobility upon him for his service in improving the schools in his district.

Everywhere he went he planted trees. His goal was to make all of Russia a beautiful garden. Trees were to him a symbol of the beauty of nature which man dare not desecrate. He was an early environmentalist. He inspected working conditions in factories and recommended improvements.

He helped build a library collection in Taganrog. Seeing that poor people had inadequate medical facilities in Yalta, he embarked on a fund-raising campaign to build what is now the Anton Chekhov Sanitarium.

Chekhov opposed the anti–Jewish pogroms of the czar. He aided the Jews persecuted in the Warsaw ghetto. He told Sholom Aleichem to translate his works into Yiddish and give the proceeds to the persecuted Jews. He broke a long friendship with his editor, Alexei Suvorin, because of Suvorin's anti–Semitism during the Dreyfus affair.

His friend Kuprin said that "Chekhov had no rest. All day long people came to see him. Scholars, writers, politicians, officers, painters, professors, society people, priests, actors, and everybody else."[10] Dying of tuberculosis, he apologized to his friend Alexander Tikhonov for coughing at night, thus disturbing Tikhonov's sleep.

Even if he had not been a great writer, Chekhov would have deserved worldwide recognition for his role as a humanitarian. Those early critics who found his stories and plays "cold" or "inhumane" could have gained great insight by investigating the private life of this remarkable man. As Kenneth Lantz (1985) has observed, "All of the critics who accused Chekhov of indifference or social irresponsibility could, taken together, scarcely compile a more impressive list of philanthropic activities."

Russian Criticism of Chekhov

Vissarion Belinsky, writing in the 1840s, postulated the role of the writer as a spiritual leader, one who would be in the vanguard of needed social and political reform. His followers, Nikolai Chernyshevsky and Nikolai Dobrolyubov, continued to rank social tendentiousness far ahead of esthetic merit in evaluating literature. Because fiction was not subject to as severe censorship as other forms of writing, the novelist (and by implication, the short-story writer) was expected to speak out directly against governmental oppression and suppression.

By the time Chekhov began to write, populism had replaced nihilism as the prevailing literary climate. Writers were expected to exalt the common people, implying that as they were granted more political power, society's problems could be solved. Seemingly apolitical, Chekhov perplexed populist critics by publishing his stories in both conservative and liberal publications. Further, Chekhov's themes were domestic or commonplace, with little value as direct political propaganda.

An additional enigma lay in the form of Chekhov's stories. Critics found few literary forerunners of his artistic philosophy and method. "He brought into Russian literature a new kind of artistic sensibility that was irreconcilable with the sensibilities of traditional Russian literature. Chekhov's artistic creativity constituted a transition from the Golden Age of the Russian novel—dominated by realism with its civic emphasis—to the Silver Age of Russian literature with its emphasis on form, esthetic values, and daring metaphysical speculation."[11] It was many years before critics understood that Chekhov's distrust of political parties and processes led him to place his hope for a better future upon the individual—the person who would not allow himself to despoil, in any way, the dignity of any other person.

Since most of Chekhov's early writing consisted of comic sketches for cheap newspapers, critics worried that a crude journalistic style would debase a possibly very creative talent. Reviewing Chekhov's *Motley Tales* in 1886, Alexander Skabichevsky warned Chekhov that the easy popularity and the hurried writing pace of the journalist would quickly drain a talented writer of his imagination and inspiration, and he would soon merely endlessly repeat himself. What a pity, mourned Skabichevsky, that at the outset of his literary career Chekhov had "immediately entered the guild of newspaper clowns."[12]

By the end of 1888 Chekhov, nevertheless, was the toast of St. Petersburg. His play *Ivanov* had received a successful premiere there, and Chekhov had been awarded the coveted Pushkin Prize for his short-story collection *In the Twilight*. Recognition had its drawbacks, Chekhov learned. Writers ignored for the prize became envious of this young man of 28, and populist critics continued to deplore the lack of preaching in his works.

The leading populist critic, Nikolai Mikhailovsky, decried the prostitution of Chekhov's great talent on such unworthy characters and themes. His indifference and apathy, Mikhailovsky said, led Chekhov to write stories that were "inhuman," depicting no moral choices nor great characters striving for worthy goals.

Others followed Mikhailovsky's direction. Peter Percov, a symbolist critic, stated that Chekhov's attitude towards creativity was that of an objective recording camera—all objects were treated equally. With no established chain of cause and effect, Chekhov's stories appeared to Percov to be fragmentary and disjointed. Roman Disterlo found Chekhov to be an indifferent impressionist, one who strolls through life merely depicting surfaces. N.S. Rusanov called Chekhov "a deeply amoral writer," and F.I. Bulgakov said his stories "seem more like a delirium or cheap talk than sensible narratives." A.I. Ertel accused Chekhov of fostering "the cult of moral indifference," and a writer, F.F. Tishchenko, woke up Chekhov in his hotel room to lecture him on his lack of ideals.[13]

Leon Shestov (1905) called Chekhov "the poet of hopelessness." Chekhov's lack of a satisfactory world-view, Shestov said, led him to try to create out of a void, a physical impossibility. Unlike nearly every other critic, Shestov found that Chekhov's deep pessimism led him to a willful desire to "destroy" his characters. Worse even than Maupassant, Chekhov took sadistic pleasure in ambushing a character, depriving him of any possible happiness. Shestov equated Chekhov's views with those expressed by his characters.[14]

Zinaida Gippius, a symbolist poet, also called Chekhov a prophet of nonexistence, whose works were emotionally and spiritually empty. Though admiring Chekhov's technical talent, she said that "Chekhov does not wish to know of any loftier values in life. He is always sad and bored."[15]

By 1898 critics began to speak of a greater tenderness in Chekhov's writing. Alexander Izmailov said that Chekhov seemed now to be undergoing the spiritual crisis that all great Russian writers encountered: esthetic concerns were fading to the background as ethical questions came to the fore. "Everywhere, behind the narrator," said Izmailov, "the subjective author is seen feeling painfully and keenly the nonsense of life, and unable not to express himself."[16] Angel Bogdanovich agreed with Izmailov that the new subjectivity deepened the content of Chekhov's works.

In 1904 N.N. Karpov said that Chekhov began a new era in Russian literature. After early periods of carefree humor and later melancholia, his final period was one of hope and faith in the future. Chekhov's best support now came from those who knew him intimately. Maxim Gorky, for example, praised Chekhov for his persistent attack upon mediocrity. Gorky found cheerfulness and optimism where others found gloom. He disagreed that Chekhov's lack of a world-view harmed his writings, saying that "from a higher point of view he sheds light on life's boredom, its absurdities, its desires, and its entire chaos." Admitting that sometimes Chekhov's effect was elusive, he averred that "one can hear with an increasing frequency the sad but strong and accurate reproach to the people for not knowing how to live." Those people who understand you, Gorky told Chekhov, say that in *The Sea Gull* and *Uncle Vanya* you have created a new type of dramatic art which combined realism and symbolism in a profound way.[17]

Chekhov's friend Ivan Bunin pointed to all of Chekhov's humanitarian work as a refutation of his alleged lack of ideas. Bunin praised Chekhov's stories for their realism and vividness, but complained that his drama suffered from a lack of knowledge of the life of the gentry. Alexander Kuprin argued that Chekhov's shyness made him shun publicity, and then people confused diffidence with indifference. Eugene Zamyatin called Chekhov "an impartial witness," whose bold and original images influenced many contemporary writers. Zamyatin called Chekhov Russia's first impressionistic writer.

Leo Tolstoy had little use for Chekhov's "plotless" and "themeless" plays, which he said were even worse than Shakespeare's. But in the field of the short story, Tolstoy said, "Chekhov surpasses me by far. He is Pushkin in prose. Thanks to his sincerity, he created altogether new literary forms, unlike any that I have ever known."[18]

Kornei Chukovsky (1945) in 1910 asserted that critics were missing Chekhov's central theme: the importance of the internal struggle between the will and the lack of will. Chekhov's literary creativity was to Chukovsky "a moral sermon," a call to a better way of life. Chukovsky said that Chekhov's writing brought one closer to God than do most pious tracts, and that the three sisters in his play of that name were full of Christian virtues. M.M. Stepanov in 1913 decided that Chekhov must have been a Christian to have so many characters who express deep faith in God and immortality.

For a short time after the Revolution Chekhov's works were regarded as a "destructive, negative tendency" by the Soviets. But in 1924 Anatoly Lunacharsky found that Chekhov was by no means outdated. His art was a model for Soviet authors to emulate, said Lunacharsky, and Chekhov had depicted and derided bourgeois vulgarity that any modern regime should likewise oppose. Mikhail Koltsov in 1928 said Chekhov was not "a poet of the twilight period" of Russian history, but a marvelous craftsman with a deep social conscience, a materialist who satirized czarist injustice. In 1930 Yuri Sobolev saw Chekhov as greatly influenced by evolution, and said that Chekhov himself had evolved from a petty bourgeois to a liberal. In 1939 A.I. Roskin took a middle stand: Chekhov was neither the wistful poet of ineffectual intellectuals nor the proto–Bolshevik as seen by Lunacharsky and Koltsov. The gloom in his works is that of the characters rather than of the author, Roskin said, adding that optimistic Chekhov was himself joyous and compassionate, even when he was critical of his own characters.

Aided by Gorky's support, Chekhov was restored in the 1930s as the writer who had foreseen the revolutionary storm. Soon Soviet critics canonized his works as classics, and except for Gorky, Pushkin and Tolstoy, Chekhov is the most widely read author in Russia today. "Between 1918 and 1947 the total publication of his books passed the eighteen million mark. He is not only widely read but also greatly loved, as one loves an intimate friend or a member of one's family."[19]

Avram Derman has been one of the leading Soviet critics of Chekhov. Derman felt that Chekhov's great innovations were first perceived where they were most evident, in the field of drama. Chekhov's subtle inventions in both fiction and drama placed strong reliance on the reader's sensitivity, Derman said. He made a careful study of beginnings and endings in Chekhov's stories. The beginnings were effective because of their brevity, and the endings he found very moving because they were both lyrical and unexpected.

In the 1950s A.P. Skaftymov showed how Chekhov used conflicting emotions to convey complex and contradictory character traits. Vladimir Ermilov (1956) said that Chekhov employed the beauty of nature as a contrast to the injustice of most human relations. Chekhov's democratic spirit Ermilov found expressed in the way he raised "little" people to a lofty place. For Chekhov, artistic talent was inextricably bound up with high ethical standards, Ermilov stated.

Ilya Ehrenburg (1962) traced Chekhov's influence upon writers all over the world. Chekhov was seen as a perennial enemy to inhumanity. One could build a complete ethical system, said Ehrenburg, from things that Chekhov had opposed.

Vladimir Lakshin summarized Tolstoy's high opinion of Chekhov's fiction. Lakshin agreed with Tolstoy that Chekhov, living in an age of great repression, reacted creatively by inventing new literary forms that would escape censorship but still achieve his human purpose. Lakshin felt that Tolstoy was inconsistent to praise Chekhov's stories highly after reading them, but then later condemn them for lacking a religious purpose. How could they move one so deeply, Lakshin asked, unless they satisfied not only one's esthetic but also one's moral sensitivity?

Alexander Chudakov (1971) noted how Chekhov, as he matured, eliminated narrator intrusions, and strained everything through the consciousness of a central character. Using quantifying measures, Chudakov demonstrated how Chekhov pioneered in fusing dialogue, exposition, and setting into an organic unity. Chudakov classified Chekhov as an impressionist who was the father of modern drama, one who could merge everything, even the commonplace, into "an eternal whole."

In 1975 G. Andreev called Chekhov's writings a great part of the tradition of Christian humanism. Hulanicki (1976) summarizes the views of a number of Soviet critics. A.A. Cicerin finds Chekhov using a deliberate vagueness in order to suggest a society with more justice and beauty. E.S.Dobin sees deep literary, psychological, and social meaning in small Chekhovian details. Vasily Golubkov detects a lyrical quality in Chekhov's stories, built by emotional phrases, repetitions, and near-poetic expression. Vadim Nazarenko analyzes Chekhov's imagery as coming from a pictorial sense rather than from conventional figures of speech. G.N. Pospelov interprets the ennui of Chekhov's characters as arising more from political repression than from personal dissatisfaction. Victor Shklovsky regrets that the suffering of Chekhov's heroes remains unavenged. V.V. Vinogradov sees in Chekhov's dialogue great depth and subtlety in delineating social and class distinctions.

In 1980 *Soviet Literature* devoted an entire issue to the recognition of Chekhov's 120th birthday. Georgi Berdnikov saw him as one who debunked populism, Tolstoyism, Slavophilism, and bourgeois liberal social theories. The lofty ideal behind Chekhov's great art, Berdnikov said, was his crusade for a more just social order. Yuri Nagibin described how Chekhov tutored young writers, telling them to be brief, to eliminate adjectives, and to make their writing natural and unpretentious. Zinovy Paperny, after studying Chekhov's rough drafts and notebooks, said that although Chekhov ridiculed falsehood, indolence, and vanity, he never lost faith in man. He wrote in his notebook: "What a delight it is to respect people."

It can thus be seen how, once Russian critics learned to read Chekhov's works sensitively, they invariably shifted from blame to praise in assessing the quality of his short stories and plays.

English Criticism of Chekhov

E.J. Dillon (1891) was the first English writer to give extensive attention to Chekhov's works. Dillon felt that Chekhov's writing suffered not only from czarist censorship but from other factors related to it: a capricious and coarse-minded public, the cupidity of uneducated editors and publishers, and the narrow limits of self-imposed critics. Dillon credited Chekhov with artistic objectivity, remarkable insight into character, and "a wonderful fidelity to nature." Unfortunately, however, the reader was repelled by Chekhov's gallery of spineless characters, said Dillon. He attributed the disparity to Chekhov's unsuccessful effort to serve two masters: medicine and literature.[20]

R.E.C. Long, the first English translator of a volume of Chekhov's tales, had a similar reaction in 1902. After praising Chekhov highly for an unerring eye that could capture the quintessence of human emotion, Long said that Chekhov's characters were so repugnant that they stripped the last rags of dignity from the human soul. The critical fashion of the period was to find each Russian writer to be an exponent of the allegedly gloomy Russian "soul." Long thus quoted a passage from Chekhov's story "The Student," and called it a typical example of Russian gloom and pessimism.[21]

Slowly a new outlook evolved. In 1907 St. John Hankin identified Chekhov as the leader of a new "Moscow school" of drama, which refused to sacrifice probability for thrills, but revealed human souls to perceptive listeners in as enthralling a manner as a Greek tragedy. The following year Maurice Baring stated that Chekhovian drama excelled in portraying life's inner struggle. As in life, one had to piece together from a gesture or a hummed tune what went on behind the mask of the character's persona.

The war was not, however, won in one battle. In 1911, when the London Stage Society put on *The Cherry Orchard*, most of the avant-garde audience stole away, act by act. The *Times* voiced the general impression: this was an inept mixture of pathos and farce, and Russians could not be such "fools" as exhibited here. Arnold Bennett demurred, calling it the best naturalistic play ever staged in England. "People never look properly at people," he said. Were any ten members of the Stage Society to be so faithfully portrayed, "with all their mannerisms and absurdities," the result would be similarly damned as gross caricature.[22] John Palmer agreed with Bennett, stating that Chekhov's plays were a trap for critics who were blind to everything but machinery; here every seeming irrelevance contributed to a mysteriously cumulative effect.

In 1912 George Calderon wrote a veritable handbook of new dramaturgy in the introduction to his translation of *The Cherry Orchard* and *The Sea Gull*, as summarized above. It was unfortunate that few persons seem to have read this important criticism of Chekhov's drama.

World War I impelled many British people to read literature about their ally, Russia. The publishing firm of Chatto & Windus began the issuance of Constance Garnett's translations of Chekhov's works (which totalled 15 volumes by 1924).

A less radical technical innovation than his plays, Chekhov's tales soon found many favorable critics. E.M. Forster said that Chekhov's poetic treatment of life's common events made them flow on, "noble, imaginative, profound."[23] Robert Lynd boldly called Chekhov the planet's greatest short-story writer. Chekhov reacted with "good-natured disgust" at the shabby lives of his contemporaries, Lynd felt, but he depicted well how an ordinary person's life was, to himself, as stirring an epic as the life of any Homeric warrior.[24]

Chekhov was now being compared with that other great master of the short story, Guy de Maupassant. Many English critics preferred Chekhov's tales for their deep understanding and compassion. Chekhov was also admired for his keen sense of humor, economy in style, and rare narrative gift. His gentle humor was seen as a welcome relief to his otherwise gray cameos. Interest chilled briefly during the Russian revolution, but Chekhov's recovery in esteem was more rapid than that of most other Russian writers. What remained was for his drama to receive the sympathetic treatment that his tales had been accorded.

The 1920s were the decade in which Chekhov's drama received its current high status. Four factors accounted for this, in both England and the United States: the popularity of his fiction; publication of his personal papers and letters; the post-war disillusionment; and visits by the Moscow Art Theatre. Katherine Mansfield led a coterie (which included William Gerhardi, J. Middleton Murry, and Virginia Woolf) that took delight in pointing out Chekhov's specific artistic achievements. Mansfield liked best about Chekhov his refusal to preach. Gerhardi believed that Chekhov's uniqueness lay in his representation of life's fluidity, complexity, and elusiveness. Murry rated Chekhov ahead of Joyce and Proust, saying that his *mysterium simplicitatus* undercut their "illimitable intellectualisms."[25] Woolf said that Chekhov's secret was to involve the reader in the "solution" to each of his works.

Chekhov's personal papers, including his diary, letters, and notebook, demonstrated that he was far from neutral on ethical matters. Careful readers were beginning to discern that the subtle figure exquisitely woven into the fabric of his writing was a veiled but sturdy protest against the violation of human dignity, in whatsoever form it might appear.

In his introduction to *Heartbreak House*, George Bernard Shaw paid great tribute to Chekhov as one who captured the idealist's feeling of disillusion as he faces a real world of war and crass materialism. Upon reading Chekhov's plays, Shaw confessed, he felt like tearing up his own—a marked contrast to his reaction to Shakespeare's drama.

Although performed in Russian, Moscow Art Theatre productions of Chekhov's plays in London evoked widespread applause for ensemble effect, subtle character delineation, and a "spiritualized realism" achieved by deliberate restraint on the part of both the playwright and the actors.

Prince D.S. Mirsky, a Russian émigré, demurred from the general accolades, saying that Chekhov's language was pedestrian and his effects pessimistic. Janko Lavrin gave Chekhov great praise, however, finding his charity superior to Maupassant's. Desmond MacCarthy also persistently praised Chekhov's plays for their gentle irony and artful use of disconnected dialogue.

In 1926 and 1927 there were eight successful commercial London productions of Chekhov's plays, and his drama had become a classic in the modern theatrical repertoire.

W.H. Bruford (1948) published a sociological study of Chekhov that gave valuable historical background on his writing. Ronald Hingley (1950) became England's leading authority on Chekhov, writing two biographies and translating and editing the Oxford Edition of Chekhov's stories and plays in nine volumes

(1964–1980). David Magarshack wrote a life of Chekhov, and then added two full-length studies of his plays. Magarshack pointed out similarities between these plays and classical Greek drama. Magarshack believed that directors often ruin his plays by ignoring Chekhov's stated intentions.

In her biography Beatrice Saunders (1960) stressed Chekhov as a humanitarian. Frank L. Lucas (1963) indicated how Chekhov defied Aristotle, stressing unity of mood rather than unity of action. Maurice Valency (1966) showed the interrelationship between Chekhov's stories and his plays. Valency believed that Chekhov had developed a dramatic polyphony unrivalled in stage history.

J.B. Priestley (1970) in his brief biography stated that Chekhov, with "the most delicate antennae in Russian literature," was a greater influence in the theater than in the genre of the short story, where it was futile to try to achieve his unique economy and restraint. Logan Speirs (1971) analyzed the relationship between Tolstoy and Chekhov, and J.L. Styan (1971) provided a detailed stage history of the leading productions of Chekhov's plays.

Harvey Pitcher (1973) not only translated many Chekhov stories but also wrote on his humor and his dramaturgy. Chekhov's plays, said Pitcher, are notable for their depiction of the complex emotional networks that exist among people. Virginia Llewellyn Smith (1972) studied Chekhov's attitude towards women, seeming to find in his works an undervaluation of their capacities for intelligence and art.

Donald Rayfield (1975), on the other hand, said Chekhov attacked misogyny, while showing his evolution as an artist. Caryl Brahms (1976) provided a brief reading of Chekhov's plays. Beverly Hahn (1977) gave some of the most profound and insightful criticism of the century. She pointed out how time and change are protagonists in Chekhov's works. She felt that Chekhov showed deep understanding of feminine psychology. Although he seemed repulsed by both trivial domesticity and primitive aggression, he identified with strong and cultured women who found sophisticated ways to protest against a confining attitude.

In a structuralist study, John Tulloch (1980) endeavored to show that Chekhov's outlook as an environmentalist doctor determined and shaped his themes. Victor Emeljanow (1981) edited an anthology of play reviews from 1891 to 1945, in which he provided a lengthy summary of early Chekhov criticism. Vera Gottlieb (1982) produced the only full-length study of Chekhov's one-act plays.

As in Russia, once they had overcome their initial perplexity and distaste at Chekhov's themes and characters, critics in England rallied to his support with immoderate praise and at times penetrating insights into his unique effects.

American Criticism of Chekhov

In 1896 Victor Yarros characterized Chekhov as one of a group of Russian decadent writers that also included Vladimir Korolenko and Ignatius Potapenko. The pessimism of these writers Yarros attributed to oppressive press censorship.

A Russian émigré, Abraham Cahan, gave a more detailed analysis of Chekhov's writings in 1899. Paraphrasing Mikhailovsky and Skabichevsky, Cahan identified Chekhov's major weakness as a lack of unity, due to the absence of an "underlying idea" in his tales. Chekhov was nevertheless called Russia's greatest short-story writer, largely because he depicted "those evanescent flinders of life which are fresh and unexpected, yet characteristic of the person and places described."[26]

Chekhov's death in 1904 evoked a tribute from Christian Brinton, who said no other writer paralleled Chekhov's unique mixture of satire and sadness.[27] The apathy of Chekhov's characters Brinton blamed on the oppressive Russian government. The invisible cathartic element in Chekhov's works, Brinton felt, was that his indictment of his society was artfully synthesized into his writings. Despite the absence of preaching, a sensitive artist had put his finger tellingly on gross inhumanity.

As in England, Chekhov's plays were puzzling critics long after his tales had been praised. Leo Wiener in 1903 said that Chekhov's dramatic characters were all fit subjects for a psychiatrist, and his dialogue "nothing but a series of semi-articulated hysterical ejaculations."[28]

In 1908 Professor Max S. Mandell of Yale translated *The Cherry Garden*, the first full-length Chekhov play to appear in English. Mandell said that in this play Chekhov left behind the hopeless conditions of Russian society to open up "a bright new page full of hope for a better future." Mandell included a letter from the actress Alla Nazimova, who called Chekhov her favorite writer, but said that the American stage, with its "star system" of acting, would have trouble doing justice to Chekhov's plays, which demanded an ensemble effect of unusually close teamwork and unity.

World War I marked the period of the triumph of Chekhov's reputation as a short-story writer. As the form increased in popularity, American writers turned to foreign models for guidance. Attacking American authors for slavish adherence to formula-like happy endings, Henry Seidel Canby recommended to them Chekhov as a "free" writer, one who gained great range and depth in characterization by not being bound to a doctrinaire theme. Reviewers of the translations by Marian Fell found in Chekhov both humor and humane feelings. Little Theater performances of his farces helped Americans discover a lesser known phase of the Slavic soul, its humor.

In 1917 Edward J. O'Brien first recognized Chekhov's greatness, in his annual yearbook of the short story. After ranking Chekhov with Poe and Maupassant, O'Brien stated his personal preference for the Russian, whose works ranged "the entire gamut of human emotion," fully equalling Dostoevsky in "sustained and varied spiritual observation." Moissaye Olgin added that Chekhov had a Greek aptitude for a peaceful and beautiful existence, and that his melancholy was a natural reaction to seeing a world of horror and ugliness.[29] Forgiveness was the keynote of Chekhov's philosophy, Olgin found, and an innate sense of modesty seemed to color Chekhov's very style.

In 1917 the March revolution spurred interest in Russian literature, but the

October revolution cooled the fervor. Despite this fact, Chekhov's tales continued their steady rise in American critical esteem.

Not so his plays, however. When Paul Orlenev, a Moscow actor silenced by czarist censorship, brought some Russian plays, including Chekhov's, to America in the 1905–06 season, a typical reviewer commented that Orlenev seemed to be trying "to make suffering fashionable in America."[30] The reviewer for the *Nation* in 1916, upon seeing *The Sea Gull* performed by the Washington Square Players in New York, said it was absurd for an American even to try to take seriously "the neurasthenic maunderings which in this play are paraded in the guise of dramatic complication." A critic for *The Theatre* called the play boring, with an uninteresting plot, depressing subject matter, and no "dramatic" scenes.

An exception to the general trend was Gertrude Besse King, who had seen the Moscow Art Theatre stage Chekhov. Speaking of *The Three Sisters*, King admired the Wagnerian use of leitmotifs to accompany characters, and the contrapuntal interweaving of the subplots to create a great crescendo. She praised the lifelike dialogue and the background mood. Above all, she found a definite catharsis, achieved by realizing how petty one's goals and ambitions usually are, and that thus one should face the world with a philosophic poise.[31]

Moscow Art Theatre tours of America in 1923 and 1924 helped familiarize Americans with Chekhov's plays. American actors and directors received lessons in orchestrated stage effects and ensemble acting techniques, all of which sowed seeds for a fuller understanding of Chekhov's drama.

Eva Le Gallienne led her Civic Repertory Theater in New York in sensitive productions of his plays, beginning in 1926. In 1929 Broadway saw five productions of Chekhov's plays, and in 1930 *Uncle Vanya*, as produced by Jed Harris, made stage history. Two other memorable productions were *The Sea Gull* by the Lunts in 1938, and *The Three Sisters*, starring Judith Anderson, Katherine Cornell, and Ruth Gordon, in the 1942–43 season. By World War II Chekhov's plays had achieved the status of modern classics. American playwrights indebted to Chekhov include Edward Albee, David Mamet, Clifford Odets, William Saroyan, Sam Shepard, and Tennessee Williams.

In 1937 Nina Toumanova published her doctoral dissertation, a biography of Chekhov using many original Russian sources. The chief value of the book lay in its disclosure of many of the plot germs of his works. Stark Young not only translated Chekhov's plays but also wrote critical articles delineating his dramatic art. Others who have written scholarly critiques of Chekhov's writings include Eric Bentley, Joseph L. Conrad, Francis Fergusson, John Gassner, Clayton A. Hubbs, Peter Rossbacher, Gleb Struve, and Thomas G. Winner.

Perhaps the best biography of Chekhov in any language was the one by Ernest J. Simmons (1962). Simmons not only drew upon many Russian sources but he also fused biography, criticism, and judgment in a very readable yet informative format.

Robert W. Corrigan (1962) stated that Chekhov reflected better than any other playwright the spirit of our troubled time. As a man he cared deeply for fellow humans, and as an artist he practiced complete objectivity. "It is the fusion of these two characteristics that makes his work great," said Corrigan.[32]

Edmund Wilson declared Chekhov to be "one of the tersest, most lucid, and most purposive of all writers." Admiring Chekhov's faith in human dignity, Wilson traced Chekhov's tales from early satirical jokes to later ironic anecdotes, with his final stories being dense but concise studies of character and situation. Eudora Welty felt that Chekhov's perception of different views of reality, with his capacity to understand all views, may have revolutionized the art of the short story. His own vision of reality was comic, Welty said, the only framework generous enough to encompass all that he saw.

Thomas G. Winner (1966) analyzed Chekhov's prose style from the standpoint of its diction, its relation to other writers, and its seminal influence upon the short-story genre. Robert Louis Jackson (1967) edited an outstanding collection of critical essays on Chekhov, including his own analysis of *The Sea Gull* as a profound study of the artist and his role in society.

Karl D. Kramer (1970) showed the Chekhovian contrast between the chameleon, the toady who lacks the backbone to take a stand, and the dreamer, the person who dares to visualize a world with more permanent moral values. Kramer demonstrated how Chekhov, in his early parodies, was feeling his way towards a serious mastery of his craft. H. Peter Stowell (1980) said that Chekhov, like Henry James, was an innovative impressionist. Reflecting modern life, literary impressionists skirt reality, Stowell averred, and the result is "the dissolution of plot, the broken cycle of causality, the relativism of time and space, and the perpetual subjectivity of characters." Stowell sees literary impressionists as being ultra-modern, for they fuse space with time, subject with object, and linear time with eternal time.

Irina Kirk (1981) wrote a brief biography which, among other things, traced Chekhov's growing dramatic artistry from broad farcical effects to serious drama employing symbols, mood, and subtext. Anthony Winner (1981) contrasted the prose of Chekhov with that of Thomas Hardy and Emile Zola. Whereas Hardy and Zola depict moderns as victims, Chekhov shows that the individual, through irresponsibility, is partly to blame for his plight, but he is nevertheless to be pitied, for he is us.

Richard A. Peace (1983) said that the topic of usurpation is both Chekhov's theme and method. In his plays characters usurp each other's positions, and in technique, daydreams usurp action, mood encroaches on plot, and direct statement is replaced by indirect commentary. In 1985 Kenneth A. Lantz published a bibliography of writings on Chekhov, particularly rich in citing Russian works, and Charles W. Meister published a bibliography of works on Chekhov in English.

As in England, American critics moved from distaste, through perplexity, to understanding and critical accolades for Chekhov's writings. If there is any dissension among modern critics of Chekhov, it is not so much upon whether his work is artful or not, but rather on varying techniques for analyzing and explaining the secrets of his art.

World Recognition of Chekhov

It is not only in Russia, England, and America that Chekhov's works are treasured. In Paris in 1924 Charles du Bos gave a series of public lectures that penetrated to the heart of Chekhov's art. The Parisian publishing house of Plon produced Chekhov's collected works in the 1920s.

André Maurois in 1960 said that the purpose of Chekhov's art was to help liberate human beings from brute force and lies, in whatever form they appear. In France Daniel Gilles (1967), Sophie Laffitte (1973), Irene Nemirovsky (1950), and Henri Troyat (1984) have written full-length biographies of Chekhov. Laffitte and Nemirovsky stress his life more than his works. Gilles charts Chekhov's changing attitudes towards Tolstoy. Troyat depicts Chekhov's inner determination to perfect his art until he became in the words of reviewer Jules Koslow "the short-story writer's writer and the playwright's playwright."[33] Numerous French critics have described how Chekhov's fiction compares with that of Maupassant, and how Chekhov's drama has influenced absurdist and existentialist drama.

In Germany, Thomas Mann acknowledged great indebtedness to Chekhov, whose modesty, Mann felt, kept back the recognition that his art deserved. Mann admired Chekhov's type of tragicomedy, and applauded his ridicule of self-righteous "progressives." Siegfried Melchinger (1972) wrote a biography stressing Chekhov's humanitarianism. Adolph Wegener saw Harold Pinter as Chekhov's heir-apparent in dramatic technique, and Arvids Ziedonis compared *Indrani* by Rudolfs Blaumanis to *The Cherry Orchard*. Willy Birkenmaier said that Chekhov was a Christian, as seen by his life and writings. When Chekhov in his letters speaks of his loss of faith, he is specifically referring to discarding dogmatic religion, Birkenmaier believes. In 1976 Horst-Jürgen Gerigk showed Chekhov's influence upon Tennessee Williams—both show human isolation and mutual incomprehension.[34]

Thomas Eekman (1960) in the Netherlands edited several valuable collections of criticism of Chekhov's works. J. van der Eng, Jan M. Meyer, and Herta Schmidt explained Chekhov's effects based on a theory of descriptive poetics. Hilda V. Yoder compared the plays of Herman Heijermans to those of Chekhov, Hauptmann, and Ibsen.

In Norway Marit B. Nielsen studied how Chekhov handled his portrayal of women. Nils Ake Nilsson (1968) in Sweden wrote a full-length study of Chekhov's narrative technique, concentrating on the way setting is used.

Peter M. Bitsilli (1983) in Bulgaria traced the influences upon Chekhov's writing, and then showed the persons influenced by Chekhov. Henry Urbanski (1973) wrote a doctoral dissertation at Wroclaw University in Poland, showing the opinions of his Russian literary contemporaries upon Chekhov's works. Iudit Lamm studied Chekhov's art of writing, on behalf of the Hungarian Slavic Studies Academy of Sciences. Peter Egri (1986) in Budapest showed the uses that Chekhov and Eugene O'Neill made of short stories in writing their plays.

In Nigeria K.E. Senanu made a comparison of Chekhov and Henry James. P. Kuranage described Chekhov's great influence in Sri Lanka. In India Amar Basu and Sankar Basu studied the narrator's "voice" in "Ward No. 6," and Sankar Basu (1985) wrote a full-length comparison of the stories of Chekhov and Tagore. Faiz Ahmed Faiz in Pakistan said that Chekhov was one of the first Russian writers whose works were translated into Urdu. Faiz feels that Chekhov's techniques have permeated those of all Indian short-story writers, because of Chekhov's lyricism, compassion, tenderness, faith in progress, and a unique brand of social idealism.[35]

J.S.M. Lau, in China, calls Ts'ao Yu a "reluctant disciple" of Chekhov as he compares Yu's *Sunrise* to *The Cherry Orchard* and Yu's *Peking Man* to *Ivanov*. Seiro Sato states that Chekhov's plays are prominent in the modern Japanese theater, and his short stories have influenced such Japanese writers as Hakucho Masamune and Kazuo Hirotsu. The Japanese are impressed, Sato says, by Chekhov's stress on beauty and gentleness, and by his constant appeal for greater human understanding.[36] In 1983 Kim Rekho described Chekhov's influence upon recent Japanese writers and scholars.[37]

The world-wide acceptance of Chekhov's works, based not only on their art but also on their humane content, justifies the earlier statement that Chekhov can serve as an important bridge of global understanding just when his values are desperately needed as inspiration for a future world of peace, brotherhood, and love.

The Education of Critics

This book will not only summarize what critics from many countries have said about specific works by Chekhov, but also provide an overview of the growth in critical acumen and insight as they cast aside traditional tools of their trade and evolved new and creative ways to account for new and creative literary effects.

For both short stories and plays, Chekhov's works will be presented chronologically. This will permit the reader to chart the growth and progress of Chekhov as a literary artist.

In addition, for each Chekhov work the criticism will be given in a chronological order. In this way one can watch the evolution of critical taste, and also assign credit for original insights to those who first furnished them. It is one thing to analyze disconnected dialogue in 1912, but quite another thing to repeat the analysis in 1982. For ease in locating them, the stories will be listed alphabetically within each time frame. Alternate titles are listed in parentheses. The reader is referred to the index for a complete listing of all references to each work.

Hopefully perusal of this book will lead even more readers to return to the corpus of tales and plays produced by this great but humble Russian physician. Scratch a modern Russian, and you will find one of Chekhov's characters underneath. If Americans and Russians—indeed, all citizens of the global village— can deepen their common humanity, and approach current problems with some of Chekhov's tenderness, compassion, understanding, and humor, we may take giant strides towards averting a nuclear holocaust. Chekhov's entry in his notebook can be our motto: "To understand is to forgive, and it would be strange not to forgive."

2. Stories: 1880–1883

"Artists' Wives" (1881)

Winner (1966) calls this a parody of romantic fiction. The ambitious setting is all countries of the world. The humor derives from improbabilities, melodrama, and high-flown language.

"At the Post Office" (1883)

The elderly postmaster keeps his young wife faithful to him by spreading the rumor that she is the mistress of the police chief. Payne (1963) finds it "a devilishly cunning evocation of an entire social landscape in two startling pages." The odd but wonderful persons at the funeral feast, Payne says, are not only outrageously funny but also grotesque and "desperately human."

"Because of Little Apples" (1880)

The stock brutal landowner catches a couple stealing his apples and forces them to beat each other. Hingley (1950) calls this "a philanthropic story," a type once popular in Russia. Hingley cites other examples: Gogol's "The Overcoat" and some of Turgenev's *Sportsman's Sketches*. Yarmolinsky (1954) says that "indignation fashioned this immature, derivative, yet obviously promising sketch of a sadistic country squire." Ermilov (1956) points out that the early Chekhov could open a story like this with a moral tirade against the orchard owner. Hingley (1976), however, calls it Chekhov's best work of 1880. True, the narrator is verbose, but the plot is good, Hingley states, and the young author's "cumbrously expressed sympathy for victims of oppression strikes a note which will echo more effectively later." Robert Louis Jackson in 1978 saw this work being influenced by Dostoevsky's "A Christmas Party and a Wedding." Both stories tell of the loss of innocence, and of a symbolic expulsion from the Garden of Eden. The stories express motifs of humiliation and sadism. Although Chekhov's story is a parody, it retains a tragic mood.[1] Eisen (1982) shows that the later Chekhov would have omitted the moralizing, thereby arousing a stronger response in the reader.

20

"Before the Wedding" (1880)

Simmons (1962) summarizes the plot: A bride-to-be is thoughtlessly subjected to cynical views on marriage by her mother, father, and even the groom.

"The Bird Market" (1883) ("In Trubny Square")

Bruford (1948) states Chekhov's ironic view: Because so many city dwellers are still rural folk at heart, "they love wild creatures so tenderly and torture them so much." Hingley (1976) labels it Chekhov's best early work in capturing the atmosphere of a place. Eisen (1982) says that "the bird market becomes a fusion of its disparate elements, its meaning inherent in the tensions of contrast which bind them."

"A Case from a Lawyer's Practice" (1883)

Harvey Pitcher, in Clyman (1985), finds Chekhov using a surprise ending for a humorous effect: The eloquent defense lawyer moves everyone to tears, including the defendant, who confesses his guilt.

"A Daughter of Albion" (1883)

A vulgar landowner strips nude in front of his English wife, to unsnag a fishing line. Avram Derman, in Bruford (1957), calls it "a vivid picture of stupid coarse nationalism." In a story that deeply impressed Nikolai Leskov, Derman averred, Chekhov defended human dignity by showing how it was outraged by some in czarist Russia. Eekman (1960) says that Chekhov, as a Westernizer, directed his ridicule as much against the unmannerly Russian as against his stoical wife. Hahn (1977) states that Chekhov creates a comic tableau out of communication failures. Although the images describing the wife are "memorably comic," she is unfairly lampooned here. "Vulnerability in certain kinds of characters sometimes impelled Chekhov early into impatient ridicule," Hahn judged.[2] Harvey Pitcher, in Clyman (1985), states that Chekhov intended to satirize both persons—the husband for being too aggressive, and the wife for being too submissive. "It is true generally of absurd comedy," Pitcher concludes, "that it is unsentimental, even brutal: it eliminates the element of human sympathy."[3]

"The Death of a Government Clerk" (1883)

Payne (1963) finds a reversal of this "grotesque and glorious parody" in the last word of the story: "died." Chekhov often did this, Payne says—one brief stroke isolates a fragment of experience, and then the whole story shines in the light of that stroke. Kramer (1970) sees a satire on czarist bureaucracy in the chagrined government clerk who dies after having sneezed on the bald head of a higher official. Here Chekhov is aping Gogol's "The Overcoat," Kramer feels. This story, says Hingley (1976), has become famous in Russia as "a perfect specimen in an admittedly lowly genre." The plot came from an actual happening told to Chekhov by V.P. Begichev, director of the Moscow imperial theaters. The skill of this minor masterpiece, Hingley believes, lies not in its trivial plot "but in the ingeniousness, verbal felicity, and playful panache with which the theme is developed."[4]

"An Enigmatic Nature" (1883)

A budding young writer ponders whether to flirt with a pretty girl in his railroad compartment, or study her psychology in wanting to marry an old general. Magarshack (*Life*, 1952) calls this a satire against Dostoevsky and his followers. Chekhov, says Magarshack, did not trust Dostoevsky's psychological insight nor like his pretentiousness.

"Fat and Thin" (1883)

Two old friends have a joyful reunion until the thin man discovers his fat friend's higher rank—he then becomes a sycophant. Alexander Werth (1925) saw this as evidence of how deeply Chekhov despised all "official" attitudes in human relations. The fat official is himself disgusted at the sudden servility of his friend. Winner (1966) notes how Chekhov depicts the thin man's embarrassment through his needless meaningless repetitions of speech. Kramer (1970) says that its expert handling makes it Chekhov's best "chameleon" story. For example, whereas his family was once his proudest boast, the thin man now finds it full of flaws. He re-introduces his family to his fat friend because the world which previously existed has been nullified. By his use of the chameleon device, Chekhov unmasks social rank as a dehumanizing influence. Hulanicki (1976) quotes Avram Derman on Chekhov's 1886 revision of this story. The later version assumes that the reader knows the cruelty of a rigid hierarchy, and stresses that the thin man should have asserted his human dignity, even in the presence of a "superior." Hahn (1977) finds a clever mixture of farce, pathos, and satire: the thin man fastens his buttons upon learning his friend's rank; his cardboard boxes seem to shrink along with him. Stowell (1980) says that the thin man dies (to his pride) and is reborn (to his chagrin). As an impressionist, Chekhov portrays the physical changes of the thin man, "a chameleon, who ever unsure of his reality, finds that only in abrupt transformations of appearance can he feel momentarily at one with his milieu."[5]

"The Flying Islands" (1883)

Three men travel to an airborne island, which drops into Havre harbor when their weight proves to be too much for it. Ralph E. Matlaw, in Eekman (1960), calls this a parody on the science fiction of Jules Verne. Hingley (1976) feels that editor Nikolai Leykin appropriately rejected this long story, since its satire is very thin.

"The Green Scythe" (1882)

Payne (1963) enjoyed this lighthearted romance of young people on the estate of a Georgian princess. Payne finds here Chekhov's first three-dimensional characters: the bullying princess, young and beautiful Olga, and Yegorov, the dashing lieutenant. These characters constantly occur in Chekhov's stories, Payne feels. Nor is Chekhov the objective narrator: "Far from being the neutral observer, Chekhov was a man who portrayed himself endlessly."[6] Hingley (1976) believes that this story is atypical for Chekhov, since the right boy gets the right girl.

"He Understood" (1883)

Caught poaching, a peasant is let off when the landowner sees the peasant's passion for hunting. Rayfield (1975) calls this Chekhov's most mature story of 1883. Rayfield liked the accurate and artful nature description, such as the simultaneous liberation of the peasant and a wasp which was trapped in the same room. Simon Karlinsky, in Barricelli (1981), notes how the crippled peasant has a limping mongrel for his bird dog. When the peasant pleads alcoholism as his excuse, the landowner, an alcoholic, forgives him.

"In the Landau" (1883)

Magarshack (Life, 1952) says this story shows the effect of Turgenev's death upon Chekhov, who at the time was attending spiritualist seances. At one of them Chekhov evoked Turgenev's ghost, who told him, "Your life is drawing to a close!" Chekhov immediately lost interest in spiritualism. Ermilov (1956) describes how 16-year-old Marfusha dislikes the gossip of her wealthy cousins. After a circular drive on Nevsky Prospect, the landau returns home. So too with all vulgarity, such as gossip, Ermilov concludes – it makes a full circle and returns on itself. Rayfield (1975) tells of how Marfusha begs her uncle not to criticize Turgenev. Since editor Leykin cut the story short, we do not know the original ending.

"Joy" (1883)

Hingley (1950) finds this a satire of Mitya's mediocre value system. Mitya is overjoyed at being known throughout Russia, despite the fact that his notoriety derives from having his name in the newspaper as a person who was run over by a carriage while he was drunk.

"The Lady of the Manor" (1882) ("The Mistress")

When a rich woman takes a handsome young peasant as her lover, the peasant family is disorganized. Hingley (1950) sees this as a satire of both the upper and the lower classes of society. Winner (1966) points up Chekhov's irony: When the distraught peasant beats his innocent wife to death, the aristocratic seductress hypocritically denounces the lack of morality in the lower classes. As Winner indicates, Chekhov differentiates character through dialogue: the mistress employs French affectation, and the peasants speak ungrammatically. Rayfield (1975) calls this pure melodrama, with the stereotyped villainous Pole, and with crude asides, à la Balzac. Eisen (1982) disagrees with Rayfield, saying that Chekhov avoids melodrama and sentimentality by revealing the peasant's submission to the lady in a very objective manner. To Eisen, this is a study in the brutalizing effects of poverty and exploitation.

"Late Blooming Flowers" (1882) ("Belated Blossoms")

Dr. Toporkov wants to marry Princess Marusya for her money, but rejects her for a richer merchant's daughter. Out of pity, Toporkov takes Marusya to France to cure her illness, but she dies. Her early hesitation and the doctor's greed led to their missed love opportunity. Hingley (1950) sees it as one of Chekhov's best early stories, a forerunner to *The Cherry Orchard*. Although it is sentimental, Hingley admits, it depicts with a touch of pathos the decline of the Russian nobility. Ralph E. Matlaw, in Eekman (1960), finds the ending improbable in this story of wasted lives. Chekhov's technique is intriguing to Matlaw: an accumulation of scenes in which "nothing happens" mounts up until the overall effect is very moving. Winner (1966) detects clumsiness as Chekhov, as narrator, boldly steps into the action. But Winner is grateful for the poetic mood achieved through sound repetitions and through personification of nature. Kramer (1970) finds the names symbolic: Toporkov means "axe" and Priklonsky (Matusya's family name) means "to bend down." Kramer discerns Turgenev's influence in the contrast between literature and life: Marusya thinks of Toporkov as a valiant Insarov, and of her brother as a "superfluous" Rudin. Rayfield (1975) identifies the "flower" as the declining nobility, Marusya and her brother. He states that greed for money kills

Toporkov's human instincts. Hingley (1976) agrees with Matlaw that the ending is both sentimental and improbable. Kirk (1981) calls this "the most thematically significant of Chekhov's early works." Here Chekhov preaches the doctrine of hard work, Kirk states, as industrious Toporkov rises in the wake of the feckless Priklonskys. Although Chekhov's style here is crude and his characters underdeveloped and unmotivated, Kirk feels that the story evokes a mood, "creating a world filled with impotent lives, wasted emotions, and the absence of communication."[7] H. Peter Stowell, in Clyman (1985), says that "Chekhov developed a tragic superstructure, but his realism, his young cynicism, his satiric portrayals, and his ultimate sense of irony do not mesh successfully." Stowell believes, however, that Abram Room's 1972 film of this story improved it by extending Marusya's life longer, and by using Hector Berlioz's *Symphonie Fantastique* well in creating mood music. Ralph Lindheim, also in Clyman (1985), feels that the story "chronicles the decline and the decadence of the upper classes, and shows how the ambition of the children of serfs was crowned by empty materialistic triumph."[8]

"A Letter from a Don Landowner to a Learned Neighbor" (1880)

A poorly educated landowner displays a pompous manner and foolish thoughts in a letter written in a baroque style, with repetitions, mistakes in grammar, and misspellings. His ideas are ludicrous; he believes, for example, that winter days are short because like all things, they contract in cold weather. Magarshack (*Life*, 1952) calls this Chekhov's first published story, in which he satirized the high-flown style used by his father, his uncle, and his grandfather. Ermilov (1956) finds the story making fun of a style which unites bombast with illiteracy, trying to give trite everyday acts a pompous dignity. Winner (1966) deems it Chekhov's first published parody, containing such inane ideas as that no one could live on the moon, since it exists only at night. Kirk (1981) was pleased to observe that even in such an early story, Chekhov shunned intrusion into the narrative by the author.

"A Living Chattel" (1882) ("Live Merchandise")

Kramer (1970) calls this one of Chekhov's most fantastic stories. Bugrov sells his wife, Lisa, to her lover Grobolsky. Now, since Bugrov is wealthy again, Lisa prefers Bugrov. Grobolsky has to pay Bugrov a further bribe to keep him from sleeping with Mrs. Grobolsky. Although David Magarshack called this story realistic, Kramer finds it very improbable. He says it is entertaining reading, but merely marks a stage in Chekhov's experiments with plot construction. Rayfield (1975) describes this as a weird *ménage à trois*, in which the husband hires the wife's lover as a servant. Eisen (1982) discovers rhythmically recurring references to a piano, which is a symbol of this loveless troika. The piano, says Eisen, is like Lisa, something to be bought and sold but never played. Just as music is absent from the piano, so is love absent from this daffy triangle.

"On Christmas Eve" (1883)

Russian critics disliked this story. V.K. Petersen in 1886 said that the husband's excessive heroism was improbable. In 1887 K. Arsenyev declared that Chekhov aimed to achieve pathos but merely created melodrama. Chudakov (1971) explained that in this story Chekhov employed literary devices that he was parodying at the time in other stories.

"The Reporter" (1882)

Jones (1959) finds in the story a serious discussion by young girls at a dance of when a girl should address her beau in the second person singular, the familiar form. Jones observes that this distinction is found in many European languages. Eisen (1982) describes Chekhov's technique, as he retells the story: A shy reporter, discovered by drunken celebrants, attacks modern society, especially the educational system. Impressed, a group of merchants pledge money for school buildings, but when they sober up, they throw out the reporter. Technically, at the start Chekhov is subjective, favoring the reporter. By the end of the story Chekhov becomes objective, with the result that the reader then identifies fully with the reporter's position.

"St. Peter's Day" (1881)

Simmons (1962) calls this a Pickwickian account of the zany behavior of a hunting party more interested in drinking than in shooting. Simon Karlinsky, in Barricelli (1981), describes this as Chekhov's attack on the cruelty of hunting. The hunters shoot everything that moves. They beat their dogs and throw stones at them. A retired general tears out the throat of a wounded quail with his teeth. The schoolboy, Vanya, along to learn to hunt, gets sick from drinking hard liquor. The scene depicted is wholly devoid of everything romantic or chivalrous.

"The Sinner from Toledo" (1881)

Winner (1966) sees this as a parody of popular romantic fiction. To save his wife from torture by the Spanish Inquisition on charges of witchcraft, the hero delivers her *dead* body to the Inquisitor! Chekhov's style fittingly here employs clichés, puns, and false etymologies.

"The Thief" (1883)

In speaking of the plot, Hingley (1976) points out that the editor Leykin disliked printing serious stories, but Chekhov replied that "a kind word spoken at Easter to a thief under sentence of exile—surely this won't ruin an issue." Chudakov (1971) notes a shift: The story begins in a neutral voice, but then "the narrative becomes more and more saturated with value judgments and emotions. These emotions belong not to the narrator but to the character himself."[9] Eisen (1982) sees this story as evidence of the further evolution of Chekhov's objectivity, with almost all perceptions being from the standpoint of the thief.

"A Thousand and One Passions" (1880)

Ralph E. Mattlaw, in Eekman (1960), describes this as a parody of Victor Hugo's romantic style. Told in inflated language, this intentionally improbable plot includes a wild carriage ride, stormy midnight atmosphere, marriage, murders, and a trip to America.

"The Trial" (1881) ("The Court")

Bruford (1948) describes the crowd relishing the unwarranted beating of a student falsely accused of taking money from his father's chest of drawers. M.H. Shotton, in Fennell (1973), feels that czarist dehumanization had gone so far that the student accepted without protest the blatant injustice and cruelty.

"The Trousseau" (1883) ("The Dowry")

Bruford (1948) finds pathos as the shy daughter of a colonel waits in vain with her homemade trousseau. When her father dies, her uncle sells the trousseau to satisfy his craving for alcohol. Rayfield (1975) denotes genteel sadness and picturesque Russian detail in the story. Eisen (1982) points out Chekhov's use of "gapping"—the major events take place in the gaps between the three scenes of the story. Eisen feels that the technique is effective, for as we infer what has happened, we feel ever more sorry for Manetchka.

"Two in One" (1883)

Yarmolinsky (1954) deems this story notable for its insight into the psychology of "the little man" in a hierarchical society. Kramer (1970) shows how the meek clerk, boisterous and bossy away from his supervisor, instantly becomes servile when the supervisor appears. Not surprised, the supervisor instantly says, "Yes, that's my clerk."

"An Unwanted Victory" (1882) ("An Unnecessary Victory")

Hingley (1950) notes the extravagant style of this romantic adventure of the life of a daughter of a gypsy violinist. Magarshack (*Life*, 1952) says this parody of romantic novels was mistaken as the work of the popular Hungarian writer Maurice Jokai. Matlaw, in Eekman (1960), says Chekhov won his bet that he could write a "romance" as good as those appearing in translation. The mass appeal is here: rapid action, sensational scenes, and flat characters. At the height of an orgy, Ilka is sold to the highest bidder. When her nobleman lover loses his title through a false accusation, Ilka poisons herself. Hingley (1976) reports that even though this was a parody, four films of this story were made between 1916 and 1924.

"What Is Better?" (1883)

Winner (1966) summarizes this story: Krokodilov, the narrator, says taverns are more important than schools, whose chief purpose is to enable people to read the sign "tavern."

"Wolf Baiting" (1882)

Karlinsky, in Barricelli (1981), states that whereas Tolstoy and Sergei Aksakov had described the thrill of killing wolves, Chekhov here shows sympathy for the animals. As well-dressed people sit in the stands watching the massacre of the terrified animals, the reader feels disgust at the cruelty of those responsible for the killing.

"Words, Words, and Words" (1883)

Bitsilli (1983) calls this an ironic rephrasing of Dostoevsky's *Notes from Underground*. Chekhov's protagonist shows some concern for the prostitute Katya, but commits himself to nothing more than words. The story is remarkable, Bitsilli feels, for its subtlety and laconic style.

Summary—Stories: 1880–1883

Since most of these stories were potboilers, there was little serious criticism of them. Many were parodies or comic sketches. Some astute critics noticed the germ of possible future mastery. Others properly concluded that here was a young writer experimenting with ways to express himself, both as to form and subject matter.

3. Stories: 1884–1885

"Abolished" (1885)

Kramer (1970) designates this a social satire upon the importance of rank in a structured society. A retired ensign wanders from office to office, but no one can tell him what he is, since all titles have been abolished.

"The Burbot" (1885) ("The Fish")

Bruford (1957) finds the plot unimportant. "The effect," he says, "depends upon Chekhov's skill in conveying the general atmosphere of a lazy summer's day, the excitement of the participants, and the suggestion of contrasted characters through the casual words they speak."[1] Chudakov (1971) notes that at first the narrator seems omniscient, but later he too must guess at the meanings of the characters' words and actions. Rayfield (1975) says that Chekhov's story of the fish that got away contains his first accurate rendering of peasant language in an unselfconscious manner. Rayfield feels that the story shows the harmony between man and nature. "Out of the story," he says, "comes a sense of a harmonious, if comically absurd, society."[2]

"The Captain's Uniform" (1885)

Bruford (1948) points out Chekhov's irony in this story. A tailor who used to make officers' uniforms laments the passing of the gentry. When he tries to collect his fee for a uniform, a captain gives him a beating. "Ah, one of the good old gentlemen from Petersburg!" says the tailor. Shotton, in Fennell (1973), denotes a borderline between Chekhov the jester and Chekhov the satirical humanist. While being beaten, the tailor smiles beatifically, as if being honored. Dehumanization has taken so sinister a turn, says Shotton, that the reader's reaction hovers between laughter and disquietude.

"The Chameleon" (1884)

Kramer (1970) made a careful study of the "chameleons" in Chekhov's writings. In this story the policeman's attitude towards a dog changes constantly, depending upon who he thinks is the dog's owner. Even the weather seems either hot or cold, Kramer slyly comments, depending upon who owns the dog. In a hierarchical society like that of czarist Russia, observes Kramer, man's concept of the external world is usually mistaken because the nature of "reality" itself constantly changes. Shotton, in Fennell (1973), declares that Chekhov here shows the unchangeability of fools. Despite his continual reversals, the fool seems unembarrassed but blindly pursues his folly in ignorance of the unfolding events. Thus, says Shotton, the story has an anti-denouement: the focus shifts from the outcome of the plot to narrow in on the character of the fool. Pitcher, in Clyman (1985), says that "within an authoritarian, hierarchical system, both individuals themselves and the relations between individuals become absurdly and harmfully distorted."[3]

"A Christmas Dream" (1884)

Rayfield (1975) sees a Dickensian touch in this story narrated from the first person point-of-view. A watchman dreams he surrenders property to poverty-stricken burglars, and awakens to find that he has done so in real life. Although he is sentenced to forced labor, the evil resides more in the system than in the watchman, Rayfield judges. The watchman creatively imagines the background of the pawned objects, which come to life as pledges for poverty, disease, and other social disorders.

"The Cook's Wedding" (1885)

Toumanova (1937) describes how seven-year-old Grisha, sure that the cook Pelagea is frightened by a visit from the huge coachman, brings her the largest apple he can find in the pantry. Winner (1966) shows how childish misunderstanding provides innocent satire of the adult world. Little Grisha wonders why Pelagea must suddenly surrender her pay to her new husband. Hingley (1976) calls the story "farce, with a hint of tears."

"The Crow" (1885)

Chudakov (1971) notes Chekhov's use of point-of-view. By restricting the reader to only what the narrator sees, a concentrated dramatic effect is achieved. Tulloch (1980) summarizes the plot: An officer, awaiting his girlfriend, calls her crow a fool for learning nothing in life. The crow replies, "We crows have no wars or brutality, nor do we surround ourselves with flunkeys, sycophants, and hypocrites."

"The Cynic" (1885)

Rayfield (1975) says that the zookeeper, who makes fun of his animals until stopped by the public, is really displaying his own secret arrogance. Rayfield adds that the censor refused to approve this story.

"The Decoration" (1884)

Winner (1966) finds a triple surprise ending in this satirical tale. A teacher borrows a medal to wear at a banquet, but is seated across from a man who knows he did not earn the medal. Chagrined to expose the medal during a toast, the teacher finds that the other man is also wearing a spurious medal—and a higher one than his! Now the teacher wishes he had borrowed an even higher medal.

"The Double Bass and the Flute" (1885)

Rayfield (1975) describes how a Laurel-and-Hardy pair of ill-matched musicians show by their slapstick incompatibility the fragility of their friendship.

"The Exclamation Mark, a Christmas Story" (1885)

R.E.C. Long (1902) summarizes the plot: Yefim, a clerk for 40 years, feels insulted when a young man chides him for not knowing how to use an exclamation point. When his wife informs him that the mark is used to show great emotion, he suddenly realizes that in the thousands of official documents he has drawn up, he has never had a chance to express anger, rapture, or terror. Eisen (1982) describes his revenge when, à la Walter Mitty, he signs his name in the guest book at his boss's Christmas party: "Yefim Perekhladin!!!" "Take that," he muttered.

"The Father of the Family" (1885) ("The Head of the Family")

After a drinking bout or a loss at cards, Stepan is mean and surly, especially toward his children. F.M. Perry (1926) observed that this seemingly plotless story has a unity organized around its illustrative purpose. Rayfield (1975) notes the irony in the father's puzzlement over why his son fears him.

"Goose Conversations" (1884)

Winner (1966) says that in this story "a flock of geese address each other by titles and fly in formation according to rank."

"The Huntsman" (1885) ("The Hunter")

Egor deserts his wife in order to be a full-time hunter. Soviet critic A.S. Dolinin in 1923 pointed out the story's similarity to Turgenev's "The Meeting" in theme and structure, but said that Chekhov's approach was less emotional than Turgenev's but more economical and more dynamic. Magarshack (*Life*, 1952) noted that the novelist Dmitry Grigorovich was so impressed by "the remarkable truthfulness of the delineation of the characters and the description of nature" that he wrote Chekhov several laudatory letters, and asked editor Alexei Suvorin to make Chekhov a regular contributor to Suvorin's large Petersburg daily newspaper, *New Times*.

Simmons (1962) found a brilliant use of dialogue to depict character. Payne (1963) says that one short sentence captures the wife's love for Egor. Upon seeing him, "ashamed of her happiness, she hid her smiles with her hand." Winner (1966) notes the similarity to Turgenev's *Sportsman's Sketches*. Nature is used symbolically, and Chekhov's objectivity in refusing to comment on Egor's cruelty deepens the pathos felt for the deserted wife. Rayfield (1975) calls this an ode to summer. At the end, as Egor disappears on the horizon, the reader sees the scene through the wife's eyes, and participates in her deep loneliness.

Hahn (1977) says this prose poem is "saturated with omens of impending separation." By erasing the author, Chekhov gets a more dramatic effect than Turgenev does. If Chekhov is not metaphysical like Tolstoy and Dostoevsky, neither is he, like Gogol and Turgenev, confined to social and psychological insight, Hahn feels. If, as an agnostic, he shows a world unyielding to human needs, then also, as a humanist, Chekhov asserts the high priority of human values.

"Intelligent as a Log" (1885)

Bruford (1948) points out the irony in this story, in which a retired military officer cannot understand why a justice of the peace has fined him for striking his valet—especially since he supported the justice during his recent political campaign.

"The Last Female Mohican" (1885)

Bruford (1948) denotes the social satire in this tale of a wife suing her husband for dishonoring their name by socializing with merchants and going hunting with his clerk. Shotton, in Fennell (1973), states that here Chekhov completely abandons the trappings of external plot.

"A Malefactor" (1885)

Denis, a peasant, is found guilty of unscrewing railroad nuts for use as fishing sinkers. He had no comprehension of the seriousness of his "crime." Magarshack (*Life*, 1952) points out that Tolstoy found this to be one of Chekhov's most profound stories. Payne (1963) describes Chekhov's reply to a lawyer who said that those who destroy state property must be punished. "I would have found Denis not guilty," answered Chekhov, "and I would have told Denis, 'You have not yet ripened into a deliberate criminal. Go, and ripen!'" Winner (1966) observes that some of the pathetic lack of communication is found in the contrast between the folksy dialect of Denis and the bureaucratic jargon of the judge. Hahn (1977) feels that Chekhov has captured "the peasant's ignorant self-righteousness which verges on deliberate though cautious insolence."

"The Marshall's Widow" (1885)

Bruford (1948) finds irony and humor in this tale of a memorial service honoring the marshall, who died of alcoholism. Although the widow expressly bans alcoholic drinks, the government officials smuggle in their bottles, and soon all are drunk.

"The Mask" (1884)

Winner (1966) and Rayfield (1975) find social satire in the surprise ending. A masked man at a ball demands a room for an orgy with a prostitute, and insults all the town dignitaries when denied. As the townspeople prepare to evict him, he reveals himself to be the town's millionaire, and the people declare it to be a great joke.

"Minds in Ferment" (1884)

Bruford (1948) describes this study in social psychology. Two men are watching starlings. Curious, a crowd gathers around them. When the police try to disperse the crowd, some educated people resist the police and are jailed for not dispersing.

"The Mirror" (1885)

Smith (1973) notes that in the original version of this story, Chekhov said that a successful love match requires cooperation from life, but never gets it. "Few writers," according to Smith, "have depicted so persistently the persecution of would-be lovers by inimical forces." Rayfield (1975) calls this a nightmare story. Looking into a mirror of the future, Nellie sees nothing but trouble: sick children, a dying husband, debts, and worries. Eisen (1982) says that a conventional romantic dream of marriage turns into a case study in neurotic depression and pathological fear. A double-distance effect is achieved as the reader perceives the action in Nellie's dreams.

"Ninochka" (1885)

Ernest J. Simmons, in Dunnigan (1960), calls this tale a transition in Chekhov's humor from anecdotal and external to accusatory, as it is here. No longer jolly or farcical, the humor is now ironic or satiric. Rayfield (1975) says that the characters are ones often used by Chekhov. The narrator, a lover of his best friend's wife Ninochka, moves into the marital bedroom and moves the husband into the pantry. The husband wants only peace, Ninochka is shallow, and the lover is ruthless but amiable, Rayfield says.

"Oysters" (1884)

Kramer (1970) states that as the onlookers laugh at the boy's dislike of oysters, Chekhov's villains become not so much cruel as indifferent. Rayfield (1975) finds melodrama in the tale of a starving boy being fed oysters, in which first his hunger and then his revulsion are well described. Stowell (1980) finds an impressionistic mingling of past and present, and of a child's viewpoint with a delirious state. When the boy passes out from eating too many oysters, he has a nightmarish dream, and awakens to find his father nearby, gesticulating. "The dream is like his waking imagination, and his waking vision of his father is dreamlike. For the impressionists all levels of reality have sensory validity and all surfaces are real."[4]

"Perpetuum Mobile" (1884)

Rayfield (1975) describes this story in which a doctor and a lawyer, going to an inquest, have differing sexual appetites. The doctor spurns the innkeeper's daughter's offers, but the lawyer seeks them out. After a quarrel, the doctor and the lawyer leave with no inquest. Rayfield finds Chekhov showing the peasants' ignorance of the law, and the fact that they receive no help from the medical profession for their mental suffering.

"Proper Measures" (1884) ("Appropriate Measures")

Bruford (1948) finds humor in this story of an examination of a grocer's shop for cleanliness. When the grocer gives the examiners vodka and sturgeon, they decide his shop is not unclean after all. Simmons (1962) says this "little masterpiece" is deserving of "an honored place in any extensive anthology of Chekhov's best tales."

"Sergeant Prishibeev" (1883)

Toumanova (1937) calls the sergeant a kind of *miles gloriosus*. Hingley (1950) points out that Chekhov escaped the censor's ban by sending this story to another paper. Ermilov (1956) said that the name "Prishibeev" came to be accepted as a symbol of authoritarian disregard for people's rights. Even though he was no doubt an unusually cruel policeman, Ermilov added, he embodied the spirit of a reactionary government, and so was a useful symbol to those desiring reform.

Winner (1966) calls Prishibeev a self-appointed supervisor of public morals. Kramer (1970) notes that instead of showing him at the height of his power, Chekhov shows him on trial for preventing religious processions, and that he is a pathetic figure trying to defend himself. Shotton, in Fennell (1973), finds disillusionment merging on misanthropy, with the laughable acquiring distinct overtones of evil. Hingley (1976) noticed that Stalin greatly admired this story, perhaps because of its accurate depiction of a potential concentration camp guard. Ralph Lindheim, in Clyman (1985), calls Prishibeev Chekhov's first "man in a case" — an inordinate legalist who exudes banality and self-satisfied mediocrity. Pitcher, also in Clyman (1985), calls this a study in hierarchy mentality. Prishibeev is so far gone, Pitcher concludes, that he tells citizens they cannot do a thing unless a precise law permits it.

"Small Fry" (1885)

Brewster (1924) points out the similarity between this story and Katherine Mansfield's "The Fly," in which frustration is vented by killing a fly. Here the clerk crushes a cockroach. "Both stories reveal the spiritual aridity of these men, but also something more deeply universal — the lower depths filled with monstrously devilish impulses, desires, and hatreds."[5] Bruford (1948) shows that the reader is torn between repugnance at the clerk's servility and admiration for his unwillingness to get ahead by stealing or by informing on fellow workers.

"Sorrow" (1885)

Grigory's wife dies as he takes her to the hospital. Not knowing she is dead, he apologizes to her for mistreating her. Iliodor Palmin, a poet, told Chekhov, "It's the best thing you've written. Full of truth to life, it leaves one both amused and sad." Ermilov (1956) describes the callous doctor, who tells Grigory, "Say goodbye to your hands and feet. Why cry? You're over 60. You've had your day."

Winner (1966) notes how Grigory's disjointed speech reflects his incoherent, stunned mind. It is ironic, Winner observes, that Grigory promises to "live anew"—for he too dies, of the cold. Hahn (1977) finds a "remarkable handling of the land-scape images, which come to act as a composite metaphor for human feelings." The storm first stands for the wife's suffering, and then for the turmoil in Grigory's mind. As he lets the reins fall, realizing that his wife is dead, it signifies the lack of direction in a man who realized, too late, how much he loved his wife. The cold attitude of the doctor towards Grigory's death, Hahn feels, gives the story an ambiguous ending.

"Surgery" (1884)

Chekhov's brother Michael explained, in Koteliansky (1925), that this story grew out of a medical student's experience, in which he in error extracted a good tooth instead of the bad one. Later the student became a famous doctor. Winner (1966) noted that Chekhov used very brief introductions in his stories. Sometimes, as here, he even starts the story with a sentence fragment.

"The Swedish Match" (1884) ("The Safety Match")

Bruford (1948) calls this a satire on legal red tape. Magarshack (*Life*, 1952) finds it a parody on Dostoevsky, in which an assistant examining magistrate (an avid reader of Dostoevsky's novels) evolves a complicated solution to a murder, only to have the "murdered" man show up unscathed. Matlaw, in Eekman (1960), says it satirizes detective stories in which the detective discards simple evidence in favor of a complex solution. There is also satire of the public for pandering to the gore found in detective stories. Kramer (1970) quotes Victor Shklovsky who praised not only the parody but also Chekhov's mastery of a complex plot.

"A Terrible Night" (1884)

An editor's note to a 1907 translation in *Current Literature* said that, like Maupassant, Chekhov was a pessimist, but with humor that saved him from the

Frenchman's morbidity. Even in this gloomy story the editor said that "a touch of humor suddenly illuminates the shadow that darkens his page."[6] Winner (1966) calls this a parody of the ghost story. Each person, returning home, finds a coffin in his room. The reason: Their friend, a coffin maker, is hiding his inventory to prevent confiscation by creditors.

"To Talk or Not to Talk" (1884)

Rayfield (1975) describes the plot: A successful womanizer tells his friend, an unsuccessful one, that the secret to a consummated liaison is to keep talking. The friend talks too much to a stranger (a plain clothes detective) and gets a two-year sentence. When the censor refused to approve the story, because of its criticism of police, Chekhov resolved to steer clear of satire so pointed as to be unpublishable.

"The Tutor" (1884) ("The Coach")

Rayfield (1975) shows how the tutor is embarrassed when the pupil's father solves an algebra problem that he could not solve. Generally, says Rayfield, to Chekhov the teacher is the epitome of exploited humanity.

"Two Journalists" (1885)

Winner (1966) summarizes the plot: Reporter Rybkin gets so depressed writing about violence that he hangs himself. His friend, reporter Schleykin, writes Rybkin's obituary under the swinging body, and then starts a series of articles on suicide. "Many of Chekhov's early works," says Winner, "satirize the cheapness and vulgarity of the Russian press."[7] Rayfield (1975) states that the story shows "a Muscovite Grub Street in which decency, aspirations, and talent are sacrificed to the routines of journalism. The jester is protesting his role."[8]

"Vint" (1884) ("Whist")

Bruford (1948) shows the fun Chekhov has at the expense of rank-happy clerks. The clerks play a card game, arranging the fifty-two cards in ranks according to authority in their office: The highest boss is the ace, the next highest the king, and the queens are the wives of the top bosses. Kramer (1970) notes how universal Chekhov's parody is, for in a highly stratified society, each role is carefully defined and proscribed.

Summary—Stories: 1884–1885

In this period Chekhov continued to write chiefly humorous sketches and parodies. His main target was the inhumanity of a rigid society that prevented upward mobility. But now his first great stories appear, and he begins to be recognized as an outstanding writer. His best work in this period includes "The Chameleon," "The Huntsman," "A Malefactor," "Sergeant Prishibeev," and "Sorrow."

4. Stories: 1886

"Agafya"

Agafya, like other women, cannot resist the charm of the idler Savka. She does not mind a beating from her husband, as long as she can spend a night with Savka. The writer Dmitry Grigorovich said in 1886 that "such a masterly way of conveying one's observations can be found only in Turgenev and Tolstoy." He advised Chekhov to nurture his great talent, which could reveal "the truth of the inner analysis, the mastery of the descriptions, and the plastic sense which sketches in a few lines a perfect picture of a cloud growing dim against the background of the sunset."[1] E.M. Forster in 1915 said that the plot flows by silently, like a beautiful nocturnal river. Each thing is specific, Forster declared. Chekhov avoids generalization, symbols, and a climax, the things that might seduce him from his theme and its poetic treatment.[2]

Winner (1966) observed that here Chekhov follows Turgenev in using an aristocratic narrator. Jackson (1967) quoted Charles du Bos on the appropriateness of concluding the story before Agafya returns home to her husband, since the theme is the irresistible attraction that certain crude idlers have on women. Chudakov (1971) agreed with Vladimir Korolenko who had said in 1888 that the point-of-view is "outside the psyches of the main heroes." Thus, the objective narrator can only report what he sees or feels, but he cannot explain why people behave so peculiarly.

Joseph L. Conrad, in Debreczeny (1977), said that by personifying natural phenomena, Chekhov links little people with the entire universe. Hahn (1977) called this an excellent study of Agafya's complex feelings about a wife's responsibilities. Her "wild, guttural laugh" while making love with Savka shows an anarchic component that Chekhov found in the female personality. Agafya is an amalgam of reckless determination, pain, and impotence. The bright green trail she cuts as she leaves Savka for her husband "epitomizes the fearful subjugation of the woman's needs and basic personality to the stern authority of her husband, while her lover is granted an enviable masculine immunity."[3] Agafya, Hahn believes, is trapped between two forms of masculine domination. Her feelings are shown only by default, for Chekhov had not yet understood the psychology of women.

"Anyuta"

Anyuta lives with medical students, helping them through medical school. They discard her when they get their degrees. An artist forces her to take her blouse off, so he can examine her rib structure. Poggioli (1957) states that "Chekhov makes Anyuta's body serve the higher purposes of art and science. In reality she serves, with both her body and soul, the blind selfishness of two human beings who consider her an inferior creature, while she is morally superior to them."[4] The artist is trying to paint Psyche, and Anyuta resembles Psyche after she lost her lover.

Alan Lelchuk believes that Chekhov showed great skill in breaking the time sequence into five action-blocks. This enables Chekhov to convey insights into his characters and control the reader's reaction, Lelchuk feels.[5] Charles E. May, in Clyman (1985), says that the story "depends upon a rhythm of reality being momentarily broken up by a significant event, only to fall back once again." The medical student tries to capture her body, and the artist her soul, but "only Chekhov can 'sound' her by his presentation of this significant episode."[6]

"Art"

Bruford (1948) summarizes the plot: Once a year lazy Seryozhka does a worthwhile act—he builds an ice cross for Epiphany rites. In the sunlight the cross sparkles like rubies. The ceremony is for the blessing of the waters, to improve fishing. People scramble for a piece of the wooden framework of the cross, for it will bring good luck all year. Rayfield (1975) says that here "only the taciturn recluse finds his place in nature." His artistic creation seems to justify all his meanness, idleness, and drunkenness. "Now," Chekhov says, "he's a servant of God." Rayfield observes that Chekhov, like his mentor Nikolai Leskov, found that art was never more genuine than when in the service of the church.

"At a Country House" ("At the Manor")

R.E.C. Long (1902) said that Chekhov, like Swift, is merciless in his satire but, unlike Swift, he does not satirize humanity as a whole. In Long's opinion Chekhov's art was wholly objective and therefore effective. A reviewer in *The Athenaeum* in 1904 said that this story allows the author to laugh at some of the aristocratic prejudices of his countrymen.[7] Gerhardi (1923) describes Chekhov's irony, in showing a father who insults his daughter's suitor, while insisting that he loves her very much.

Simmons (1962) shows how the suitor bursts the father's pomposity. Hingley (1978) finds Chekhov in a rare use of overstatement, devoting most of the story to an egoist's self-praise. "So deft is the handling, so richly realized the theme of mutual misunderstanding, that this must rate among the author's masterpieces," Hingley states.[8] Chekhov even briefly flirted with a rehabilitation of the father, Hingley thought, but then abandoned the idea in order to remain true to the story's primary focus.

"At the Mill"

Winner (1966) admired the excellent depiction of the peasant characters. Andrew R. Durkin saw the smallness of the selfish miller who only reluctantly gives a small coin to help his needy brother: "Monstrous as the miller may be, the hints of other emotions in him, which he ruthlessly suppresses, make him an object of horrified sympathy rather than of easy condemnation, a creature trapped in the coils of his own self."[9]

"Champagne"

Under the influence of champagne, the narrator describes his fascination with his wife's aunt. Smith (1973) finds that the aunt exuded a strange perfume of beauty and corruption, and comments that Chekhov's beautiful women often have a vaguely alarming air of evil about them.

"Children"

The contrasting personalities of brothers and sisters are shown in a game of lotto. James Gibbons Huneker says that this is a story that Dickens, had he had more art, would have been proud to have written, for "it is as full of Tolstoy as of Chekhov—and not a little of Dostoevsky."[10]

"The Chorus Girl"

Pasha, the young chorus girl, is forced to return to her lover's wife not only a cheap bracelet he gave her but also many of her personal possessions. An unperceptive reviewer in 1920 called it "a vivid study of a man lured from his wife by a chorus girl and restored to a sense of conjugal duty by the sight of his wife's humiliation before his mistress."[11] Werth (1925) stressed the "continuity of emotional significance" that Chekhov achieved by having his protagonist engage in a characteristic act at the story's end.[12]

Toumanova (1937) saw the irony in Pasha's admiring "the lady" for her "refined manners." Poggioli (1957) found further irony in the husband's remorse over having his wife visit such a "low creature" as Pasha. The wife seems to resent only the husband's loss of property, not of morality. Pasha's moral superiority is shown, Poggioli feels, by the fact that she is the only one of the two women aware of the impression she makes upon the other. Smith (1973) believes that by arousing too much pathos, Chekhov fails to strike a balance between sympathy for Pasha and an exposé of the sordidness of prostitution. Rayfield (1975) finds that the story owes much to Maupassant's *Boule de suif.*

"Difficult People"

A father and his son regret that they are incompatible. Ermilov (1956) says that the original version of the story had a final reconciliation. The son opines that everything has its price—even gentleness and kindness are attained only through hard lessons and sacrifice. Rayfield (1975) believes that in depicting an obdurate father, Chekhov was exorcising his own feelings toward his father's tyranny.

"The Dramatist"

Gottlieb (1982) shows Chekhov making fun of playwrights who steal from foreign plays. The dramatist describes his technique: He has his sister translate a French or German play, inserts Russian names, and announces the new play as his own.

"Dreams" ("Daydreams")

A tramp dreams of a free life in Siberia, but his guards try to disillusion him. Serge Persky (1913) said that in Chekhov's Russia, the only happiness possible is that found in dreams.[13] Winner (1966) calls this a subtle treatment of the vanity of illusions. He finds Chekhov creating personifications of nature with highly concentrated poetic images, and he notes that all of the tramp's features are described in diminutives. Kramer (1970) notes that Chekhov's dreamers tend toward either the mysterious or the mystical. They have utopian visions but, as here, are usually overcome by the vicissitudes of everyday life.

Debreczeny (1977) points out the tramp's reluctance to reveal his identity—he feels he has many identities. Which identity of ours is the "true" one? One of his guards stops questioning, realizing that a person has a right to privacy over who he is and who he would like to be. Autumn is used structurally: The season reminds the tramp of previous happiness and present dismay. Hahn (1977) interprets the characters as spineless and negative, crushed by an oppressive environment. She believes that Chekhov's pessimism predominates here: "Pondering the vast difference separating them from freedom, all three men are robbed of any air of effective initiative."

"Easter Eve"

Crossing on a ferry, the narrator encounters Jeronim, a lay brother mourning the death of the good monk Nikolai, who wrote creative psalm-like songs of praise. In 1915 Henry Seidel Canby used this story as an example of "free" fiction. Chekhov does not slavishly follow literary convention, as American writers do, said Canby. This story, with little plot and no "punch line," is "an unforgettable portrait of wistful hero-worship." If an American editor told Chekhov that his stories must "move," Chekhov's stories would reply: We pause, as life does. We have no foregone conclusions, any more than life does. Canby says that in a few pages, this interesting story conveys "much of Russian spirituality and more of universal human nature."[14]

Gerhardi (1923) recalls Chekhov's letter to Suvorin about this story. Merezhkovsky, said Chekhov, calls my monk who composes songs "a failure!" How so? God grant us all a life like his: He believed in God, had enough to eat, and had the gift of composing poetry. What more is required for success in life? Was Napoleon a success? It would take a god, said Chekhov, to be able to tell human successes from failures.

George Ivask, in Eekman (1960), noted that when Jeronim saw the merchant's beautiful young wife he experienced no erotic feeling but is rather reminded of the tender beauty of Nikolai and his radiant Church Slavonic music. Chekhov captures Jeronim's simple angelic nature without sentimentalizing him. Rayfield (1975) finds a magical charm in the story, noting too how well the language is differentiated for the characters. The river is used symbolically, as a divider between the lay and the holy worlds.

Hahn (1977) says the story is poised on tension between the night-sense, having a religious intensity and strength, and the dawn-sense, when religious values seem numbed. Chekhov the humanist is here "stating the problem correctly," as he would say. In contrasting the two worlds of the workaday ferry and the uplifting church, the story uses intense poetic imagery to achieve a concentrated emotional pitch. "This," says Hahn, "is not the art of a skeptic, but of an extremely sensitive empiricist," who can show how life feels different at different times. Charles E. May, in Clyman (1985), sees Chekhov sharing his own creative credo as he describes how Nikolai wrote his songs: Everything must be harmonious, brief, and complete. In every line there should be tenderness. The psalm should be written so that the worshipper will both rejoice and weep, and his mind should be so stirred as to throw him into a tremor.

"Excellent People" ("Good People")

Vladimir, a lawyer and would-be literary critic, incurs the wrath of his sister, a doctor, for attacking Tolstoy's doctrine of non-resistance to evil. He dies, forgotten, and she volunteers to do medical work in the provinces. Hingley (1950) feels that Chekhov's sympathy lay with the sister. Magarshack (*Life*, 1952) believes that in this, his first Tolstoy story, Chekhov deserts his usual objectivity in preaching a doctrine of work.

Ermilov (1956) finds in the story Chekhov's political skepticism but also his search for truth. In Ermilov's opinion Chekhov had an inherent feeling that there were falsity and affectation in Tolstoy's doctrines. Winner (1966) notes that in later revisions Chekhov weakened the Tolstoyan viewpoint in the story. Hingley (1976) sees the story as a sign of the battle going on in Chekhov's mind between his two professions: should he desert his mistress, literature, in order to serve as a doctor to the poor?

"A Gentleman Friend"

In 1920 Francis Hackett noted Chekhov's use of a trick ending, something rare for him. Underneath, however, Hackett found great sensitivity and humane feeling, for Chekhov's faith is in intelligence. To those who would call that not much of a faith, Hackett replies, "Well, the other sort of thing, riding the world from one Holy War to another, has not proved a startling success."[15] Poggioli (1957) summarizes the plot: A stripteaser is so poor that she cannot dress well. She visits the office of a "customer," a dentist, to ask for a loan. Seeing herself in a mirror, she recovers her dignity and is no longer Vanka the prostitute but the simple girl Nastasya. But, failing to recognize her, the dentist pulls her tooth and extracts her last ruble in payment.

"Grisha"

Winner (1966) points out how Soviet formalist critics said that Chekhov here intentionally "made it strange," that is, shifted the plane of reality in order to achieve his effect. Grisha, a two-year-old, is taken by his nanny to a rendezvous between the nanny and a sailor. Innocent Grisha resents the loss of his comfortable nursery for the sailor's bedroom where things are dark and strange, and where even an oven fork has two horns. H. Hamburger in 1972 made a structural study of this story, using a theory of point-of-view based on an analogy with a movie camera.[16] Stowell (1980) finds this the best of Chekhov's children's stories; it allows him to experiment with raw and seemingly unintellectualized perceptions. Grisha's movements through space constitute an expansion of his consciousness. He ends up in a morass of uncertainty—in Chekhov's words, "there are so many papas, mamas, and aunts that there is no knowing who to run to."

"The Husband"

A love-starved woman dances gaily with soldiers in a provincial town, until her husband takes her home early from the ball. S.P. Mais (1921) says that "the final paragraphs of the story, in which we see the wretched couple walking home in the dark, the mud sloshing under their feet, choking with hatred of each other, are inimitable."[17] Bruford (1948) notes that the husband is not satisfied until he sees that the happy look has disappeared from his wife's face.

"In Court"

Toumanova (1937) admires Chekhov's artistic economy, as she relates the plot: On trial for murdering his wife, an old peasant asks the guard to testify for him—the guard is his son! Shotton, in Fennell (1973), feels that this story reveals, in a Tolstoyan manner, the injustice of the prevailing legal system.

"In Spring"

Bruford (1948) observes how the coming of spring is eagerly awaited and richly celebrated in cold Russia. Nature, says Chekhov, now seems to be smiling like a man recovering from a serious illness. Simmons, in Dunnigan (1960), says that although the narrator is not Chekhov, his thoughts about art resemble Chekhov's. The treatment of nature here, Simmons feels, looks forward to the lyrical landscapes of the later tales.

"Ladies"

Bruford (1948) describes this story of injustice: An aging teacher loses a position as secretary of a district home to a rich, but less qualified, young actor. Pressure from the wives of "important" people forces the school superintendent to go against his humane instincts.

"The Lodger"

Yarmolinsky (1954) sees young Brykovich as one of the many persons Chekhov portrayed as being "betrayed by weakness into a cruelly frustrating situation and unable to break out of the trap." Brykovich is simply a "lodger" in his wife's boarding house, for that is the way she treats him.

"The Long Tongue"

Winner (1966) enjoyed this parody, in which the heroine uses affectations, endearments, needless repetitions, and ludicrous Russianized foreign phrases.

"A Lot of Paper"

Bruford (1948) described this satire on bureaucracy. Finding an epidemic, a village elder requests that schools be closed on November 19. After 36 letters have been written, permission is granted on February 22, long after the epidemic has ended.

"Misery" ("Despair") ("Grief") ("Heartache")

Iona's son has just died, and no one will listen to his expression of grief, so he pours it out to his horse. Poggioli (1957) notes how each person takes out frustration on those with lower social rank. Winner (1966) observes the symbolic use of snow: It not only isolates Iona from the world, but covers him as each new customer shakes his snow off onto Iona. Kramer (1970) notices that part of Iona's problem is in his own inarticulateness. Hahn (1977) feels that Chekhov nearly broke his unwritten rule not to humiliate a character, when the hunchback hits Iona. Although the story borders on sentimentality, Chekhov here shows a strong human and moral concern, as well as the ability to project his view of the world through imagery.

Despite the lack of response from his customers, Iona's efforts to communicate improve his skill at it, thus helping ease his grief, in the view of Joan D. Winslow.[18] After discerning a similarity between this story and Katherine Mansfield's "The Life of Ma Parker," Walter Allen says that, failing to understand common people, Mansfield produces sentimental characters. "The cabby's customers in Chekhov's story strike us as representative figures from a real world whereas those in 'The Life of Ma Parker' do not," Allen feels.[19] Soviet critic A.N. Vasileva, in an excellent stylistic analysis, shows how the first paragraph forecasts the direction the story will take. The mood, says Vasileva, is one of death-like immobility and despair.[20]

"Misfortune" ("A Calamity") ("A Disaster")

Ignored by her husband, pretty Sophia keeps chasing away the lawyer Ilyin, who wants to make love to her. As her resistance weakens, she says to herself, "You're an immoral woman." A reviewer in the *Nation* in 1915 says that Sophia acts as if hypnotized "not so much by passion as by calamity."[21] Winner (1966) detects an influence of *Anna Karenina* upon this story. Rayfield (1975) agrees, stating that "her innate insincerity, her 'leech-like' sexuality, and the author's condescending comments on the 'triviality and egotism of a youthful nature' all betray a too recent reading of Tolstoy."

Hahn (1977) contrasts D.H. Lawrence with Chekhov. Whereas Lawrence conveys feelings through images of a solipsistic kind, "Chekhov conveys by dialogue and dramatic suggestion feelings of whose existence the woman herself is not yet consciously aware." At the age of 26, "Chekhov was already writing with unexpected authority about the collision between conscience and instinct in the sexual life, about the romantic overtones of feminine sexual desire, and the self-delusion by which women in particular avoid recognizing sexual impulses in themselves." Virginia Llewellyn Smith says that Chekhov feared women and rarely portrayed a fulfilled sexual relationship. But Hahn distrusts Smith's judgments, for Chekhov's sympathies are often with women who are bullied by men, and his understanding of women and his presentation of their problems grew continually until he finally achieved the "magnificently realized feminine personalities" of *The Three Sisters*.[22]

Eisen (1982) shows Chekhov's use of objective correlatives, situations which reveal Sophia's entire state of mind. Examples are her feeling as frustrated as a bee trapped against a window pane, or considering her life as monotonous as railroad cars clinking over the rail joints, or feeling that her conscience stands like a sentry on guard to protect her morality. Andrew R. Durkin observes how "seemingly objective but potentially metaphoric objects (stifling heat, or a church with a rusty roof) not only orient the reader in a specific setting but also subtly align him perceptually and emotionally with the central character."[23]

"A Nightmare"

Kunin, a district board member, wants to open a church school, but is appalled by Father Yakov's poor appearance and incompetence. When he learns of Yakov's poverty, hard work, and charitable acts, he is sorry he criticized Yakov. Sean O'Faolain in 1937 noted Chekhov's eye for details. When Yakov hangs his hat on a large misshapen nail, Kunin spitefully says that even nails are bent in this run-down house.[24] Chudakov (1971) observes that Chekhov here discards the omniscient narrator, and restricts everything to Kunin's point-of-view. "In this way," says Chudakov, "an objective method of description arises even in a narrative related to an internal world." Chudakov mentions that Chekhov could not keep himself from stepping into the story at the conclusion to condemn Kunin.

Shotton, in Fennell (1973), detects irony in that Kunin, a lifelong wastrel, criticizes Yakov, a thrifty person, for being careless with money. Rayfield (1975) states that this story was well received by the public. Some letters to the editor suggested that readers felt that Chekhov had identified a new field of social action.

"Not Wanted"

Anne Friis in 1946 showed how Katherine Mansfield's "Marriage à la Mode" resembles this story. Both deal with a hardworking husband who visits his wife in the country on weekends, only to be crowded out by the wife's bohemian friends. Although Mansfield's story seems to be original, she shows Chekhov's influence not only in the plot but in the creation of atmosphere and the description of intricate psychological phenomena.[25]

"On the Road" ("On the Way")

Grigory, a widower, meets single Marya on an overnight stop at an inn. After a long discussion they fail to fall in love, due to his reticence. This story was an instant success. Chekhov's brother Alexander said it caused a furor in St. Petersburg. Grigorovich praised it, and the critic L.E. Obolensky wrote an article showing that Chekhov was a greater artist than Korolenko.[26] Long (1902) called it "the most brilliant and despairing story Chekhov ever wrote." Grigory, Long felt, is admirable even in his extravagance and pathos. Chekhov's sharp eye enables him to compress "into a single vivid but untranslatable sentence a whole life of vulgar emotion." Chekhov achieves an extraordinary effect through repetition of banalities. He turns base metal into gold, being "at his best when his characters are at their worst. By some strange reversal of the ordinary laws of art," Long said, "the more aimless his motives, the more monotonous his background, the more vapid his characters, the more glowing and lifelike are his pictures. He dazzles by analysis of the simplest things. That this is art of a high order is beyond question."[27]

A reviewer in 1903 said that this story showed "a typical Russian, enthusiastic and speculative but in actual life ineffectual and despairing." Though his stories are gloomy, said the reviewer, Chekhov shows a unity, a restraint, and a complete subordination of details to the overall effect which makes him a master of the short story.[28] In 1911 another reviewer said that an illuminating sentence from this story describes much of Chekhov's work: Russians have an inquiring mind, a tendency to speculate, and an extraordinary capacity for belief, but all of this is wasted by their laziness, wastefulness, and fantastic triviality.[29]

Magarshack (*Life*, 1952) pointed out that Sergei Rachmaninov said that his *Fantasy for an Orchestra* owed its origin to this story, Kramer (1970) calls this Chekhov's best story of 1886. Each detail of setting is used organically, Kramer notes. He disagrees with Caroline Gordon and Allen Tate, who had said (in *The House of Fiction*, 1960) that it is Grigory's reticence that barred a love relationship. Kramer feels that the pair created their own unhappiness through their inability to respond to each other. Rayfield (1975) states that the composer Peter Tchaikovsky liked the story so much that he sent Chekhov a fan letter praising it. Rayfield sees Grigory as a superfluous man, like Turgenev's Rudin, unable to make love to Marya, who pities him.

Savely Senderovich, in Debreczeny (1977), sees the story as a chain of momentary impressions, with the switch among impressions being accomplished by a shift in point-of-view. Chekhov used this mosaic of impressions because Grigory's life has been a chaos of shifts and changes. As man and woman meet, everything merges into one massive impression of ecstasy, even though the relationship is never consummated. Chekhov captures the atmosphere of impressionism just as the impressionistic painters capture the evanescence of beauty by breaking it into a series of discrete images. As these painters eliminate geometrical perspective, so does Chekhov overthrow spiritual perspective. This story's spiritual atmosphere culminates, Senderovich feels, in the Christmas carol.

This story is not about love, Senderovich adds, but about the Russian capacity for faith, and the meaning of faith in Russian life. When the reader discovers the story's special poetic composition, she says, the true meaning of the story is revealed.[30] Tulloch (1980) points out that Grigory has futilely chased every ideal—America, science, socialism, Tolstoyism—while ignoring his immediate goal, Marya. In the final pathetic scene he is on the road in the snow, dragging his daughter by the hand, still seeking. This story beautifully anticipates Jack Kerouac's *On the Road*.

"The Orator"

Zapoikin, the orator, delivers a funeral oration on the wrong person—he thought it was the old assessor, not the young one, who died. Bruford (1948) notes that the old assessor feels it mockery to say "He would never take a bribe" about a living person. Winner (1966) finds a long list of rhetorical clichés in the oration. Hingley (1976) calls this the best of Chekhov's early comic stories, noting that the old assessor dislikes hearing his fondness for alcohol mentioned so publicly.

"Other People's Misfortunes"

Vera, the young bride, is reluctant to dispossess the Mikhailov family from their dilapidated country estate, but her husband Stepan sees it as an opportunity to experiment with scientific farming. Yarmolinsky (1954) finds Chekhov living up to his admonition to "be humane to the tips of one's fingers," as he depicts the pathetic decline of the landowning gentry. Ermilov (1956) sees this story as biographical: Chekhov's feelings were mixed when his bankrupt father fled to Moscow, and the new owners would have a lot of painting and papering to cover over "other people's misfortunes"—scratches, cracks, and graffiti.

"The Privy Councillor"

Bruford (1948) describes the privy councillor as such an obnoxious guest that his sister gives him money to travel abroad rather than to have to put up with his ingratitude and surliness. Later, Bruford (1957) saw in the story a contrast between city and rural manners. Although he is ignored by his uncle, the nephew pities him because of his loneliness, and shows love toward him. Bitsilli (1983) sees this as a comic allegory. Since the narration is a recollection of childhood, there is an ironic contrast between the past and present narrator. The story is thus viewed as an experiment by Chekhov to see what effects can be achieved through manipulation of points-of-view.

"The Requiem" ("Mass for the Dead")

Merchant Andrey has a requiem mass for his daughter Marya, whom he calls a "harlot" because she was an actress. Toumanova (1937) finds pathos in Marya's early death, especially since she knew death was coming. Bruford (1957) notes that, for an unbeliever, Chekhov always handled ecclesiastical themes with singular delicacy. Poggioli (1957), on the other hand, believes that the priest may be a hypocrite, kowtowing to popular expectation to honor a well-known actress. Andrey may not even know the meaning of the word "harlot," Poggioli feels. In this view the story becomes a study in misunderstanding: between Andrey and Marya, and between Andrey and the priest.

Winner (1966) recalls that Marya loved nature, but that Andrey said it simply took up space without giving anyone a profit. Also, as Andrey listens to the choir, the forbidden word "fornicator" reveals unconsciously that his attempt to feel kindness is superficial sentimentality. Kramer (1970) quotes Poggioli on how a vulgar word, uttered in innocence, can spark a highly meaningful incident. The circle of misunderstanding is a sign to Kramer of life's eternal isolation. Yarmolinsky (1973) cites Chekhov's letter to Suvorin in 1886, conceding that the ending is bad and that a cut should be made there.

"Romance with a Double Bass"

This tale is a fantasy in which a musician hides a nude princess in his double-bass case. Smith (1973) says the comedy is enhanced by a pseudo-delicacy of style and sentiment. For example, offering her the case, the musician felt he might be profaning sacred art.

"The Schoolmaster"

Dying of tuberculosis, teacher Sisoyev destroys the festive mood at a banquet by attacking a fellow teacher. However, when the school inspector praises Sisoyev as a good teacher, everyone lauds him. Ermilov (1956) notes how well Chekhov describes tuberculosis symptoms. Hingley (1976) says that "what happens here" is not as important as "how it felt." In Hingley's opinion this story is "a biography of a mood."

"Slime" ("Mire")

When men come to collect their debts from Susanna, she gives them their reward in bed. M.P. Willcocks in 1922 said that Chekhov "bleaches" a tale of primitive lust until the reader forgets that a man is telling the tale. Only a "free" artist like Chekhov could give such dispassionate reporting, Willcocks believed.[31] Bruford (1957) remarks that sexual lust is as irrational as death itself. He notes the contrast between the natural beauty outside Susanna's home, and the filthy disorder in the interior. Winner (1966) declares this to be a naturalistic description of a nymphomaniac. He recalled Chekhov's defense of his topic to Maria Kiseleva. Chekhov said that he too personally disliked such literature, but "a writer must be as objective as a chemist. He knows that evil passions are as much a part of life as good ones." Rayfield (1975) observes the vivid imagery in the story, and says that "slime" is misused sex. Hingley (1976) seems grateful to report that "the erotic aspects of the plot are handled by discreet allusion." The title of the story is itself condemnatory.

"Talent"

Bruford (1948) summarizes the plot: An unskilled young painter drinks vodka and dreams of when he will be famous. He calls himself "a free spirit," but he seems to have nothing to offer but conceit and indolence. Kramer (1970) observes that his lover's dream about the artist's success is more "real" than his because, in Chekhov's terms, it is unselfish.

"A Trifle from Life" ("A Common Trifle")

Little Alesha tells his mother's lover Belyaev that his father resents Belyaev being with his mother, but swears Belyaev not to mention his father's dissatisfaction. Instead, Belyaev indignantly complains to the mother, who scolds Alesha for still seeing his father. F.M. Perry in 1926 sees Chekhov avoiding melodrama, even when tempted here. The boy is shocked by a man's betrayal of his confidence, but Chekhov lets the situation evolve its own emotional effects.[32] Bruford (1957) states that the broken home is seen from three angles: that of the husband, the lover, and the son. The stress is on the contrast between Alesha's keen sense of humor and Belyaev's broken word. Kramer (1970) finds Alesha deeply hurt to discover that the values he had been taught to respect are frequently ignored in the adult world. Shotton, in Fennell (1973), says that Chekhov's vision of the human potential for goodness is revealed in a belief (à la Rousseau and Tolstoy) in the fundamental innocence of children.

"A Trivial Incident"

Bruford (1948) tells the plot: A prince squanders his fortune through generosity. His abnormal timidity keeps him from marrying a wealthy neighbor. Hingley (1976) calls this "a pathetic study of hopeless yearning for an unattainable love object."

"An Upheaval"

A boorish homeowner so offends a sensitive young governess, Mashenka, while looking for a missing brooch, that Mashenka resigns. Hahn (1977) feels that Mashenka has not been wronged as badly as Nikolai, the homeowner's husband, whose wife has taken all of Nikolai's property from him, including the brooch. Nikolai admires Mashenka for standing up for her dignity — something he cannot do. "Compared with Nikolai, whom she holds in contempt, Mashenka hardly knows what an outrage is." Thus Hahn finds irony in that "the supposed victim of the story ends up the slightly callous victor." Andrew R. Durkin, in Clyman (1985), remarks on the homeowner's gluttony. Her finicky taste terrorizes the household, and her gluttony utterly ruins Mashenka's appetite.

"Vanka"

Vanka, an eight-year-old orphan apprenticed to a shoemaker, writes a letter to his grandfather complaining of mistreatment and asking to be taken home, but addresses it simply to "Grandfather Konstantin in the village," and so the letter is never delivered. Winner (1966) calls it good child psychology, and notices that even nature is personified in childish images. Victor Shklovsky, in Hulanicki (1976), deems it the saddest Christmas story ever written. All Vanka asks for for Christmas is a sugared nut, and he does not even get that. Joseph L. Conrad, in Debreczeny (1976), finds that here Chekhov reaches a new high in nature description: "The poetization of Vanka's dreams acts as an effective counterpoint to the objective conditions of his real life."

Hahn (1977) believes that "Chekhov captures superbly the emphatic emotional imperatives of the child's voice," while artfully avoiding sentimentality. Leon Shestov may have thought it "cruel" of Chekhov to have Vanka misaddress the envelope, says Hahn, but it is Chekhov's "way of realizing the irrecoverability of that special sense of childhood belonging in any life in which it has been lost." Vanka, of course, does not realize that one cannot recapture one's childhood, but if he can retain the deep capacity for love, as revealed in his letter, he shall see much happiness in life. Kirk (1981) finds the pathos heightened by the fact that, even knowing the disadvantages of life at home, Vanka craves it as an improvement over his apprenticeship. Nathan Rosen, in Eisen (1982), says this story is not so much social protest as a study of psychological mechanisms, such as dreams of earlier happiness, which we use under stress to survive in a hostile world. Rosen thus differentiates between the consciousness of Vanka and that of the narrator.

"Who Was to Blame?"

Hingley (1950) comments on Chekhov's view of faulty classical education, as seen in this story. A character voices this view: Whenever I see a classical play, all I can think of are irregular verbs and the ablative absolute. Even as an adult I am full of terror, as I was as a schoolboy!

"The Witch"

In 1886 Chekhov admitted to Grigorovich: "You're right. When I saw this story in print I myself felt the cynicism you mentioned. It wouldn't have been there had I three or four days to write the story, instead of one!"[33] Bruford (1948) points out the failure of this church-arranged marriage. When the parish clerk dies, church authorities tell his widow to marry his successor, and the older man, jealous of her beauty, accuses her of being a sorceress who attracts men to her. Bruford (1957) says that, seeing the story through the old man's superstitious eyes, the reader feels the devil's hand raging in the winter storm. Rayfield (1975) also applauds "Chekhov's powerful evocation of sexual languor and his romantic technique of projecting the tormented passion of the 'witch' into the blizzard raging outside."

Joseph L. Conrad, in Debreczeny (1976), notes that the opening snowstorm is described in war imagery. The personification of nature, Conrad says, "brings out both the hero's primitive understanding of his environment, and his wife's earthy sexuality." Hahn (1977) feels that "Chekhov captures the pathos of the sexton's growing sense of his wife's attractiveness as her mysterious powers slowly remove her from his reach." Feeling that her husband is from a lower social class, the wife directs her sexual energies elsewhere. But "the comic conception of the 'witch' commanding the demons of bad weather to bring her a man from out of the cold is too exaggerated to convey any very serious understanding of sexuality." In a linguistic analysis, Bitsilli (1983) observes how Chekhov uses varying forms of the Russian infinitive "to say" ("skazat"), according to the emotional context.

"The Wolf" ("Hydrophobia")

Magarshack (*Life*, 1952) notes that this story uses Chekhov's famous phrase about moonlight gleaming like a star reflecting from a broken bottle. Chekhov told his brother that a writer needs to notice small details like that, but in *The Sea Gull* Magarshack feels Chekhov used the phrase to show Trigorin's lack of art. Rayfield (1975) states that this story grew out of the rabies epidemic of 1886. Unlike many of Chekhov's later doctors, Dr. Ovchinnikov is "wisdom incarnate," says Rayfield. Bitsilli (1983) believes that the story was influenced by Turgenev's "The Dog," for both stories deal with mad animals.

"A Work of Art"

A doctor disposes of an unsightly candelabra given him by a grateful patient. The patient retrieves it from a second-hand store, and gives it to the doctor as a mate to the supposed first one. Paul Selver, a translator in 1915, said that the story was not pointless or vague but among the most "witty and ingenious" stories ever written.[34] Durkin, in Clyman (1985), notes the comic effect achieved through differing perceptions of the same object.

Summary—Stories: 1886

For the first time Chekhov was seen as a major short-story writer. His most common theme in 1886 was mistreated or misunderstood women: "Agafya," "Anyuta," "The Chorus Girl," "A Gentleman Friend," "The Husband," "Misfortune," "The Requiem," "An Upheaval," and "The Witch." A number of his children's stories attracted critical attention: "Children," "Grisha," "A Trifle from Life," and "Vanka." Perhaps his three best stories, in the view of contemporary and subsequent critics, were "Easter Eve," a tender and sympathetic picture of sincere religion; "Misery," a clinical study of grief at the loss of one's child; and "On the Road," a psychological insight into the tremendous price paid for excessive timidity.

5. Stories: 1887–1888

"The Avenger" (1887)

Fyodor goes to a gun salesman – he plans to kill his wife, her lover, and himself. But then he reflects, why go to Sakhalin over such pigs? So instead he buys a quail net. An early critic said that here "Chekhov indulges in flippant merry-making at the expense of the flabby creature who wants to cope with this gigantic monster – Life."[1] Another voiced similar sentiments: "The little Othello who goes to buy a revolver to kill his guilty Desdemona will always end up by buying a net for catching birds," since "cuckoldry is his natural condition."[2] Winner (1966) notes the use of a zero ending, as there is a gradual fading away of tension.

"The Beauties" (1888)

The narrator describes the effect of two young beautiful girls upon the men who see them. Gerhardi (1923) says that Chekhov uses a melodic style to capture the sweet sadness of Masha's beauty. Peter Quennell in 1927 observed that Chekhov here indulges in feeling for its own sake. Despite the fact that the story has no construction and no development, Quennell avers, still it is "brilliantly successful."[3] The sadness evoked, states Bruford (1948), is over the fact that beauty must die. Hingley (1950) observes that this sadness is similar to the effect readers were finding in 1888 in Chekhov's stories. "The physical frailty of both heroines is stressed as their most delicious quality," said Hingley (1976).

A.V. Chicherin, in Hulanicki (1976), notes that Chekhov uses an ugly background to contrast with Masha's beauty, which is mysterious but powerful. Beauty evokes sadness, Chicherin believes, because it reminds us of how beautiful all of life should be, and also that even for beautiful people, life is far from a happy existence. Hahn (1977) remarks that both beauties are seen on journeys, suggesting that most people see beauty fleetingly and accidentally. The two girls are in unlovely settings where their youthful beauty seems cruelly out of place and wasted. Chekhov ambitiously but unwisely tried to account for beauty's effect. For once, says Hahn, Chekhov does not even "accurately state the problem." The reader is confused, because the reason never is given why beauty evokes sadness. Because the narrator is not clearly distinguishable from Chekhov, the story loses some of its unity and coherence.

"The Beggar" (1887)

A beggar is reformed not by a work schedule but by the fact that a kind cook chops wood for him. Simmons (1962) calls this "a pure Tolstoyan creation," for in reply to critics who asked for a message in his works, Chekhov "sought in the teachings of Tolstoy for elements of moral and social conviction." Winner (1966) remarks that a clever-twist ending facetiously carries out Tolstoy's non-resistance theme.

"The Boys" (1887)

William Lyon Phelps says that this charming picture of how James Fenimore Cooper influenced two impressionable young Slavs could have happened in New Haven. Phelps states that the most attractive elements in Chekhov's works are the solid ethical foundation and a profound love of children coupled with sympathy with their imagination.[4] Toumanova (1937) gives the plot: Twelve-year-old Chechevitzin says he is not Russian but Hawk Claw, an Indian leader. With a penknife and several sandwiches, he and his friend Volodya will cross the Bering Strait and go to California. When picked up by police and returned home, Volodya is greatly relieved. Kramer (1970) feels that the story shows how the crass world distrusts dreamers for challenging its values. Final victory goes to Chechevitzin, says Kramer, for he writes in his notebook at home: "Montigomo, the Hawk Claw," and the dream persists.

"Cold Blood" (1887) ("The Cattle Dealers")

A cattle dealer has to bribe trainmen, a stationmaster, and a guard in order to get his cattle to market. A critic in the Russian journal *The Week* in 1891 said that the blithe acceptance of corruption spoke volumes on how evil the entire system was. E.J. Dillon that year agreed, commenting on the good humor with which the bribes were given and accepted.[5] N.K. Mikhailovsky in 1897 said that Chekhov's choice of themes was haphazard. For example, what relevance has the title "Cold Blood" for a story of cattle dealers?[6] Edward Garnett (1921) found this story a slice of life delightful in its human byplay. Chekhov's sensitive observation, said Garnett, shows even the unhappy cattle penned in their trucks "in a soft, restful atmosphere."[7] Bruford (1948) said that the story showed that governmental supervision was so ineffectual that one railroad company got away with stealing 300 cars from a rival, repainting the cars and using them as its own.

"The Cossack" (1887)

A sick Cossack begs food from Maxim and his wife Lizaveta, who are returning from church on Easter. Lizaveta says that their Easter cake cannot be cut before they get home, for it has been blessed. Maxim disagrees, they quarrel, and their marriage seems jeopardized. Winner (1966) finds this an exemplification of Tolstoy's doctrine of the vanity of all earthly goods. Shotton, in Fennell (1973), states that the story proclaims Tolstoyan virtues of charity, humility, and simplicity.

"The Doctor" (1887)

As a young boy is dying of brain tuberculosis, his mother and the doctor quarrel over whether the doctor is the boy's natural father. Shotton, in Fennell (1973), notes that as the boy dies, two adults suffer their private misery, "unable to offer each other the comfort which both desperately need."

"Enemies" (1887) ("Two Tragedies")

Dr. Kirilov, mourning the death of his son, reluctantly goes to treat the seriously ill wife of Abogin. But the wife was not ill—she has run off with a neighbor. Abogin is angry, and so is the doctor, and the two sufferers berate each other unmercifully. A reviewer in 1903 said that Chekhov "holds up to solemn mockery the weaknesses which men display under the stress of great grief."[8] Another reviewer praised the nature description in the story.[9] Hingley (1950) quotes Vladimir Ermilov as believing that Chekhov had a deeply buried preference for the hard-working doctor over the well-fed Abogin. Ermilov (1956) states that every detail enhances Kirilov's human dignity and points up Abogin's parasitism and vulgarity.

Ehrenburg (1962) said that Chekhov trusted his readers so much that he could dare to show good traits in Abogin and bad ones in Kirilov. Lionel Trilling felt that Kirilov's insistence that he be thought to be Abogin's moral superior greatly diminished his stature.[10] Marija Rev in 1969 showed how Chekhov achieved great economy from skillful use of dialogue, employment of parallels and antitheses, and apt laconic comments.[11] Kramer (1970) finds that the two grief-stricken men attack each other over resentment at each other's unhappiness.

Rayfield (1975) feels that Chekhov's message is that "it is human nature, not ideas of justice and humanity, that is intractable and in need of treatment." Avram Derman, in Hulanicki (1976), observes that Chekhov, as narrator, takes time out to philosophize over the inadequacy of words to express joy or sorrow.

Hahn (1977) says that Chekhov, like George Eliot, shows the relativity of moral claims: "Equally compelling human needs are found to be diametrically at odds." Here Hahn finds Chekhov writing as a humanist rather than as a dispassionate observer. Chekhov is saying that it is more important to respond to people's needs, howsoever absurd they may seem, than to perform an obvious act of heroism. The story is an eloquent plea for human understanding. Anne Frydman in 1979 said that this study of unhappiness was a culmination of Chekhov's previous work and a new departure for his future stories.[12]

"The Examining Magistrate" (1887) ("The Coroner")

A coroner says that a woman accurately predicted her death in childbirth. The skeptical doctor says the woman probably committed suicide, perhaps because of an unfaithful husband. The shocked coroner confesses that he is her husband. V.V. Vinogradov greatly admired Chekhov's deftness in portraying the inner struggle within the coroner.[13]

"A Good German" (1887)

Ivan, a German steelworker, comes home to find his wife in bed with a stranger. He writes her parents, calling her a swine. Chudakov (1971) observes that Chekhov here uses three types of narration: objective, intrusive, and interior monologue.

"Happiness" (1887) ("Fortune")

Young shepherd Sanka hears his 80-year-old grandfather rave about buried treasure, which he would be too old to enjoy, even if found. Sanka now realizes the fantastic, fairy-tale nature of human happiness. Constance Garnett (1920) said this story grew out of one of Chekhov's nanny's tales, which were always "of the mysterious, the extraordinary, the poetical." Ermilov (1956), Simmons (1962), and Kramer (1970) find the story's meaning in the old man's statement that there is enough happiness in life to satisfy everyone, if people only know how to seek it. Ermilov states that the beautiful steppe yearns for some sort of meaning; this story is an overture, introducing all the main motifs of Chekhov's works. Simmons adds that it is a sad allegory of Chekhov's own life, telling of a person's eternal search for life's meaning.

Laffitte (1971) recalls that the painter Levitan called the landscapes in the story "the height of perfection. The pictures of the steppes, the tumuli, and the sheep are truly astonishing," said Levitan. Shotton, in Fennell (1973), says Chekhov here achieves a total harmony between the setting and the characters' moods. The story has no narrative pattern, Shotton says, but instead the style is controlled by the psychology of the characters. Rayfield (1975) felt that lyrical nature descriptions replace the plot, and that sounds are used ominously.

Hingley (1976) said that Chekhov and the critics considered this story to be his best work so far. Joseph L. Conrad in Debreczeny (1977), noted how the nature description creates an atmosphere of anticipation. Disagreeing with the general consensus that this is an allegory of the search for life's meaning, Hahn (1977) believes that Chekhov's main concern here is how the characters conceive of happiness. Suddenly they feel the need for assurance that life does have some value. Many images are a fascinating blend of Christian legend, folklore, and demonology. By showing each character's preference for happiness, Chekhov is saying that there is no single road to it, Hahn feels.

"Home" (1887)

Toumanova (1937) recounts the plot: An intelligent father notices with amusement that his six-year-old son, whom he wants to punish for smoking, answers all of his complaints with a peculiar brand of child's logic. Bruford (1948) finds two messages in this affectionate portrait: Chekhov's love of children, and the fact that children are the same the world over. Kramer (1970) detects that a child can instinctively grasp a more Christian set of values than can his well-meaning father. Ralph Lindheim, in Clyman (1985), states that the father cannot understand why Serezha draws people that are larger than horses, not realizing that to Serezha, people are more important than horses.

"In Passion Week" (1887)

Bruford (1948) relates the plot: An eight-year-old boy feels starved, fasting between confession today and communion tomorrow. After communion, everyone seems to share his feeling of relief and freedom—but he still feels superior to his playmate Mitka. Rayfield (1975) notes that Chekhov captures well the boy's joy at absolution, as well as the appeal of the half-intelligible church language. The story was written on a visit to Taganrog, when Chekhov's mind was in an ecclesiastical strain.

"In Trouble" (1887) ("A Catastrophe")

In Bruford (1948) we read the plot: Merchant Avdyeyev knew *something* was wrong at the local bank, but continued to sign loans as a member of the auditing committee. Ignorant of bookkeeping, he slowly realizes in court that he will be found guilty. Hingley (1976) called the story "egregiously Tolstoyan." But realizing that he was never good at preaching, Chekhov excluded it from his collected works.

"Kashtanka" (1887)

Mirsky (1927) called this story a masterpiece, a wonderful blend of humor and poetry, even though it sentimentalizes animals. Toumanova (1937) states that this delightful tale is told from the point-of-view of the dog. A little boy recognizes that his lost dog has now been trained to do circus tricks. Seeing the boy in the circus crowd, the dog abandons his tricks in order to rejoin his former master. Simmons (1962) recalls that Chekhov's view of children's literature was not to write down to their level but rather to select for them something artistic, written for adults but containing an appeal for children. This story and "Whitebrow" admirably exemplify Chekhov's theory.

"The Kiss" (1887)

Shy Lieutenant Ryabovich, kissed by mistake in the dark, dreams of romantic love encounters but fails to find a lover. Felix Grendon in 1913 said that Chekhov had provided merely "thirty pages of suffering. How did Chekhov's work ever cross the Atlantic," Grendon asked, "untouched as it is by the passion, energy, and resurgent willfulness of the modern spirit?"[14]

Persky (1913) said that the story showed life's absurdity. To Ryabovich, life is senseless, "an absurd mystification." Gerhardi (1923) pointed out that the flowing river symbolized time's passage in a meaningless monotony. Hingley (1950) said that Chekhov showed how much story can come from so little plot, by having the protagonist both comical and pathetic. Nature descriptions evoked vivid moods, he thought. Magarshack (*Life*, 1952) indicated that the background of the story came from the artillery battery Chekhov encountered in 1884 at Voskressensk.

Winner (1966) sees this as a story of isolation and missed opportunities. A subtext is provided by the nightingales, by the peasants picking cabbage, and by the general's sheets hung out on the line. Kramer (1970) said that Chekhov here penetrates his hero's inner world. No girl at the party can measure up to the one in Ryabovich's imagination, for she is a composite of all the beauty he has ever desired. Lobytko, the foil of Ryabovich, helps turn his "romance" into an everyday affair. Shotton, in Fennell (1973), says that both plot and language revolve around the hero's inner world. Descriptive details match the character's emotional state.

Rayfield (1975) feels that the hero's exaggerated self-consciousness finally becomes neurotic. Nathan Rosen sees the kiss releasing the hero's repressed life force, and his newly released imagination identifies his new life with the von Rabbecks. When they do not invite him for another visit, he is "destroyed."[15] Stowell (1980) says that the kiss creates a new identity for Ryabovich. He now perceives the world differently, and in turn is perceived differently. But try as he may, he cannot really perpetuate the new pleasant persona. As his memory fades, his dreams take over, but he learns that to share his precious experience is to lose it.

Wilks (1982) points out that the name "Ryabovich" implies "pock-marked." Bitsilli (1983) calls the story a reworking of the old comic theme from a fabula: the hidden kiss. Chekhov departs from tradition in having no recognition scene (as he did in "The Mask"). Lindheim, in Clyman (1985), shows that the hero's painful awareness of his diminished existence leads him to isolate himself from life, so as to guard against further disappointment.

"The Letter" (1887)

A deacon, writing a letter of remonstrance to his son for living with a married woman, adds a humorous postscript which undoes the seriousness of the intended correction. Simmons (1962) states that Chekhov's mingling of pathos and humor shows that "life's misfortunes may be intensified by humor or softened by its wise, gentle smile." Winner (1966) notes that oblique devices such as speech mannerisms or a slight cough create characterization. Also, Chekhov employs here a typical stylistic trait—triads of descriptive adjectives.

"Lights" (1888)

Ananyev, a railroad engineer, chides a young student for being pessimistic at such an early age. Ananyev describes his remorse over his seduction of a former schoolmate. The narrator sees the receding lights of the railroad camp huts until they vanish in the darkness. The only moral he gets from Ananyev's story is that "there is no making out anything in this world." Two of Chekhov's friends, Suvorin and I.L. Leontiev-Shcheglov, chided him for raising problems he did not solve. Chekhov replied, "I feel ashamed of it. It is frightfully dull, with too much preaching and discussion. But I need money." Later he added, "I get annoyed with critics who attach any importance to this story. I fancy I deceive them with my work just as I deceive many people with my face, which looks serious or overly cheerful."[16]

In another letter Chekhov admitted that the minor characters Masha and Nikolai are overemphasized. He said that he inserted their final dialogue as a replacement for the last scene between Ananyev and his former schoolmate

schoolmate Kisochka. Chekhov said that he became overanxious while writing a long story.[17] Berating himself, he said that he did not have enough passion to be a great writer, and thus not enough talent. But he saves this story by following one of his rules, "Give people people, and not yourself."[18]

In a letter to Suvorin in 1888 Chekhov said that the writer's job is not to solve the problem of pessimism, but rather accurately portray it. Here, he said, I merely depict two Russians discussing pessimism. Anyway, he added, "the time has come for writers to admit that in this world one cannot make head or tail out of anything, as Socrates and Voltaire admitted."[19] V.K. Stukalich in 1888 said that the story gave a faint hint of contemporary spiritual movements. To show the hero's regeneration would have required "more colors and a greater sense of artistic completion."[20] Toumanova (1937) recalls that Chekhov called the story mere "resin with vinegar." Bruford (1948) says the story shows the inadequacy of nihilism as a philosophy. If one denies the dignity of the human personality, then no philosophy of any kind is possible.

Ermilov (1956) said the story showed that Chekhov had entered the battle against the reactionary forces of his time. Ananyev warns the student that false thoughts lead to false actions. Leonid Gromov in 1958 found in the story an appeal for sympathy with the plight of educated women, and was happy that the critic A.M. Skabichevsky had also read the story that way.[21] V.I. Linkov in 1971 said that the story explores the role that ideas play in determining personality and behavior. Ananyev says that one must "live" ideas before using them as the basis for a worldview. The reader cannot accept the ideas of Chekhov's characters at face value, Linkov warns, but must evaluate them critically within the context of the work.[22]

Speirs (1971) says that from this story on, all of Chekhov's work is art, that is, an expression of one's spiritual aspirations and discoveries. The railroad, a symbol of progress, causes one to think: what is progress? In vain Ananyev tries to teach the student, for each person must find life's answers for himself. Rayfield (1975) says that the story teaches that early pessimism can lead to moral turpitude. To be a pessimist, one must earn it through life's frustrations. Hingley (1976) says that this "Tolstoyan" story did not achieve its purpose, proving that good moralizing may be bad art. No wonder, Hingley concluded, that Chekhov excluded the story from his collected works.

Hahn (1977) calls this "a classic story actively engaged with epistemological problems and systems of thought which are seminal to twentieth-century consciousness." The setting is surreal, especially in the evoked chaos of the railroad camp. The student expresses the nihilist view of how transitory human values are, but Ananyev sees long-range progress at work. Ananyev's description of his seduction of Kisochka shows a "kind of explicitness concerning masculine sexual calculation which would have been impossible for reputable English writers at the time." In Ananyev's self-criticism, the values asserted are moral responsibility, respect, and love. In Kisochka we see Chekhov's current problem: "Generally in sexually direct situations his women characters tend to lose their strength as fully realized women." Kirk (1981) said that Chekhov found it hard to write on political themes, but here he discusses nihilism. Neither a psychologist nor an author, Chekhov said, should pretend to understand what no one understands.

"The Meeting" (1887)

Winner (1966) says that this tale of a thief regenerated when his victim refused to report him is a sign that Tolstoy's theory of non-resistance to evil works. Rayfield (1975) understood why Chekhov omitted this story from his collected works, since it "shows a noticeable falling-off of tension and involvement."

"The Name-Day Party" (1888) ("The Party")

Pregnant Olga is overworked and tense serving as hostess at her husband's name-day party. Resenting his flirtations and his shallow political views, she confronts him after the guests leave, and they quarrel. She lapses into delirium and delivers a stillborn baby. Her husband Peter moans, "Why didn't we take care of our child?"

In a letter to Suvorin Chekhov said, "I know my hero is worthy of further development. I know I waste good material. I would gladly have spent six months on this story, but I have no such time to spare. I let myself go at the beginning but by the middle I fear my story will be too long, and so the end, like that of a short sketch, is fireworks. In planning a story one selects one main character, and all others revolve around that character."[23]

Chekhov admitted trying to "balance out pluses and minuses in this story, but I'm not balancing conservatism against liberalism, which are not the main thing for me, but the falseness of the heroes against their truthfulness. Peter lies and plays the buffoon, but he is a softhearted person by nature. Olga lies at every step, but this lying pains her."[24]

A reviewer in 1917 called the story "a terrifying piece of realism, indicting the ordinary artificialities of life like breaking a butterfly on a wheel, were it not that we are made to feel that an existence made of these artificialities is spiritually ruinous."[25] Katherine Mansfield disagreed with Edward Garnett that it took a doctor to write this story, for what made the story effective was Chekhov's subtle understanding of feminine human nature.[26] Edward Garnett designated the story a brilliant social picture fusing artistic and scientific insights. "For atmosphere and subtle inflections of tone," Garnett added, "it leaves most of contemporary art in the shade." [27] Alexander Werth said that Maupassant, in "La Mère aux Monstres," discusses emotionally the harm done by corsets worn by pregnant women, but Chekhov, although a doctor, "speaks of the psychological causes and effects of a clinical case, never of the case itself." Thus Chekhov is never sordid or crude, but simply accurate.[28]

In America, *Harper's Magazine* broke a long silence on Chekhov in 1926 to admit that this story belonged among the great short stories of the world.[29] Mirsky (1927) called it "the biography of a mood developing under the trivial pinpricks of life." Magarshack (*Life*, 1952) noted that Chekhov was pleased that women praised the accuracy of his description of childbirth. Bruford (1957) said that here Chekhov shows the clash of opinions between educated people. Olga's inward voice tells her that, worse than Peter's insensitivity, is her own insincerity. She differs from a character in Kafka or in existentialist literature in having the remembrance of a well-ordered society in her youth.

Kramer (1970) believes that Chekhov here is the victim of his own characters, and creates effects not intended. For example, Olga is sometimes the victim and other times the perpetrator of corruption. Oddly, Olga seems indifferent to the stillborn child, but Peter now rejects his persona in favor of a deeper, more honest self. Speirs (1971) compares the quarrel with that of Vronsky and Anna Karenina: "In each case the woman is acutely aware of the indignity which her dependent position involves her in." Peter is of little help—"he understands that she does not mean what she says, and yet he will never be able to convince himself of this."

Shotton, in Fennell (1973), states that Chekhov need never have felt guilty about the lack of a message in his stories. Here the teaching is strip off the sham of conformist behavior, and follow the instincts of your better nature. Rayfield (1975) notes how nature is integrated into the story's psychology. A storm, for example, parallels Olga's emotional outburst leading to the premature delivery. Charanne C. Clarke, in Debreczeny (1977), says that the theme is really Olga's state of mind, doing trivial things while deeply absorbed over her baby.

Hahn (1977) sees Chekhov far ahead of D.H. Lawrence in depicting feminine emotions. He shows the intensity of "masculine isolation at the time when the carrying of the baby gives a special, private fulfillment to the wife. The sad irony is that Olga's mounting distress at what she interprets as her husband's falsity should be a reaction to that same necessity of adopting a public personality which she feels as such a burden on herself." Peter's own anxiety over an ugly lawsuit, and his attempts to mask it from Olga and others, make it clear that husband and wife are bound to intensify each other's troubles.

Hingley (1980) sees Tolstoy's influence at work in this rejection of sophisticated life. In his revision Chekhov cut out some of the Tolstoyan treatment. Several critics reacted to this story in Clyman (1985). Durkin finds the entire story filtered through Olga's consciousness. Since what she perceives is often the incongruity between her notion of reality and the true state of affairs, this character in Chekhov is often, as here, cast in the role of a victim. Lantz describes how the petty social hypocrisies accumulate, giving the characters false images of themselves and creating the confusion that leads to the tragedy. Lindheim notices that Olga cannot recall a single person about whom she can say something good. Rayfield finds in the story "an embarrassingly high number of coincidences with *Anna Karenina.*"

"A Nervous Breakdown" (1888) ("An Attack of Nerves") ("The Fit")

Law student Vasiliev reluctantly visits several brothels with two friends. He is appalled at the human indignity he encounters. After fretting all night over ways to abolish prostitution, he suffers a breakdown the next morning, and is taken to the doctor to see if he is mentally ill.

In 1884 Chekhov and two other medical students visited a brothel on notorious Sobolev Street, ostensibly for research on why women become prostitutes. This story, which Chekhov called "sad, depressing, and serious," aroused considerable comment, mostly favorable. Tolstoy, who liked the story, said that Vasiliev should have partaken of the brothel's wares.[30] In a letter Chekhov said that "in this story I have told of the spiritual agony of such rare men as Garshin."[31] He felt satisfied that he had accurately described the medical disorder, and he advised Suvorin to attack the dreadful evil of prostitution.[32] Chekhov was bothered that only Grigorovich noticed the symbolism of the virginal white snow. If only I had better critics, he lamented, I could learn faster how to be a better writer.[33]

Persky (1913) said that the public's indifference to the vast evil of prostitution crushes Vasiliev, whose values are too fine for society. A reviewer in 1915 said that the sensitive young man was overcome by swarms of painted faces from all over the world, with eyes speaking of unfathomable loss. Ironically, the doctor writes Vasiliev a prescription, as if it could cure him of the malady of pity.[34] Ermilov (1956) says that everything at the brothels is coarse and vulgar, to disguise the humanity of the girls. Chekhov, says Ermilov, had much in common with Vasiliev. "No one but Chekhov could combine in one story the coarsest sides of life with true poetry."

Winner (1966) said that Vasiliev considered himself abnormal because he could not react the way his friends did. Joseph L. Conrad in 1969 reported that Chekhov here uses many stylistic devices similar to those found in Garshin's works.[35] Kramer (1970) relates that Garshin's own story of a prostitute, "An Occurrence," influenced Chekhov as did Gogol's story "Nevsky Prospect." Chudakov (1971) admired the use of interior monologue. Laffitte (1971) commented that not only Garshin's suicide but also Gleb Uspensky's mental breakdown inspired this story.

Sonia Gotman in 1972 found irony in the fact that the reader could see what Vasiliev could not detect—that as a law student he should have been able to suggest a solution to the social problem that caused him so much pain.[36] Shotton, in Fennell (1973), says that Vasiliev experiences a typical Tolstoyan spiritual awakening. He now puts love of all human beings ahead of gratification of his primal instinct, and realizes that only by the rule of conscience can the world be improved. Crass society meanwhile thinks that, like Dostoevsky's "idiot," he is insane.

Rayfield (1975) sees the story as an indictment of state-tolerated prostitution. It was published in a book dedicated to Garshin's memory. Vasiliev breaks down when he finds himself doing what the others do—consider prostitutes as conveniences rather than as human beings. Hingley (1976) states that, although he was no prude, Chekhov objected to vulgar displays of feminine nudity. In its moral indignation the story is Tolstoyan, Hingley says, but it lacks Tolstoy's recommended solution.

Debreczeny (1977) provides studies of the story by Phillip A. Duncan and Marena Senderovich. Duncan observes that this experimental narrative exemplifies the physiological and environmental determinism that Zola prescribed for the experimental novel. Senderovich notes that Chekhov uses complex color symbolism to portray the breakdown, which occurs as a result of the collapse of Vasiliev's Christian moral values. Tulloch (1980) calls Vasiliev inauthentic for his inability to suggest a solution to the problem. The doctor is even worse, offering a mere anodyne for a social problem that requires not an escape but a confrontation.

Eisen (1982) reports several counterpoints to Vasiliev's torment: the snow; the doctor's cold detachment; the noisy glee of the students; the prostitutes' indifference to their plight. Bitsilli (1983) finds the ending symbolic, as Vasiliev is overwhelmed by the ineradicability of evil. Joseph L. Conrad, in Clyman (1985), says that like Chekhov, Vasiliev was gifted with "a talent for humanity."

"Panpipes" (1887) ("The Shepherd's Pipe")

Old Luka, a shepherd, complains about man's desecration of nature. Rayfield (1975) describes how Luka's panpipes seem to be weeping because of the disorder that humans bring into nature. Tulloch (1980) tells of Luka resenting that Time has destroyed the gentry, and with them the fertility of the soil. Karlinsky, in Barricelli (1981), finds in the story a modern understanding of ecology. Luka says that when man cuts down the forests, river water levels go down, and birds and fish decline. Along with the natural decay comes the degeneration of the people inhabiting the land. Luka attributes the condition to God's warning that the end of the world is near.

"Polinka" (1887)

Young Polinka's tearful effort to get sympathy from the salesman who loves her is hidden in the small talk of prices and dress goods that she is buying for her mother. Ermilov (1956) describes the subtle irony in that Polinka knows that her student boyfriend does not love her, but she is so dazzled by him and his possible future that she spurns the salesman's love. Poggioli (1957) notes that the sales counter serves as both a bridge and a barrier. He also emphasized the contrapuntal interplay between whispers of private talk and shouts of sales talk. Ehrenburg (1962) states that when the salesman covers Polinka's tears with loud sales talk, the vulgar shop terms have "the ring of high poetry." Simmons (1962) calls this a subtle mingling of pathos and humor, an outgrowth of the disharmony between people's hopes and reality.

"The Post" (1887)

The postman is surly all day because the postmaster has him drive his nephew to the railroad station, breaking regulations. "What do I care," asked critic N.K. Mikhailovsky in 1897, "if the postman tumbles out of his jostling carriage?" He called Chekhov indifferent to human values.[37] Magarshack (*Life*, 1952) notes that Chekhov has the clouds whisper, and the harness bells laugh and cry. He later attacked this anthropomorphism in Gorky's writing. Rayfield (1975) pointed out the contrast between the surly postman and the glorious countryside.

"The Runaway" (1887)

Pasha, seven, is in the hospital, awaiting amputation of a diseased arm. When a man in his ward dies that night, Pasha gets frightened and leaves the hospital. He is further frightened at a cemetery, and returns to the hospital. F.M. Perry (1926) observed what Chekhov substituted for plot unity: unity of time; unity of point-of-view; and emotional climax and unity as an inexperienced boy encounters a strange and frightening environment.[38]

"The Shoemaker and the Devil" (1888)

A shoemaker, resentful over having to make boots on Christmas Eve, dozes and dreams he has exchanged his soul to the devil for riches. But then he learns of all the rich people's worries, and awakens. Now he does not feel so bad, knowing that the rich are as bad off as the poor.

A reviewer in 1920 said that the story teaches that there is nothing in life for which one need ever give the devil even a tiny scrap of one's soul.[39] Winner (1966) says the shoemaker is satisfied when he learns that the rich will some day burn in hell fire. Hingley (1980) said that at first Chekhov was ashamed of this "mawkish rubbish," but later he revised it and included it in his collected works. The reception from critics was mixed. N.A. Leykin said that this charming story was more Tolstoyan than Chekhovian.

"Shrove Tuesday" (1887)

Stepan, ten, is forced to eat meat, eggs, and milk products, foods that will be banned on the morrow, when Lent begins. Bruford (1948) describes the people stuffing themselves until they hiccough. On the way to confession, each person falls down at the others' feet and asks forgiveness for the year's sins.

"Sleepy" (1888)

Varka, 13, a babysitter, is dead tired. As she tries to stay awake, her mind wanders. She has nightmares involving work, mistreatment, and punishment. In a daze she strangles the baby, and falls into a deep sleep.

N.K. Mikhailovsky in 1897 was shocked at this cold-blooded tale of murder. Too bad Chekhov lived in such a repressive time, he said, for otherwise his talent would have radiated light and warmth.[40] A critic in 1906 called it "one of Chekhov's strongest and most characteristic pieces, one which symbolizes the feelings of modern Russia — stagnation, revolt against the baseness of life, and inability to cope effectively with one's problems. The tedium of life — this is the keynote of Varka's tragedy, and this is what a vast people is trying to throw off."[41]

Mirsky (1927) called it "a real masterpiece of concentration, economy, and powerful effectiveness." Tolstoy praised it, Mirsky said, and wrote a very similar story 18 years later, "Alyosha Gorshok." Noting the extreme similarity in plot, mood, and detail to Katherine Mansfield's "The Child Who Was Tired," Elisabeth Schneider called Mansfield's story unconscious memory rather than plagiarism.[42] Gleb Struve in 1960 (printed in Lantz, 1985) said that Chekhov's story was probably influenced by Grigorovich's "Karelin's Dream." Winner (1966) called "Sleepy" "a masterful treatment of the child's dreams, subtle use of recurrent images, and impressionistic description. Its musical construction anticipates many of Chekhov's mature works."

Joseph L. Conrad in 1972 stated that "by the end of 'Sleepy' we do not feel the same sense of frustration as at the close of 'Vanka.' Like Varka, the reader experiences a sense of relief, despite the horrible act brought on by the girl's maddening fatigue."[43] H. Peter Stowell calls the story a prose fugue, for its juxtaposition of contrapuntal levels and its overlapping fragments of the heroine's perceptions. He finds the story moving through four levels toward the crescendo of its "inexorable conclusion."[44] On the other hand, Victor Shklovsky, in Hulanicki (1976), finds that, despite the psychological build-up, the strangling is improbable. He finds the ending based on the insanity not of Varka but of the entire social order.

Debreczeny (1977) presents the views of Charanne C. Clarke, Jerome H. Katsell, and H. Peter Stowell. Clarke sees the story as a masterpiece of compression, skillfully depicting the relationship between dreams and reality. Chekhov's theory of dreams stated that the sleeper's environment suggested dream motifs

and moods. Katsell finds the story's themes to be the meaning of death, its occurrence in life, and its relationship to the need for survival. Death imagery permeates
the story, which begins and ends in darkness. Ultimately, says Katsell, one must
experience death as a part of the life process. Stowell shows how Varka identifies
the baby with all the things that are preventing her sleep. Her act turns the baby
into an object, the obstacle keeping her from the much-needed sleep.

Stowell (1980) describes Varka's four levels of reality: First is the real world,
full of commands that must be obeyed immediately; second, distorted images of
diapers, black trousers, and their shadows on the ceiling; third, a surreal vision of
people dragging themselves along a road that leads to their death; and fourth, the
memory of her father's death rattle tied in with the baby's lullaby. The common
denominators of all levels are death and the baby. The "vicious cycle of exploitation
needs to be broken—she must sleep to avoid going mad or she must go mad in order
to sleep."

Clyman (1985) presents the views of Andrew R. Durkin, Charles E. May, and
H. Peter Stowell. Durkin notes that by relegating the strangling to a subordinate
phrase, the reader's attention is shifted to the atmosphere and Varka's
psychological state. It also intensifies the final impact by leaving the aftermath
undescribed. May calls the story "a half-way point between the symbolic use of the
hypnogogic state by Poe and its being pushed to surrealistic extremes by Kafka."
Stowell calls it one of Chekhov's best stories, with a greater potential for a film version than any other. "It is a highly imagistic story," Stowell believes, "with a surrealistic use of spatial and temporal shifts, and its transitions between dream and
reality are based on sensory associations." Stowell shows how the film version
(*Desire to Sleep* by Maurice Fasquel) changes Varka's dream about falling into mud
into having her dying on a pretty couch in a palatial room.

"The Steppe" (1888)

Egorushka, nine, is being taken across the vast steppe to high school by his
uncle, Kuzmitchov, a merchant. The sights and sounds of the steppe fascinate him.
For a long while he travels with a wool wagon train, and hears the drivers talk of
robbers and storms. In a letter Chekhov described his difficulty in writing such a
long story as this. Since he is unused to long works, Chekhov admits, each page
has a compact unity, seeming to be a story in itself, and as a result there are no
smooth transitions and no unity of overall effect, but just a succession of pictures.
In 1888 Pleshcheyev wrote Chekhov: It is so charming that I am in wild ecstasy
over it. Vsevolod Garshin is crazy about it. Peter Boborykin (the novelist) is madly
enthusiastic over it, and considers you to be the most gifted of all living fiction
writers.[45] Pleshcheyev praised the poetic descriptions of nature, but N.K.
Mikhailovsky said that this shapeless work showed that Chekhov was not at home
in long fiction.[46] Peter Kropotkin mentioned that "admirers of Zolarism and minute
descriptions of nature would find in it the same methods applied to the prairies of

south Russia."[47] Chudakov (1971) reports the reaction of a number of contemporary critics. R.A. Disterlo in 1888 said that Chekhov's style had many independent fragments as well as useless details. Evgeny Garshin in 1888 said Chekhov was not in control of his impressions, which "carry him away and heap themselves up in ridiculous literary conglomerations." P.N. Ostrovsky in a letter to Chekhov on March 4, 1888, complained that although many scenes are vividly rendered, the lack of transitions or connection between them disturbs the attentive reader and damages the unity of his impression. Ostrovsky recommended to Chekhov a study of how Turgenev achieves a unity of impression in his nature scenes. The critic of the *Weekly Review* (Moscow) in 1888 quoted Turgenev: no picture in a story can be accidental, but so organic to the whole that to remove it would be detrimental. But here there are many scenes which can be eliminated.

Kazimierz Waliszewski (1900) was confused as to Chekhov's intent. He noted that Chekhov here used Turgenev's technique of mingling the child's feelings with nature description, but felt that Chekhov's result was artificiality. When Chekhov has the grass singing and weeping, this seemed to Waliszewski to be beyond the child's imagination.[48] In 1902 R.E.C. Long said that this story convinced Russian critics that a young eagle had arisen in their midst, as "the hundred indefinable impressions of an endless journey are sketched with unerring skill." Chekhov, said Long, could compress a whole lifetime of emotion into a single vivid sentence. Like an alchemist, Chekhov transmuted base metal into gold. "By some strange reversal of the ordinary laws of art," said Long, "the more aimless his motives, the more monotonous his background, the more vapid his characters, the more glowing and lifelike are his pictures. That this is art of a high order is beyond question."[49]

Christian Brinton in 1904 found Chekhov's style to be like that of Turgenev, "but the shifting panorama of the steppe seen through Egorushka's eyes has never been interpreted with such charm, verity, and poetic intuition."[50] A reviewer in 1915 said that Russia's infinite distances and her stoical peasantry came alive in this story—along with Egorushka, the reader can almost smell the hot earth.[51] E.M. Forster that year found Chekhov full of humor and tenderness, with this story showing an artistic arrangement of life's common events that made them flow on "noble, imaginative, profound."[52] J. Middleton Murry said that old criteria of plot and theme are irrelevant in evaluating Chekhov's works, since the prevailing tone unified seemingly random episodes, as in this story, into a satisfying whole.[53]

Katherine Mansfield called the story "one of the great stories of the world—a kind of *Iliad* or *Odyssey*. A touch of Chekhov's pen made this story immortal."[54] Not, however, to a reviewer in the *Nation*, who said that "a flagrant want of constructive skill" turned the story into "merely a series of detached impressions."[55] Edward Garnett agreed with Mansfield—Chekhov's fluid consciousness faithfully reflected the vast bosom of the steppe—variegated, wild, and elusive.[56]

Gerhardi (1923) liked the way Chekhov was able to bring universal meaning out of the ordinary events of life. Brewster (1924) found Chekhov and Mark Twain alike in "their spiritual outlook on the essential tragedy of man's loneliness.

One saw life through the lens of exaggerated humor, the other through the lens of a tranquil realism. Under more propitious conditions Mark Twain might have been as great an artist as Chekhov."[57]

Werth (1925) observed how Chekhov built atmospheric effects through appeals to all five senses. The impressions "shape themselves into a description which is a picture, a poem, a number of perfumes, and a symphony all in one. It is the highest achievement of purely descriptive literature."[58] John Cournos told of how Chekhov in a letter had described how he had unified this "encyclopedia of the steppe" by keeping the focus on Egorushka throughout the story.[59]

Bruford (1948) liked 80-year-old Father Christopher, who has a smile for everyone because he has found peace of soul. Hingley (1950) analyzed Chekhov's successful technique: He selects a specific incident, links the descriptive passage to the characters' moods, personifies plants and animals, and uses everyday phrases in a novel context, "as though someone had struck a match across the sky." Magarshack (Life, 1952) found the story built upon letters Chekhov had written during a trip to the Don steppe in 1887.

Ermilov (1956) felt that the story showed Chekhov's love of his country, his poetic conception of life, and his faith in a better future. Bruford (1957) said that, as the landscape dwarfs the characters, Chekhov shows something like the pantheistic nature worship of the earlier Romantic writers. George Ivask, in Eekman (1960), found Father Christopher's good nature growing out of his love for the beauty of God's creation. Simmons (1962) saw the story as important in Chekhov's development, for it gave him the confidence to show that he could succeed in nontraditional forms.

Winner (1966) notes the picaresque structure—these are the things that happen to travelers. It resembles Gogol, but replaces his biting satire with poetic reflection. Some of the weaknesses include: the author intervenes; apostrophes to the reader; occasional lack of restraint; and the inconclusive ending. Many of Winner's insights were like those of the structuralist Roland Barthes. For example, when a grave is called "audibly silent," the structuralist would call this a "high-cost" phrase, since it violates the traditional categories of association, as nature seems to cry out in protest against the tragedy of neglected graves.

Nilsson (1968) says setting provides two functions: it is beautiful in itself, and it gives the background for the action. Here nature is not so much a nurturing agent as indifferent to mankind's problems. Kramer (1970) reports that Soviet critic Zinovy Paperny called this a patriotic hymn to the land and its people. Chudakov (1971) observed that the narrator bypasses Egorushka's consciousness to provide philosophical and lyrical monologues. Laffitte (1971) finds on almost every page "prose poems which are all variations on the same theme: the ecstasy of being alive, the joy of being young, the love of beauty, and the deep inexpressible melancholy of man's condition."

D.E. Maxwell identifies a linguistic unity of plot, character, and setting achieved through a variety of verbal forms based on the Russian root "makh" (waving, gesticulating).[60] Urbanski (1973) noted that Evgeny Garshin felt a lack of unity—that Chekhov had let his "impressions carry him away, accumulating into unthought-through conglomerates."

Rayfield (1975) called the story Chekhov's masterpiece. He detected many Gogolian influences: episodic construction; anonymity of towns; and reflections on the Russian character. The style combines two elements—the richness of steppe life and the simplicity of Egorushka's outlook. On the steppe all humans fit into a hierarchy, and thus the human world is as unified as is the natural world.

Hingley (1976) said that Chekhov's enemy V.A. Goltsev reported that this story lacked ideas, plot, psychology, and even ethnographic interest. Following this story, Hingley notes, Chekhov was never again a prolific short-story writer. Hulanicki (1976) gives the views of Soviet critics Victor Lakshin and Victor Shklovsky. Lakshin praised the story by quoting the Polish writer I. Dombrowski: "We Europeans only flirt with nature descriptions, but Russians capture its essence—smells and all. A Frenchman describes dew as a rainbow; a Russian makes you feel the dampness in your boots." Shklovsky liked Chekhov's subtle way of indicating Egorushka's love of home life. When he sleeps on a manure pile, Egorushka sets aside the coat which had hung in Mama's closet, because he wants to keep pure his memory of her.

Debreczeny (1977) has comments by Joseph L. Conrad and Karl D. Kramer. Conrad detects in the story a musical counterpoint of leitmotifs. Surviving the thunderstorm, Egorushka has completed his rite of passage into the adult world. Kramer finds a complex interplay of theme and seasons, and observes how the narrator advances and recedes from the hero's voice. Rufus W. Mathewson finds an influence of Thoreau upon Chekhov.[61] Hahn (1977) agrees with Chekhov's own strict appraisal: "I lose the consistent thread of the narrative, grow weary, do not speak out, and am not serious enough in manner." Hahn identifies as a unifying principle the ironic thought that the journey to school educates Egorushka more than school itself will.

Jerome H. Katsell explains the coordination of points-of-view: the narrator deals with the steppe itself, and Egorushka with the journey. The mystical quality of the story fits in well with the outlook of a nine-year-old boy, Katsell feels.[62] Soviet critic Evgeny Evtushenko says that despite its small plot, an excellent film of the story has been made by Sergei Bondarchuk. "In this film," says Evtushenko, "the steppe performs like an actress of genius."[63] Hingley (1980) finds this story unique among Chekhov's mature works in having a child as the protagonist. What Chekhov called his "purple patches" of long nature descriptions are among the story's strong points, Hingley says.

Stowell (1980) says the journey through the steppe is really a search for identity, but their changeability keeps the characters from a unified sense of selfhood. Like Henry James, Stowell says, Chekhov shows how *little* children know when they think they know so much. Tulloch (1980) notes how a woman's song seems to mourn her lost youth and beauty, stolen by the heat and drought of the steppe.

Karlinsky, in Barricelli (1981), observes that the cart driver Vasya has a "Buddhist" regard for the sanctity of all of life. On this journey through ecosystems, Chekhov shows the interrelationships among animals, plants, water, and weather. Kirk (1981) reminds us that P.N. Ostrovsky felt that the story had neither a center nor an inner principle of organization. Eisen (1982) recalled that Nils Ake Nilsson found the narrative technique here similar to that in *What Maisie Knew* by Henry James.

Bitsilli (1983) finds two main themes interweaving: the life force, and exclusion from life. He notes Chekhov's daring use of personification: the steppe is alternately joyous or sad. Troyat (1984) remembers Chekhov's confession of writing the story slowly, "as a gourmet savors a woodcock." Lantz, in Clyman (1985), says that the journey is a carefully delineated picture of Egorushka's learning process.

"The Story of Miss N.N." (1887) ("Lady N——'s Story")

Peter, an examining magistrate, feels that Natalya, a wealthy lady, is above him socially, and so their promising love relationship dissolves. Kramer, in Debreczeny (1976), quotes Chekhov on this story: "Country acquaintances are charming only in summer; in winter they lose half their charm." The story ends in a hopeless struggle of dying fireplace embers to endure. Stowell (1980) states that the fluidity of time produces both ecstasy and loss. Winter, sleep, and death await those who can no longer believe in the presentness of the past. Tulloch (1980) sees the story as a struggle between nature, which is trying to unite the lovers, and social custom, for gossip speaks against the union.

"A Story Without a Title" (1888)

During the Dark Ages a Father Superior left the monastery for three months, then returned disillusioned, telling of seeing half-naked women in sinful taverns. The next morning the monastery is deserted—all of the monks have gone to town! Simmons (1962) calls this a satire on the unreality of Tolstoy's moral preaching. Smith (1973) says that "the element of comedy in this does not detract from its cynicism, which gives the story its impact."

"Thistledown" (1887) ("The Rolling Stone") ("Uprooted")

At a large religious festival, the narrator shares his room with a converted Jew, Alexander, who has been a tramp and a mine foreman. The narrator befriends him, as he starts out on a long foot journey across Russia.

Simmons (1962) says that this story is based on a visit Chekhov made to a monastery. He later found out that his roommate there was a disguised police spy. Rayfield (1975) calls this "a poetic evocation of the wholeness of ecclesiastical life, its harmony with creation and with the passage of the seasons." Alexander, the wandering Jew, is a social misfit who finally finds a peaceful sanctuary in the monastery, but still has the urge to wander. Bitsilli (1983) detects Gogol's influence in this story.

"Typhus" (1887)

Navy lieutenant Klimov has typhus, which causes him to have delusions and nightmares. After a long sleep he awakens, cured and happy. But alas, his sister Katya, who had been nursing him, caught typhus from him and died. Now his joy is mixed with the sorrow of bereavement.

Hingley (1950) says that Chekhov's descriptive skill, plus his knowledge of medicine, makes this a very effective story. Jackson (1967) sees this as evidence of Chekhov's awareness of the role of chance in human fate. Kramer (1970) notes the contrast in the way reality appears between a delirious person and a normal person. Leonard Polakiewicz admires Chekhov's use of the full sound potential of words to show Klimov's mental disorientation.[64] Stowell (1980) notices that delirium gives Klimov a new unifying power. At the end, "typhus has opened a bewildering world of joined polarities and disparities."

"An Unpleasantness" (1888) ("An Awkward Business") ("A Trivial Matter")

A doctor is brought to trial for striking his assistant in a fit of anger. Chekhov said he was ashamed of this story, because of all of its philosophizing. Yarmolinsky (1954), however, felt that it had more substance, including plot, than many of his other tales. By depicting the unhappiness of the intelligentsia, Yarmolinsky feels, Chekhov is declaring that something is rotten in Russia. Winner (1966) believes that the doctor was frustrated to discover that he was as stupid as those around him.

Kramer (1970) finds the doctor overreacting, considering such things as a duel and an apology. Although his error was a private one, he feels that his only avenues of satisfaction are public ones. Seldom, said Hingley (1976), did Chekhov ever write such "an inconclusive study of inconclusiveness." Hingley (1980) further points out that a medical assistant has an indeterminate status, so the judge is confused over how to decide the case. Ironically, the doctor is sorry to win the case, for he felt that if he had lost, his "debt" to the assistant would have been paid.

"Verochka" (1887)

Shy Ivan cannot bring himself to returning Vera's love. On the verge, he returns to her home but cannot muster the courage to enter. Tolstoy and V.V. Bilibin praised the story, and Grigorovich said it proved that Chekhov's "horizon completely embraces the motif of love in all of its most intimate manifestations." N.A. Leykin advised Chekhov to stick to writing shorter sketches, but he may merely have been jealous because the story appeared in a rival source, Suvorin's *New Times.* [65] A reviewer in 1920 called it a picture of "the sadder poetry of life," written by someone "like Shelley, who has bled upon the thorns of life and can transmute the experience into a lovely sonnet." [66]

Sean O'Faolain in 1937 called the story an ironic attack upon the two main characters for the falsity of their adjustment. No writer matched Chekhov, said O'Faolain, in his "mercy tempered by justice, sympathy ordered by understanding, and love restrained by irony." His characters experience epiphanies of self-revelation, such as when Ivan, leaving Vera, realizes that a precious part of his youth has vanished forever. O'Faolain said that Chekhov's "restraint was immense because his emotions were powerful, his heart so kind."[67]

Simmons (1962) thought that perhaps Ivan was expressing Chekhov's own reluctance to make a love commitment. Winner (1966) notes Ivan's obtuseness: When Vera confesses her love to him, his feeble response is, "Are you ill?" Joseph L. Conrad says that this story parodies Turgenev's style, especially as seen in his "Asya."[68] Kramer (1970) shows how the tale demonstrates that recollections can double back on oneself with ironic bitterness.

Conrad, in Debreczeny (1977), points out that, whereas Turgenev used nature to mediate the narrator, Chekhov uses selective but generalized details, along with phrases like "it seemed," to create an impression of haziness and fluidity. Stowell (1980) says that Chekhov's characters, like William Faulkner's Quentin Compson, see life as a pond with a stone creating ripples that flow on forever. A straw hat, like T.S. Eliot's "objective correlative," keeps reminding Ivan of his meeting with Vera. Her love declaration "challenges the fixed stability of his statistical world," and he chooses security over romance. Stowell sees this as a pivotal story, helping launch Chekhov into "a more mature, controlled, and complex period of impressionism." Bitsilli (1983) declares that the story captures a keen sense of time's passage and of lost opportunities.

"Volodya" (1887)

Volodya, 17, is embarrassed because his mother never pays her debts, and bullies him at every opportunity. He has a brief love affair with Anna, 30, the wife of an architect. When Anna spurns him, he unloads on his mother all of his suppressed complaints, and then commits suicide.

A reviewer in 1917 said that what saves Chekhov from naturalism is that a character like Volodya has many redeeming features. "Hapless mortals, striving mainly for self-fulfillment; frustrated in the end, but not ignoble—such are the figures with which this little world of Chekhov's is peopled."[69] Winner (1966) finds the vulgarization of the sexual relationship overshadowing the moral issue. Rayfield (1975) states that a wave of adolescent suicides prompted Grigorovich to ask Chekhov to write on this topic. Chekhov made his story a work of protest. "To know what suffering is," he told Grigorovich, "you must have suffered yourself." Volodya's basic values are too sound to permit him to aggress upon his mother, except verbally. His breakdown occurs because of his shame over the illicit love affair, Rayfield feels.

Summary—Stories: 1887–1888

In October 1888 Chekhov received the Pushkin Prize from the Russian Academy of Science for his short-story collection *In the Twilight*. By that time most of the stories described in this chapter had been written.

Critics labeled many of these stories Tolstoyan, because of their obvious effort to inculcate moral teachings. These stories include "The Beggar," "The Cossack," "In Trouble," "The Meeting," and "The Shoemaker and the Devil." As usual, Chekhov wrote a number of religious stories: "In Passion Week," "The Letter," "Shrove Tuesday," and "Thistledown."

Many stories depict the price paid for timidity or undue sensitivity: "The Kiss," "A Nervous Breakdown," "The Story of Miss N.N.," and "Verochka." Some, like "The Name-Day Party," show an equal penalty for persons with too little sensitivity. Some stories embody protest themes. "Cold Blood," for example, exposes corruption among railroad companies and their regulators.

As Chekhov matured, he sought for a satisfying philosophy of life. Some of his best stories during this period seem to be trial balloons in an effort to come to terms with life's realities. "The Beauties" contains his musing on the inexplicable mystery of beauty. "Happiness" amounts to a philosophical treatise on the subject. "Lights" defines pessimism, as the characters try to answer whether human society shows any progress. "Sleepy" is a clinical study of fatigue, as "Typhus" is of the delirium accompanying that disease.

Paradoxically, his best story to date, "The Steppe," contains little reflection. Critics praised it, however, for its lyricism, its poetic descriptions of nature, and its ability to evoke the very atmosphere of the vast plains of Russia. Some applauded the choice of a sensitive nine-year-old boy as the protagonist, for he could react with fresh wonder and delight at the many natural beauties he encounters. Early critics bemoaned the absence of a formal plot, but later ones found unity provided in the setting, the mood, and the characters. Most critics agreed that the center of interest was not so much Egorushka as the steppe itself, almost personified as it speaks of the natural beauty existing in the world before man besmirches it.

6. Stories: 1889–1892

"After the Theater" (1892) ("Joy")

Magarshack (*Life*, 1952) and Simmons (1962) call this a charming study of an adolescent girl's dreams of love. Reeve (1966) summarizes the plot: Nadya, 16, after seeing *Eugene Onegin*, thinks of herself as Tatyana. She thus wishes to be spurned in love, like Tatyana, but cannot decide whether to write a love letter to a young officer or a student, both of whom have shown her some attention.

Hingley (1971) said that Chekhov first published this story under the pseudonym "The Rook," but in 1892 published it in the Petersburg *Gazette* under the title "Joy" and carrying his signature. Shotton, in Fennell (1973), calls this a clinical study of an adolescent girl in her first amorous raptures.

"The Bet" (1889) ("Skazka: A Tale")

J. Rives Child in 1941 pointed out the origin of this story: To win a bet, an American named Walter Hastings on 2 May 1860 allowed himself to be put into solitary confinement in a small room in Lord Cecil's home in London. He was given books, writing materials, and food from servants he was not allowed to see. Hastings kept his word and collected £10,000 ten years later. But although he was only 35 years old, he looked twice that age. He returned to America and died four years later.[1]

Chekhov's story closely follows the real one. A lawyer bets a banker two million rubles that he can remain in solitary confinement for 15 years. He spends his time reading books on religion, philosophy, history, and languages. Near the end, the banker wants to kill the lawyer to save the payment, but finds a letter in which the lawyer says that he will come out five minutes early, to show that he has renounced all earthly things. When he does this, the banker hides the letter, to save face.

In an alternate ending, Chekhov had the banker retrieve the renunciation letter, to win a bet with a millionaire over whether anyone has survived so long in confinement. But the lawyer returns, recants his renunciation (saying that he now loves wine and beautiful women), and asks the banker for a loan of 100,000 rubles. The banker, chagrined, tells the millionaire, "You have won! I am ruined!"

Chekhov improved over the life story, Child says, by showing the philosophic growth in the lawyer. He also substituted a highly imaginative ending, showing "life as those who are capable of seeing beneath the surface of things view it. It is that which constitutes great literature."[2]

Persky (1913) says that the lawyer scorns humanity because he feels that all of its efforts are doomed to oblivion when the next ice age comes. A reviewer in 1915 detected a worldly ennui in this story, a gray mood of melancholy in Chekhov at having been overwhelmed by life's banality.[3] Toumanova (1937), on the other hand, saw this as a beautiful story which declared all earthly things to be transitory. She heard Chekhov admonishing us to live as Marcus Aurelius taught, ready to meet death at any time.

Hingley (1980) noted that the revised ending reversed, somewhat clumsily, the earlier Tolstoyan emphasis. Leslie O'Bell in 1981 showed that Chekhov used the skazka, or fairy tale form, in order to better portray the clash of ideas and ideals. Soviet critics point to the lawyer's raving as a sign that he has lost his mind. Chekhov was wary of systematic philosophy, and especially wanted to avoid the twin pitfalls of the didactic and the sentimental.[4] Leonard Polakiewicz, in Lantz (1985), reads the story as an example of Chekhov's deep humanitarian concern over confinement as a type of criminal punishment.

"A Dreary Story" (1889) ("A Boring Story") ("A Tedious Story")

A professor, 62, in poor health, looks back on his life and considers it a failure. His only happy memories are his lectures and his guardianship of Katya, a young actress who is squandering her fortune. "No one can find in my statements," he says, "what is called a central idea or the spirit of God in man. And if this is lacking, then there is nothing."

Describing this story, Chekhov said, "It's a weighty piece, weighty enough to kill a man. It's awkward and clumsy. It touches on a new theme."[5] The new theme, he went on to say, was "the miserable state of mind I could not shake off all summer." Chekhov told his editor that he hoped the story would draw some abuse, since "abuse is the sister of advertisement." The editor, Pleshcheyev, replied, "You have never written anything so strong and deep as this work. The tone of the old scholar is marvelously well kept up, and the arguments with a subjective ring to them, your own, do not damage the whole."[6] Chekhov refused to follow the editor's advice and change the title of the story.

N.K. Mikhailovsky in 1890 grudgingly confessed that "if this story is so beautiful and true to life, it is because the author has endowed it with his own sufferings." But he said that the professor, like Chekhov, had an "indifferent" attitude. How could the professor, who knew Pirogov, Kavelin, and Nekrasov, have lived without a "central idea," Mikhailovsky asked. "I know of no sadder sight than that of this talent being vainly wasted," he concluded.

Jackson (1967) said that Mikhailovsky was wrong to state that Chekhov lacked a "central idea." In a letter to Pleshcheyev in 1888 he had stated his credo: "I would like to be a free artist, and that's all. Pharisaism and stupidity dwell not only in the houses of merchants; I see them in science, in literature, and among the youth."

R.A. Disterlo in 1889 said that despite its lack of plot and clear structure, this story was very interesting and rich in content: "In its every aspect we sense an authentic artistic creation."[7] L.E. Obolensky in 1890 said that the professor's pessimism grew out of the spiritual vacuum caused by his lack of religion. D.M. Strunin that year preferred Tolstoy's "Death of Ivan Ilyich" to this story, feeling that Tolstoy not only gave a fuller picture of the falsity of his hero's life, but he also provided the solution to the hero's search for meaning.

Paul Milyukov praised Chekhov's honesty in not giving a trumped-up ending to the story. Chekhov, he said, "describes the sufferings of two people with the same complaint: a consciousness of the aimlessness of life." Although not very comforting, the end "is more natural than any farfetched theory of an abstract love of humanity, or a still more fanciful worship of the 'non-existent.'"[8]

E.J. Dillon (1891) said that Chekhov had gracefully donned Turgenev's mantle, and that his work gave the impression of "great power studiously kept in reserve."[9] Dillon saw the professor as a tragic figure who might have done great things in a society that did not have so many governmental regulations and restrictions.

Later that decade Dmitry Ovsianiko-Kulikovsky asserted that Chekhov was the best exemplar of Zola's sought-after "experimental" writer. Here Chekhov scrutinizes the psychological state of gloominess. The professor is found to have two main traits: a penchant for scientific analysis, and a profoundly misanthropic outlook.[10]

In 1903 S.A. Vengerov identified this story as a turning point in Chekhov's career, away from the early comic sketches and towards a serious, if pessimistic, appraisal of society. One forgives "the absence of precisely defined social attitudes" because his characters constantly long for a better world. He remains the historian of "the period of neurasthenic enfeeblement of Russian society," Vengerov said.[11]

Shestov (1905) was less sanguine. Chekhov, he said, destroyed whatever he touched: art, science, love, inspiration, and ideals. Chekhov's heroes are faced with the impossible task of trying to create something (a meaningful philosophy) out of nothing (an absence of conviction). Why, he asked, would anyone be interested in "this prodigious monster," the professor? When a character like Katya shows "new and noble" thoughts, Chekhov becomes interested in her only when she has grown "weak and despondent." Life, Shestov admitted, contains many dreary stories, but he doubted that any of them were fit subjects for literature.

In 1915 Gerald Gould said that this story is largely pathological: "The mental states of senile decay are, of course, fit subjects for art, and one finds them treated by Chekhov with all the reticence and gentleness of the artist, but they should be the conditions, not the substance, of the artistic problem." Despite this retraction, Gould found Chekhov to be "a man of indisputable genius," with "a luminous understanding, a tenderness towards human error, an ironic appreciation of human virtue, and a real if philosophical sense of humor."[12]

An equally kind critic in 1916 said that Chekhov had a talent for humanity, and that his tales were the best possible introduction to the mind and literature of Russia. This story is "a fragment of universal life, touched with Chekhov's autumnal melancholy."[13] Less kind was the reviewer in 1918 who said that the story's title was the keynote of all of Chekhov's art: "Russian life, observed through Chekhov's prism, is a dreary vegetation of victims of circumstances. The higher the intellect of the individual, the deeper his tragedy. Intellect, idealism, and imagination have no outlet in this freezing atmosphere."[14]

A contrary view was presented by Mais (1921), who found in this story "a magnificent description of the fascination of lecturing." After granting that Chekhov was "obviously puzzled by the why and wherefore of existence," Mais said that "his main feature is his incurable optimism, his unbounded faith in the future."[15]

Chekhov's brother Michael, in Koteliansky (1925), said that the professor's attack upon the theater sounds exactly like Chekhov's own comments on the subject. Edmond Jaloux in Paris in 1925 said that anguish and nostalgia form the basis of Chekhov's work. "His art," said Jaloux, "consisted in finding the means to express this anguish and nostalgia, not in lyricism but in the humblest pictures of everyday life, using them to show us, in the cheap mirror of this life, what is universal and human."[16]

Werth (1925) took issue with Shestov that Chekhov's writing showed only despair. Even the professor had lived a worthwhile life, Werth said. How many more students like Katya had been inspired by him? What is excellent characterization of the professor need not be the guidepost to our appraisal of him.

Rereading this story, Arnold Bennett reported that "it now seems to me quite fresh, full of new powers and beauties, and one of the finest things I ever did read."[17] The French critic Charles du Bos agreed with Bennett that this was Chekhov's finest story. Chekhov's characters are universal, du Bos alleged, and treated with such fairness that one could not tell when Chekhov agreed with them.[18]

Mirsky (1927), like Vengerov, saw this story as a watershed in the evolution of Chekhov's literary technique. Here he brings out with great power the leitmotif of mutual isolation, and from here on we find in his stories "the Chekhovian state of mind," an atmosphere of disillusionment. By ending the story on a minor note, he leaves the reader feeling depressed.

Hingley (1950) said that much of the story was written shortly after the death of Chekhov's brother Nikolai, when he was feeling depressed. Although Chekhov kept saying that the professor's views were not his own, Hingley finds the same views in Chekhov's letter to Suvorin in which he states that "reasoned life without a definite outlook is not a life but a burden and a terror."

Magarshack (*Life*, 1952) reported that although the story was widely discussed when it appeared, Chekhov received relatively little abuse from the critics over it. Magarshack (*Dramatist*, 1952) noted that Katya was a forerunner to Nina of *The Sea Gull*. Both are actresses who have a child out of wedlock, and the child dies. But Katya, unlike Nina, leaves the stage forever, feeling that she lacks dramatic talent.

Ermilov (1956) says that Alexander Gnekker in the story is the typical intellectual poseur found as a parasite among artists. This is not a dreary story but one full of *Weltschmerz*. It illustrates the bankruptcy of bourgeois intellectuals who, in their search for a "great idea," were blind to the possibility of a revolutionary cause.

Thomas Winner, in Eekman (1960), agrees that this is Chekhov's best story to date. Winner found many reasons for the professor's unhappiness: his overdedication to science; his lack of a prevailing purpose in life; the isolation of the famous; the despair of the aged; and disillusionment in art in general and in Katya in particular.

Ehrenburg (1962) stated that despite Chekhov's denials, he and the professor shared many outlooks. Both, for example, knew the wide chasm between indifference and impartiality. Thomas Mann raved about this story, saying that it was not boring but profoundly moving: "It is an absolutely extraordinary, entrancing piece. Nothing like it can be found in the whole of literature. The power of its effect, its special character lies in the quiet sadness of its tone."[19] Calling it Chekhov's best work of the 1880s, Soviet critic F.I. Evnin in 1963 said that here Chekhov first realized the hollowness of his milieu.[20]

Winner (1966) avers that in this story Chekhov shows the inhumanity of the purely scientific outlook. He also notes how impending disaster is often presaged by sound effects, such as a bird call, a mysterious moan, or a noisy gate hinge. Jackson (1967) refutes Shestov's charge of Chekhov's pessimism by pointing to the early comic stories, the faith in mankind's future, and his lifetime of humanitarian works.

Logan Speirs in 1968 preferred this story to Tolstoy's "Death of Ivan Ilyich," because at least Chekhov's professor discovers himself in the process of discovering life's emptiness. This makes him more alive and interesting than Tolstoy's Ivan. Also, where Tolstoy's story expresses his own fear of death, Chekhov confines himself to his hero's terror.[21]

In 1970 I.A. Gurvich (printed in Lantz, 1985) cautioned us not to accept at face value the professor's assertion that he "lacks a general idea," for he is too critical of himself, and tends to mistake temporary phenomena for permanent ones. Hingley (1970) calls the story a hymn to despair, full of harangue, but by common consent one of Chekhov's best tales. In reply to those who considered it a story of sexual perversion, with the professor coveting his ward Katya, Chekhov responded, "Why then would one bother to write about it?"

Kramer (1970) said that this story and "Ward No. 6," Chekhov's two most powerful stories, represented a creative catharsis for him. Finally Chekhov was able to show both the strengths and weaknesses of the dreamer. Kramer says that too much is made of the professor's lack of a central idea. Marxists like Ermilov say he needs a plan to advance society, and Christians like Boris Zajcev say he needs religious faith. More important is to recognize the professor's struggle for identity. The original title of the story was "My Name and I." The professor finally is able to dissociate himself from his name and his name's reputation. Katya, the professor's alter ego, "finally realizes that she must escape from the trap of non-identity into which the professor has fallen."

In 1972 Peter Hodgson approached this story as metaliterature, that is, literature about literature. Hodgson thinks that Chekhov gradually and subtly undermines his narrator by exposing the narrator's rhetoric. When the professor boasts of his lecturing, the reader begins to question his reliability.[22]

Lantz (1985) tells of two additional critical approaches to this story in 1974. A. Fejer sees the professor as a victim of banality: "He is neither unfeeling nor insensitive but is simply overwhelmed by life's vulgarity." M.M. Smirnov examines the relationship between the author and the narrator: "The author reveals the bankruptcy of the narrator's views by showing why he believes the things he does, and by pointing out the discrepancy between his image of reality and reality itself."

Rayfield (1975) says this is Chekhov's best work, as far as form is concerned. Remarkably modern, it is a confession story which lays bare existential absurdity. "Its vision of life is too complete to be enlarged." Critics who compared it to Tolstoy's "Death of Ivan Ilyich" "failed to see the chasm between Tolstoy's morality and Chekhov's elegy of life, between Tolstoy's miracle play and Chekhov's irony."

Hingley (1976) said that this "superb" story "surpasses all of Chekhov's other clinical studies put together." At once his most pessimistic and most exhilarating story, it established Chekhov as the finest Russian fiction writer of his day.

M.P. Gromov in 1977 found "hidden quotations" from Dostoevsky in this story. Hahn (1977) found Chekhov completing what Tolstoy had started with Ivan Ilyich. Chekhov replaced Tolstoy's incipient sarcasm with a wider range of tones, from nostalgia through regret to irritation. Chekhov better shows not only a person's unpreparedness to face death but also the fate of mankind's best values, as people go through old age into death. The professor, like a doctor diagnosing his own condition, "is morally superior, braver, and more in control" than Ivan. Chekhov here indicates that art might entail quite direct forms of social and moral responsibility. Ivan discovers selfhood in death but the professor, facing death, becomes separated from his hitherto meaningful life. Like all people, the professor partially falsifies the values by which he supposes himself to live. But his innate sense of justice makes him struggle to preserve his human dignity and his Christian values. Because most of us are in a similar dilemma, this story has great significance for us. Ironically, each time Katya tries to come closer to the professor, they become estranged. The professor, like Chekhov, refuses to give Katya a formula-like prescription on how to live life. Chekhov's honesty keeps the story from being either pessimistic or negative.

Stowell (1980) says that as the professor relives his life, he sees time as a flux, "the dissipation of the past, the despair of the present, and the fear of the future. His narrative follows the structure of a maelstrom. It begins with a calm exterior surface and slowly moves inward toward the heart of turmoil." Seeing how many different roles he has played "creates the effect of a man dissociated from himself—shades of the Underground Man, Prufrock, and Herzog. With each almost psychoanalytic session Nikolai finds he is able to break in at a deeper level." Unable to find a unity in his life, he is thrown back into impressionism. But the reader perceives the unity that is hidden from Nikolai, the professor.

Tulloch (1980) recalls how enraged Chekhov was at critics who called this an unnatural relationship between Nikolai and Katya, for he felt that he had clearly portrayed how apathy and pessimism had paralyzed contemporary intellectuals. Kirk (1981) says that Gnekker, though shallow, will easily become the family leader upon the professor's death, because the professor was never really that leader. The professor's final strategy is, if one's life cannot be a work of art, perhaps one can at least make it seem like one. Although the professor cannot externalize his inner world, the reader, like Katya, senses his inner goodness.

Bitsilli (1983) remarks that the professor's final separation from Katya marks his emotional death. Troyat (1984) said that one reason that Chekhov understood the professor so well was that he too suffered from the cheap adulation given successful people.

Clyman (1985) provides critical views of Charles E. May and Victor Terras. May reports that Chekhov here uses a theme later used by Franz Kafka and Katherine Anne Porter—"the conflict between the presentational self and the problematical 'real' self. The result is a lack of genuine communication between the central characters and others." Terras recalls that a number of contemporary Russian critics pointed out the influence upon this story of Paul Bourget's novel *The Disciple*.

"The Duel" (1891)

Laevsky, 28, is bored with his girlfriend, Nadya, who has deserted her husband to live with him. Von Koren, a zoologist, resents Laevsky's irresponsible and carefree attitude. Planning to abandon Nadya, Laevsky borrows money from his friend, genial army doctor Samoylenko, who in turn asks Von Koren for a loan. Von Koren will lend the money only if Laevsky agrees to stay with Nadya. Laevsky resents Von Koren's meddling into his private life; eager Von Koren challenges Laevsky to a duel. Laevsky discovers that Nadya is living with a police captain. Laevsky intentionally misses Von Koren in the duel. A kindly deacon's shout distracts Von Koren, whose bullet merely grazes Laevsky's neck. Laevsky is a changed man. He marries Nadya, and works hard to pay his debts. Now Von Koren respects him. As Von Koren leaves in a rowboat, Laevsky says that the search for truth is like the boat's course: two steps forward, then one step backward.

Writing this long story wearied Chekhov. He told Suvorin that Von Koren's name could not be changed, since Germans had permeated Russian science. Dmitry Merezhkovsky praised the story, but called the ending improbable. P.A. Voevodsky agreed, stating that the only thing missing was the indication of the moral grounds upon which Laevsky re-accepted Nadya. A.N. Pleshcheyev also felt that the ending was arbitrary, since Laevsky's regeneration was unmotivated. V.I. Nemirovich-Danchenko called it Chekhov's best story to date. J. Yasinsky deemed the story Chekhov's answer to Tolstoy's *The Kreutzer Sonata*.

Paul Milyukov echoed the general sentiment in 1892, when he said that "the motives are weak, and the regeneration takes place under the influence of contempt, but the story shows great powers of observation."[23] A.M. Skabichevsky noted that "the end of the story smacks of falsehood and mediocrity." K.P. Medvedsky was even more harsh in 1896, declaring that Chekhov's works have no point to them because he was a superficial writer who could not see into the human heart.[24] Shestov (1905) considered the story another example of Chekhov's gloomy philosophy.

By 1917 a quite different attitude prevailed. One reviewer felt that Chekhov had achieved the highest reaches of realism, by taking account of "man's most delicate emotions and most mysterious impulses." This is the tale, he said, of a strong man wanting to kill a weakling, "a wonderful study in the conflict between good and evil, between the merciless ethics of science and the merciful ethics of Christianity." The characters "are all blind and well-meaning—in short, they are human. Like a thrilling personal experience, the story is one to ponder for a lifetime."[25]

Another reviewer that year, after praising Chekhov, wondered whether to blame Americans for early stupidity or congratulate them on finally recognizing Chekhov's merit. Chekhov was seen as a relentlessly realistic photographer who at the same time was the most broadly sympathetic among modern writers. Small town life was said to be depicted with fascinating variety and humor, dispelling the charge that Chekhov's works were all depressing and sad.[26]

Edward Garnett (1921) found in Chekhov the perfect fusion of science and art. He quoted Chekhov's statement that the artist's instinct and the scientist's brains had the same purpose and nature, "and that perhaps in time as their methods become perfect they are destined to become one vast prodigious force." Garnett said that Chekhov is far ahead of us "by the way in which his scientific knowledge sharpens ordinary insight, and his humanity corrects scientific narrowness."[27]

To J. Middleton Murry in 1924 the regeneration in the story was not only credible but inspiring. "Von Koren gropes in vain after some understanding of the impossible Laevsky," Murry said, "until at last the rigidity of his honest mind is melted by a simple intuition into Laevsky. The reconciliation which ensues is as profound as any in the great drama of old." Thus Chekhov, the non-preacher, "in reality preached no less than this—a reconciliation here and now, achieved not from the mind but from the soul, or more truly from a reborn soul."[28]

Werth (1925) found all of Chekhov's outstanding strengths centered in "The Duel." Selfish Laevsky clashes with the Darwinian concept of the survival of the fittest, and weakness survives. When asked whether the souls of the duelers could be saved, the humane deacon replied that if God could accept the religious school inspector, who had fed him bread having sand in it, he would surely accept the misguided duelers. The plot was a conflict between two mechanical types that Chekhov disliked, the cold scientist and the impractical idealist, Werth said, and the outcome was the scourging and reconciliation of the two extremes.

Again Prince D.S. Mirsky (1927) dissented. Since Chekhov could not "feel" ideas, as Dostoevsky did, the dialogue is in "colorless journalese." This story, Mirsky felt, was "especially disfigured by harangues. No Russian writer of anything like his significance used a language so devoid of all raciness and nerve. This makes Chekhov easy to translate," but keeps him from literature embodying deep thought, in Mirsky's opinion.[29]

William Gerhardi called Chekhov "the real modern genius of reconciliation," and pointed to the closing scenes of this story for his proof.[30] In 1940 A. Kviatkovsky praised Samoylenko as one of Chekhov's most memorable characters. Chekhov's brother Michael, in Chukovsky (1945), said that the germ of this story came from arguments that Chekhov used to have with Vladimir Wagner, who later became a prominent zoologist. When Wagner said that heredity determined a person's actions, Chekhov replied that the human spirit, especially if reared in a wholesome environment, was powerful enough to overcome inherited limitations. Chekhov here was very close to Laevsky's position.

Bruford (1948) felt that Chekhov gave a fairly sympathetic portrayal of four positions: Laevsky, the philosophical idealist; Von Koren, the scientific positivist; Samoylenko, the good-natured doctor; and the deacon, with a strength growing out of a childlike religious faith.

Magarshack (*Life*, 1952), after deploring the *deus ex machina* reconciliation, said that Chekhov here shattered "Tolstoy's argument in *The Kreutzer Sonata* that the ideal of Christian love was incompatible with sexual love." Bruford (1957) tended to agree with Magarshack that the ideas in the story are in a state of suspension, rather than solution, and thus they protrude, making the work read more like an essay than a story. But Merezhkovsky was wrong, Bruford said, in saying that Von Koren was Chekhov's mouthpiece.

Eekman (1960) brought forth views on "The Duel" from George Ivask, Ralph E. Matlaw, Charles B. Timmer, and Thomas G. Winner. Ivask admires the deacon's enthusiastic appreciation of the beauties of God's creation. Timmer studies the rôle of the bizarre in this story: Von Koren does not admit its existence; Laevsky fights it only to become its victim; and Samoylenko blithely accepts the bizarre as an intrinsic part of life.

Matlaw feels that "The Duel" is as close as Chekhov came to writing a traditional novel. It is his most "literary" work, constantly quoting literary references. Laevsky often compares himself to Hamlet, and to the "superfluous" men of Russian literature. Matlaw sees Bazarov in Laevsky, and the duel in this story resembling the one in *Fathers and Sons*. The strengths of this story are the vivid characters, the organic use of the setting, and "the dogged reality of the ending." Chekhov's theme is the meaning of human love: how it helps humans to understand their place in the universe. Winner saw that however shallow he might be, Laevsky quickly spotted Von Koren's inhumane balance towards science.

Simmons (1962) notes how Laevsky grew in responsibility until he finally realized that Nadya's infidelity was caused by his mistreatment of her. Lucas (1963) felt that modern Marxists had adopted Von Koren's view by outlawing all dissent. Some are killed or sent to Siberia, "others he would break by disciplinary measures; he would have anyone shot who stepped outside the circle of our narrow conservative morality, and all this in the name of improving humanity."

Soviet critic S.V. Kalacheva in 1964 saw the influence of the Sakhalin trip on this story: Von Koren is much more austere than his early counterpart, Dr. Lvov in *Ivanov*. Winner (1966) found this duel to be a parody of all literary duels – no one seems to know how to proceed!

Jackson (1967) quoted the view of Charles du Bos that Chekhov's supreme realism is seen in the fact that even characters that Chekhov despised are presented fully, fairly, and with conviction. Jackson also quotes Soviet critic Dmitry Chizhevsky as finding Chekhov to be an impressionist, one who shows decisive changes in human life as either unmotivated or due to minor causes. V.B. Kataev in 1967 saw the story as an indication that Chekhov recognized the relativity of "truth."

Hingley (1970) liked the local color and the characterization, but said that Chekhov stooped to "a bathetic reconciliation and ending." Small wonder, said Hingley, that Chekhov liked to avoid solving problems in his literature, judging by what happened here. Kramer (1970) tended to agree with Hingley. He saw Laevsky as a blur between a parody and a serious person. The tone of the story is out of control: Laevsky is too weak to be a hero and Von Koren too strong to be a villain. Since Laevsky's regeneration is not accompanied by an intensity of feeling, the ending is melodramatic, Kramer feels.

Chudakov (1971) observed that each chapter of the story is saturated with the language of the character who is the prime focus of that chapter. V.Y. Linkov in 1971 showed how Laevsky differed from previous "superfluous" men.[31] Speirs (1971) found this story to be Chekhov's answer to Tolstoy's position in "What Is Art?" He also noted how the clash between Laevsky and Von Koren resembled that between Andrey and Pierre in *War and Peace*.

Smith (1973) believed that the "fallen" woman, Nadya, was more decent than her hypocritical friend Mariya, "whose homily on womanly virtue is one of the finest satirical pieces Chekhov ever wrote." Urbanski (1973) commented on how Chekhov used nature to reflect moods. On the way to the duel Laevsky saw rocks

as dark and wet, resembling a bottomless pit. Returning, he sees raindrops spar-
kling in the sun like diamonds.

Rayfield (1975) found this symmetrical plot to be dramatic, staged in five major
confrontations. The truth is found in neither major character, but in silence, as one
listens to the forces of nature outside of man. When Laevsky forgives Nadya, it is
"perhaps the only place in Chekhov where Christian love moves in when sexual love
is dead." Hingley (1976) disagreed, stating that the ending constituted the worst
writing to be found in Chekhov's mature work.

Hahn (1977) says that "The Duel" asserts, against Tolstoy's formulas, life's own
power to shape people's lives into new forms. Chekhov here captures the atmosphere of a Black Sea port, with its sultry heat and its constantly changing sen-
sual stimuli. This is a good setting for both romance and listlessness. Chekhov's
leisurely syntax copies the quality of Nadya's life. Through images, Chekhov
renders Laevsky's restlessness. Disliking himself, Laevsky is vexed that Nadya continues to accept him. Von Koren's callous acts make nonsense of his supposed love
of the human species. He has incorporated into his Darwinian outlook elements
from Herbert Spencer and Nietzsche which accord with his arrogant and single-
minded temperament. "The Duel" anticipates Chekhov's major plays in the manner
in which the tension tightens and in the way the mental duel becomes a physical
one. Although Nadya seems imperfectly realized, Chekhov showed insight in having
her rationalize her infidelity by the thought that she is at least saving her "soul" for
Laevsky. "At its deepest level, Chekhov's realism is that no choice in life is positively
final," Hahn states.

In 1977 the German critic Christine Scholle examined this story in the context
of Russian literary duels, and found that Chekhov's contribution was to suggest that
perhaps humility was a better solution than bullets for reconciling differences.
Charles B. Timmer, in Bristow (1977), notes how Chekhov uses the bizarre in this
story. When Von Koren and Samoylenko are about to come to blows, the deacon
remarks bizarrely, "Our bishop always travels on horseback." This comment cools
off the heated duo by suggesting that perhaps, like the bishop, they too should be
humble.

Tulloch (1980) indicates that Chekhov, always accurate on scientific matters,
shows Von Koren's ineptitude by having him select the Black Sea, a poor area for
marine study, as the site for his research. In this story Chekhov opposes the view
of Max Nordau that rapid degeneration was a byproduct of modernity. Von Koren
is not the only destructive person—Laevsky too wants Nadya's husband out of the
way. Laevsky's regeneration begins the moment he begins to treat Nadya as
something more than an object. The peripateia at the end is by no means arbitrary.
Laevsky has changed from being an inauthentic hero, who rejects the world and
is crushed, to being an authentic hero who, with a vision of knowledge and suffering, will endure.

Kirk (1981) points out that Nadya resents more criticism of her clothes than of
her immoral conduct. Kirk feels that Chekhov put Tolstoy's gospel of moral

redemption through Christian virtues into a more mundane but more humanly acceptable perspective. Chekhov deals here with modest self-knowledge in which a person learns to accept his own mediocrity. Bitsilli (1983) discerns parallels between this story and works by Pushkin and Michael Lermontov.

Troyat (1984) recounts how Chekhov said that writing "The Duel" cost him "a pound of nerves." Troyat feels that the optimistic ending cannot hide "the bitter, violent strain running through the work. In the figure of Laevsky Chekhov settled his account with a large portion of the intelligentsia. He had nothing but contempt for brilliant but idle minds, empty hearts, and loose tongues."[32]

Clyman (1985) has the views of Kenneth A. Lantz and Donald Rayfield. Lantz notes that despite the fact that he complained of being ruined by his milieu, Laevsky is able to gather up the fragments of his life and face the future with newly found strength. Rayfield states that Chekhov greatly admired the explorer of central Asia, Admiral Nikolai Przhevalsky, and that some of Przhevalsky's descriptions of his explorations influenced Chekhov in this story. Egri (1976) considers this story a rewrite of *Ivanov*. It thereby gave Chekhov an opportunity to give "adequate treatment to an ambiguous figure, an unheroic hero, and a characterless character."

"The Grasshopper" (1892) ("The Butterfly")

Olga, 22, apologizes to her artistic friends for her "uncreative" husband, Dr. Dymov. While he works hard and secures a good medical reputation, she flutters about bohemian circles and has an affair with the artist Ryabovsky. Dymov dies of diphtheria contracted from a patient. Too late Olga realizes that her husband had been the great man she had sought for so long.

Gerhardi (1923) notes that when Dymov tells Olga of achieving his lifetime goal of a readership in general pathology, she ironically worries about being late for the theater. Chekhov's brother Michael, in Koteliansky (1925), said that the germ of this story came from the illicit love affair between the painter Isaac Levitan and Sophie Kuvshinnikov, the wife of a police doctor. In 1930 Soviet critic I.V. Sobolev stated that Chekhov had created a very unpleasant character in Olga because he so disliked her real-life prototype, the writer Tatyana Shchepkin-Kupernik.

Magarshack (*Life*, 1952) said Chekhov blundered by lampooning his friend Levitan and Mrs. Kuvshinnikov. But the story gave a brilliant picture of Moscow's artistic milieu, "and its main theme, the facility with which people overlook real greatness and fool themselves into mistaking tinsel for gold, is admirably developed."

Ermilov (1956) felt that in Dymov Chekhov had created a hero who was a humane scientist. Many Russian scientists, he added, found Chekhov to be their favorite author. One of them, K.E. Tsiolkovsky, often remarked, "I wish to be a Chekhov in science." Beneath the disguise of pseudo-beauty, Olga's affair with Ryabovsky is tinged with vulgarity. Tolstoy liked the fact that Olga's "remorse" was short lived—she would always be nothing more than a social butterfly.

Simmons (1962) declared that Olga's philistinism keeps her from appreciating either true beauty or human worth. She feels she justifies her seduction by saying of her husband that "the happiness he has had is enough for an ordinary man like him." The actor A.P. Lensky recognized himself as the "fat actor" in the story. Seeing himself depicted, Levitan threatened a duel, and did not speak to Chekhov for several years.

Don W. Kleine in 1963 said that this story was the source of Katherine Mansfield's "Marriage à la Mode" (rather than Chekhov's "Not Wanted," as alleged by Ronald Sutherland in *Critique* in 1962). There are numerous plot similarities in the two stories, but Mansfield shifted the emphasis. Where Chekhov primarily exposed Olga's egotism, Mansfield focused more on the parasitism of her friends.[33]

Winner (1966) exposes the irony of a woman stupid enough to prefer a mediocre painter to a great doctor. Kramer (1970) felt that Olga's emotions were so strained and artificial that the story became melodrama. He observed that Soviet critics like Ermilov and Golubkov praise Dymov as the prototype of a socialist realism hero. Chudakov (1971) observed how the narrator borrows speech habits from the characters. As the focus centers in on Olga, the narrative becomes increasingly saturated with her bohemian vocabulary.

"Highly charged with irony," says Hingley (1971), "this work has a neatness and symmetry such as Chekhov often eschewed." Chekhov here uses food symbolism: coarse Olga eats and drinks too much, but saintly Dymov often foregoes food and drink as a sacrifice to his work. Hingley found Chekhov doing two unusual things: using his friends as direct plot material, and then denying having done so.

Shotton, in Fennell (1973), calls Dymov the only perfect hero in Chekhov's fiction. Chekhov permits him to be unflawed "only because in the story he rarely appears, is not psychologically revealed, and his heroic qualities are fully disclosed only after his death. Thus, Chekhov avoids the technical difficulties and esthetic danger of showing his own notion of absolute virtue." Smith (1973), while conceding that the story is a damning indictment of woman's triviality, disagrees that Dymov is an ideal husband—after all, Olga describes his face as "that of a Bengal tiger."

A.P. Chudakov in 1974 said that in noting how Chekhov altered real life persons into his characters, one can see Chekhov's artistic vision at work.[34] Rayfield (1975) said that the characters were too black or white to be depicted in a wholly convincing fashion. In this, the last of Chekhov's Tolstoyan morality studies, Chekhov's intermittent misogyny is seen in his portrait of Olga, Rayfield felt.

Hingley (1976) said that in later revisions, Chekhov eliminated some details that referred specifically to Levitan and Kuvshinnikov. After a three-year estrangement, their mutual friend Tatyana Shchepkin-Kupernik reconciled Levitan and Chekhov by stating that what Chekhov had really done was to turn the love affair into a masterpiece. Later, when married, Chekhov found that the Olga of his story was a forerunner of his wife Olga Knipper, in Hingley's opinion.

Hulanicki (1976) gives V.V. Golubkov's appraisal of this story. He says that early titles of it were "The Philistines" and "A Great Man." Olga says of her husband that "he oppresses me by his magnanimity." Dymov's excellence is brought out by the testimonials of other people. For example, Chekhov's own view seems exposed in Korostelev's funeral eulogy, which extols the beauty of the human soul.

Hahn (1977) said that although Olga is one-dimensional, Chekhov shows insight into feminine psychology in having her vacillate between disregard for her husband and love for him, "according to whatever area of self-gratification is uppermost in her mind." In the liaison between Olga and Ryabovsky, we see "intimacy in its inverted form." The lovers feel close enough to trade insults, and such intimacy heightens our pathos at Dymov's suffering.

One might have predicted that after being placed on such a high critical pedestal, Dr. Dymov was due for a fall. The toppling of the statue was done by Roger Freling in 1979. Dymov is not a great man, Freling charges, but a "medical mediocrity." His name means "smoke" in Russian. He is so servile to Olga as to lack dignity and self-respect. He often dangerously cuts himself doing postmortems, and his death can be attributed to his own carelessness. The title of the story comes from Ivan Krylov's fable "The Grasshopper and the Ant." True, the grasshopper does no work and hence will not survive. But Dymov, the ant, is a plodding drone who serves the queen ant, and "there are no great ants."[35]

Troyat (1984) recalls how indignant many people in the world of art were with Chekhov's thinly veiled lampoon of his friend Levitan. Basu (1985) admired Chekhov's technique of exposing Olga's superficiality by small traits, such as calling her husband by his surname.

"Gusev" (1890)

Gusev and Pavel are sick ex-soldiers, sailing home from service in the East. Pavel protests against military tyranny and civilian hypocrisy. Gusev has delirious visions of home life, and wishes to return home to help his parents. But both men die and are buried at sea in gunny sacks.

Edward Garnett (1921) finds a spiritual aura hovering over Chekhov's works so that even here, dealing with "the gloomiest, most sardonic facts of death," the reader can experience a catharsis. This story shames other modern writers by being "so humanly broad, so tender, so infallibly true in its spiritual lightings, conveying the mystery of nature with sharp precision." It captures "life's pulsating forces, its inescapable laws and its evasive rhythms." By incorporating a tinge of science into its fluid unity, it even bests Tolstoy's wonderful "Three Deaths," Garnett said.

Gerhardi (1923) describes how weak-willed Gusev envies the relentless determinism of the never-ending waves as they break on the prow of the equally determined steamship. Chekhov's restraint in depicting death makes the effect on the reader all the more profound. S. Hoare in 1923 marvelled at Chekhov's ability to

get symbolic meanings out of everyday events. Chekhov was able, said Hoare, to
reveal a universal quality by giving to his subject its greatest particularity."[36]

The American novelist Henry B. Fuller in 1924 said that the quintessence of
Chekhov could be extracted from "Gusev." One finds in the story Chekhov's con-
ciseness, his seemingly passionless objectivity, his physician's eye, his comprehensive sympathy, and his imaginative pity. While Henry James tiptoes around a car-
cass with a penknife, Chekhov expertly wields his scalpel, making every brief cut
count. The only possible flaws in the story, Fuller concluded, are the absence of
humor and the extreme contrast between human misery and the triumphant beauty
of nature.[37]

Thomas G. Winner, in Eekman (1960), says that "Gusev" deflates the self-
importance of intellectuals. For example, Pavel, after showing that he understands
everything in life, dies. Winner (1966) feels that his Sakhalin trip gave Chekhov a
feeling of moral responsibility to present social problems in his works. Ironically,
the activist Pavel dies before the acquiescent Gusev. Nature is seen in two aspects:
indifferent to man's suffering, but extremely beautiful to contemplate. Rufus W.
Mathewson in 1968 showed how the response to the beauty of nature is linked with
death.[38]

Hingley (1970) said that this story tries to straddle social classes, from a soldier
to an intellectual. Returning from Singapore on his Sakhalin trip, Chekhov had seen
two men buried at sea, as in the story. In 1974 V.V. Kataev found Pavel scornful
of the humanity he ostensibly loves, and his relationship with Gusev shows how ineffectual Pavel's protest is.[39] Rayfield (1975) feels that the story depicts the peace
of death. The sea reminds man that he lives and dies in obscurity. Now nature is
the reservoir of all the beauty that has disappeared from human life.

Kenneth A. Lantz in 1978 stated that even though the polarities in the story
are not resolved in the ending, nonetheless their perfect balance provides a catharsis. The sunset, often a symbol of hope in Chekhov, here is refulgent in glory, a
symbol of the possibility of a better life. The shift in point-of-view from Gusev to
the omniscient narrator is a sign to Lantz that there has been a shift from the temporal to the eternal.[40]

Milton Ehre in 1979 found a three-level symbolic picture of the universe, with
man in the middle, between a lower realm of chaos and an upper realm of
"unspeakable magnificence." Unlike the symbolists, however, in Chekhov's view
the higher realm is immanent in nature.[41] Also in 1979 James McConkey, comparing E.M. Forster and Chekhov, said that the end of "Gusev" presented Chekhov's
vision of life: The lower world has pure Darwinian survival but the sunset reveals
an ocean which has "tender, joyous, passionate colors for which it is hard to find
a name in the language of man." Anyone having trouble perceiving Forster's unity
in *A Passage to India* can find in "Gusev" the key to solving that riddle, McConkey
said.[42]

Kirk (1981) declared that perhaps readers called Chekhov a pessimist because
of this story. She found its five sections to resemble a five-act play which depicts

the unreflecting man of nature versus the conscious protestor against life's injustices. Gusev often dreams of a blind bull, the subconscious embodiment of unthinking brute force. His conscience reminds Gusev how he thoughtlessly beat up four innocent Chinese laborers. Before he dies, Gusev sees the blind bull on a cosmic plane as the symbol of a hostile universe.

Bitsilli (1983) detects that the characters are in moral isolation, as shown by their indifference to the death of a fellow traveler. In addition, there is cosmic indifference: The shark plays a game with the dead body before eating it. McConkey (1984) notes that here as usual Chekhov used characters that reveal competing aspects of his own personality. More than any other Chekhov story it discloses Chekhov's spiritual essence, "the degree of his insight into that desire for freedom which for him underlies all of our values."

Ralph Lindheim, in Clyman (1985), admired the great moral strength shown by Pavel and Gusev. The cause of Pavel will always speak out against the exploitation of the weak by the strong. Gusev will live as a symbol of strong family values, and "the will and spirit of both men will not be broken." To Lindheim the beautiful final sunset symbolizes the need for persons never to surrender their dreams of a better world.

"Horse Thieves" (1890) ("The Devils") ("The Thieves")

Ergunov, a hospital aide, is wary when he stops at Chirikov's tavern, a hangout for horse thieves. Chirikov's daughter stops him from checking his horse, and hits him on the head while her boyfriend steals Ergunov's horse. Ergunov is fired by the hospital, and wonders if maybe *he* should contemplate stealing something.

Hingley (1950) calls this the most outspoken of Chekhov's fictional manifestos in favor of freedom. Magarshack (*Life*, 1952) notes that Chekhov resented those critics who said he should have condemned stealing. Magarshack feels that Chekhov here may have been betrayed by his medical training, for "it is impossible to dissociate human conduct from its purely moral consequence." Yury Nagibin in 1959 said that no sickly ascetic of an author could have sympathized so obviously with the rebellious spirit of the protagonist.

Simmons (1962) recounts Ergunov imagining how wonderful life would be if he could have the carefree existence of the thieves. Winner (1966) recalls Chekhov's reply when Suvorin asked him to attack stealing in the story: "When I write, I put all my faith in the reader, presuming that the subjective elements which are lacking will be supplied by him."

Hingley (1970) says that in Chekhov's day there were approximately one million German settlers in Russia. Most of them were more peaceful than the ones who put out the eye of Filya, the horse thief. Hingley finds this Chekhov's most successful picaresque tale; like Gogol's work, it shows an obsession for colorful rogues. With no message to preach, it is merely "the biography of a mood."

Kramer (1970) sees the real villain of the story as deadly societal conformity. Ergunov envies not only the thieves' freedom but also their mystery and passion. His irony is that in seeking shelter from the violence of a storm, "he has fallen into the hands of thieves whose life force is a freedom and violence unfamiliar to him." Bitsilli (1983) deems this an obvious reworking of Lermontov's "Taman": A girl keeps a traveler busy while thieves do their work. Chekhov admired "Taman," said Bitsilli, saying that in it not one word could be taken away or added.

"In Exile" (1892)

A Tatar, 25, resents his penal assignment on a Siberian ferry. He wants his wife and mother to join him in Siberia. The veteran ferryman Simon says that Siberia is no place for women. He tells the Tatar the story of an aristocrat, in the penal colony for forging a will. The aristocrat's wife deserted him for a free man, and his daughter died of tuberculosis.

In 1912, J. Berg Esenwein called the story a masterpiece, stating that Chekhov's "workmanship, power of characterization, and subtle, sardonic humor" gave him a place alongside Andreyev but below Dostoevsky, Tolstoy, and Turgenev.[43] Katherine Mansfield in 1920 said, "I do think a story like 'In Exile' or 'Missing' is frankly incomparable."[44]

Bruford (1949) notes differing types of Siberian exile. A rich person can buy an estate and lead the life of the gentry. Simon has adjusted to life as a ferryboat-man. The young Tatar insists on his innocence and resents his mistreatment. Charles B. Timmer, in Eekman (1960), says that although the Tatar is illiterate, he understands hidden relationships and chides Simon, "God made man that he should be alive, but you want nothing—you are not alive, but a stone." Kramer (1970) and V.V. Golubkov, in Hulanicki (1976), summarize Simon's defense from the Tatar's attack as indifference, and the Tatar too had better cultivate indifference in exile, or he shall suffer great sorrow.

Hingley (1976) observes that the absence of women in the penal colony is felt deeply. Sympathetic with the Tatar, Chekhov is saying that Tolstoy's philosophy of non-resistance will not work here. In revising this story in 1894, Chekhov had the aristocrat's daughter desert him, just as his wife had done. McConkey (1984) says that exile can reduce even a person who affirms life, like the Tatar, "to a level as animalistic as that of a Simon who would deny human love and all hope." In his grief, the Tatar howls like a dog. But the reader feels sympathy even for Simon, understanding how he lost his humanity.

"In Moscow" (1891)

Magarshack (Life, 1952) calls this a "brilliant and merciless exposure of a Moscow highbrow." Hingley (1976) deemed it a "bilious and disparaging article on Moscow affairs," reviving briefly for Suvorin's *New Times* what Chekhov had once contributed to Leykin's *Splinters*. Tulloch (1980) states that this story reveals the bankruptcy of a Russian literary critic.

"A Moscow Hamlet" (1891)

In a long monologue, the narrator exposes himself as bored with life, in love with himself, and contemptuous of anything positive he encounters. Edward Garnett in 1927 called it "a crushing satire on the Asiatic barbarous element in the Russian character which Chekhov, like Turgenev, warred against all of his life."[45] Bruford (1948) describes the narrator as saying, "That's from Molière," when it is by someone else. He lives in filth, and no story meets his allegedly "high" standards.

"Neighbors" (1892)

Peter dislikes the fact that his sister Zina is living with a married man, Vlasich. He visits the couple in order to protest, but Vlasich explains that he had married his wife just to keep her out of prostitution, and now she has left him, will not divorce him, but seeks support money. Peter reluctantly accepts their living arrangement, musing that life's values are as muddled as the murky pool he is passing.

Long (1902) says that the theme of this story is that most people avoid misfortune through stupidity and banality, rather than by intelligent choice. Gerhardi (1923) praised Chekhov for not trying to postulate a cheap ending to one of life's tangles. "What is an impasse today may be a practical proposition tomorrow," Gerhardi opined. Werth (1925) found only one long road comparable to that facing Vlasich at the end of the story—"the road in all the best sadly humorous Charlie Chaplin films."

Magarshack (*Life*, 1952) quoted Chekhov that this story should never have been published, for it lacks both a beginning and an ending. This story contains the famous line from Lydia Avilov's letter to Chekhov ("If ever you want my life, come and take it") that was used as Nina's message to Trigorin in *The Sea Gull*.

Ermilov (1956) states that Marxian critics warmly greeted the story, for it shows how threadbare were the views of both the populists and the zemstvo liberals. Simmons (1962) calls the story an expose of the futility of a union made up out of politics rather than love, for Zina had lived with Vlasich because she admired his "progressive" views.

Kramer (1970) interprets Peter's remorse as feeling that Zina had accepted Vlasich out of pity rather than out of love. Hingley (1971) agrees that the incipient liaison has too shabby a base to augur well for a happy future. Bitsilli (1983) calls this a zero-resolution plot, since instead of scolding Vlasich, Peter feels closer to him when he understands his plight. Basu (1985) quotes Soviet critic M.E. Elizarova as stating that Peter portrays the bankrupt intelligentsia. Elizarova states that "the most dangerous thing according to the author is any kind of self-satisfaction. Even not knowing the way out is not so frightening as intellectual and moral stagnation."

"Peasant Wives" (1891)

Matvey tells of how Mashenka poisoned her husband over love of Matvey. Sentenced to 13 years of labor in Siberia, Mashenka died on the way there. Another peasant's wife earns money through sexual relations with the priest's son. She would like to poison her husband, an alcoholic hunchback, and his father. The women are interested only in themselves, and constantly scold one another.

Constance Garnett, having just translated this story in 1906, doubted that John Galsworthy would like it, saying "I am afraid you will think it too grim and ugly." A reviewer in 1918 said the story "describes the emotional inception and barbarously callous end of a liaison in low life."[46]

Magarshack (Life, 1952) calls it "one of his most ruthless studies of a type of sanctimonious bully and hypocrite." Simmons (1962) felt that the story might have been influenced by Tolstoy's The Power of Darkness, which Chekhov admired. Simmons found the ending gruesome, for he felt that the women would commit the murders they were plotting.

Ehrenburg (1962) believed that Chekhov presents even inhumanity in a humane fashion. Thus even the hypocritical Matvey is decent enough to adopt Mashenka's son when she dies. Winner (1966) disagrees, pointing out that Matvey mistreats the boy. Winner calls Matvey's speech "phony ecclesiastic"—he blames Satan for overpowering him when he seduced Mashenka, and he is constantly crossing himself while thinking evil thoughts. The people's view of him acts as a chorus, condemning him.

Hingley (1970) says that the presence of a Jewish woman suggests that this story took place in the Pale of Settlement, to which Jews were confined at this time. Matvey's self-congratulatory narrative exposes his outrageous treatment of his mistress. Hingley felt that Chekhov showed great faith in human nature here, for he spent his time castigating its vices in this story, assuming that the reader's ethics would ultimately prevail.

Kramer (1970) found a divided focus in this story. Should one condemn the women, Matvey, or both? Many of the women would sympathize with Mashenka, because they too had been forced into an unwilling marriage. Smith (1973) feels that Chekhov arouses compassion for unfaithful and potentially treacherous peasant women.

Rayfield (1975) finds this story Tolstoyan in depicting the layers of ritual, inhibition, and passion. Matvey's evil infects his listeners. One group of peasants, hearing the story, pronounced judgment: "Mashenka is guilty!"[47]

"The Princess" (1889)

Princess Vera is cordially received at her visit to a monastery. She thinks that she spreads joy wherever she goes, but in actuality people realize that her charity is meager and ostentatious. A doctor who formerly worked for her derides her as a tyrant, but then apologizes—and Vera once again feels magnanimous.

Bruford (1948) finds it ironic that the monks spend three days preparing for Vera's visit, but all she has ever given them is 100 rubles. Ermilov (1956) says that when the doctor blushes while apologizing to Vera for having scolded her, he is actually ashamed of being apologetic for having told the truth. Simmons (1962) praised the characterization in this "almost sordid revelation of the parasitism of a wealthy lady who excuses her incredible self-indulgence by false piety and hypocritical almsgiving."

Winner (1966) states that the princess is narcissistic. Shifts in points-of-view reveal her hypocrisy. The Father Superior uses the particle "s" terminally, which indicates subservience. Vera likes this. Here Chekhov used bird imagery to suggest a destructive woman. Vera likes to think of herself as a bird, but after the doctor's tirade she feels she resembles a bat. She is depicted as a glutton, one of Chekhov's signs of a villain.

Hingley (1970) notes how Chekhov describes Vera in positive terms, but allows her actions to debase the use of the terms. Chekhov considered this a protest story, a type that he felt he had not mastered. Kramer (1970) observes the irony: not only does the doctor's tirade not change Vera, but it even makes a hypocrite out of him. L.S.K. LeFleming in 1970 showed how in later revisions Chekhov removed strong language, so that the reader would focus on the story itself rather than upon the language.[48] Rayfield (1975) sees Tolstoy's influence at work in this story, for the good and the evil are presented in exaggerated forms.

"Terror" (1892)

Dmitry, a farmer with a college degree, tells the narrator that his great fear is not what happens after death but rather whether his wife Marya loves him. He is convinced that she married him merely out of desperation. One night, alone with her, the narrator makes love with Marya, and Dmitry catches them in the act. He leaves her, and so does the narrator. Later Dmitry returns to live with Marya.

Hingley (1971) quotes Chekhov on 25 December 1892: "Yesterday I spent the whole day on the soul-destroying job of concocting a Christmas story." Berenice C. Skidelsky in 1917 listed three other things that Dmitry feared: everyday routine, lies, and the way people mistreat one another. If life is for enjoyment, Dmitry reasons, then most people are superfluous. Skidelsky felt that in this story Chekhov was showing a preference for contemplation over action.[49]

Chudakov (1971) points up the role of coincidence in the story. Dmitry's fear of life, more awesome than that of death, is triggered by some patches of fog he sees that remind him of ghosts. Tamara Kaszurkewicz in 1974 showed that small details are quite functional in the story, a blend of symbolism and impressionism.[50] Albert Leong that year demonstrated the three kinds of terror in the story: philosophical, psychological, and sociological.[51] A.V. Chicherin, in Hulanicki (1976), said that Chekhov here employed long strings of "but" clauses in an "adversative" style.

G.V. Ivanov in 1977 showed that Chekhov's story differs from Maupassant's of the same name by locating the source of the terror in everyday events rather than in supernatural ones.[52] Eisen (1982) interprets Dmitry's abnormal fear not as a neurosis but as a general cultural malaise.

"Ward No. 6" (1892)

Dr. Ragin tries to improve the administration of a corrupt and filthy hospital, but gets no cooperation. The porter Nikita beats inmates in Ward 6, the mental unit. Ragin's only diversion consists of long intellectual discussions with inmate Gromov, a once wealthy man now suffering delusions of persecution. Even though he finds Gromov saner than most townspeople, Ragin will not free him, but tells him to accept his plight stoically. Gromov refuses, vowing to protest constantly against the outrageous conditions both in the hospital and in the outside world. Townspeople remove Ragin as the hospital administrator. One day Ragin loses his temper and is placed in Ward 6. Nikita beats him, and he dies of a stroke.

N.K. Mikhailovsky in 1892 found the story inferior to Garshin's "The Red Flower," and said that Chekhov's talent continued to lack focus. Suvorin told Chekhov that the story lacked "an alcoholic kick." Chekhov agreed, stating that all modern art and literature were purely "lemonade."

The year 1893 brought forth many critical comments in Russia. The writer Alexander Ertel called it "a masterly and profound piece, though not without defects from the point of view of Pushkinian clarity and soberness."[53] A.L. Flekser found the characters psychologically convincing, except that Gromov's madness did not ring true. Nikolai Leskov said, "Ward No. 6 is Russia," where good people are considered insane, and cynical people given state jobs. Paul Milyukov said that Ragin's lax administration and lack of willpower led to his eventual incarceration and death.[54] A.M. Skabichevsky said it was wrong to say that Chekhov lacked ideals; he simply does not formulate his ideals systematically. Does Ward 6 symbolize Russia, or is Ragin a satire on the conservative intelligentsia? The fact that both might be true was a sign to Skabichevsky that the story embodied ineffable art.

A. Volynsky demurred, stating that Chekhov lacked philosophic depth and a compelling world-view.

An English reviewer in 1897 conceded that this psychological study compelled the reader to deep thought, but he found the description "repulsively realistic," especially the death of Ragin.[55] M.O. Menshikov in 1899 called the story a picture of "a contemporary Oblomov." He felt that the story attacked both the ineffectual intelligentsia and Tolstoy's doctrine of non-resistance to evil. Waliszewski (1900) agreed, finally finding in Chekhov an effort to take a stand at solving society's problems. N.K. Mikhailovsky in 1900 praised Chekhov's effort to postulate worthy ideals.

Long (1902) liked the portrait of Russian provincial life, but decried the pessimism. He found in Chekhov's characters "no ambition, ardor or exaltation, and no enduring passion. There is an inherent cowardice and irresponsibility in the human soul which so controls things that great crises in Chekhov are inevitably determined by petty accidents."

A reviewer of Long's translations in 1903 disliked reading of unjust suffering, but said that Chekhov, despite his pessimism, wrote stories that were excellent works of art, with the vividness, unity, and restraint found only in the masters of the short story.[56] Shestov (1905) stated that Ragin's demise showed how futile it was for a Chekhov character to try to create a meaningful life out of a void. Arnold Bennett wrote in his journal in 1909 that "to say that anything is as good as 'Ward No. 6' wants a bit of nerve."[57] Esenwein (1912) tended to agree with Shestov, saying that what was probably Chekhov's greatest story was a "pitiless tragedy disclosing the ultimate breakdown of all that is noble in body, mind, and spirit."

N. Bryllion Fagin in 1921 called Chekhov "the master of the gray short story." One by one Chekhov's characters are defeated by life, Fagin said, but his art is flawless in depicting people and settings with great vividness and realism. Fagin saw Gromov carrying Chekhov's view that it is both insane and inhumane to surrender supinely to ignorance and tyranny.[58] A reviewer that year pointed out the similarity between this story and Padraic Colum's play *Thomas Muskerry*, both dealing with administrators who end up as inmates in their own institutions. Chekhov's story, said the reviewer, is "developed with that degree of introspective analysis that is so much a part of Russian art." The reviewer said that Chekhov compared with Maupassant in France and O. Henry in the United States.[59]

Reading "Ward No. 6" for the third time, Arnold Bennett was still impressed by its vividness, calling it "one of the most violent instances of Chekhov's preoccupation with Russian slackness and corruption."[60] Werth (1925) asked who but a doctor could have given such a clinical description of a hospital. Mirsky (1927), however, called it "the darkest and most terrible of Chekhov's stories," although he praised its suggestive symbolism.

Avram Derman in 1929 found in the story "a typically Turgenevan overview of the heroes' past lives, detailed psychological characterization, and an unhurried beginning, an invitation to join the author at the scene of the action."[61] I.N.

Kubikov found that Chekhov's Sakhalin trip told him that Aurelian stoicism is inadequate, and so the story encourages more active social protest.

In 1936 Montgomery Belgion contrasted Chekhov with Dostoevsky. Chekhov was admired for leaving "the underlying belief about life" to inference, but Dostoevsky was said to have achieved a more profound effect in *The Possessed* because this world was, despite its abnormality, at bottom "moral." Belgion said that what makes "Ward No. 6" a great story is the fact that it applies not only to hospital situations but wherever insensitivity and cowardice fail to alleviate human suffering.[62]

Bruford (1948) liked that Gromov found "a kind of selfishness in thinking too much of one's own salvation or peace of mind." Hingley (1950) listed the "ravings" of the "maniac" Gromov: town life is boring; people should have higher interests; we need better schools, honest newspapers, a theater, and a lecture series; crooks are well fed while honest men have crumbs; and violence tramples justice. Chekhov disliked this story, Hingley reported, for it lacked a love interest.

Magarshack (*Life*, 1952) calls the story a fully integrated work of art, whose serious purpose flows naturally out of the characters. Refusing to confront evil, Ragin commits evil and finally falls prey to it. Chekhov gave Suvorin permission to edit out direct tirades against Tolstoy's beliefs, but then, disgusted with Suvorin's reactionary politics, submitted the story to the liberal journal *Russian Thought*.

M.P. Gushchin in 1954 agreed that the tale is an attack upon reactionary thought.[63] Ermilov (1956) called the story a rallying point for protest against autocracy. He noted that Ragin had a powerful build but a high tenor voice — implicit strength but explicit weakness. Bruford (1957) reported that after reading the story, Lenin said he felt as if he too were locked up in a ward. A.P. Skaftymov in 1958 said that Chekhov's adversary here was not Tolstoy but Schopenhauer, the philosopher whose views Ragin's most closely resembles.[64] Thomas G. Winner, on the other hand, saw the story as a parody of Tolstoyan ethics.[65]

Eekman (1960) presented further views of Winner and Sophie Laffitte. Laffitte felt that the story showed how far apart were the views of Chekhov and Tolstoy. Winner said that the story demonstrated that intellectualism can interfere with a direct attack upon life's pressing problems. That year Z.C. Paperny, as quoted in Basu (1985), said that in this story Chekhov stated with artistic integrity that "the whole of contemporary life is like a prison."

In 1961 E.B. Meve studied the influence of Chekhov's medical career upon his writings. Rufus W. Mathewson, in Dunnigan (1965), shows how society corrupts individuals in this story. Winner (1966) quotes Gromov: "How ridiculous it is to look for justice when society accepts violence as a reasonable necessity!"

In 1969 Randall Jarrell sided in with Chekhov against Tolstoy. For society to improve, each individual must merely do his everyday best.[66] Kramer (1970) reported that Soviet critics see the corrupt hospital as a symbol of czarist Russia. But the ultimate order under attack is any unjust society which classifies dissenters as insane, and is thus applicable to some modern countries. Kramer finds irony in the story. The porter Nikita wants "order" but the building he keeps is filthy. Also, the more reasonable Gromov's statements become, the more sure his attendants are he is insane. Kramer sees Gromov as a Tolstoyan; his protests are peaceful, and his ideas are in works by Tolstoy like *The Kingdom of God* and *Resurrection*.

Laffitte (1971), on the other hand, brings out how Ragin's stance is a burlesque of Tolstoy's views: Why relieve suffering if people are better off dead? If Pushkin and Heine suffered, why should not these little people suffer? Hingley (1971) calls it "a symmetrically constructed work," one which has had great impact upon readers both inside and outside Russia. The argument of Ragin versus Gromov is one of Chekhov's own interior monologues. In 1900 an Archangel editor asked permission to print the story, in an effort to get officials to improve a mental hospital.

In 1974 N.M. Fortunatov used "Ward No. 6" to illustrate how a story uses a dynamic unfolding process rather than a spatial narrative.[67] Rayfield (1975) says that this story is more tragic than any of Chekhov's plays, for in Ragin one finds hamartia, hubris, catastrophe, nemesis, and catharsis. In Russia this is Chekhov's most influential work. One echo of it is seen in Solzhenitsyn's *Cancer Ward*.

The year 1976 saw many critical views on "Ward No. 6." Angus Calder saw Chekhov as a "reverent agnostic" subtly taking issue with Tolstoyan ethics.[68] Elena Chervinskene believes that the story reveals Chekhov's universal standard for humanity as "a civilized, humane, and enlightened attitude which reveals itself in respect for others, sensitivity, intelligence, talent, a capacity for work, and a love of beauty."[69] Hingley (1976) calls it Chekhov's finest work, noting how he cleverly put his own views in the mouth of the supposed lunatic Gromov. Damir Mirkovic stated that this story discovered two key sociological terms – labelling and the stigmatization process – long before sociologists knew of them.[70] G.N. Pospelov, in Hulanicki (1976), identified Ragin as a victim of the deceit and cowardice typical of the Russian intelligentsia at that time.

Hahn (1977) demonstrates that the dialogue of ideas is firmly grounded in each character's background. Flogged in his youth, Gromov now rebels. Ragin, having had a comfortable childhood, is passive in the presence of cruelty. Although its ideas differ from Tolstoy's, the story employs a Tolstoyan structure. From Tolstoy Chekhov learned to abstain from the use of color, and so everything in the story is white, gray, or black.

Susan S. Smernoff, in Debreczeny (1977), notes the similarity to Solzhenitsyn's *Cancer Ward*. Dr. Dontsova, in *Cancer Ward*, contracts cancer, and finds out what her patients have been suffering. Both works are critiques of repressive governments. Ragin's tragic outcome preaches Chekhov's moral: theories must never become, especially for a doctor, a substitute for relief of suffering.

Ober (1979) states that Ragin's determinism exemplifies modern existentialism. Mariya Rev in 1979 found this story to belong to the tradition of Voltaire's *conte philosophique*.[71]

Tulloch (1980) reports that zemstvo mental hospitals already had alienists by 1890, but here Chekhov is describing a non-zemstvo hospital. Andrew R. Durkin in 1981 said that in this story Chekhov rejects both "Gromov's Dostoevskian hypersensitivity and Ragin's pseudo-Stoic indifference. Neither global moral awareness nor aesthetic solipsism constitutes a valid response to the human condition," for both are evasions in the direction of literary clichés. "The implied golden mean," says Durkin, "is found in awareness tempered by reason which leads to feasible acts." Characters are in the grip of Dostoevskian illusions which Chekhov forces them to abandon in order to confront life's problems.[72]

Anthony Winner (1981) called this tale an example of "twilight fiction," that which is produced when traditional assumptions have grown dim or uncertain. Chekhov's characters live in a world lacking conviction, and thus they cannot bridge the gap between their private personalities and real life problems.

Bitsilli (1983) finds the same plot here as in "Gusev": doom in a hospital ward. Each story has only one "protector," who dies. Patients are victims of indifference and irresponsibility about them. The characters are not highly individualized, for they have become inhuman as a result of the inhuman treatment they receive.

Clyman (1985) presents views by Andrew R. Durkin and Donald Rayfield. Durkin says that Ragin justifies his moral indifference through misuse of philosophy; "his certitude is crushed and illumination comes, but only when it is too late for him, if not for the reader." Rayfield believes that Chekhov's view of the world as a hospital may derive from the basic image presented by Charles Baudelaire.

"The Wife" (1892)

Pavel, 46, is writing a history of railroads, but is bothered by a famine raging among the peasants. He cannot find a way to help them. His estranged wife Natalya, 27, works well with the peasants, and organizes a successful drive for their relief. Jealous, Pavel tries to assist her, is told what an egotist he is, and leaves home. Two of his friends assure him that he has been too selfish in his attitude towards his wife. He returns to her a more modest person, and finally finds his peace.

Bruford (1948) states that Pavel finally realizes that his unhappiness stems from having treated people as means rather than as ends. Simmons (1962) says that the story is drenched in a typical Chekhovian atmosphere, "as gentle, penetrating, and poetic as a Chopin nocturne." Pavel learns that institutionalized giving, such as through alms or orphanages, is no substitute for the giving that comes straight from the heart.

Winner (1966) reports that in 1891 Chekhov took active part in famine relief. But in his story didacticism pushes out art, Winner feels. The landowners stuff themselves at a dinner held to discuss ways to help the peasants. Even Natalya's motives are questionable, since she is seeking recognition for herself, and at the same time trying to spite her husband.

Kramer (1970) quotes Avram Derman, who said that Chekhov wrote this story to prove to critics that he was not "cold" to social issues. Maybe so, replies Kramer, but he notes that no character in the story is purged in that way. Pavel goes through a process of regeneration but the price he pays is his virtual destruction. His final return to his wife is as an abject slave, not as a man.

Hingley (1971) states that Chekhov was surprised that none of the story was censored, since the government was suppressing information about the famine. Shotton, in Fennell (1973), notices that Pavel is honest enough to admit that his work as a railroad engineer, built on the pessimistic assumption that all things die, is vastly inferior to that of the carpenter Butyga, who works in the belief that human values are paramount. Petty good deeds are a conscience salve to escape coming to grips with the cause of the problem.

Summary—Stories: 1889–1892

Probably because of his trip to the penal colony in 1890, Chekhov's stories show a definite social purpose during this period, and some of them embody social protest. For example, "The Princess" and "The Wife" are attacks upon the wealthy. Two stories directly reflect the Sakhalin trip: "In Exile" shows varying attitudes towards life in a penal colony, and "Gusev" permits the beauty of nature to provide the catharsis from the Darwinian struggle for existence found in life at all levels.

Chekhov's attitude towards Tolstoy was in a flux during these years. "A Dreary Story" (1889) tends to substantiate Tolstoy's stress on the importance of literature having a "great idea," but "Ward No. 6" (1892) seems definitely to show the suffering that results from an attempted application of Tolstoy's doctrine of non-resistance to evil.

The constant revisions to the ending of "The Bet" show how carefully Chekhov strove to achieve the best presentation of his material. In "The Grasshopper" Chekhov finally presented a "positive" character in Dr. Dymov, but in the story he is secondary in importance to his wife Olga. Chekhov drew criticism for not attacking robbers, in "Horse Thieves." It is notable that Chekhov did not present a single praiseworthy peasant woman in the story "Peasant Wives."

Three of Chekhov's best and most praised stories were written during these years. "A Dreary Story" depicts Chekhov's own search for a satisfying philosophy of life. "The Duel" showed that, on occasion, Chekhov could use a conventional plot and a happy ending, but the story was widely attacked for its improbability. "Ward No. 6" was immediately praised in Russia and ultimately lauded in the West for its clinical accuracy, its condemnation of inhumanity, and its symbolic picture of an autocratic Russia.

7. Stories: 1893–1897

"All Friends Together" (1897)

Hingley (1976) calls this "a notable study in non-rapprochement." He says that perhaps Chekhov is explaining here why he postponed marriage so long. Relatives have decided to marry Nadya, 23, to her childhood friend, lawyer Misha. But Misha is appalled to see Nadya's white neck—it is "not altogether nice." He also hates to see Nadya's flesh-colored stockings when her skirt billows up. "Disconcerted by these sinful glimpses," he takes the first train to Moscow to resume life as a bachelor.

"Anna on the Neck" (1895) ("The Order of St. Anna")

Anna, 18, married government official Modest, 52, for his wealth. But he is very stingy, and she longs for youthful romance. At an official ball, she catches all the men's eyes, including the governor's. She is now coveted by the men of the town. The governor decorates Modest with the order of St. Anna, and tells him he now has three Annas: one on his lapel and two on his neck. Anna now treats Modest condescendingly.

V.I. Pokrovsky in 1907 summarized early Russian criticism of this story. Leonid Grossman in 1914 noted that Chekhov here uses a technique also employed by Flaubert and Maupassant: an ordinary woman is completely transformed by her experience at a fancy ball. Gerhardi (1923) feels that Chekhov blends irony with melancholy in this tale. Anna changes from a hen-pecked wife to being a bully of her husband—but her smallness is there all along. In 1963 F.G. Svetov traced the origin of this story, showing that the crystallization of Anna's character constitutes the plot.

Hingley (1965) sees Modest as one of Chekhov's implacable villains. He notes that Chekhov made extensive additions to the story for his collected works, something unusual for him. Winner (1966) states that Chekhov used many labial consonants, which suggest lip smacking, in depicting Modest's gluttony. Chekhov also uses alliterative linkages to point out the contrast between the young wife and the older husband. Winner finds numerous parallels between Anna and Tolstoy's Anna Karenina.

V.V. Golubkov, in Hulanicki (1976), says that powerful imagery is used to show Anna's fear of authority. The story contains two types of characters: predators and their victims. The mazurka dance is described masterfully – aware of her beauty, Anna gets her partner, a stiff officer, to dance like a teenager. Her character comes through: when the notorious flirt Artynov leered at her greedily, it is obvious that she enjoyed it. She grows increasingly ashamed of her father, fearful that his plain manners might interfere with her upward social climb. As he goes down, she goes up, but she loses her morals and "all that was good in her before her marriage."

Tulloch (1980) notes the teeter-totter structure: just as Modest mistreated Anna when he held the power, so she mistreats him when the power shifts to her. Wilks (1982) recalls how, in his revision, Chekhov intensified the satirical portraits of small-town society and stressed the complete alienation of Anna from her family. Bitsilli (1983) commented on the story's imagery. At first Modest overpowers Anna like a huge bear; at the ball, when an officer invites her to waltz, she feels as if she is sailing away from a violent storm, leaving her husband behind in it.

"An Anonymous Story" (1893) ("The Story of an Anonymous Man")

The anonymous narrator serves as footman to Orlov, a government official, hoping to get a chance to murder Orlov's father for political reasons. Orlov takes married Zinaida as his mistress, but mistreats her and then deserts her. The narrator quarrels with Orlov's friends, and goes to Italy with Zinaida. Zinaida delivers a baby, then dies of self-inflicted poison. Orlov arranges for Zinaida's child to be reared by Zinaida's husband. Orlov admits that upper-class life is useless, but that no change is possible. The narrator's radical politics have faded, but he still tells Orlov that life should be lived boldly and nobly.

A.L. Flekser in 1893 admired Chekhov's talent, but said that these characters seem unmotivated. Paul Milyukov that year felt that Zinaida's suicide came because of unrequited love for Orlov. "The situation is treated with depth of feeling and faithfulness to life," said Milyukov, but the lack of motivation of the characters he attributed to "the prevalent fashion for symbolism."[1] A.M. Skabichevsky in 1895 stated that even in such a gloomy story as this, Chekhov's basically healthy scale of values can be seen. In 1897 K.F. Golovin identified this story as the best of an undistinguished lot of stories that were indifferent as to ideology, and which failed to separate significant details from trivialities.[2]

Waliszewski (1900) says this story is reminiscent of the literature of the 1840s, with a plot dealing with intrigue against a government official. The weakness is the lack of organic connection between the characters and the plot. William Lyon Phelps in 1917 found excellent characterization of the business executive Pekarsky.

To Pekarsky all persons were in one of two classes: competent and incompetent.[3]

Gerhardi (1923) said that the story showed life from two angles of vision—the active narrator and the passive Orlov. The narrator makes Orlov look weak and foolish, but he also condemns himself by the stands he takes on issues. Chekhov clothes a plot of naked irony with pity and human understanding, Gerhardi feels. Orlov, Chekhov's closest approach to a conventional villain, says Werth (1925), is one who can never be more than a *bon vivant*. In Werth's opinion Chekhov's villains are merely fools, that is, persons who undervalue love, sincerity, intelligence, and talent. Perry (1926) finds the story's chief attraction in Orlov's character—he is selfish and abnormally sensitive to annoyances, and incapable of reacting seriously to any of life's problems.

Bruford (1948) discovers in the story the atmosphere of the disillusioned Petersburg intellectuals of the 1890s. Their speech is full of sarcasm as they gossip and play cards out of boredom. Orlov is disappointed when Zinaida leaves her husband to live with him, for he covets no domesticity. Pekarsky voices the view of the governing class: "It is not intelligent to believe in God but religion must be preserved, for the common people need some restraining principle, or they will not work."

Ermilov (1956) said that Chekhov was debunking the populist terrorist, who all too easily abandoned his ideals. Zinaida, on the other hand, was one of Chekhov's great heroines; she truly loved Orlov, but her ideals see through his shallowness. The poet F.D. Batyushkov was wrong, Ermilov felt, in saying that the narrator eventually discarded isolated conspiracy in favor of "a mass protest against the common evil." In fact he had deserted his principles, thus leading to Zinaida's suicide.

Ehrenburg (1962) finds in the narrator many of Chekhov's own views. The narrator observes Zinaida's moral superiority to him, for she is willing to surrender her life to a great cause. Like Tolstoy, Chekhov had no use for the violence of revolution, Simmons (1962) declared, so the narrator is rather poorly depicted. Liberal critics attacked the story because of the narrator's loss of integrity. But Chekhov's friend, I. Gorbunov-Posadov, said that reading the story caused "a joyous feeling in my soul."

Chekhov is closer to the narrator than to Orlov, Jackson (1967) believed. The narrator sounds like Chekhov when he says, "One would like to make history so that future generations will not say of us: 'They were an insignificant lot.'" Kramer (1970) calls the story a variation of Turgenev's *On the Eve*, but more like a farce based on mistaken identity. Zinaida wishes to assist a revolutionary hero, but her men keep failing her. Kramer likes the way Chekhov unifies the story lines of love, revolution, and human relations.

Hingley (1971) sees Chekhov depicting one of his inner struggles—his domestic side favored Orlov but his freedom-loving nature preferred the narrator. Zinaida smacks of the predatory female. Since there were no important Russian political assassinations in the 1890s, it is little wonder that the narrator failed in his mission.

Chekhov did not like the ending, feeling that it was "all bunched up." He planned to expand the story into a novel, but never did. Laffitte (1971) says that the post-Sakhalin Chekhov has characters saying that suffering shows a person his destiny, which is love and self-sacrifice for one's neighbors. Zinaida says what many of Chekhov's lady friends told him: "You respond with irony and coldness to my foolish love."

One of Chekhov's weakest works, this story is ruined by the Dostoevskian atmosphere and melodrama, believes Rayfield (1975). G.N. Pospelov, in Hulanicki (1976), finds the narrator a true hero who evolves beyond political ideals to higher moral values, searching for a life which is "holy, lofty, and solemn like the vault of heaven."

Bitsilli (1983) identifies several flaws in the story, such as narrative clichés and an epilogue that is not worked into the texture of the narrative. Ralph Lindheim, in Clyman (1985), finds the narrator atoning for his life of violence by his solicitude for Zinaida's child.

"Ariadne" (1895)

Ivan tells of beautiful Ariadne, whom he admired even when she was the mistress of married Lubkov. Paying all of their bills, Ivan notices that she is shallow and conceited. Ivan lives with her for a month, and now is trying to "dump her onto a prince." Ivan is now a confirmed misogynist.

V.I. Pokrovsky in 1907 analyzed this story and its origin. In 1916 Robert Lynd said that "there has never been so wonderful an examination of common people in literature as we find in Chekhov's stories. Though he describes moral and material ugliness with tolerance, he never leaves us in doubt as to their being ugly." Here he shows the woman from the perspective of the disgusted rather than the attracted lover. It is a sensitive man's picture of a woman more greedy than beautiful.[4]

Bruford (1948) calls Ariadne's love attempts "a study in cold sensuality and love of power." Chekhov is here satirizing the Russian habit of constantly philosophizing, says Hingley (1950). Simmons (1962) denies that the attractive actress Lydia Yavorskaya was the prototype of Ariadne, as many critics alleged. "One of the most cruelly dissected Becky Sharp types in all of Chekhov's fiction," Ariadne uses men for her own purpose. "Whatever shred of conscience she has left she employs, not as a guide, but as a kind of accomplice in designing schemes of self-betterment. Affectation and pretense are the loose ornaments of her conversation," Simmons feels.

Hingley (1965) believes that Chekhov had no interest in depicting a love triangle, for "sex did not interest him very much." He found it boring to read about sex. But perhaps he is a little too hard on Ariadne, Hingley observes. Although she is shown with no redeeming feature, she has been "served up with three of the most ineffective and exasperating men that can ever have crossed a woman's path."

Winner (1966) finds that Ariadne is an inversion of her namesake in classical mythology, who was deserted by Theseus and then married Dionysos. Her lovers are also inversions of Theseus and Dionysos. This story shows the effect of hypocrisy upon love. The double narrator, producing a tale within a tale, gives the story greater depth, Winner believes. Smith (1973) sees Ariadne as Chekhov's most obvious villain. He often used this theme of how a woman, through her sexual power, threatens a man's happiness, Smith states.

S.E. Shatalov in 1974 found a deep influence of Turgenev upon Chekhov. Rayfield (1975) detected not only Turgenev but also Maupassant and Dostoevsky's *The Gambler* in this story. Ariadne's actions are not wholly her fault, Rayfield said, for woman's position is ambiguous, fluctuating from slave to goddess. Ivan's solution is for men to give women equal education and opportunities, and then cease worshipping them.

M.L. Semanova in 1980 points out both the positive and the negative influences of Tolstoy's *The Kreutzer Sonata* on this story. The stories have similar structures, but Chekhov is careful to distinguish the views of the narrator from those of the author.[5] Tulloch (1980) believes that Chekhov here echoes the *History of Sexual Authority* which he outlined in 1883. Following Herbert Spencer, Chekhov believed that women should have equal education with men, and then not be restricted to selected roles in society.

Peter Meller in 1982 stated that this and other Chekhov stories dealing with man/woman relationships can be better understood when observed in the light of Tolstoy's position on marriage, as seen for example in *The Kreutzer Sonata*.[6] Donald Rayfield, in Clyman (1985), observes that the story concludes with a Schopenhauer-like diatribe against cunning, aggressive women.

"At Home" (1897)

Hingley (1976) summarizes the plot: Attractive young Vera is gradually demoralized by trivial life on a country estate. She succumbs, and marries lugubrious Dr. Neshchapov, one of Chekhov's few unsympathetic doctors.

Bruford (1948) points out that Vera's aunt forbids her from talking to peasants. Simmons (1962) feels that after surrendering her high ideals, Vera's only escape is to feel that one is merging oneself with the eternally luxuriant steppe. Hingley (1975) states that the plot is one familiar to Chekhov — mortgaging the family estate. Kramer (1970) formulates the theme: To believe that one is free of the past is to be trapped by it. G.N. Pospelov, in Hulanicki (1976), says that the lyrical description of the steppe dominates the story and provides the story's unity.

Debreczeny (1977) gives several new insights. Joseph L. Conrad notices how the decaying countryside contrasts with the eternally roaring waves of the Crimean

Sea. Karl Kramer says that although the story begins and ends in June, a season of promise, it is winter, a season of deadness, which dominates the story. Tulloch (1980) points out that in isolation, Vera finds the steppe beautiful, but "encountering it in a degenerative relationship with her debased family, is crushed by it."

"Big Volodya and Little Volodya" (1893) ("The Two Volodyas")

Sofia, 23, married wealthy Colonel Yagich (Big Volodya), 53, partly to spite her lover Vladimir, 33 (Little Volodya). Dissatisfied by Big Volodya's neglect, Sofia has a frustrating liaison with Little Volodya. She envies her friend Olga, who has found peace and happiness in a nunnery.

Chekhov was incensed at how the censors cut his story, calling it "purely childish chastity, and amazing cowardice. They sliced off the middle, gnawed off the end, and my story lost so much that it turned my stomach."[7] Persky (1913) reported that frustrated Sofia sees no way to happiness for women of her station and condition. Simmons (1962) observes what good friends the two Volodyas remain throughout the plot changes.

Zygmunt Rukalski in 1969 showed how both Chekhov's story and Maupassant's "Mount Oriol" portray selfish and shallow extra-marital love.[8] Toby W. Clyman in 1974 demonstrated that the story depicts woman's hopeless lot: Sofia is trapped into marrying a man she does not love; the spinster Rita lives a barren life; and the nun Olga insulates herself from the world's frustrations by suppressing all of her emotions.[9] Rayfield (1975) defends Sofia by delineating Little Volodya's earlier rejection of her. He notes how here, as usual, Chekhov uses church bells to suggest eternal bliss.

Hingley (1978) says that Chekhov, like all fiction writers, is better at depicting the negative characters than the positive ones. He is also more effective as a negative moralist, that is, pointing out how people should not behave. Chekhov conceded that the story is cynical, but he felt that it would have been better for the censors to reject it than to butcher it.

"The Black Monk" (1894)

Kovrin, from Moscow, visits his former guardian Pesocky, a horticulturalist, in southern Russia. Kovrin tells Pesocky's daughter Tanya the legend of a black monk whose image floated around the world a millennium ago, and who is now due to return. Alone, Kovrin sees the black monk, who tells him that Kovrin is hastening the coming of the kingdom of eternal truth. Feeling sorry for her, Kovrin marries Tanya, but she and her father consider Kovrin demented and have him institutionalized. Cured, he is released, but now he no longer sees the monk, and he is crabby and unhappy. He runs away with another woman. Tanya tells him, in a letter, of Pesocky's death and of her hatred of him. But the black monk returns to console him, and he dies happy.

Chekhov said he wrote the story in order to describe megalomania. "The monk floating across the country was a dream, and when I woke I told my brother Misha about it."[10] F.A. Kumanin, editor of *Artist*, considered the story "not an important thing, very watery and unnatural," but he said that it would be awkward not to print anything bearing Chekhov's name.[11] Tolstoy called the story charming. A.M. Skabichevsky in 1894, however, said that here Chekhov shows a lack of philosophic depth and absence of a compelling world-view. N.K. Mikhailovsky in 1900 welcomed this story as a sign that Chekhov was now affirming positive ideals. A reviewer in 1903 said that this mingling of fantasy and symbolism revealed Chekhov's philosophy of despair by having a thinking man succumb to a cruder friend.[12] Shestov (1905) says that Kovrin is confused—at times the black monk seems very real, but at other times Kovrin's friends convince him that the monk is a delusion. Shestov observed that Chekhov often took the side of abnormal people, like Kovrin, in his stories.

Leonard Woolf in 1917 stated that after Kovrin's death, the reader feels that for him, "the most complicated part is just beginning."[13] A reviewer that year called the story "a wonderful study of madness. It illustrates how closely the higher realism is bound up with the same imagination as the poet's."[14] George Sampson said that Chekhov's tales were "supreme examples of artistic detachment." Chekhov was never sentimental or cynical. This story is one "on the highest plane of imaginative invention, and is told with a wealth of detail and description. From the mouths of Chekhov's characters you can collect a varying but vital criticism of modern life," Sampson concluded.[15]

Mais (1921) was surprised to see a realist like Chekhov cross the border into mysticism in this story. Normally a foe of superstition, here Chekhov fared "deep into the spiritual world and comes into line with Dostoevsky." Werth (1925) found a poetic beauty in the description of Kovrin's hallucinations. Mirsky (1927) said that this story was Chekhov's only definite failure, caused by his abandonment of "the limits of strict realism."

Edward J. O'Brien in 1928 selected this story (over "The Bet" and "The Darling") as one of the fifteen best short stories of the world. Like Dostoevsky or Emily Brontë, Chekhov here achieves "nothing less than a synthesis of the spiritual life of our time," O'Brien said. "Here all temptations are encountered, all sins committed, all hope for the future abandoned; but life makes its final affirmation from the brink of the grave."[16]

George Z. Patrick in 1932 found expression of Chekhov's philosophy in Pesocky's explanation of his success as a gardener: "I love my work." "In these words," said Patrick, "is heard Chekhov's appeal. Life pleads for purposeful occupation and the wise distribution of human energy."[17] Yarmolinsky (1947) declared that the story examines madness as a possible gateway to transcendental reality. Magarshack (*Life*, 1952) calls it "a careful scientific study of mental disorder."

When people wondered about Chekhov's own mental health in depicting Kovrin's troubled state so accurately, he said that he wrote the story "not under the influence of gloomy thoughts but with cool deliberation."

M.P. Gushchin in 1954 used this story to show that Chekhov strongly opposed reactionary thoughts. Ermilov (1956) discovered "a profound poetical undercurrent" in the story. Here, said Ermilov, Chekhov the doctor merged with Chekhov the artist. The story castigates disease and shows "the false beauty glorified by the morbid art of decadence." George Ivask and Thomas G. Winner commented on this story in Eekman (1960). Eekman quoted Shestov in declaring that Chekhov hated philosophy, and hence a character like Kovrin philosophizes unconvincingly. Winner sees Kovrin as a victim of the intellectual hubris of scientism. When he asks the monk, "What is eternal truth?" the monk vanishes. Kovrin is Chekhov's warning, says Winner, that a person who aspires to be a superman may be insane.

In 1961 E.B. Meve wrote on Chekhov's career as a doctor, including material on Chekhov's descriptions of abnormal mental states. Winner (1966) says that here Chekhov tries to solve no problems, but rather lets the reader be the jury. Not only mystics but also artists and scientists are seen as persons apart from common humanity. Although Kovrin thinks of himself as a modern Faust, in actuality he is a mediocre "superfluous" man. In Chekhov's symbolism the black monk is Kovrin's frustrated goal, a projection of his repressed ego. Setting and music are used to enhance the characters' moods. Like Henry James, Chekhov tried to present a complex perspective of the inner life of the individual, Winner states.

A comparison of this story with Gogol's "Notes of a Madman" was made by Peter Rossbacher in 1969. Sane Kovrin is merely a typical suffering hero but insane Kovrin is an antitype—he no longer suffers, for he can proceed beyond the point where the literary type got stuck. He stands for Chekhov's desire for a world where happiness is the norm.[18]

Kramer (1970) notes that Kovrin is a more productive scholar before being cured of his hallucinations. Pesocky's split personality shocks Kovrin—in his garden Pesocky is creative but his scholarly articles are full of hateful poison. Kovrin often sees the black monk after Tanya sings a song describing an insane girl who hears beautiful music. In 1970 N. Ulianov studied Chekhov's mysticism, calling him "a mystic by nature," since many supernatural elements appear in his works, and mysterious forces often govern the lives of his characters. In 1972 V.T. Romanenko reviewed critics' comments on this story. He felt that they often overlooked Chekhov's often-used theme: a person's moral responsibility for his thoughts and actions.[19]

The black monk may be a projection of Kovrin's megalomania, concedes Shotton, in Fennell (1973), but "in an insanely petty world the penalty for, or the mark of, idealism is mental instability." Urbanski (1973) feels that Chekhov's medical knowledge and literary art united to give a convincing picture of mental illness.

The story is seen as written in sonata form by N.M. Fortunatov in 1974. Two contrasting themes interplay in a three-part musical structure.[20] Rayfield (1975) says that the garden symbolizes the earth's beauty. Although implausible and inferior to Garshin's "The Red Flower," the story unites beauty and horror in a new way for Chekhov. V.B. Kataev in 1976 notes that Chekhov often relied on mythology; in this story it is the myth of Faust.

In 1977 M.M. Girshman detected complex disharmonious elements beneath Chekhov's apparently smooth style, and M.P. Gromov found hidden quotations from Dostoevsky in this story.[21] Jerome H. Katsell, in Debreczeny (1977), notes the symbolic use of the seasons. Kovrin's insomnia, Katsell feels, prepares him to face death, here symbolized by the black monk.

Hingley (1978) states that part of Chekhov's material came from a conversation Chekhov had with peasants concerning mirages they had seen. Kovrin may have mistreated Tanya, but he resented her effort to domesticate him, lest it strip him of his personality. Even death is preferable to trivialization, Chekhov is saying. As in "Ward No. 6," Chekhov's protest against mediocrity is put into the mouth of a lunatic. David Matual that year disclosed Byron's influence upon the story. Chekhov's letters show that he admired Byron very much, Matual observes, as he points up parallels between Chekhov's black monk and the black friar in *Don Juan*.[22]

Tulloch (1980) shows that Chekhov carefully details the social pressures which may have caused Kovrin's *mania grandiosa*, including his addiction to the ideas of Nietzsche and Max Nordau. Kirk (1981) believes that Kovrin overrates his genius, and that his final smile of mystical ecstasy is hard earned, coming at the expense of other people's happiness. L.M. O'Toole in 1981 sees the story as built around a series of concentric circles surrounding the estate. The characters are defined by their movements among these circles. V.I. Kuleshov in 1982 studied symbolism in this story.[23]

O'Toole (1982) says that their names reveal their personalities: Pesocky comes from "sand" (he likes the outdoors), and Kovrin from "carpet" (he prefers indoor life). Tanya has a constant need for an enclosure, or shelter. The black monk originates at infinity and "moves centripetally in proportion to Kovrin's centrifugal process. This reciprocal movement charts the course of the hero's megalomania."

Bitsilli (1983) explains Chekhov's artful use of "it seems" to deepen mysticism, as when Chekhov says, "It seems that if one were to walk along the path, it would lead to a most supernatural and mysterious place." I. Sukhikh in 1983 surveyed current Russian criticism of the story, concluding that it illustrates one of Chekhov's fundamental beliefs, the moral equality of human beings.[24] Troyat (1984) observes that Chekhov tried to purge himself of his nightmare by writing this story. Although some critics called it a masterpiece of fantasy and others a sneer at intellectual mystics, Chekhov was simply glad that a person like Tolstoy enjoyed the story.

"A Daughter of Albion" (1893)

Gryabov makes fun of his English wife, who cannot speak Russian. When his fishing line gets snagged, he tries to get her away, but she remains. So he strips naked, to unsnag the line, stands in front of her, and says, "This isn't England, you see!" But she coolly continues to fish.

Gorky in 1920 said that "the dear public, when it reads this story, laughs but hardly realizes how abominable is the well-fed squire's mockery of a person who is lonely and strange to everyone and everything. In each of his humorous stories I hear the hopeless sigh of sympathy for men who do not know how to respect human dignity."[25]

"The Head Gardener's Story" (1894)

Chudakov (1971) recounts the plot: Karlovich, a Swedish head gardener, is a very gentle man. He tells a Swedish legend of a very talented and loving doctor, whom everyone loved for his good deeds. Instead of robbing him, thieves would take off their hats and offer him something to eat. One day his murdered body is found. The murderer is tried and found guilty but the judge frees him, saying, "It is impossible to imagine that any human could sink so low." Townspeople agreed. The gardener's grandmother said that for such faith in humanity, God forgave the sins of the town: "He rejoices when we believe we are in His image, and grieves when we forget human dignity."

L.M. Dolotova in 1974 showed how this story developed from entries in Chekhov's notebooks.[26] V.V. Golubkov, in Hulanicki (1976), marveled that no townspeople protested the decision. Hingley (1978) calls the story "an example of direct didacticism rare in Chekhov's mature work." Censors cut out a passage in which Chekhov said, "It's easy to believe in God. The Inquisitors did. So did tyrants. So did Alexander I. *You* believe in *man!*" Leonard Polakiewicz in 1983, in a study of Chekhov's views on crime and punishment, said that the story exhibits Chekhov's deep humanitarian concerns.[27]

"The Helpmate" (1895) ("His Wife") ("The Mate")

The surgeon Nikolai has a useless wife Olga who is keeping up a love match with young Michel. Nikolai bawls out Olga when she receives an amatory telegram from Michel. Olga ignores him, and complains about losing a purse with 15 rubles in it. Nikolai promises her 25 rubles if she will be quiet. She confesses her infidelity. Nikolai wants to give her a divorce and a passport to go to Michel, but she prefers the security of being Nikolai's wife. She keeps asking Nikolai for the 25 rubles.

Gerhardi (1923) states that this story reveals that human nature is too subtle to be classified. When the narrator stops trying to classify the doctor, he finally understands him. Simmons (1962) feels that Tolstoy's praise of the story's misogyny resulted from Tolstoy's feud with his wife. Hingley (1965) quotes Chekhov's brother Michael, who said that this was practically the biography of A.A. Sablin, the former chief finance officer at Yaroslavl. Winner (1966) notes that Olga behaves like Anna Karenina. Olga is described like a bird frantically beating its wings against a window, trying to escape. Desiring the prestige of Nikolai's name, she will continue to torture him with her faithlessness. Hingley (1976) feels that Olga is virtually a "creation by anticipation" of Olga Knipper, whom Chekhov had not yet met.

"The House with the Mezzanine" (1896) ("An Artist's Story")

The narrator is a landscape painter in love with quiet Genya. Genya's sister Lida is very outspoken, and is organizing a group of intellectuals to oust the tyrannical mayor. The narrator refuses to support Lida's plan for a medical center, saying that what is needed is a complete economic change: Machinery should alleviate the peasants' hard work; everyone, including doctors and priests, should do several hours of physical work daily; and universities should be available for all citizens. When Lida sees that Genya and the narrator are getting serious about each other, she sends Genya abroad. Years later the artist still pines for Genya.

Jeronim Yasinsky in 1896 said that Chekhov cluttered the story with unnecessary details. For example, why need this house have a mezzanine story? F.D. Batyushkov hailed the tale as a breakthrough in Chekhov's fiction, in which he was asking for a fundamental change in the Russian way of life. Other Russian contemporary critics, however, seemed to miss the story's point. The most liberal Russian newspaper, *Russian News*, simply called the artist another of Chekhov's gloomy characters. Another liberal paper, *Stock Exchange News*, preferred hardworking Lida to the inactive artist.[28]

Robert Lynd in 1916 said that this beautiful, sad story could have been written by Turgenev. Egoism is what offends Chekhov the most, even when it is, as here, the egoism of good works. "I know of no writer," said Lynd, "who leaves one with the same vision of the human race as the lost sheep of the house of Israel."[29] George Z. Patrick in 1932 said Chekhov creates situations in which his characters can discuss life's meaning. The artist is Chekhov's mouthpiece when he says that "the highest vocation of man is spiritual activity. When science and art are real, they seek for eternal truth, for God, for the soul."[30]

Hingley (1950) notes that time erased love's impressions, so that when the artist tried to recapture his affair with Genya, the poignancy of the deeply felt emotion was already half buried in memory. Magarshack (*Life*, 1952) felt that the artist destroyed Tolstoy's followers in one sentence: "The people have been entangled in a great chain, and you do not cut through that chain but merely add new links to it." Ermilov (1956) says this, one of Chekhov's most poetic works, underscores the poverty of liberalism. The story's beauty lies in Chekhov's mourning over two kinds of lost happiness: love for the individual, and social change for the whole society.

Simmons (1962) reports that Lida's action projects were ones that Chekhov was working on, and hence, despite his chiding her zeal, he seems closer to her viewpoint than to the artist's. V.A. Nazarenko rebuts Ermilov's position, saying that the artist really loves Lida but spurns her to focus on his art. Chekhov is stressing how seriously artists should take their calling.[31] Hingley (1965) states that Chekhov often shows an ineffectual person as preferable to a priggish do-gooder. This story's theme is that one's private life is more important than public postures. Chekhov's brother Michael said that the prototypes of these characters were the owners of the estate at Aleksin, where Chekhov rented a house in 1891.

Winner (1966) reports that Lida finally drove the village tyrant from office. Kramer (1970) doubts that Lida is the villain of the story. The narrator exaggerates Lida's evil to make himself look good—he is lazy, and untrustworthy as a narrator. Genya too is so subservient that perhaps she instigates Lida's bullying of her. Chudakov (1971) is impressed at how fairly Chekhov presents Lida's ideas, considering that they are not his.

A.A. Belkin in 1973 stated that the story illustrates Chekhov's beliefs that truth is liberation from illusions.[32] Smith (1973) finds the story a cross between a love tale and a sermon, but the love tale wins out because the lyrical introduction and conclusion establish a dominant romantic tone. She quotes French critic E. Triolet as saying that Lida kept her sister from having the artist because she wanted him for herself. In 1974 Soviet critic A. Fejer surveyed previous criticism of this story and showed its similarity to Turgenev's works.

Rayfield (1975) also noted Turgenev's influence. It is Lida's attitude rather than her actions that is wrong. Lida and the artist spar more over control of Genya than over ideology—both characters reflect differing aspects of Chekhov's own convictions. V.V. Golubkov, in Hulanicki (1976), says the poetic ending—"Misyus, where are you?"—arouses in the reader a dissatisfaction with the present and a thirst for a brighter future. Hingley (1976) feels that Chekhov may be mocking himself in his portrait of Lida, for at the time he was interfering with his sister Marya's attempted marriage.

Kirk (1981) observed how nature descriptions harmonize with major plot changes. Although Soviet critics consider the artist as a socialist visionary, Chekhov here is actually politically ambiguous. Bitsilli (1983) points out that here, as in many of his stories, Chekhov describes a cross "burning" in the setting sun. Basu (1985) disagrees with Soviet critic Z.S. Paperny, who says that both Lida and the artist oppose the interests of the poor. Lida is the cruel intellectual who can destroy an innocent love match, Basu says, but the artist dreams of a beautiful world where callous intellectuals like Lida would have no power.

Clyman (1985) expresses the views of Charles E. May and Harvey Pitcher.

May finds the satire in the artist feeling that he is a person "above facts." Pitcher discounts Lida's community projects in the light of her bullying her sister and her mother. Pitcher concludes that Lida may be on the way towards political fanaticism.

"In the Cart" (1897) ("On the Cart") ("The Schoolmistress")

Marya the schoolteacher is returning from collecting her 20-ruble annual salary in town. She meets landowner Khanov, whom she would like to marry, but knows that she will never be asked. Returning home, she recalls childhood pleasures.

Simmons (1962) sees this as a crushing indictment of the plight of rural teachers. Based on the experience of a Talezh teacher, the story illustrates Chekhov's technique of filtering a topic through his memory until only the quintessential details remain. Insensibly Marya begins to sink to the level of her peasant students, cringing before each petty official. Hingley (1965) regrets the failed love match, because each person needs the other. Caroline Soëp in 1965 describes how Chekhov drew upon letters received from teachers in writing this story.[33]

Jackson (1967) quotes Dmitry Chizhevsky as calling this the typical Chekhov style, as Marya reminisces about her past. We see "the 'flitting past' of reality, the unexpected, unmotivated, and mutually contradictory experiences," related in an impressionistic manner. In 1971 D. Breshchinsky found that time was a major theme in this story. The heroine cannot connect herself to her past or her future. The story has three layers of time: the heroine's present while on her journey; "the larger present of her unchanging everyday life; and her past and future."[34]

Smith (1973) believes that artistic economy makes this a superior story, as Chekhov presents the contrast between her present dreary existence and the lyrical remembrances of past happy family life. V.V. Golubkov, in Hulanicki (1976), denotes this "a lyrical symphony," employing a contrapuntal technique of repeating musical phrases. The main episode is Marya's imaginary meeting with her mother. H. Hamburger in 1976, as seen in Lantz (1985), studied the component of time as used in this story. Hingley (1976) credits Chekhov here with sympathy for women's misfortunes — "a tribute to those who persist with unrewarding work under hopeless conditions."

Karl D. Kramer, in Debreczeny (1977), notes how the season of springtime correlates with Marya's romantic recollections. Stowell (1980) sees Chekhov as an impressionist. As Marya waits for a train to pass, Chekhov's scene fragments and dissolves the material landscape, like a Monet or Turner painting. In Stowell's view, "the elements of impressionism are here: visual perspective, motion and stasis, harmony of feeling, formlessness of colors and shapes, random and isolated detail, and the pervading source and reflection of light at a particular time of day. In a sense," says Stowell, "Chekhov's career seems to have been pointed towards this passage," the impressionistic epiphany, which combines dream and reality, past, present, and future, and subject and object into "an atmospheric moment of presentness." After moving in the cart, Marya is caused to stop—the stasis, after the motion, gives her pause to reflect and integrate her impressions. Kenneth A. Lantz, in Clyman (1985), observes that the daily grind of the overburdened teacher shows vividly how environment can erode a person.

"The Murder" (1895)

Persky (1913) describes the plot. Disillusioned by the worldliness of the monks, novitiate Matvey leaves the monastery. He founds a sect, then tries to destroy it to return to the Orthodox Church. His cousin Jacob and Jacob's wife Aglaia are converts who are religious fanatics. When Matvey uses oil on food during the Holy Week fast, Jacob begins to throw him out of the house, and Aglaia hits him with the oil bottle, killing him. They are caught trying to dispose of Matvey's body, and are sent to Sakhalin. There Jacob renounces his fanaticism, and wants to return to a religion of love and pity for all mankind.

Concerning this story, Chekhov wrote in his notebook that "most people in Russia, even freethinkers, hate people who have some special kind of religion of their own." Sean O'Faolain in 1937 observed how the snowstorm is used organically: "It impresses us with a sense of the mute suffering, as of beasts in a winter field, that holds these peasants together in a kind of fatalistic effortlessness." The murder's effect is "that of one poor brute killing another."[35]

Bruford (1948) noted that in 1753 Russia abolished the death penalty, except for political crimes. Some prisoners, he adds, died of legal beatings. Charles B. Timmer, in Eekman (1960), cites as an example of the bizarre this accidental murder, "a terrible eruption out of the smooth current of everyday life." Simmons (1962), calling this one of Chekhov's few stories reflecting his Sakhalin trip, says it gives a vivid glimpse of the horrors of the penal colony. Hingley (1965) shows that some of the details in the story came from the town of Uglich.

Chudakov (1971) says that now Chekhov uses a narrator whose every position in space is always precisely indicated. Chekhov also depicts clearly the thoughts and feelings of Jacob in all of their complexity and inconsistency. Chudakov notes that A.A. Shevelev in 1895 had complained that Chekhov did not make clear whether Jacob's "conversion" in Sakhalin cured him of his extreme arrogance.

Shotton, in Fennell (1973), summarized the plot as "rival religious fanaticisms lead a man to fratricide." L.M. Dolotova in 1974 showed how entries in Chekhov's notebook establish links between the Sakhalin trip and this story.

Rayfield (1975) said that this story was highly praised. Ivan Bunin thought it was the best of Chekhov's later stories, because the objective narrator lets the shocking conduct make a great impact upon the reader. E.S. Dobin, in Hulanicki (1976), emphasizes that the quarrel was over potatoes—Matvey put some oil on them. After Aglaia hits Matvey with the oil bottle, Jacob hits him with a flat iron. After the incident, nothing seemed to Jacob so frightful as the blood-stained potatoes—he is careful not to step on them. Potatoes thus carry the imprint of the murder.

E.A. Polotskaya in 1977 studied this story in the light of Chekhov's religious upbringing and his Sakhalin trip. His religious rearing helped him create the story's atmosphere. The Sakhalin trip gave him prototypes for his characters as well as material on the psychology of murder.[36] Bitsilli (1983) finds a subtle use of symbolic imagery. All episodes occur during a snowstorm, which fluctuates in accordance with the characters' moods. The senseless and unexpected murder of Matvey is prepared for by the storm's symbolism. The demonic possession of the religious fanatics is suggested through color and olfactory images.

"My Life" (1896)

Tired of the lies and bribes in his town, Poloznev turns his back on his aristocratic heritage and becomes a house painter. Everyone in town looks down on him for this, especially his father, an architect with atrocious taste. Poloznev gets a job as a railroad laborer, then marries Masha, the daughter of the railroad superintendent. Dr. Blagovo, an intellectual, marries Poloznev's sister Kleopatra. Masha and Poloznev try to help the peasants, but they do nothing but steal and lie. Impatient with the peasants, Masha and Blagovo run off together. Kleopatra and Poloznev keep helping the peasants. Kleopatra dies in childbirth—Poloznev, now a contractor, rears her child.

Since the story was published in a family magazine, The Meadow, the censor deleted many passages. Incensed, Chekhov restored the cuts in the book version. In a letter Chekhov gave his view of railroad contractors: "They are vengeful people. Refuse them a trifle and they will punish you for it all your life—it's their tradition."[37] A. Lugovoy-Tikhonov, literary editor of The Meadow, told Chekhov in 1896: At first I thought you had made a mistake by omitting the characters' motivation, but then I realized that you were flattering the reader by leaving these things to his inference.

Constantine Balmont in 1898 commended the skillful delineation of Russian provincial life in this story. Balmont summarized Chekhov's "original gift": "He has unusual powers of observation, and vigorously seizes the situation before him and the psychological details; without visibly aiming at effects, he succeeds in producing a deep impression on the reader by straightforward realism, with all its heartlessness, cruelty, and tragic color."[38]

Persky (1913) states that Poloznev describes the peasants' ignorance: They will mow your field for six liters of brandy but not for 20 rubles (which would buy eight times as much brandy). But Chekhov's peasants here have the most important quality: a deep sense of justice. A reviewer in 1920, however, found Chekhov a naturalist with little typical Russian compassion. He said that Poloznev's kindly nature "serves to accentuate the qualities of the people in that grey and dishonest town."[39]

Francis Hackett in 1920 was more kind to Chekhov. At first, Hackett says, one is repelled by the Darwinian Dr. Blagovo and the crude peasants. "But only the unduly purposeful man is likely to be fooled by this cruel candor. Soon Chekhov shows another side of the peasant. He is not committed to the Tolstoyan view or the bourgeois view. He relates both views to his object, the portrayal of Poloznev."[40]

Conrad Aiken in 1921 called Chekhov "a master of mood," able to portray a broad range of states of consciousness which are kept unified by "a unity of tone."[41] Mirsky (1927) called "My Life" Chekhov's best story, better than his others because "its sweep and range are wider; it is like the ultimate poetical synthesis of his intuition. This life of Chekhov's only hero, the delicate man haloed by continuous defeat, is his *Odyssey* or his *Purgatorio*, a true poem of immense symbolical pregnancy. The very vagueness and generality of its titles make it something like an *Everyman.*" Here Chekhov finally escaped the "lullaby" effect of his style, said Mirsky, in which a Chekhov tale generally trailed off into an indefinite ending.[42]

V.S. Pritchett in 1943 found the story "a scathing picture of corrupt people in an awful provincial town," linked with the social and spiritual problems of the day. The story bears reading not only for Chekhov's great indignation but also for his acute knowledge of social problems. No one, said Pritchett, can suggest more between the lines than Chekhov. Here Chekhov's plea is for personal integrity and social compassion.[43] Orlo Williams was less generous, finding the story "just another long narrative of frustration. The particular point of it is not really obvious to the foreigner. It is certainly a fierce indictment of provincial life without that mixture of pathos and humor found in *The Cherry Orchard.*"[44]

Bruford (1948) cites specific protests. The railroad engineer acquires three estates near where the new railroad line will be laid. Although the drinking water is contaminated, rich people squander their time gambling, saying that the town cannot afford a sanitary water supply. Hingley (1950) says that the story attacks Tolstoy's doctrine of simplification. Chekhov seems to agree with Blagovo when he scolds Poloznev for not developing his higher intellectual powers. Magarshack (*Life*, 1952) agrees that this is a story of the tragedy of people who try to apply Tolstoy's teachings.

Ermilov (1956) notes that Poloznev's first name, Misail, means "little use." Ermilov sees Masha as the heroine, for she realizes that something more radical than superficial palliatives are needed to solve the peasants' problems. Simmons (1962) asks, If Tolstoyism is not a tenable philosophy, what is? Perhaps Chekhov's conviction that happiness and progress depend more upon truth than upon love. Hingley (1965) states that Chekhov tended to regard Tolstoyism, or any ism, as an obstacle to human freedom. The troubles that Poloznev and Masha have in building a school for the peasants indicate that perhaps the effort should never have been made.

Nevertheless, said Hingley, Chekhov himself built three schools for the peasants in the Melikhovo area.

Winner (1966) notes Chekhov's characterizing devices: Blagovo's weakness is shown by the use of diminutives describing him. One peasant, Redka, constantly quotes proverbs. Masha's father always takes showers, as if trying to wash off his peasant background. Kramer (1970) detects four town rebels in this story. Two are unsuccessful: Masha's motto is "All things pass," and Blagovo dodges current reforms in the name of a coming millennium. Kleopatra and Poloznev succeed through persistence.

Chudakov (1971) sees Poloznev's triumph not in his ideals but in his everyday kindness toward his family and friends. Struve (1971) comments that Chekhov, who gave careful attention to his titles, disliked this one because the word "my" was in it. Struve called this a triple love story, one using a rare first-person narrator.

A.P. Kuzicheva in 1974 examined the moral judgments made in the story, especially how vulgarity affects those who rebel against conventional standards. Also that year Josephine M. Newcombe chose a middle course in the Chekhov-Tolstoy controversy: Chekhov was deeply influenced by Tolstoy, but as in this story, neither disseminated nor attacked his doctrines.[45]

Rayfield (1975) called this story Chekhov's richest work by far in the realm of ideas. It is the first of his stories with strong political implications. Neither condemned nor deified, the peasants are presented accurately: "only their love of righteousness raises them above the bourgeoisie." Poloznev, a "natural Christian," is one of the meek whom Chekhov would like to see inherit the earth, in Rayfield's opinion. Avram Derman, in Hulanicki (1976), notes that Chekhov begins this story *in medias res*, a technique he learned early while writing very brief stories. Hingley (1976) feels that Chekhov is attacking Tolstoy here. Poloznev is satirized for seeking the simple life, but his many friends are shown in comfortable surroundings, with no hint of sarcasm.

Hahn (1977) believes that Chekhov uses Blagovo to voice some of his own misgivings about peasants. Poloznev exceeds Blagovo in having greater courage, higher morals, and capacity for growth. Tulloch (1980) states that Poloznev's father, the architect, builds houses of oppression, with façades that look hard-hearted. Even with serfdom gone, Poloznev finds exploitation under the new capitalism, and he wonders how much progress there has been since the Tatar occupation. Kirk (1981) finds Poloznev's belief that he must obey "the moral law" weak compared to Blagovo's impassioned faith in humanity's future.

Bitsilli (1983) shows that Chekhov uses "animating metaphors." For example, the house built by Poloznev's father had "a vulgar roof, with flabby chimneys," implying qualities in the designer. Basu (1985) disagrees with Soviet critic M.A. Gribanov, who had said that both Masha and Poloznev were on the right path in solving their problems—only Poloznev seems to show the strength of his convictions. Tagore, in his story "The Renunciation," depicts a revolt against inhuman customs similar to Poloznev's revolt. Egri (1986) detects in "My Life" the proto-theme of *The Three Sisters:* Here is a corrupt village in which only young girls have moral purity; there is heavy stress upon the need for work; and the discussion of happiness between Poloznev and Blagovo anticipates the talk between Vershinin and Tusenbach.

"Patch" (1895) ("Whitebrow")

Hingley (1965) describes this story: A she-wolf carries Patch, a dog named for a white spot on its forehead, to her lair, mistaking it for a lamb. When someone whistles, she drops Patch, but Patch follows her to her lair. She suckles Patch along with her cubs. By the following winter both she and Patch are in poor health. Chekhov's brother Alexander said that Chekhov owned a dog with Patch's marking. Simmons (1962) comments that this "altogether charming tale," although written primarily for adults, is universally enjoyed by both adults and children.

"Peasants" (1897)

Nikolai, a waiter in a Moscow hotel, takes ill and returns to his home town with his wife Olga and his daughter Sasha. Nikolai finds his relatives living in filth, ignorance, and poverty. When a fire burns down a peasant's cottage, only a student organizes effective fire fighting. Nikolai dies, and Olga and Sasha leave on foot for Moscow, begging as they go.

Laffitte (1971) observes that while writing this story, Chekhov had daily contact with peasants. He was building a school at the neighboring village of Novoselki. He saw how they got drunk as a refuge from meaningless lives. This story was his farewell to his peasants. He wrote Suvorin that "from a literary point of view, Melikhovo has run dry for me and lost all its value, after 'The Peasants.'"

Simmons (1962) reports that no other tale of Chekhov's raised such a furor. Most reviews were favorable, as were many letters that Chekhov received from readers. The *Northern Herald* said we are reminded of that glorious time when a new novel by Turgenev or Dostoevsky appeared. Other positive reviewers in 1897 were Ilya Ignatov and Jeronim Yasinsky.

Struve (1971) said that the censors eliminated some material said to be too harsh on peasants. The Marxist Peter Struve praised the story, and Yuzhin-Sumbatov, the actor and playwright, said that like Shakespeare's work, this story seemed written by nature. Hingley (1976) points out that the Marxist journal *New Word* liked the story, since Marxists were attacking the backwardness of rural Russia. But the populist journal *Russian Wealth*, led by N.K. Mikhailovsky, felt that Chekhov had shown only the negative side of peasant life. Mikhailovsky chided Chekhov for not using his full talent as a writer. The characters were said to be vague and unreal, and village life was portrayed in somber colors.

E.A. Solovyev in 1897 said that this is not a story but just a picture, for it has no beginning or ending. Other negative reviewers included N. Ladozhsky and K.P. Medvedsky. When Chekhov applied for membership into the Writer's Union for Mutual Assistance in 1897, he narrowly missed being blackballed for what was called this "reactionary" story. The liberals thus had their own kind of censorship, almost as stringent as the czar's.

L.A. de Bogdanovich in 1897 said that this beautiful but gloomy story "portrayed so vividly, with such artistic truthfulness, the cheerless life of the Russian village, that it could not be better described in hundreds of novels, or in treatises crowded with figures."[46] Another reviewer that year, after deploring the depressing picture, agreed that this psychological study was thought-provoking, probably written to call attention to a serious problem needing a remedy. Chekhov showed great talent at describing people and scenes—in fact, "everything that he writes is carefully finished."[47]

Waliszewski (1900) agreed that the peasants' lives were depicted with great power, but he found no art in the story. Gogol and Turgenev created more accurate peasants, showing them with hearts and souls. Chekhov's peasants are heavy brutes, lacking moral purity. In 1902 Peter Struve called Chekhov the outstanding representative of post-populist literature. This story, however, was a pessimistic and oversimplified portrait of brutality.

A reviewer in 1909 said that Chekhov had great merit as a writer. This graphic picture of dismal peasant life seemed, however, to lack a prevailing theme.[48] Nowhere could one learn more about peasant life than in this story, said a reviewer in 1915, since Chekhov had "that highest gift of lending to the lives of individuals an apparently universal significance."[49] A critic in 1918 found a ray of hope in Olga, saying that "the gloomiest moment in the village is suddenly illuminated by a shaft of light, of profound religiosity."[50]

Edward Garnett (1921) said that Chekhov's portrayal of peasants was much more accurate than that of Turgenev and Tolstoy. Chekhov captures the peasants' intuitions, but Tolstoy betrays the upper-class mind at work. J. Middleton Murry in 1937 used this story to discuss political change. This "luminous and unforgettable picture" was Chekhov's protest against the sentimental description of peasants by the populists. Seeing their brutal life, Murry wondered how the Soviets could have raised them so fast, but he quickly added that there should be no revolution in England.[51] Toumanova (1937) quoted history professor Maxim Kovalesky, who recalled that liberal critics had opposed the story as a possible deterrent to reform.

Bruford (1948) said that the peasants' huts were so filthy that even bedbugs avoided them! The peasants' religion is purely external, said Nemirovsky (1950). They love the Bible and will not eat meat in Lent, but they abandon the aged, beat children and animals, and are often unfaithful in wedlock. Magarshack (*Life*, 1952) recalled the trouble Chekhov faced from both liberal and conservative critics. M.P. Gushchin in 1954 asserted that the story indicated Chekhov's strong opposition to reactionary policies.

George Ivask and Charles B. Timmer expressed their views in Eekman (1960). Ivask noticed that Olga always wept upon hearing the Church Slavonic word for "until," for to her it had an angelic ring. Here Chekhov was not being satirical but factual. Timmer feels that Sasha is used to show the suffering of innocent people because of poverty. Young Sasha perceives the hidden relationships of life, including its injustice. Timmer notices the bizarre touch when Nikolai dons his former waiter's coat at midnight, and is reminded of his former dignity and happiness—the irony is that normally the coat would be a badge of servitude and humiliation.

In 1961 John W. Harrison pointed out how symbolic action united a loosely connected series of incidents. Stripping, he says, is the unifying factor in the story. The town's nickname, "slavey town," strips it of dignity. The squire's men humiliate Fyokla by stripping her nude. The father strips himself of needed winter fodder by selling his hay. Drunken men strip themselves of money and self-respect. To a great extent, the peasants are their own oppressors.[52] Despite their bestial existence, says Simmons (1962), Chekhov brings out the humanity of those whose gentle natures cause them to suffer more than the rest. Their chief vision of a better world comes through church services.

Hingley (1965) says this was Chekhov's most famous story in Russia during his lifetime. A great work of art, it is scarcely more than a series of sketches. People were curious to read about peasant life. Just because they had been exploited, Chekhov was not going to manufacture excellence for them, as if in expiation. The story has humor, but no satire or sarcasm. Tolstoy called it "a sin against the common people," but most readers accepted its accuracy. S.I. Bychkov, a waiter at the Great Moscow Hotel, where Chekhov sometimes stayed, was the prototype for Nikolai.

Winner (1966) points out that the lyrical description of nature contrasts with the lack of beauty in the peasants' lives. Their religious faith may give them hope for living, but it may also interfere with their efforts to improve themselves. As they leave the church, they go to the tavern. They look forward to death. Chekhov uses naturalism, as "each individual is characterized by a metonymic detail."

Tolstoy and Chekhov were contrasted by Speirs (1971). Tolstoy depicts peasants as unique people, partly because of their closeness to God. Chekhov, whose father had been a serf, sees peasants as like other people. Tolstoy trusts folk wisdom, but Chekhov does not.

There are two themes in this story, said Rayfield (1975): the village is a potential paradise (were it not for the tavern), and the village is constantly raided by outsiders, such as the police and tax collectors. Permanently in debt, the village keeps taking things away from the residents. The authorities contribute nothing. The Bible moves peasants to tears, but the church only tells them when to feast and when to fast. To the peasants, the New Testament exalts carpenters and fishermen, and condemns church officials, the governor, and the king. Peasants dream of the coming of the kingdom of heaven. Some resent emancipation—as a matter of record, peasants ate less and died younger in the 1890s than in the 1850s. This story brought Chekhov more praise than all of his other works put together, and it doubled his income in 1897.

Hulanicki (1976) presents the views of Avram Derman and E.S. Dobin. Derman tells why Nikolai's coat episode is so effective: It is simple, it seems innocuous, it leaves much to inference, and it is very original. The actor and playwright Juzhin said that when Nikolai put away his tailcoat, he was discarding his chance for a better life: "I could not read any further, I was so overwhelmed," said Juzhin. Dobin said that Chekhov made the reader feel the bureaucratic coldness of the officials. Hingley (1976) calls this Chekhov's most controversial story, a picture with sociological precision that broke with the tradition of idealizing the peasants.

Hahn (1977) regretted the absence of a story line, and found the tale a mere "*tour de force* rendering of what it means to live that squalid life." It counters Tolstoy's romantic picture of peasant life with specific details, but is still "little more than a postscript to the once powerful engagement of Chekhov's art with Tolstoy's." Apparently Chekhov had already lost touch with the lower class, for "though informed by a special spirit of humane understanding, it projects only a flat image."

Savely Senderovich, in Debreczeny (1977), finds an impressionism similar to Seurat's pointillism. Seen up close, the effect is not good, but at the proper esthetic distance, one perceives the beauty of the work. Charles B. Timmer, in Bristow (1977), judges that Nikolai's trying on the coat at night is his final bizarre effort to recapture happiness and dignity.

A group of peasants in 1978 agreed that people should live better than those reported in the story, but also said that the story should have shown the positive side as well as the negative side of peasant life.[53]

L.M. O'Toole says the setting in this story serves as "a moral touchstone by which to evaluate human actions and a tenuous bridge from an unbearable reality to a potentially better life." Chekhov shows the effect of urbanization upon Russian provincial life. Most of the story takes place at night, the time of fear and despair. Following the peasants' practice, Chekhov focuses more on Orthodox holidays (especially those relating to the Virgin Mary) than on general Christian holidays.[54]

Wilks (1982) states that the peasants use every church holiday as an excuse for a drunken spree. Living on the brink of superstition, the peasants are easy prey for the predatory. Chekhov shows that alcoholism, epidemics, and venereal disease were worse in the 1890s than in the 1850s. He does, however, find some vindication for their behavior. Wilks points out that Bunin and Grigorovich described peasant life in even gloomier scenes. Bitsilli (1983) states that although the social milieu is in the foreground of the story, in the background is chaos.

Clyman (1985) encompasses the views of Kenneth A. Lantz and Ralph Lindheim. Lantz shows Olga's reaction to her dishonest and drunken relatives: "Yes, they were frightful people to live with. Still, they were human beings, and there was nothing in their lives for which an excuse could not be found." Lindheim recounts how the idyllic calm of the Russian countryside is shattered by noise pollution: shouts, cries, curses, orders, pleas, yelps, growls, and drunken roars.

"The Pecheneg" (1897) ("The Savage")

A lawyer spends the night at the home of Ivan Zhmukhin, a retired Cossack officer nicknamed "Pecheneg" after the wild tribe in the Caucasus. Animals live in with the people, and the teenagers take target practice by shooting hens. Ivan refuses to send his sons to school, as their mother requests. Ivan tells his wife that she should quit thinking so much.

Hingley (1965) says that the farm is so coarse that it is called "The Savage Farm" by neighbors. There is some compassion for Ivan as he nears the end of his life, but clearly his wife has superior values. The wide open spaces would have fostered a rich culture among the Cossacks, Chekhov believed, had it not been for the ignorance of the ruling officer class.

"Rothschild's Fiddle" (1894)

Winner (1966) summarizes the plot: Jacob the coffin-maker sees everything in terms of business. He grumbles when people die out of town. While his wife is dying, he takes her measurements, makes her coffin in the same room, and enters it into his profit-and-loss statement. Returning from her funeral, he has nostalgia for their dead child. When Jacob himself must die, he improvises a melody so beautiful that whenever his friend Rothschild plays it on the violin, Rothschild and the audience weep. As he dies, Jacob does his one good act—he gives his fiddle to Rothschild, even though he hates Jews. The fiddle thus becomes an instrument of reconciliation.

Francis Hackett in 1920 commented on Chekhov's tenderness. "Yet tenderness does not induce Chekhov to give the stupid undertaker fine perceptions. The story is marvelously faithful to the dumbness and numbness of the old peasant."[55] Simmons (1962) calls the story "a perfect little study in the harmony of mood and tone." Here Chekhov combines the grotesque with the farcical. Winner (1966) notes that Jacob hates deficits. His view leads to the final absurdity: the most economical state is death. To achieve an impression of ugliness, Chekhov employs alliteration and assonance in a pejorative onomatopoeia. He also uses sibilants and other harsh sounds to reinforce Jacob's dislike of Rothschild.

Avram Derman, in Urbanski (1973), comments that as Jacob, on his deathbed, reflects about life's meaning, the effect is to get the reader to do likewise. Hulanicki (1976) presents the views of E.S. Dobin and Victor Shklovsky. Dobin is grateful that Jacob finally asks, "Can't a person live without always thinking of losses? Why do people always quarrel? Think of the losses that come from hatred and malice!" Shklovsky denotes catharsis in Jacob's donation of the violin. Also, disgust at his worthless life led Jacob to write such a beautiful song that it always moved listeners to tears.

Hingley (1978) marks irony: Jacob curses his wife for dying after he has sold the coffin he has made for her. Hingley resents Chekhov's preaching here, feeling that he was always more effective at purveying a doctrine of love by showing its lack. Robert Louis Jackson in 1978 made a connection between Jews and Russians as suffering people. The theme becomes a universal one as references to music and to Psalm 137 create a "poetry of suffering."[56] Charles E. May, in Clyman (1985), says this is close to being a parable. Bernard Malamud writes stories about Jews that are similar to this story, May observes.

"The Student" (1894) ("At Evening")

Ivan, a religious student, feels cold, hungry, and pessimistic on Good Friday. He pauses to chat with two widows, a mother and her daughter. Ivan tells them the story of Peter's denial of Christ. His tale is so moving that it brings the women to tears. Now, although the landscape is as desolate as ever, Ivan revives his humanitarian hope. Since that garden weeping of Peter can still be real after 1900 years, Ivan sees how the past runs into the present, and how life does contain, after all, beauty, truth, and deep meaning.

D.S. Merezhkovsky said that this story proved that Chekhov did not conceive of Christianity as an enemy of progress. But F.D. Batyushkov quoted a letter by Chekhov in which he said that the mysticism of Dostoevsky's God was insufficient for building "the truth of the real God."

Long (1902), quoting Ivan's early pessimism and ignoring the story's conclusion, called Chekhov "a philosopher of despair." A reviewer that year concurred, stating that if human beings were as Chekhov paints them, they would be better off as apes.[57] Trivialities seemed immense to an observant physician who was also a sick patient, said Esenwein (1912). Thus, although this story seems to show little hope for the future, one must commend Chekhov for his honesty, and seek beneath the surface for the veiled protest against an unjust order that must be changed.

V.D. Goldiner in 1940 viewed "The Student" as Chekhov's first expression of his mature outlook, that human beings are entitled to a happy life. Z.M. Paperny in 1954 interpreted the story as a landmark in Chekhov's newly acquired faith in "the people." Gunnar Jacobsson in 1960 saw the student as Chekhov's mouthpiece: one can move from pessimism to optimism by seeing that the permanence of truth and beauty give life significance and meaning.[58]

George Ivask, in Eekman (1960), praises Chekhov's bravery in de-romanticizing nature in this story, while evoking sincere appreciation of the biblical tale. Ivask likes the effect Chekhov gets by describing the Garden of Gethsemane as "quiet, quiet, dark, dark." Simmons (1962) says Chekhov here "achieved to perfection that exquisite harmony of form and content, of mood and substance which Tolstoy had in mind when he described Chekhov as the Russian Pushkin in prose." V.N. Ilin in 1964 said that many of Chekhov's characters are lost persons who find salvation. Ilin feels that his works argue in favor of the existence of God.[59]

Kramer (1970) says that Ivan believes he has found the relationship between the past and the present, what T.S. Eliot calls "the still point in human history." But the vision is not all positive: Ivan also recalls the cruelty and suffering present throughout human history. L.M. O'Toole in 1971 used this story to demonstrate how a structural analysis can illuminate a story's parts and purposes. Here the chief theme is catharsis, or "the power of tragedy to move and inspire."[60]

A.A. Belkin in 1973 found the meaning of the story in the fact that values such as compassion are eternal, especially as transmitted by art. The optimistic triumph of goodness, Belkin states, is Ivan's and not necessarily Chekhov's. Urbanski (1973) observes how the reader is moved to reflect on life's meaning. John Glad pointed out in 1974 that Soviet writer Valentin Tublin's story "Until the Ship Arrives" is an adaptation of "The Student." Although poles apart ideologically, the stories are impressionistic and structurally similar. Modern Soviet writers, says Glad, are conservative, looking to the past for literary models.[61]

Rayfield (1975) calls the story a parable about how art can overcome despair. All the details of the setting are mirrored in the story of Peter's betrayal. Suddenly the reader realizes that now is a part of eternity. Verbal rhythms parallel the student's epiphany – at first the style is harsh and laconic, but later it becomes rich and gentle. Avram Derman, in Hulanicki (1976), strangely states that this is the most "materialistically grounded" of all of Chekhov's stories, and that its theme is not religion but youth.

Hingley (1978) calls this a fictional sermon, as if by a fervent Christian, which Chekhov was not. "Still, to reject the dogma of the various Christian denominations is not necessarily to be wholly unsympathetic to the spirit of Christianity. No believer, Chekhov nevertheless respected religious faith in others, provided they were not given to excessive proselytizing." He also thought that women believers got into less mischief because of their beliefs than men did. Chekhov said that it was his best story, and used it as an example of his optimism. It does an effective job of portraying the essential unity of all peoples in all ages, but it is nowhere near as artistic as many other Chekhov stories, in Hingley's opinion.

David Martin in 1978 observed that Chekhov used Luke's story of Peter's denial, but actually the gospels read at the Good Friday service would have been from Matthew and John. Martin concluded that apparently Chekhov preferred Luke's version for the story's emotional atmosphere.[62] Jefferson Hunter in 1980 contrasted Chekhov's treatment of Peter's denial with Rembrandt's painting of the theme and with Bach's *St. John Passion.* Unlike Rembrandt and Bach, says Hunter, Chekhov sees the biblical story as showing the possibility of self-knowledge, and of the ability to be moved.[63]

Stowell (1980) says that the women's tears recall Christ's tears to Ivan, and so the link is made from past to present. Charles E. May, in Clyman (1985), denotes this as one of Chekhov's mystical tales. Chekhov believed that the eternal can be realized only esthetically. Here the esthetic mingles with the religious to form an unbroken chain through time.

"The Teacher of Literature" (1894) ("Mediocrities")
("The Russian Master")

Bashful Nikitin finally proposes to happy Masha. As a literature teacher, Nikitin feels guilty over never having read Lessing's *Hamburg Dramaturgy*, but he is happy in marriage. After the death of a colleague, Nikitin feels guilty, as if he has been insincere. He now quarrels with Masha, says he is bored with everyday people, and resolves to go to Moscow to save his sanity.

G. Kacherec in 1902 felt frustrated at the abrupt ending. Long (1902) calls Nikitin "another spiritless weakling," driven to the verge of insanity by his feeling of inadequacy as a teacher. Shestov (1905) states that Nikitin is following Chekhov's own advice (from the play *Ivanov*), but still Nikitin is bored to death. Shestov believed that Chekhov enjoyed it when his protagonist broke down in despair.

Gerhardi (1923) says that Nikitin's early happiness is so excessive that it cloys him. Gerhardi notes how Chekhov captures human isolation—one's personal emotional epiphany is ignored by others. For example, when Nikitin shares the joy of his coming marriage to Masha with an old colleague, all the colleague can say is that Masha was weak in history but had not done badly in geography.

Perry (1926) reported that Chekhov did not reveal a cause-and-effect world. "He labors to conceal the real significance" of his story, and substitutes "a realistic scene presenting the irritation and trifling annoyance that accompanies rather than induces Nikitin's awakening." Mirsky (1927) says that a Chekhov story has a buried plot, which deviates from the straight-line plot at the surface. Here the straight line is the teacher's love, but the curved-line buried plot is Nikitin's dissatisfaction with his unfulfilled ambitions. Hingley (1950) agreed with Mirsky's analysis, adding that unfortunately as a Chekhovian character gets more sensitive, he also generally grows less happy.

Nikitin's revolt is against complacency and conformity, said Ermilov (1956). Winner (1966) sees the story as a conflict between beauty and banality, a struggle raging within Nikitin. Animals dominate Masha's life. She constantly talks of horses, and her sister Varvara is identified with a growling dog. Nikitin addresses Masha in a letter: "My dear little rat." Eventually Nikitin feels cheated in his marriage. Kramer (1970) explains Nikitin's inconsistent behavior as due to his moodiness. When Nikitin says that "man is the creator of his own happiness," he is ironically right for the wrong reason: "He believes his happiness is something real which he has created, but it exists only in his imagination."

Domestic details led Nikitin to consider sex as a trap, says Rayfield (1975). E.S. Dobin, in Hulanicki (1976), observes how Chekhov can characterize with one telling phrase: Shelestov keeps remarking, "It's caddishness." Small tiffs increasingly interrupt an idyllic marriage. Soon Nikitin is fearful of asking for a glass of milk, lest it upset Masha's "orderly" milk bottles. Now Nikitin feels irritated at the cat, because it reminds him of knuckling under to Masha on the milk issue.

Hingley (1976) states that when Chekhov read the original story, then called

"Mediocrities" or "Philistines," to his family, they insisted that he keep a happy ending, and Chekhov then called it a "sloppy" story. Five years later he inserted the unhappy ending, changed its title, and then considered it to be one of his best stories. Hingley (1978) observes that Chekhov develops his anti-romanticism with the greatest subtlety. It is with gentle nudges, rather than with sledgehammer blows, that domestic bliss is undermined. Nikitin is destroyed by the methodical complacency of the always-eating Masha, "a potential monster." Wilks (1982) notes that Chekhov called this story "a light-hearted piece of nonsense from the lives of provincial guinea pigs." Chekhov's satire, says Wilks, is conveyed with a light touch. Nature itself changes, paralleling the growing disgust of Nikitin for his commonplace life.

"Three Years" (1895)

Laptev, a wealthy Moscow merchant, marries Julia, who accepts him to please her father, a doctor. When Laptev's sister Nina dies, they rear her two daughters, replacing their own child who died in infancy. Laptev resents his father, a tyrant both at home and at his dry goods firm. Yartsev, a shrewd but idealistic scientist, lives with Laptev's former girlfriend Polina, who resents being jilted by Laptev for pretty but vacuous Julia. The dry goods business thrives, and Julia begins to love Laptev, who now grown stoical, has hope for a happy future.

Of this story Chekhov said, "My intention was one thing, but what has come of it is something different." He would like to write about devils or terrible women, he continued, but the public demands happy stories of Ivans and their wives.[64] When the censors eliminated a number of passages dealing with religion, Chekhov told Suvorin that "it takes away any desire you have to express yourself freely—you feel there's a bone stuck in your throat."[65] Chekhov compared his story to the novel *The Pass* by P.B. Boborykin, but unlike "Three Years," the novel shows merchants in a favorable light.

V.P. Burenin in 1895 brought out the old charge that Chekhov had no philosophic depth, as seen in this story. A critic for the Moscow *Russian Review* that year blamed Chekhov for the indeterminate ending—life, he said, has beginnings and endings to its episodes. Leonid Grossman in 1914 found a similarity between this story and Maupassant's "Une Vie": both were comprehensive accounts of a woman's life.

Gerhardi (1923) called this an objective treatment of subjectivity. When Laptev loves Julia, she is cold. When she loves him, he does not respond. N.F. Byelchikov, in *Chekhov and His Milieu* (1930), suggested that Chekhov himself had the inferiority complex found in Laptev—a product of his oppressed childhood. A.G. Gornfeld in 1939 called the indeterminate ending a conscious and effective artistic device. It was appropriate for characters whose life showed no structured form, he said. Moreover, the indeterminate ending connected oneself back to life in an infinity, "that triumphant life-affirming infinity which is immutably revealed to us in any genuine work of art."[66]

Bruford (1948) calls this story a small-scale *Forsyte Saga*, epic in scope. Seeing his father's mismanagement, Laptev fears taking over the firm, lest he too become a slave to power. Magarshack (*Life*, 1952) sees this as Chekhov's last attempt to write a novel. Yartsev, predicting a coming change for the better, is Chekhov's mouthpiece, says Ermilov (1956). Eekman (1960) finds Chekhov's love for Russia in this story, even though Chekhov probably agreed with Yartsev in opposing Laptev's Slavophile beliefs. When Laptev says that Europe must be saved by Russian idealism, Yartsev replies, "From what must Europe be saved?"

Simmons (1962) designates the story "a profound psychological study of character," as well as a picture of the deterioration of a merchant family. Although many of Chekhov's contemporaries disliked the story, "in the richness of its detail, its leisurely pace, and the psychological analysis of its characters," it is the closest thing to a novel that Chekhov ever wrote, says Simmons. Reeve (1966) notes how Chekhov identifies Julia with her parasol. The tension of Chekhov's language is the tension of life. "For us, as for Laptev," Reeve states, "the ironies of love can be encompassed only by the formal irony of comic tragedy."

Winner (1966) finds the story satirizing various theories of love and marriage. The secondary characters have positive outlooks and active lives, in contrast with the Laptev family. Chekhov depicts well how Laptev's brother Fyodor's "purely businesslike attitude" towards people eventually drives Fyodor insane. Laptev and Julia are trying to escape their pasts, in marrying each other, says Kramer (1970). One sign of their change is that both discard their religious faith.

Chudakov (1971) notices that the characters' extensive biographies and interior monologues are given in the narrator's words. Laffitte (1971) points out that the character Polina is modeled on Chekhov's girlfriend, Olga Kundasova, who had accompanied him as he sailed up the Volga at the beginning of his Sakhalin trip. He enjoyed her company, but lampooned her poor taste in dress.

Speirs (1971) contrasts Chekhov's treatment of "small people" with Tolstoy's. Chekhov understands them but Tolstoy does not. Tolstoy wants to direct the education of the peasants, but Chekhov wants them to be free to bring out their own individuality. Laptev is a coward who brings out the reader's innate cowardice; Tolstoy depicts courageous people, in an effort to develop courage in his readers. "Train journeys, in Chekhov as in Tolstoy, give the illusion of freedom, although all routes are circular." Like Levin in *Anna Karenina*, Laptev hates to meet his brother, for he sees his own weaknesses reflected in Fyodor. Laptev's deep fear that he will be "merely an average man" dissolves when he finally realizes that there is no such person.

Shotton, in Fennell (1973), states that, like Chekhov, Laptev is spiritually stunted as the result of a fanatical religious rearing. Here Chekhov abridges a novel by using time-lapses and selecting a few moments to reveal a whole life, says Rayfield (1975), but the compression weakens the structure. Chekhov intended

Laptev to be a typical Muscovite, torn between Asiatic falsehood and European honesty. Its weaknesses are the story's rambling plot and the hasty denouement. Its strengths are its lyricism and its carefully delineated minor characters. In a mystical vision Chekhov presents a prophecy of Russia's future, Rayfield felt.

G.N. Pospelov, in Hulanicki (1976), finds the meaning of the story in Laptev's moral development. The oppressed son of an oppressed mother, he finally comes to understand the reason for his fears. Hahn (1977) says that here Chekhov shows us how time changes people. By being a freer man than his brother Fyodor, Laptev can escape the harm caused by the family's mores and morals. Nature, unlike man, seems unchanged by time. Chance seems to be the shaping factor in life. Chekhov himself seems impatient with Laptev's blindness to his opportunities. As Logan Speirs says, Chekhov's uncertain voice makes him very modern. Nicholas Moravcevich, in Bristow (1977), finds in the story a vivid description of Isaac Levitan's impressionistic painting "Quiet Cloister." Levitan's art, says Moravcevich, influenced Chekhov's impressionistic style.

Hingley (1978) observes that Chekhov gives a detailed and, for him, rare description of Moscow life. Laptev's haberdashery is copied from Gavrilov's, where Chekhov's father worked. The plot is a reversal of Pushkin's *Eugene Onegin:* Love's perversity is seen in that when Laptev loves Julia, she spurns him – and vice versa. Chekhov denied that Laptev's father was based on his own father: "Father is still what he has been all his life: a small-calibered person of limited range."

In depicting Laptev's growing love for Julia, says Bitsilli (1983), Chekhov uses the phrase "it seemed" effectively. Seeing a landscape painting, Julia imagines a trip down the path into a supernatural world. In a dream, Yartsev envisions a cruel world, a contrast to the peaceful one in which he lives. Grown cold towards Julia, Laptev develops great affection for his dead sister's children; often in Chekhov love for an orphan becomes an emotional outlet for guilt or sorrow. Andrew R. Durkin, in Clyman (1985), remarks that "an ordinary umbrella becomes a symbol of love first for Laptev and then for Julia, but neither can tell the other what the umbrella means, nor could the other share that meaning fully."

"A Woman's Kingdom" (1894)

Anna, 26, has inherited her father's large factory. As sole owner, she feels guilty, collecting all the profit while the workers have bad working conditions. She would like to return to a simple life, marry a worker, and have children. She meets a handsome worker, Pimenov. She advises her servant Mishenka to marry her maid Masha, but he refuses. At an evening card game, one table is for the rich ladies and another for the servants. A pilgrim woman advises Anna to marry. She confesses that she wants to marry Pimenov. Everyone laughs at her for even considering a marriage below her class. She tells Masha she will not marry, saying, "Oh, what fools we are!"

Paul Milyukov in 1894 said that Anna's father, a conceited fool, can be found in Ostrovsky's comedies, and that Anna, through acquiring an education, "has lost the energy of her will and become a moral nonentity: another variation on the Nietzschian theme of the utility of egoism and the injurious effects of civilization."[67] Long (1902) says that in this story "the familiarity of an imprudent servant is enough to wreck a nascent romance": Mishenka warns Anna that Pimenov would not even know how to hold his fork properly, when dining with a neighboring general.

Edward Garnett (1921) calls this an incomparable story for showing the complex web of labor/capital relationships. Good-hearted Anna is "paralyzed by her false position between her aristocratic friends who sponge on her and the exploited work-people who strive to cheat her." Chekhov depicts human nature caught up in an industrial juggernaut, but he paints his picture with delicacy and tenderness. Chekhov's scenes, Garnett concludes, always pulse with the ocean of humanity.

James T. Farrell in 1937 used this story to debunk the critical tenet that a short story should create a single or a unified impression. "This is a story of class relationships in czarist Russia, a cross-section of many phases of that life. One gets from it impressions of class relationships, of characters, of moods." Chekhov's stories refute dogmatic literary standards, for they are "like doors of understanding and awareness opening outward into an entire world."[68] Magarshack (*Life*, 1952) indicated that this story was based upon Chekhov's experience as a factory medical inspector.

Simmons (1962) found the story's excellence in its good characterization and in its realistic scenes in the factories, the workers' hovels, and Anna's kitchen on Christmas Eve. Winner (1966) notes that Anna receives the common people on the first floor of her house (where it smells of icons) and the wealthy on the second floor (which is clean and well furnished). Her democratic tendencies are shown in her preference for the downstairs people. This is an important story, says Jackson (1967), in which fate overcomes Anna only because she permits it. Chekhov is here saying, "Be brave—make your own fate!"

Kramer (1970) observes the ironic contrast in this Christmas story between Christ, the Lord of humanity, and Anna, a laborer's daughter who has become the mistress of 2000 workers. Struve (1971) notes that this "impressionistic story of isolation and lack of understanding" covers only one day in Anna's life. The story had enough material for a novel, Rayfield (1975) feels, and thus the tale suffers from compression. Life in this factory town is hellish, Rayfield says, and Anna's charity leads simply to scandal. Although Anna has nervous energy and primitive goodness, she lacks the courage to make bold decisions.

Hahn (1977) shows that D.H. Lawrence used a similar plot of an upper-class woman attracted to a working-class man in *The Lost Girl*, but he could not maintain Chekhov's objectivity. Lawrence's Alvina is overcome by primal passion, so there is really no conflict. Chekhov, however, shows both inner and external reasons why Anna cannot submit to Pimenov. Someone of Anna's temperament has not only a primal urge but also background, cultural tradition, education, and inhibition as a part of her makeup. Like Chekhov's plays, this story has four parts: night, morning, evening, night, and thus the story moves from loneliness to hope to loneliness. As a study of isolation and of class dynamics, this story resembles *The Three Sisters* in many ways.

Hingley (1978) reminds us that Anna is as much a victim of the factory system as are her workers. She really should have either taken over effective management of the factory, or sold it. But then, says Hingley, if all humans made sensible decisions Chekhov would have had little material for his stories. E.M. Sakharova in 1982 pointed out that Alexander Blok's essay "Anarchy" conveys the same sense of Russian life as this story does.[69]

Anna speaks "as if to herself" in Mishenka's presence, says Bitsilli (1983), because she despises his vulgarity. The reason she dislikes her own wealth is that it deprives her of simplicity. Clyman (1985) shows views by Andrew R. Durkin and Donald Rayfield on this story. Durkin denotes an ironic disparity between the protagonist and the reader—the reader's perception exceeds that of Anna through most of the story. Rayfield detects Zola's influence here, in the documentation, the naturalism, and the set of attitudes permeating the work.

Summary—Stories: 1893–1897

Now an established author, and with some income from his plays, Chekhov during this period wrote fewer stories than previously, but now the stories are longer and better. There is little humor and not much satire in these stories. Now completely free from Tolstoy's domination, Chekhov is very objective in his approach, but now he begins to take a very firm stand on social issues.

The story which attracted the most attention during this period was "Peasants." Detractors chided it for not showing the positive side of peasant life; those who liked the story praised its honesty, objectivity, realism, and vividness. Probably the best stories that Chekhov wrote during these years were "The Black Monk," "My Life," and "The Student." "The Black Monk" was admired for its mysticism, symbolism, and study in abnormal psychology. "My Life" dealt effectively with problems of love, marriage, the peasants, and social reform. "The Student" was a penetrating portrait of sincere religion.

Several other lengthy stories drew much critical attention. "An Anonymous Story" struck most critics as proof that Chekhov's forte was not political intrigue. "The House with the Mezzanine" was generally favorably received for its effective handling of the themes of love, social reform, and anti–Tolstoyism. "Three Years" also was liked for its depiction of love, marriage, and the factory system.

Chekhov could not stand bullying. In two stories women are bullies ("Ariadne" and "The Helpmate"), and in two others women are bullied ("A Daughter of Albion" and "In the Cart").

"The Head Gardener's Story" was an unsuccessful fantasy. "The Murder" studied the problems of religious fanaticism. Just as "Rothschild's Fiddle" satirized egoism, miserliness, and anti–Semitism, so did "The Teacher of Literature" satirize banality. Finally, "A Woman's Kingdom" was praised by most critics for its excellent presentation of love, shyness, social stratification, and the problems of the factory system.

8. Stories: 1898–1904

"About Love" (1898)

Alekhin carries on a platonic love relationship with Anna, wife of a court official. He is warmly welcomed in her home, where her children call him "Uncle." When she moves away, Alekhin finally breaks down and kisses her at the railroad station. They now both feel remorse as well as ecstasy.

Alexander Izmailov in 1898 stated that Chekhov was no longer objective, for in this story the subjective author is everywhere visible in the narrator. Izmailov felt that Chekhov was undergoing the same spiritual crisis that all great Russian writers encounter: art moves to the background, and religion and ethics to the foreground.

A reviewer in 1918 professed to find the secret of the success of the Russian revolution in this story. A character alleges that educated Russians intellectualize everything, including love. The Russian passion for the truth, the reviewer feels, allows them to be, despite ignorance, cruelty, and worship of wooden theories, "one of the noblest and most intelligent of peoples."[1]

Avilov (1950) recalls how Chekhov directed her attention to this story, a parallel, she felt, with their real-life love affair. Chekhov's theory of love is that it is a mystery about which one cannot generalize, avers Hingley (1950). Magarshack (*Life*, 1952) says there are many indications that this story did refer to the love affair between Chekhov and Lydia Avilov, and that by giving artistic form to his secret feelings, he finally cured himself of his love for her. Simmons (1962) disagrees that the story referred to the Chekhov-Avilov relationship, finding more differences than similarities between the life situation and the story.

Valency (1966) calls this "a beautiful story that takes account of the social uncertainties that inhibit the elemental requirements of the heart." Chekhov gets us to understand Alekhin chiefly by the things he does not do or say, because "the things that most interested him as a writer were often too intangible for direct communication. In consequence, he developed a tangential method of approach." The reason Alekhin refuses to consummate the love match, says Winner (1966), is that he realizes his own limitations—he would simply be taking Anna from one dull life to another.

Kramer (1970) feels that Alekhin is "a man in a case," like another Chekhov protagonist, since he cannot take action. In the story Alekhin is likened to a squirrel in a cage. Hingley (1975) agrees that the shackles on Alekhin's love are self-imposed. Hingley quotes an entry from Chekhov's notebook about this story: When you love, you discover such a treasure of tenderness inside you that you cannot really believe yourself capable of so much love. The positive ending is stressed by Rayfield (1975): The sun drives away the rain, and Alekhin's confession of his illicit love thoughts gives the reader the sensation of great energy about to be released. David E. Maxwell, in Debreczeny (1977), notes that Chekhov employs the subjunctive mood to indicate lost opportunities. He also uses nature as a contrasting element—as Alekhin's perspective narrows, the frame of the story gradually widens.

Three critics study this story as one in a trilogy that also includes "Gooseberries" and "The Man in a Case." Maxwell observes that all three stories have the same characters, narrators, structures, and themes. Each story is made unique by having its own relationship among the component parts. Rich Wear in 1977 found the common theme in the "possession" of a person by some idea or emotion that keeps him from understanding other people. Ivan is not Chekhov's spokesman, Wear states, for he is pretentious, hypocritical, and overly moralistic.[2] L. Lieber in 1982 said that Chekhov, like Gogol, used geographical space as a humanizing factor. Lieber finds the characters in all three stories living in a narrowly circumscribed and oppressive space.[3]

"At Christmas Time" (1899)

A married couple, illiterate, hire ex-soldier Yegor to write a letter to their daughter, whom they have not seen for four years. As a prank, Yegor does not follow their dictation but writes a lot of nonsense about army life. The daughter is disappointed, for she had hoped to hear about her parents. Her husband, a tyrant, has been neglecting to mail her letters to her parents.

Here, says Charles B. Timmer in Eekman (1960), Chekhov uses the bizarre not as an ornament but "here it is the canvas on which the story is embroidered." Hingley (1975) calls the tale an important addition to Chekhov's panorama of Russian rustic life, as he contrasts life in St. Petersburg with life in the provinces. Hingley (1976) mentions the pathos of weak poor people mistreated by callous associates.

"The Betrothed" (1903) ("The Bride")

Nadya, 23, is about to marry Andrey, the town idler. But her friend Sasha convinces her not to, saying she would be wasting her life, since "only enlightened and holy people are interesting – the more of such people there are, the sooner the kingdom of Heaven will come on earth." Nadya takes Sasha's advice, and goes to the university instead. When she returns home a year later, everything seems altered. She now realizes that the great change is coming soon. Even Sasha's death cannot dim her spirits, as she leaves for the university, full of optimism.

Chekhov's friend, Dr. S.Y. Elpatievsky, in 1903 said that "here a new, no longer somber note was to be heard in Chekhov's work. A big change had taken place in his mood, in his artistic perception of life."[4] Less sanguine, Valery Bryusov in 1904 said that the story contained many powerful scenes but had the customary sad Chekhovian characters.[5]

Hingley (1950) reported that once Nadya perceived her life as vulgar, she was bound to change it. Magarshack (*Life*, 1952) observes that in this, Chekhov's last story, Nadya is sorry to see Sasha, like Chekhov himself, dying of tuberculosis. Ermilov (1956) recalls how V.V. Veresayev quarreled with Chekhov over Nadya's character, saying, "That was not how girls go into the revolution." "There is more than one way," Chekhov replied. In 1957 Y.O. Zundelovich showed that the constant use of the phrase "for some reason" created an atmosphere of vagueness and provided a departure from the rigidly analytical psychologizing.[6] E.N. Konshina in 1960 showed the changes Chekhov made in the various stages of creating the story. V.D. Goldiner and V.E. Khalizev in 1961 demonstrated that "in successive drafts Chekhov shifted the story's conflict from external to internal, intensified its emotional currents, and relied more on expressive details to convey his meaning."[7]

We are moved by Chekhov's truthfulness, said Ehrenburg (1962), in leaving the ending ambiguous – we know Nadya's life will change, but we are not given all of the details. The first version had Sasha voicing revolutionary sentiments, said Simmons (1962), but Chekhov deleted them, perhaps because of the censor. Here again we see Chekhov's faith in gradualism: Society is slowly improving itself. Payne (1963) states that Chekhov's final style shows no decline in strength, but it is a bare style, language stripped free of ornaments. Although Chekhov loathed the thought of a Russian revolution, in a way this arch-conservative was the most subversive writer, for "his stories are hosannas in praise of freedom, of the wanderings of the human heart in search of its own peace. And so, with the insidious power of genius, he prepares us for the revolution of the future."

In 1963 Thomas G. Winner found the three main parts of the story progressively charting Nadya's realization of the inadequacies of her environment. The story's theme is achieved through the interplay of elements of beauty and vulgarity.[8] Winner (1966) further analyzed the structural principle of the story: Musical counterpoint plays off the motifs of beauty and vulgarity against each other with increasing intensity. A typical Chekhov device is to hold many plot elements static in order to set off Nadya's character change.

In examining the three different manuscripts of this story, Kramer (1970) found that the later versions indicate that perhaps Nadya will keep going through a series of changes, never really finding herself. Chekhov may have been deliberately ambiguous, showing that life is ambiguous too. Laffitte (1971) feels that the lyrical passages are more frequent in his later works. Here, for example, he speaks of "a mysterious, beautiful, rich and holy life, beyond weak sinful man's understanding, burgeoning under the vault of the sky."

In this story, says Toby W. Clyman in 1974, Chekhov finally depicts a woman strong enough to escape victimization. This happens only after Chekhov admits that it is possible for one person to communicate meaningfully with another.[9] David Maxwell that year made a structural approach to the role of setting in the story. Time plays a crucial role – characters must either move forward with it or surrender to stagnation. By keeping the setting static, Chekhov provides a background against which Nadya's progress can be measured.[10]

Hingley (1975) says that to call Nadya a Marxist, as some Soviet critics have done, is "to descend into bathos." True, some of Chekhov's contemporaries saw Nadya as a revolutionary. Tolstoyist I.I. Gorbunov-Posadov told Chekhov: "How charming your 'Bride' is! What a pity that she fell for the Marxist line!" Chekhov's use of phrases like "somehow" or "for some reason" indicates a slackness to Hingley. This story, along with "The Bishop," helped give Chekhov the reputation as a self-pitying pessimist. Sasha's contemplation of his imminent death gives pathos "but not necessarily literary distinction to the material." Sasha is Chekhov's mouthpiece. Chekhov endows such mouthpieces with "absurd or pathetic characteristics skillfully designed to muffle the didactic impact of their pronouncements." Here it is the traces of sputum left by the dying Sasha. "No other story of Chekhov's provides such a rich array" of variant texts, says Hingley. He worked on revising this story for over a year.

Rayfield (1975) states that Trofimov in *The Cherry Orchard* is a reworking of Sasha, who denounces the filth and lack of ambition in the small town. Saturated with a feeling of death, this story has a more vigorous affirmation of life than all other Chekhov stories. The life-giving quality of the garden contrasts with the sterility of the people inside the house. "Instead of building up an ethical, esthetic, and religious system as a framework within which to write fiction," says Rayfield, "Chekhov broke down the extraneous structures of thought on which his characters and scenes might so easily have been superimposed. Chekhov evolves as an artist by withdrawing as a philosopher. He takes away the lies that are outside us and leaves with the truth that is in us."

A.V. Chicherin, in Hulanicki (1976), notes that Chekhov often used the adversative displacement, that is, described a complex situation by opposites, or by vague phrases such as "it seemed" or "for some reason." Often after describing something as attractive, he follows with a "but" clause. For example, Nadya is ecstatic over a glorious May day, "but for some reason she wanted to cry." We can infer from signs in the story that it is because, enmeshed in her conventionality, she cannot be as free as nature is in the springtime.

V.B. Kataev in 1977 accounts for the fact that, in his revisions, Chekhov makes the ending more vague. It is to give the story a broader symbolic significance as a general picture of youth breaking away from tradition.[11] Debreczeny (1977) provides the views of Jerome H. Katsell and H. Peter Stowell. For Chekhov, Katsell says, death is part of a natural process necessary for inner growth. Thus, Nadya lives through death at many levels, including the death of her former self, in order to find her true self and grow into her full potential. Townspeople chide her for not marrying Andrey, not realizing that she "sees her life in the flux of a constant marriage with the future. For Chekhov as well as Proust, identity is linked to time and time to death and death to only a possible rebirth," in Stowell's opinion.

Stowell (1980) finds "The Betrothed" to be Chekhov's most elusive, most solipsistic, and most misunderstood story. Karl Kramer, he feels, correctly perceives the story's ambiguity: Will Nadya find a more free existence, or will she go through an endless cycle of disillusionments? "Nadya centers her life on an ever-present hope of future change, not realizing that she is in its midst, that each moment is itself change." The story is impressionistic—time gets Nadya homesick. Everything that changes is subject to Nadya's perception of change. Nadya is in a catch-22: time means change (which she desires) but it also brings a sense of loss (which she would like to avoid). So here we have Chekhov's final statement on change: It is exhilarating but constricting, static and dynamic, timeless and temporal—above all, impressionistic. Chekhov uses seasons and times of the day to show Nadya's rituals of change. Even though she is on the threshold of marriage, she is unhappy. Garden images remind her of the freedom she may be losing. Nadya is Chekhov's most impressionistic character. Her impressions never crystallize, and thus she never knows whether it is she or her environment (or both) that is changing. "She remains in the swirl of relativistic flux to the end," Stowell feels.

Kirk (1981) observes that most Soviet critics call this Chekhov's finest story, seeing it as a prediction of the coming revolution. But they ignore the fact that Nadya is a dreamer whose impassioned dreams often lead her to disillusionment. The story is one of her process of self-discovery, as she checks her dreams against reality. Just as she has rejected her mother, Andrey, and Sasha, so might she also reject her utopian dreams. Her early conflict is between the kitchen and the garden—domestic life versus freedom. Andrey is depicted negatively: He is always eating, and he has poor taste in furniture and paintings.

Bitsilli (1983) feels that Chekhov uses vague phrases like "it seemed" to convey the impression of Nadya's comprehension of the "unreality" of her situation. The first three paragraphs of the story constitute a prose-poem: They have equal length, similar sentence structure, and similar style. The lack of vitality in the story shows that it was written when Chekhov was near death.

Kenneth A. Lantz, in Clyman (1985), notes that Chekhov always keeps his characters free, that they are in continual evolution. Thus even Nadya's final departure reads "she left town, as she supposed, forever." Egri (1986) shows how the contrasts between the rich and the poor foreshadow *The Cherry Orchard*. Sasha's diatribes prefigure those of Trofimov. Having mastered the short story form, Chekhov was learning to master dramatic form in stories like "The Betrothed."

"The Bishop" (1902)

Bishop Peter is tired from his long hours of Holy Week services. Ailing and lonely, he thinks back upon his happy childhood. He resents the fact that even his mother calls him "Your Holiness"—he wants to be accepted merely as a person. On Holy Saturday he catches typhoid fever and dies. Soon he is forgotten by everyone except his mother.

Chekhov's brother Michael, in Koteliansky (1925), explained the origin of this story. Chekhov's friend Stepan became a bishop at an early age but was deprived of his see and sent to "rest" in a monastery. The prototype for Bishop Peter, he often visited Chekhov in Yalta. Concerning this story Chekhov wrote to the editor: "If the censor crosses out only one word, do not print this. I already cut too much, with an eye to the censorship."[12]

A reviewer in 1915 observed that women and children in Chekhov's stories are not as "aimless" as the men characters. And his best male characters, like Bishop Peter, have much of the woman and child in them. Although his stories may seem "mere pinholes compared to Tolstoy and Dostoevsky's wide casements, through these pinholes one receives a strangely vivid impression of life and of its devious ways with the human heart."[13]

Another reviewer felt that Chekhov's great art was "to illuminate not only the ordinary sympathies of men, but their unlooked-for depths of sentiment, aspiration, and degradation, where they lie concealed under some unpromising or misleading exterior." In this story, "where the feeling penetrates every pore of the characterization, his success is complete in revealing the pathos of the humbly born bishop, whose elevation has withdrawn him from the familiar affections which his simple heart yearns for."[14]

Edward Garnett (1921) discerned an "element of tenderness and sweetness of understanding that forms the spiritual background of many of Chekhov's tales, which dominates invisibly the coarse web of human struggle and the petty network of human egoism. It is seen to perfection in that golden tale, steeped in hues of dying sunset, of the death of the Bishop."[15]

W. Somerset Maugham in 1934 assessed both Chekhov's strengths and weaknesses. His greatest weakness was his actionless plot, Maugham felt. For example, if the bishop died of eating tainted food, the death should not be ascribed to typhoid. Chekhov's stories are not slices of life, but are events chosen "to square with the prepossessions of a sick, sad, and overworked man." But his strong points are that his stories are very interesting, the beginnings are unusually good, and "no one had a greater gift than he for giving you the intimate feeling of a place, a landscape, a conversation, or (within his limited range) a character." He lets the reader see the very spirit of his characters. "I do not know that anyone but Chekhov has so poignantly been able to represent spirit communing with spirit," said Maugham.[16]

Bruford (1948) points out that this town has 42 churches and six monasteries.

Every peasant's home has an icon. Religious consciousness is so acute that everyone who looks at the bishop feels guilty. This story raises an interesting question, Hingley (1950) remarks: Why does childhood seem so much more pleasant in retrospect than it actually was? George Ivask, in Eekman (1960), commented on Chekhov's ability to portray sincere religion. His religious characters usually have a deeper understanding of the mysteries of life and death than other characters have. Ivask quotes Boris Zajcev on the ultimate secret of Chekhov, "the good Godless Christian": "Maybe God loved him more than he loved God."

Simmons (1962) concurs on Chekhov's ability to evoke a religious atmosphere, feeling that he surpasses the Christian Dostoevsky at it: "Chekhov's quiet realism, a series of exquisitely related homely impressions, movingly evokes the faith of the old bishop and creates the hallowed atmosphere of the Church that gives meaning to his faith." "In the portrait of the dying biship," Payne (1963) feels, "he painted himself." Reeve (1966) finds the bishop's tragedy in his lack of self-knowledge – he would not mind dying if he knew *who* was dying.

Nilsson (1968) found that here Chekhov uses setting not for its independent beauty (as in an early story like "The Steppe") but only as an integral backdrop for the plot and theme. Nature is not now completely indifferent to man, but something of a nurturing agent. Constance Curtin in 1969 showed that Chekhov used bridging devices, such as word repetition and sound effects, to bind together the various elements in this story.[17]

Kramer (1970) believes that this story is the culmination of Chekhov's studies of the uncertain nature of man's existence in a world he cannot fathom, and where all truths are relative. Ambiguity is a part of Chekhov's impressionism: a cloud of doubt hangs about the bishop's existence. This story shows the immutability of life, says Chudakov (1971).

Chekhov here abandoned his reticence, says Laffitte (1971), and for once bared his heart. He himself is the bishop, a tragic man superior to his surroundings, misunderstood and condemned to solitude – a man who cries out for a beautiful life, unattainable on this earth, and who dies as much alone as he lived. Urbanski (1973) notes that when the bishop sees his mother, he starts to cry, and soon the whole congregation is crying. "This mass-scale weeping for no apparent reason creates a huge lyrical subtext which convincingly reaches the reader. One feels the influence of some higher force, which in the end saves the bishop. Through his unique lyricism, Chekhov succeeds in his efforts to convey the harsh realities of life convincingly and artistically."

Hingley (1975) believes that this story reflects Chekhov's unhappiness because of his failing health. Although it is a fascinating example of Chekhov's art, Hingley says, its importance has sometimes been exaggerated by critics. Rayfield (1975) detected that the church's music and wholeness were as beautiful and uncontaminated to the agnostic Chekhov as nature itself. His idea of art was remarkably religious. As the bishop approaches death, the past becomes more meaningful to him than the present. The goodness of life is seen in the face of death. The bishop's fever causes hallucinations which merge with Holy Week themes. The moonlight, for example, suggests Christ's agony in Gethsemane as well as the bishop's final illness. Chekhov evokes "a whole chaos of sensations and memories" and resolves "their discord into a harmonious set of images." As the bishop nears death, Church Slavonic forms blot out the Russian language. Now "all that lies between the bishop and euphoria is a sense of something missing." This missing element is his estrangement from his family because of his office. As he grows weaker, he seems more childlike, and the estrangement diminishes. He dies dreaming of walking across sunlit fields. In this story the verbal rhythm creates a prose poem in which virtually every resource of the Russian language is exploited. The story expresses Chekhov's desire to be loved for himself, not for his fame.

H. Peter Stowell in 1975 noted how the bishop searches for his identity, which seems to be in question. This cloud of uncertainty makes it look at times as if his very existence may have been a dream of his mother.[18] Hingley (1976) admits that Chekhov is so sympathetic towards religion here that one could scarcely know that he was an unbeliever. V.B. Kataev in 1976 showed that Chekhov often relied on literary tradition. Here, he uses the "myth" of Christ's death and resurrection.[19]

Debreczeny (1977) provides insights from Charanne C. Clarke and Jerome H. Katsell. Clarke, seeing it as one of Chekhov's most impressionistic stories, says that in it time boundaries dissolve, and scenes alternate between dream and reality. "The use of light and color to create vivid yet static scenes," says Clarke, "suggests that there was more than an awareness on Chekhov's part of the work of the French Impressionists." Katsell states that the form of the story derives from "clusters of images relating to light and darkness; time present, past, and future; stasis and motion; and as always in Chekhov's mature prose, in the prescient detail." A strong motif is also "the silent but illuminated intensity of nature, the moon at night and the bottomless azure sky during the day."

Stowell (1980) feels that the bishop's existence is ambiguous: as his mother's son, he should respect her, but as a church official, she should respect him. Like impressionist painters, Chekhov believes that "appearances are reality, and that perceptions are subject to the caprices of both the subject and the object. The bishop's death before Easter allows him to rise on Easter Sunday and become one with the world of man, God, and nature."

Wilks (1982) observes that the whole story has a dreamlike quality. Ivan Bunin, says Wilks, called this story "amazing," saying that only an author "who himself has experienced these hellish torments can understand this work in all its beauty." Alexander Kuprin stressed Chekhov's astonishing accuracy of observation. Like Tolstoy's Ivan Ilyich, the closer the bishop comes to death the happier he is. This is "a perfect work of art," in the opinion of Wilks. The bishop's final delirium brings him peace of mind and spiritual illumination, and he is relieved to once again feel like a normal person. Chekhov employs counterpoint tellingly: After the bishop's death on Easter Eve, he is forgotten, but after Christ's death (and resurrection), He will always be remembered.

Compared to his earlier stories, says Bitsilli (1983), Chekhov here uses images and motifs more effectively. The structure of the story is built around a pilgrimage. The life cycle is shown, through the bishop's memory and his death. His death brings catharsis, a release from the bishop's "I," "a transcendence of its empirical limitations and its isolation."

Troyat (1984) concedes that this story is so imbued with the atmosphere of the church that it seems to be the work of a man of faith. Kenneth A. Lantz, in Clyman (1985), sees this as a story of how the bishop attained release from the constraints of his office. In this life the release comes from his childhood memories. As he dies, he finally achieves the freedom he had sought for so long.

"The Darling" (1898) ("Dusechka")

Olga always needs someone to love—she speaks her husband's language, waits on him faithfully, and is a darling wife. In her childhood she loved her father, her aunt, and her French tutor. Married to Kukin, a theater manager, she helps him at the theater. When he dies, she is despondent, and mourns his death. Three months later she meets and marries Pustovalov, a timber merchant. She learns timber terms, and they are happy until his death. Olga then boards Smirnin, a veterinarian, who is separated from his wife. When Olga starts using medical terms, Smirnin becomes bored and moves to Siberia. Olga's life is now pointless and dull. But Smirnin returns from Siberia, Olga begins to "mother" his son Sasha, and her life once again seems fulfilled.

Tolstoy said that Chekhov, influenced by the feminist movement, wanted to ridicule a woman who lacked ideas or opinions of her own. But the true poet in Chekhov shone through, making it impossible to satirize this loving woman, and so he paints her devotion faithfully and unbiasedly. Like Balaam in the Old Testament, who came to curse the Israelites but instead blessed them because of an angel's influence, so Chekhov's guiding poetic angel had him do the opposite of what he had planned.

Tolstoy liked the story so much that he read it aloud to friends on four consecutive nights. Chekhov was pleased to hear this, but wondered why Tolstoy ignored serious stories like "Gooseberries" for lighter ones like "The Darling." A reviewer in 1916 said that Tolstoy was wrong—there is no sign of contempt in the story. Chekhov, an artist for art's sake, came to neither praise nor blame but to reveal. "Without the subtlest sympathy he could not understand and reveal as he does," said the reviewer, "and the effect of reading his tales is to be washed free of petty impatience and acerbity of judgment."[20] Robert Lynd that year found Olga to be ludicrous even when she is most unselfish. Lynd saw a strange marriage of sympathy and disgust in Chekhov's tales. He would be a pessimist but he lacks despair. "The genius of gentleness and love and laughter," said Lynd, "makes him the greatest short-story writer to have appeared on this planet."[21]

Katherine Mansfield in 1922 called Tolstoy's view of this story "a small master-piece of stupidity."[22] Gerhardi (1923) noted Chekhov's ability in this story to characterize a person in one sentence. However simple-minded Olga may be, Gerhardi said, she is rich in kindliness and love, and could be the beginning of a cultural tradition which centuries from now will develop in mankind the spirit we call God. Brewster (1924) felt that the story demonstrated Chekhov's zest for living.

M. Robinson in 1927 asked if Olga was a failure. True, she does not protest against life, and she seems weak and flabby. Yet she continually rises to something beyond herself. "Moral qualities," said Robinson, "are complete in themselves. To demand that they should be balanced out by success or prosperity or heaven hereafter is not the demand of a mature judgment." Chekhov makes "weak" people heroes, with "courage the greater because it is hopeless, selflessness the purer because it is unconscious. And so one comes to realize that in that kind alone is success possible, because it alone is worthy of humanity on its divine side." This vision, Robinson concluded, made Chekhov a true prophet.[23]

Evelyn May Albright (1928) said that although the story's four steps appear to be downward, they are actually upward to a perfect love. Tolstoy's interpretation was wrong, she felt, for of all of Chekhov's stories this is "one of the most deliberate and conscious artistry, with its carefully crystallized stages of action, with the rise and fall of her personality as love is withdrawn or supplied, and with the clever climactic development to the supreme level bestowed upon the one who offers the least return." Olga's law of being was to love and to be loved.

N. Elizabeth Monroe in 1941 contrasted this story with Virginia Woolf's *Jacob's Room*. Chekhov's method of integrating the story elements is far more subtle, since the bonding agent is love. "By the mysterious alchemy of love, Olga transforms herself into the men she loves, and they in turn become phases of her devotion. We know little of Jacob, but we understand everything about Olga, and love her despite her silly foibles."[24]

Lenin used Olga as a symbol of intellectuals who lack the backbone to take a stand and hold it, said Ermilov (1956). Poggioli (1957) observed that Olga called her successive husbands by similar names, as if they were interchangeable. People call Olga "Dusechka," meaning "little soul," except when she has no man to love, for then it seems she has no soul. Dusechka was a Russian version of the Psyche myth, as used by Ippolit Bogdanovich, an 18th-century Russian poet.

Saunders (1960) and Simmons (1962) doubt that Tolstoy's interpretation of the story was correct. Simmons adds that Tolstoy never perceived Chekhov's tenderness for people who suffered. Tolstoy said that the story was "like lace made by a chaste young girl," who depicts her dreams of happiness in her lace patterns. Embarrassed, Chekhov simply replied, "There are many misprints in the story."

Winner (1966) quotes Poggioli's theory that Olga realized unconsciously what Psyche failed to understand: that love is blind and must remain so. But Olga and her lovers are "lower versions" of the myth—none of the lovers is an Eros, and

Olga, too naïve to see past one love, cannot be a proper Psyche, Winner feels. Zygmunt Rukalski in 1969 found a parallel to this story in Maupassant's "Happiness," where Suzanne also shows unselfish love of her husband. Olga's shallowness we forgive, says Rukalski, because of her love.[25]

Kramer (1970) differs from most critics in saying that perhaps Olga is no darling, after all. She loves so much that she destroys—her husbands do not last long. She completely dominates her men, and young Sasha resents her very much. Michael A. Sperber found mental illness in Olga. In this view she has an emotional disturbance in which her relationship to life lacks genuineness but functions outwardly as if it were complete. Lacking a sense of self, she becomes dependent upon a series of men whose behavior she imitates.[26]

A.S. Melkova in 1974 supported Tolstoy's contention that Chekhov changed Olga from a ridiculous character to an endearing one. Hingley (1976) said that Chekhov seemed to break his rule here, for he shows us not only one, but three, successful marriages. Hahn (1977) also supports Tolstoy's interpretation. Nevertheless, despite the reader's affection for the story, "the sources of its pathos are relatively facile," Hahn believes. Olga embodies an exaggerated aspect of womanhood, and "if we respond to her, it is still not with complete belief."

P. Kuranage in 1980 reported that Chekhov is the most popular European fiction writer in Sri Lanka, and that Sri Lanka's leading author, Martin Wickramasinghe, said that "Chekhov's genius inspires our writers." In "The Darling," said Kuranage, "I did not see Olga but the wife of a current official, a kind and sentimental woman with a soft smile."[27] A.M. Turkov in 1980 used this story to show how Chekhov's attitude towards women differed from Tolstoy's.[28] Kirk (1981) points out that Olga's maternal solicitude towards her first husband encourages his indulgent self-pity, which proves fatal to him. Her doting love also stifles Sasha, who cries out in his sleep against her.

Barbara Heldt in 1982 stated that, just as Flaubert makes us doubt the devotion of the heroine in "A Simple Heart," so does Chekhov make us question our initial favorable reaction toward Olga.[29] Bitsilli (1983) reminds us that everything changes in the story except Olga. She continues to need to love in order to exist.

"A Doctor's Visit" (1898) ("A Case History")

Young Dr. Korolyov visits a factory to treat the owner's daughter for a heart attack. He finds her not ill but yearning for a lover, and conscience stricken over the way the factory exploits the workers. The doctor wonders why so many people have to work so hard just so that the governess can have fine wine and sturgeon. He says, "At least we are worried about these problems. They will have been solved in the next fifty years."

Edward Garnett (1921) notes how cautious the doctor is not to be too harsh in his criticism of the factory system. Albright (1928) says the story shows that

Chekhov disliked tasteless and garish luxury as much as the squalor of poverty.
George Z. Patrick in 1932 stated that Chekhov believed that a truly educated person would respond with compassion to a fellow human's suffering. Thus Chekhov
shows here how "Liza, sick in mind and body, has benefited more from a few gentle
words of Dr. Korolyov than from any medical treatment."[30]

Bruford (1948) remarks that the doctor does not blame the rich owners for the
exploitation, but the devil, in whom he does not believe. He sees the factory windows shining like two eyes of the devil, with a chimney belching out smoke and fire.
Liza's depression is a healthy sign, says the doctor, because it indicates a moral
code that could lead to reform, in the opinion of Hingley (1950) and Ermilov
(1956). Ehrenburg (1962) agrees that Chekhov is exposing the evils of capitalism.
Winner (1966) notes how the sharp clang of a piece of metal striking the hour
reminds the doctor of the harshness of factory life.

To Kramer (1970) this story has many incongruities. A doctor of medicine is
asked to cure a spiritual disease, and is forced to attribute the disease to possession
by a devil. Here even the owners suffer; only the governess benefits, so that the
master is slave to the servant. In this corrupt system it is not only the strong exploiting the weak, but everyone is suffering, including the wealthy. Kramer finds
Chekhov employing the absurd, but for a serious purpose. Hingley (1975) points
out that the villain, the governess, is once again depicted as a glutton.

Avram Derman, in Hulanicki (1976), observes that Chekhov avoids a trite
"rounding off" ending by employing several unpretentious "lowering" lines, which
return the reader to commonplace life after a very idealistic statement. Hingley
(1976) feels that Chekhov only sketches in the industrial workers, since he did not
know them as well as he knew peasants. In his years of physical decline, Hingley
adds, Chekhov's cry for social justice became ever more prominent.

"Gooseberries" (1898)

Ivan tells of his brother Nikolai, who always dreamed of owning an estate that
would have even gooseberry bushes. Nikolai marries a wealthy widow, and when
she dies he buys such an estate. but he mistreats his peasants, grows lazy, and says
of sour gooseberries, "Aren't they delicious!" Ivan, ashamed of his brother, advises,
"Be not weary in well-doing. Only virtue lasts—not happiness!"

Studying the technique of a story-within-a-story, Mark Schorer in 1950 found
that the anecdote and its "frame" illuminate each other. The frame judges the anecdote (Ivan's story) and reveals the confusion of fact and dream that it contains.[31]
This story shows that Chekhov was no fatalist, Magarshack (Life, 1952) declares.
Chekhov felt that the writer should "knock on the conscience of mankind," and
awaken people to action to improve society.

Sour gooseberries are used to expose the unjust nature of selfish happiness,
says Ermilov (1956). Ivan gives the story's moral: Life cannot go on as it is.

F.G. Svetov in 1963 showed how the story crystallizes around the main character and the one idea he represents.[32] Winner (1966) sees Ivan as asserting that rural withdrawal is selfish monasticism—one should identify not with a small piece of land but with the whole earth. The idyllic setting at the beginning of the story contrasts with Nikolai's estate, where the stream is polluted by factories.

Jackson (1967) quotes Boris Eichenbaum as declaring that Chekhov himself was "the man with the gavel," who in the story is supposed to knock on the door of every happy home reminding the owner that misfortune exists. Kramer (1970) detects a contradiction between Ivan's words and actions. He lingers longest in the pool, enjoying himself, and he tells Nikolai to change but says that he himself is too old to change. Burkin suspects some lingering falsehood in Ivan's story, which was trying to prove and disprove its point at the same time.

Milton A. Mays in 1972 also questioned Ivan as a narrator, feeling that by no means does he draw the proper moral from the story. Like Nikolai, Ivan is "excessive," trying to reduce life's complexity to a single maxim. His pipe's bad smell helps show readers Ivan's insensitivity.[33] Shotton, in Fennell (1973), says that this story shows people "encased" in materialism, complacency, and narrow self-indulgence. The "case" is a personality outlook "which confines man's consciousness, restricts his freedom of spirit or imagination, and hinders the achievement of his higher aim—the realization of his full potential as a human being."

Hingley (1975) states that Chekhov is concerned here with inequality. In his notebook Chekhov wrote: "Even happiness has something sad about it. We must train people in conscientiousness and clarity of mind." The characters conclude that happiness is based upon other people's misery, Rayfield (1975) finds. David E. Maxwell, in Debreczeny (1977), says that the story shows the devastating effects of delay and inertia. People waiting for their opportunity to act find that the opportunity never comes. At the end of the story, expectations are unfulfilled: Nikolai's gooseberries are sour, Alekhin and Burkin dislike what they have heard, and Ivan's hopes as to the effect of his narrative are unrealized.

Richard Wear in 1977 argued that Ivan is not Chekhov's spokesman, and that each story in this trilogy shows a person "possessed" by some idea or emotion that interferes with human understanding. Ann E. Berthoff in 1981 stated that Ivan's pipe is not a metaphor, but a means of identifying him: It suggests that he has the leisure to speculate about human misery. But it bothers him to have such leisure, and so he attacks the notion of human happiness.[34] L. Lieber in 1982 observed how the characters exist within a very confined space. Z.S. Smelkova that year explained how a close examination of the word "gooseberries" discloses new meaning in the story.[35]

Wilks (1982) finds in the story many Gogolian overtones, especially the comparison of people to pigs. In this story, Basu (1985) says, Chekhov shows the need for social reform. Basu quotes Boris Eichenbaum that here Chekhov moves from mere diagnosis to recommended treatment. Clyman (1985) shows the views of Andrew R. Durkin and J.L. Styan. Durkin notes a reversal: Gooseberries symbolize bliss to Nikolai but disgust to Ivan. Here Chekhov experiments with the ironic use of a symbol, and his "usually careful presentation of the character's subjective world is deliberately and totally reversed." Styan explains why seemingly irrelevant details are used— they not only intensify the illusion of reality but also challenge the reader to judge which items are significant.

"In the Ravine" (1900) ("The Hollow")

Grigory, a greedy shopkeeper, is the only wealthy person in Uklivo, a town located in a ravine. He cheats the public whenever he can, his one love being his family. His older son Anisim is serving six years at hard labor for counterfeiting. His young son Stepan is weak, deaf, and listless. Aksinya, Stepan's wife, is jealous of Lipa, Anisim's wife, for being heir to the family estate, so she throws scalding water on Lipa's baby, killing it. All the powers of the household pass to Aksinya, and old Grigory, who has lived all of his life in a rut, in a wicked ravine, is reduced to begging from Lipa.

To those shocked by the plot, Chekhov answered that a child being scalded to death is often encountered by a country doctor. Reacting to this story, Tolstoy called Chekhov "a prose Pushkin," a great impressionist whose random splashes of color suddenly congeal into a unified art object. He called Chekhov "an artist without equal. He created new forms. Without any false modesty, I tell you that from the point of view of technique, Chekhov is far superior to me."[36]

Defending Chekhov of charges of gloominess, Gorky in 1900 said that Chekhov's works are full of courage and the love of life. Gorky declared that "as a stylist Chekhov is unequalled. Future historians of literature, speaking about the development of the Russian language, will say that this language was created by Pushkin, Turgenev, and Chekhov." Gorky told of reading this story to some peasants, and soon both he and they were crying. Chekhov's detachment permitted him to show life as it is, said Gorky, and led readers to the conclusion that life as it is must be changed. Better than anyone else Chekhov showed the struggle between a person's striving to be a better person and striving to succeed in the eyes of the world.

M.O. Menshikov in 1902 stated that this story shows the catastrophe that ensues when capitalism hits village life. He noted three feminine character types: Aksinya, the predator; Varvara, between good and evil; and Lipa, the meek Christian, who is really the strongest. D.N. Ovsianiko-Kulikovsky in 1909 agreed that the rural bourgeoisie were motivated only by a desire for profit.[37]

Persky (1913) found catharsis in this tragic story. Although evil and injustice seem to triumph with revolting cynicism, Varvara's honesty and goodness "seem to be something strange, joyous, and free, like the lights that glow before the saintly images" in Chekhov's works. Lipa and her mother not only endure suffering, but also give alms to the poor, through their faith in God: "Big as the evil is, the night is beautiful and calm. Justice is and will be calm and beautiful on God's earth also."

Leonid Grossman in 1914 said that this story repeats on a small scale Emile Zola's *The Earth*. There is the same naturalistic description, and the same sensuality, cruelty, and violence. A reviewer that year agreed that the misery and barbarity were vividly depicted, but noted that Chekhov "observes gently and dispassionately, blocking his characters out with salient lines and expressive traits which leave a softness of tone over them."[38] The following year a reviewer said that, although no one showed the shopkeeping class better than Chekhov did, in actuality his characters can be found in every country, for he has tapped their universal characteristics.[39]

Discussing this story in 1921, Conrad Aiken called Chekhov "a poet of the actual." Turgenev may create a deeper impression of character, but in Chekhov's characters one finds "an infinitely fine and truthful sequence of mood. Chekhov's sympathy, pity, and tenderness were inexhaustible. He lived, and thus permitted us to live, everywhere."[40] Edward Garnett (1921) agreed that despite the Aksinyas of life, Chekhov felt that in the long run truth and beauty would prevail in life.

Werth (1925) says that the story's message is that man cannot know everything, but he knows all that he needs to know. Mirsky (1927), not given to praising Chekhov, called this story "an amazing piece of work, remarkably free from excessive detail, and infinitely rich in emotional and symbolic significance." The story's atmosphere is like that of Maeterlinck. Here Mirsky found something rare in Chekhov, a keen moral judgment.

Toumanova (1937) said that Lipa had no bitterness at Aksinya's terrible act but only surprise. Her deep love and forgiveness show the Christianity of the Slavophiles, who considered Moscow to be "the third Rome." They believed that Russia had to be crucified to atone for the sins of the world, and that only suffering brought atonement. Bruford (1948) observed that Aksinya had been an efficient, if unscrupulous, manager—her brickyard always showed the greatest profit. Hingley (1950) saw the story as a classic treatment of the rise of the kulak, or wealthy peasant.

This is a somber tale of village life, full of pity for the common people, painting their daily heroism with severe detachment, said Magarshack (*Life*, 1952). George Ivask, in Eekman (1960), pointed out that Chekhov sometimes ridicules insincere clergy. Here the priest savors a salted mushroom as he tells the mourning mother, "Do not mourn your child, for theirs is the Kingdom of Heaven."

John W. Harrison in 1961 called this a dynamic story, in which Chekhov uses counterfeiting to unify the plot and convey the story's social criticism. Anisim's counterfeiting symbolizes the hypocrisy of the village. Anisim is not only a detective who passes false money but he is also a counterfeit husband to comely Lipa. Grigory is a counterfeit merchant who sells tainted food and illegal vodka. Aksinya is the biggest counterfeiter of all, criticizing Lipa as a convict's wife, and killing her baby out of greed and envy. Most of the merchants are engaged in illegal trade, in contrast to the peasants, who are honest and hard-working people.[41]

Simmons (1962) observes that this story has more characters than the usual Chekhov tale, but each has a distinctive personality. In reviewing the generally favorable criticism of the story, Simmons said that Chekhov found Gorky's praise of it "balm for his soul." Victor Mirolyubov shed tears over the story; I. Gorbunov-Posadov said it revealed not only Chekhov's talent but also his tender sympathy for suffering humanity; and A.F. Koni said that it was Chekhov's best, "one of the profoundest productions of Russian literature."

Winner (1966) noted the similarity between this story and Tolstoy's *The Power of Darkness*. He called attention to Chekhov's use of imagery: Lipa resembles a singing bird, and Aksinya is described in snake images. He also found that sound effects are used symbolically in this story. Hugh McLean in 1968 showed how Chekhov keeps in balance many polarities: the specific world and its general significance; metonymy and metaphor; objective description and emotional appeals.[42] Chudakov (1971) observed that by now Chekhov can switch the point-of-view back and forth among the characters, with no loss of unity.

Laffitte (1971) was amazed to see that Lipa, mourning her lost baby, found her sorrow matched by "the beauty and serenity of the night" and "that truth, equally beautiful and serene, would always exist in the world." In this grim story, says Speirs (1971), the "old peasant whose life has been a hell wishes to go on living another twenty years" to see "more of the good. Great is our Mother Russia!" The old man's religious faith carries him through, as he tries to console bereaving Lipa. Chekhov uses impressionism in this story, says Urbanski (1973). For example, carrying her dead baby, Lipa asks two strangers, "Are you holy men?" and they reply, "No, we are from Firsanov." The disconnected dialogue establishes a lyrical mood.

Hingley (1975) says that this story, along with "Peasants," ranks as Chekhov's best fictional work in the rural idiom. The plot is superbly managed. Chekhov's brother Michael said that the central plot incident came from Chekhov's Sakhalin experience. Politically naïve, Chekhov insisted that the story contradicted Marxist beliefs, even though Marxist critics welcomed the story. Even Soviet critics cannot claim Chekhov as a Marxist, but they can say that he truthfully depicted reality, and that their version of reality coincides with his.

Rayfield (1975) finds in the story Gorky's influence toward social protest. Industry divides the peasants into workers and masters. The air and the river are polluted by the factory, which also pollutes the morals of the managers. Predatory images in the story create terror, but the carpenter Crutch is a Christ-like figure. Catharsis comes from Lipa's great strength, some of which she seems to absorb from the sounds of nature. Hingley (1976) reports that Chekhov expected the magazine *Life* to reject the story for not glamorizing peasants.

Hahn (1977) finds that Aksinya's blind instinct to achieve wealth and thus power "at whatever cost to other people's lives, disturbs Chekhov more than anything else." Aksinya exercises "a tyranny of tears": to get her way all she has to do is throw a tantrum. That she can murder a baby shows the perversion of her maternal instinct. Since she has no child, the factory becomes her surrogate baby. Because Chekhov had trouble creating characters for whom he had no affinity at all, Aksinya is not quite real—the imagery depicting her is overly explicit and dehumanizing.

Thomas G. Winner, in Debreczeny (1977), notes that joyful bird cries are chorus-like, singing, "Life is given only once—enjoy every minute of it." After noting that Chekhov uses "eloquent silence" to achieve his ironic purpose, Paul Debreczeny in 1978 came up with the novel interpretation that Lipa is not the heroine of the story but rather the target of Chekhov's satire for inappropriately practicing Tolstoy's non-resistance.[43]

In 1982 G.A. Bialy compared this story to Tolstoy's *The Power of Darkness.* Both show "the power of darkness" to be greed, ignorance, and squalor. Morality has been replaced by custom in both works, and despite their gloomy atmosphere, goodness ultimately prevails in the play and the story.[44] Simon Karlinsky, in Barricelli (1981), finds Chekhov ahead of his time in attacking industrial pollution.

Nabokov (1981) notes how Chekhov slyly reveals that Anisim's friend Samorodov has been a counterfeiting accomplice, by having the same beautiful penmanship, used in Anisim's letters, accompany Anisim to Siberia. "In her innocence," says Nabokov, "Lipa never thought of telling people it was Aksinya who killed her baby." The family believed that Lipa had accidentally scalded the baby to death. Wilks (1982) lists the story's social themes: Rapid industrialization disintegrates village life. Greed brutalizes the kulaks. Despite the pollution and corruption, there is catharsis—Chekhov shows that those who suffer and endure can eventually triumph.

After pointing out parallels between this story and "Peasants," Bitsilli (1983) showed that here the characters are more highly individualized. Here, says Bitsilli, Chekhov achieves Shakespearian tragedy, by portraying the struggle between the eternal feminine principle (as seen in Lipa) and the demonic woman principle (as depicted in Aksinya).

Clyman (1985) presents comments on this story by Kenneth A. Lantz, Ralph Lindheim, and Donald Rayfield. Lantz observes that Lipa never descends into the moral ravine in which the other characters live. Lindheim believes that the story indicates "how the development of capitalistic alternatives to the feudal tradition reinforces rather than eradicates physical and moral savagery." Rayfield detects in this story the same Old Believer faith that Nikolai Leskov used in his work.

"Ionych" (1898) ("Dr. Startsev")

Dr. Ionych Startsev courts Kitty Turkin unsuccessfully. She tells him she likes him but can never love him. Four years later she wants to marry him, but he refuses. Several years later he is wealthy, fat, and crabby—but single. Kitty also has not married.

Mirsky (1927) applies his technique to this story: The straight-line plot is the doctor's love for Kitty, and the curved-line buried plot is his relapse into egotistical complacency as a successful provincial doctor. Avram Derman in 1929 called terseness Chekhov's most characteristic trait. Here it is seen in the laconic beginning and ending, the rapid development of the theme, and the selection of only one or two details to denote the change in the doctor's social status. For example, from not even owning a horse, Ionych improves to having a troika with a liveried servant.

Magarshack (*Life,* 1952) finds great compassion in this story. In 20 pages a whole provincial town springs to life, and the descriptive passages evoke the inmost feelings of the characters. The debasement of Ionych, says Winner (1966), is artfully portrayed by subtexts and by changes in the narrative style. The Turkins never change; they are forever banal but happy. Ionych, destroyed by banality, ends up isolated and cruel to his patients.

Zygmunt Rukalski in 1969 showed how both Chekhov and Maupassant depict the vanity of human existence. Chekhov shows Ionych revolting in defiance of his creator, and Maupassant's "Moiron" has the demented teacher accusing God of creating death to amuse Himself. Rukalski adds that both writers have uncanny insight into human nature, and both give numerous examples of both selfish and selfless love.[45] Kramer (1970) notes that Chekhov uses a muffled ending in the form of a recognition scene to overcome the lack of drama inherent in the short story genre.

Three different points-of-view are used, said Chudakov (1971), to help show the doctor's change of character, and to give a denunciatory tone to the story. Chekhov early sows character traits that make probable the change from Dr. Startsev to Ionych. Hingley (1975) observes that Ionych eats too much, a sure sign of a Chekhov villain. Chekhov's style in this story is poetic, Rayfield (1975) says; he uses alliteration, assonance, internal rhyme, and triads of nouns and adjectives.

Ionych falls for Kitty, who has large breasts, "a sinister portent in any of Chekhov's fictional young women," asserts Hingley (1976). Their timing is bad— when he is ready for love, she studies piano in Moscow, and when she returns, ready for him, he is a land speculator with no time for love. "In an exquisitely symmetrical plot, both miss happiness which each might have found with the other had they not been characters in Chekhov and therefore by definition precluded from all prospect of united bliss," Hingley comments sarcastically.

Eisen (1982) points out that the four-part structure of the story (built around visits by Ionych to the Turkins) follows the form of a four-act play. Basu (1985) feels that Chekhov uses nature passages lyrically. Waiting for Kitty, Ionych perceives the soft moonlight as a cradle of mystery, suggesting eternal life. But Kitty does not come, and a cloud over the moon makes it hard for him to find the gate in the darkness.

Clyman (1985) has critical comments from Kenneth A. Lantz and Ralph Lindheim. Lantz says that Ionych "has retreated into a safe world of routine where he can cultivate an indifference that need not put his feelings at risk." Lindheim notices that by the end of the story, Ionych cannot even talk like a human: all of his utterances are either commands or rhetorical questions.

"The Lady with a Dog" (1899)

Gurov, a philanderer, likes to leave his wife and three children in Moscow while he hunts for women. One day in Yalta he sees young Anna with her white Pomeranian—she pleases him, and soon they are in bed. When she leaves him, he cannot forget her (as he usually does with picked-up women). He visits her at her home, evading her husband. Gurov and Anna arrange regular trysts at a Moscow hotel. For the first time in his life Gurov is in love, and Anna returns his affection. Both hope that some day the big break will come that will allow them to be together permanently.

After reading this story, Gorky told Chekhov that he was killing realism. "After even the least important story of yours," Gorky said, "everything seems coarse, as if written not with a pen but with a stick." But it was time for realism to go, Gorky added, for it had reached a dead end.

Leonard Woolf in 1917 appreciated Chekhov's "delicious irony": Gurov dares to mention his illicit liaison, and his companion replies, "You're right—the sturgeon was a bit too strong."[46] Mais (1921) said Chekhov gave a note of optimism "just where the normal writer would be pessimistic," as the frustrated lovers on the seashore hear the waves breaking, seeming to offer hope for a brighter future.[47] Gerhardi (1923) notes how Chekhov focused on a seemingly insignificant detail in a moment of high emotion: Gurov, wondering whether Anna will receive him in her town, concentrates on an inkstand with a headless figure on horseback adorning it.

Mirsky (1927) applies his usual criterion thusly: the straight line is Gurov's assuming that this is simply one more affair, and the curved line is his growing all-consuming love for Anna. Peter Quennell in 1927 found Chekhov's settings both beautiful in themselves and also contributing to the overall effect: "His effects are often so concentrated as to be nearly painful, like water reflections that trouble by their distinctness and disturb us by their veracity and beauty."[48]

Magarshack (*Life*, 1952) calls this "a remarkable story of a great love arising out of the pick-up of a young unhappily married woman by an old roué." Z.M. Paperny in 1954 studied how Chekhov presented love, feeling that in this story he showed that love can call forth a person's best qualities. B.S. Meilakh in 1956 compared Anna with Anna Karenina. Tolstoy's Anna perishes, he feels, because of her society's harsh standards, but Chekhov's Anna still has hope of finding a solution to her love problem. George Ivask in 1959 compared this story with Innokenty

Annensky's "Parting." Both stories are impressionistic, use understatement, find
the tragic in everyday life, and are built on similar themes. In 1960 K.M.
Vinogradova showed how in revising the story, Chekhov put greater stress on signs
of Gurov's regeneration.[49]

The first literary fruit of Chekhov's Yalta life, this story is permeated with the
resort's atmosphere, Simmons (1962) states. He finds a Maupassant flavor in this
tale of adultery. Like *Anna Karenina*, this story shows the conflict between beauty
and banality, says Winner (1966). Just as Chekhov's lovers are of a lower intensity
than Tolstoy's, so the denouement is pathos rather than tragedy. The concluding
mood is gentle melancholy. Rufus W. Mathewson in 1968 found that "Gurov's
esthetic response to the sea is transformed into an ethical insight, and he is liberated
from the empty forms of his public life."[50]

Kramer (1970) finds the story ambiguous, not knowing whether this is a new
experience or not for Gurov. Chudakov (1971) says that here Chekhov uses short
stacatto sentences to capture the breathless pace of action. Gurov feels that in life's
very indifference maybe there is "a pledge of eternal salvation." In this passage the
repetition of sibilant sounds, in the Russian, creates a poetic effect. Chudakov
quotes E.A. Solovyev, who in 1900 called this story an unfinished fragment, with
its last lines suggesting "some impending cruel drama of life."

In 1971 N. I. Prutskov differed with B.S. Meilakh, stating that in Chekhov love
does not destroy, but it regenerates his characters to help them change for the better. Wolf Düwel in 1973 said that Gabriele Selge was wrong to call Chekhov a
modernist — this story shows him to be a realist and a humanist.[51] Shotton, in Fennell (1973), says that this story illustrates how nature shows man beauty: "Man is
mortal, mankind immortal. The life of the individual has meaning only when he sees
his mortal span as one link in an unending chain."

Smith (1973) says that Anna is a symbol of the ideal love Chekhov could en-
visage but not embrace. This story, she feels, is the best picture of Chekhov's attitudes towards women and love. Although the plot is banal, Chekhov's artistry
preserves a careful balance between the poetic and the prosaic, and achieves vivid
characterization through the use of half-tones. Gurov is a story of everyman, and
his fate is Chekhov's: true love had come too late, and thus complete happiness is
impossible.

Hingley (1975) called this Chekhov's most profound exploration of love, and
possibly his best known story. This is the only Chekhov story set in Yalta, Rayfield
(1975) states. Gurov is fascinated by Anna when he cannot fit her into one of his
three classes of women: sensualists, who repel him by their gratitude; intellectuals,
who bore him by their conceit; and predators, who offend him by their coldness.
Gurov finally realizes that man destroys beauty when he forgets about the higher
aims of his being.

G.P. Berdnikov in 1976 closely analyzed this story, finding the characters to
be both individualized and universal. Z.S. Paperny that year showed the origin of
this and other stories, after an examination of Chekhov's notebooks.[52]

Hulanicki (1976) provides further views by Avram Derman, E.S. Dobin, V.V. Golubkov, A.G. Gornfeld, and V. Lakshin. Derman calls this Chekhov at his highest level of creativity, with the story having an ending that points towards a new beginning. Dobin says that Anna, who considers her husband a good man but a flunkey, does not even know where he works. Golubkov finds that Gurov differentiates between the persona and the person when he says that we all lead two lives: one is open, but conventional and false; the other is secret but not deceitful, sincere but hidden. Gornfeld, who studied Chekhov's endings, said that Chekhov had the reader identify so intensely with the hero that when the story ends, the reader postulates what happened to Gurov. Lakshin reports how Gurov, seeing an ugly grey fence near Anna's house, fears that Anna has forgotten him, confessing "that would be quite natural for a young woman who had to look at that damned fence from morning to night."

Hahn (1977) says that the story traces the conversion of desire into love. The mellowness and tolerance in the story reflect Chekhov's awareness that he was dying. As in Mozart, Chekhov developed a quiet confidence that life is worthwhile, built upon his mastery of his art. But Chekhov's "generalized speculation about our 'unceasing progress toward perfection' comes with disastrous heaviness in a story otherwise so delicate." Anna's "unconsciously reproduced posture of a classical Magdalen is made to express a genuine shame and humility which gave Anna a new depth in our eyes" and in Gurov's. When he writes of Moscow, Chekhov deserts the slow Yalta rhythms for a crisp, energetic prose. Written during his dramatic period, the story has a dramatic structure: there are few characters, with the main focus on Anna and Gurov. Like the plays, this story has four parts, each capturing a different phase of the love affair. Had this been a novel, the reader would have wanted more details about his wife and her husband, and moral considerations could have ruined the esthetic effect. When their relationship grows difficult, Chekhov portrays it through "a whole sequence of images of hardness, constriction, and enclosure." This story, Hahn feels, is a "testimony to Chekhov's belief in the worth of human love. Few of his stories manifest such mellowness and so lyrical a tone."

Karl D. Kramer, in Debreczeny (1977), says that here Chekhov confronts the disparity between aspiration and reality. Self-deception is the keynote of the story. Gurov is finally "convinced that only in his secret life with Anna is he sincere and free from self-deception." The ending gives the story's message: their continuing relationship will be both marvelous and exasperating. Jan van der Eng in 1978 evolved a descriptive theory of poetics to account for this story's narration. The main issue stressed is Gurov's growing self-knowledge.[53]

Stowell (1980) calls this story Chekhov's finest impressionistic achievement. It surrounds every impression, thought, and feeling with "the opacity of ambiguity and change. Gurov perceives only bits and pieces of his past and present. Love becomes the perfect impressionistic subject, because it is so responsive to change, so evanescent, and so dependent upon the subjective perceptions of both lovers.

Part One suggests the languid filling of time, Part Two the oppressive atmosphere of timelessness, Part Three the winter grayness of loss, and Part Four their drift toward their uncertain future." Anna grows to become central to the core of Gurov's being. His whole attitude towards women changes because of Anna.

A.M. Turkov in 1980 discussed Tolstoy's and Chekhov's attitudes on women and love, as seen in their differing comments on this story. Kirk (1981) noted Anna's change. At first she has conscience pangs about the adultery. By the end of the story she has love pangs over the breakup of the romance. Nabokov (1981) observed that the story begins *in medias res*. "The unexpected little turns and light touches," Nabokov says, "place Chekhov, above all Russian writers of fiction, on the level of Gogol and Tolstoy." Despite the fact that he broke all of the traditional rules of story telling (no problem, no regular climax, no point at the end), Chekhov gave us "one of the greatest stories ever written." Chekhov's typical features are a natural method of narration; exact and rich characterization; no message; waves of shades of mood; and a story that does not end, any more than life does. Nabokov believes that the seemingly insignificant trifles create the real atmosphere of the story.

Basu (1985) disagrees with Soviet critic N.Y. Berkovsky, who said that the love of Anna and Gurov is "without character as they themselves are." Chekhov clearly shows, says Basu, "that love brings about great spiritual changes in the lives of Gurov and Anna," changes that "love without character" could not achieve. Just as Tagore in his story "Punishment" uses the eve of a storm to presage the tension of a murder scene, so Chekhov uses the eve of a storm to imply the breaking away from the old values by Gurov and Anna, Basu says.

Clyman (1985) provides views on this story by Kenneth A. Lantz, Ralph Lindheim, and Victor Terras. Lantz admired the gradual release of exposition concerning the facts of Gurov's life. Lindheim found all of modern Russian life castigated: provincial towns for banality, and Moscow for card playing, gluttony, and drunkenness. Terras believed that this story may have been Chekhov's polemic response to an 1891 story that Tolstoy liked, "Mimochka Taking the Waters" by L.I. Veselitskaya. Tolstoy disliked "The Lady with a Dog" because of its Nietzschean blurring of the distinction between good and evil.

"The Man in a Case" (1898)

Burkin, a teacher, tells Ivan, a veterinarian, the life story of Burkin's fellow teacher Belikov, who carried his pen in a case, his umbrella in a case—indeed, he himself seemed as if he were always wrapped up in a case. He loved to prohibit students from doing things. After many years of bachelorhood he fell for Varvara, sister of a geography teacher, but he keeps postponing the marriage. One day he sees Varvara and her brother riding bicycles—this is entirely too modern for Belikov, and so he chides the brother for misconduct. The brother throws Belikov down the stairs—seeing him there, Varvara laughs at him. A month later he dies and is put into his final case: a coffin. Burkin concludes his story saying that most of us are in some sort of a self-made case.

Chekhov's diary for 18 August 1896 suggests that Belikov was modeled after the journalist M.O. Menshikov. Angel Bogdanovich in 1898 stated that Chekhov's striking objectivity, which led to his being called indifferent, is not found in this story, since he often uses Ivan as his mouthpiece. K.P. Medvedsky that year said that Chekhov lacked philosophic depth and a compelling world-view.[54] A.L. Flekser in 1900 praised Chekhov for probing the spiritual depths of modern man.

In 1916 M.V. Trofimov called this story the high point of Chekhov's creative genius, for "the delightful compactness of form, the keen observation, the graphic painting, the pessimistic idealism inspired by shallowness of life and longing to see it sublime."[55] Chekhov's brother Michael, in Koteliansky (1925), said that Belikov's prototype was a Taganrog teacher, Alexander Diakonov, who always dressed and talked the same way, and who never forgave a breach of school rules.

Werth (1925) felt that this tale is weakened by its unusually satirical tone. The story is both entertaining and frightening. Belikov's big fear, that "something might happen," could be stifled only by death. In 1935 A.M. Linin published an anthology that included a study of the biographical sources of this story.[56]

Bruford (1948) found this to be far more than an amusing anecdote. Belikov is suspicious of any projected change, even the formation of a drama club. On his trip to Sakhalin Chekhov found people on the Amur River freely expressing their beliefs aloud, something no one would dare do in Moscow. Ivan states the theme of the story: "Not to declare openly that you are on the side of the honest, free people — no, we cannot go on living like this." M.P. Gushchin in 1954 pointed up Chekhov's criticism of reactionary social policies.

Ermilov (1956) declared this story remarkable for its poetic atmosphere of freedom. Belikov, he said, was not only fearful but ridiculous and pitiable. "Chekhov's optimism," said Ermilov, "was of the hard kind, uncompromising and austere." Avram Derman in 1959 used this story to show the workings of Chekhov's poetics. Vadim Nazarenko in 1961 demonstrated that the story's "frame" fit very well into the chain of imagery, giving it a much broader range of application.[57]

Simmons (1962) found Belikov not only ridiculous but sinister, for he demanded that everyone else should be in a shell, preferably his. In 1966 Joseph L. Conrad stated that the story presented two of Chekhov's favorite themes: concern for personal freedom and for moral responsibility.[58] Winner (1966) noted how Belikov always covered himself with his clothing, wearing high collars and dark glasses. As Chekhov says, the ancient languages he taught were the galoshes and umbrella behind which Belikov hid from life's realities. Burkin says that Belikov's influence on a town is to make everyone fearful of everything.

Kramer (1970) finds ambiguity in Chekhov's use of the "case" or "shell" concept. For example, at the story's end Ivan sees the whole village as in a shell, but a pleasant one of peace and serenity. Chudakov (1971) deemed the exaggerated manner of character depiction very uncharacteristic of the mature Chekhov.

Hingley (1975) sees Belikov as one of Chekhov's most famous characters, the one who most wholeheartedly sacrificed freedom, Chekhov's highest value, for elaborate and unnecessary restrictions, some of which are self-imposed. Chekhov's notebook on this story said, "Lying in his coffin, he seemed to smile, having attained his ideal." Rayfield (1975), finding a Gogolian grotesqueness in Belikov, says that he preys by denouncing others.

E.S. Dobin and Vadim Nazarenko criticized this story in Hulanicki (1976). Dobin views it as unusual for Chekhov to state a straightforward message through Ivan: "Do we in the city lead a better life, wasting our time in playing cards, idle conversation, and gossip?" Nazarenko comments that Chekhov finds excellent "staging" for his stories. Seeing Mavra, the church elder's wife, Ivan is reminded how wasteful it is for so promising a person to remain uneducated and unappreciated. He is thus motivated to deliver his tirade favoring change.

M.M. Girshman in 1977 showed how, in this story, beneath Chekhov's apparently smooth style lay complex, disharmonious elements. David E. Maxwell, in Debreczeny (1977), asserts that the story's organizing principle is repetition. Most repetitions relate to Belikov's efforts to isolate himself, or to restrict the actions or imaginations of town dwellers. The phrase "You can't tell what might come from it" occurs seven times in the story. The subjunctive mood is used a lot, for people are either hoping or fearing that something will happen. Richard Wear states that Ivan is not Chekhov's spokesman, and that the theme of the story is the "possession" of people by an overwhelming concern that inhibits their communication.[59]

Kirk (1981) reports that the novelist Joseph Conrad found parallels between Belikov and Dostoevsky's "underground man," except that where Belikov enslaves others, Dostoevsky's man wishes to free them. L. Lieber in 1982 showed that, like Gogol, Chekhov "humanized" space, so that the characters exist within proscribed and oppressive containments. In this allegory, Belikov is the only Chekhov character who reacts to stimuli like an animal, whereas Gogol had many such characters, avers Bitsilli (1983). Harvey Pitcher, in Clyman (1985), quotes Ronald Hingley that this story shows the style of the early Chekhonte, Chekhov's pseudonym when he was writing sketches for popular humorous magazines.

"The New Villa" (1899)

Rayfield (1975) summarizes the plot: Kutcherov, an engineer, builds a new villa near the village where he is supervising the construction of a new bridge. He and his wife try to help the peasants, but they steal materials, break fences, and let their pigs trample the villa's garden. When the bridge is finished, Kutcherov and his wife move back to Moscow. When the bridge deteriorates through lack of maintenance, the peasants say, "We never wanted a bridge here."

Peasants view life differently than Kutcherov does, says Kramer (1970) – here Chekhov is showing the relativity of truth. Laffitte (1971) notes how Chekhov can suggest ugliness by brief but ferocious similes; in a fight between a father and a son, they are likened to foul beasts, spiders, and monstrous puppets. Hingley (1975) observed that in the year that Chekhov wrote the story, he built himself a new villa in Yalta. The engineer can bridge the river, says Hingley, but not the gap separating him from the peasants. The professional class and the peasants live in two different worlds, according to Hingley (1976). The blacksmith Rodion and his wife are one of the few happily married couples in Chekhov, Hingley states, and this may be attributed to the fact that, as peasants, they are uneducated. Nabokov (1981) notices that Chekhov wisely makes the old peasant who mouths pithy maxims not the traditional "wise man," but a crabby, lazy person—and the effect is more realistic.

"On Official Business" (1899) ("On Official Duty")

The plot is summarized in Rayfield (1975): Lyzhin, a young deputy examining magistrate, is investigating a suicide. Delayed by a snowstorm he spends a night in the hut where the man killed himself. He talks to the village constable, who describes the monotony of his work on official business. Lyzhin also spends a night at the home of the cultured Von Taunitz family; the contrast with the peasant life shocks him. Lyzhin has a nightmare in which the dead man's corpse returns to say, "We take all the burdens of life—ours, and *yours!*" When he awakens, Lyzhin feels that all people are part of a universal whole, and hence there must be some link, however dimly discernible, between the life of the peasants and the life of the cultured class.

Ermilov (1956) reports that after his nightmare, Lyzhin feels a deep responsibility to help bridge the gap between the rich and the poor. Tolstoy admired the warm human sympathy shown in the story, said Simmons (1962). The storm symbolizes life, to Kramer (1970). Lyzhin says that he too would have been a victim of this village, of boredom if not of murder. In fact, Lyzhin feels like a murderer, realizing that people have to live in the provinces so that he can live in Moscow. Chekhov imposes the pattern of a detective story over the plot, says Kramer, thereby intensifying Lyzhin's feeling of guilt.

Jerome H. Katsell in 1974 stated that Chekhov's technique of using a few significant details enables him to compress the complex process of character development and change.[60] Hingley (1975) finds Lyzhin a mouthpiece for Chekhov, and says the overworked constable is based upon the one that Chekhov had worked with in Melikhovo. Hingley (1976) notes that by now Chekhov shows a deep concern for social justice, such as he revealed in his stand on the Dreyfus affair. Avram Derman and G.N. Pospelov discuss this story in Hulanicki (1976). Derman finds the ending very effective—Chekhov uses no tricks, but brings out an old but hidden thought, thereby provoking the reader to think about the story's theme. Pospelov is pleased to see that the great contrast between the carefree life of the landowners and the hopelessness of the peasants' life disturbs Lyzhin deeply.

Maurice Valency, in Barricelli (1981), says it may have been the symbolist influence on Chekhov that led him to describe Lyzhin's unexpected flash of insight: "Everything is filled with a universal idea, everything has one soul, one aim." Valency said that Chekhov had periodic intuitions of a world soul, possibly Hegelian in character: "It was a concept that sorted badly with his generally skeptical and scientific materialism, but it served to rationalize the idealistic strain that was at the core of his feeling of kinship with humanity, and the real concern for the suffering of others that eventually sent him to Sakhalin." Egri (1986) finds this story sounding the theme of *The Three Sisters*. Meeting the cultured daughters of Von Taunitz, Lyzhin feels sorry for their being cut off from contact with higher centers of culture.

"A Visit to Friends" (1898)

Rayfield (1975) tells the plot. Lawyer Podgorin tries to help the Losevs save their estate. He knows he is expected to propose to their beautiful daughter Nadezhda, but he is too shy. Poems spoken by his friend Varya disturb him, and make him dream of some ideal future, but meanwhile he sacrifices a good present.

Yarmolinsky (1954) felt no great sympathy for the Losevs in this "tale of disenchantment that mixes melancholy with scorn." The note of revolt in this story is found only in the late Chekhov, Yarmolinsky believes. Ermilov (1956) says Podgorin's reluctance to marry Nadezhda grows out of his fear that her conventional view of marital happiness would bore him. He prefers a woman who would see love "as a challenge to new forms of life, elevated and rational, on the eve of which we perhaps already stand." Chekhov perceived, said Ermilov, that a new beauty was about to enter life.

Chudakov (1971) analyzed Podgorin's character. As a lawyer he is arrogant, but as a private person he is timid. He leaves all difficult decisions to the judge and the jury, for he becomes upset if he has to make decisions. Smith (1973) identifies Chekhov with Podgorin; both would like to talk about "the new noble way of life," but not engage in it.

Toby W. Clyman in 1978 noted that this story has characters, plot elements, scenes, and situations that parody Pushkin's *Eugene Onegin*.[61] Bitsilli (1983) called this story an experiment in experiencing the present as it retreats into the past. He quotes Chekhov's description of Podgorin: "He loved Nadezhda and Varya dearly but more, it seemed, as memories than as they really were. The present seemed unreal and alien to him." Podgorin, Bitsilli notes, is the prototype for Lopakhin in *The Cherry Orchard*.

Summary—Stories: 1898–1904

Some of Chekhov's best stories, in the opinion of critics, appeared during these years, when he was at his peak as a major modern dramatist. Several critics commented on how dramatic form was used as a structural principle in these stories.

Five stories of this period rank among Chekhov's best. "The Betrothed," an excellent character study, was seen by some to presage the coming revolution, and by others as the struggle and the cost of making a brave personal commitment. "The Bishop," all agreed, was a study in personal identity which tenderly evoked a sincere religious atmosphere. Most critics agreed with Tolstoy that Olga, in "The Darling," seems ludicrous and yet she loves in order to live—disagreement ensued over how much of this ambiguity was intentional on Chekhov's part. "In the Ravine" was praised by Tolstoy, Gorky, and most critics for its plot, characters, and theme. The story showed how industrialism ruins a village, bringing in its wake pollution, selfishness, envy, cruelty, and false lives. Virtually all critics applauded the characterization in "The Lady with a Dog," in which a roué finds out for the first time what real love is like.

This period saw a rare Chekhov trilogy of stories, all using the same "frame" of characters and themes, and all dealing with a "possessed" person who acts in an abnormal fashion. "About Love" shows the frustration of platonic love. "Gooseberries" is a diatribe against selfishness. "The Man in a Case" shows the social cost of an individual whose fear of life is pathological.

Two stories depict frustrated love: "Ionych" and "A Visit to Friends." As he neared death, Chekhov became more explicit in writing stories of social protest. "At Christmas Time" exposes the exploitation of a wife by her husband, and of an old couple by an ex-soldier. "The New Villa" attacks the backwardness of peasants. "On Official Duty" is an impassioned protest against the rich for exploiting the poor.

Finally, Tolstoy's influence on Chekhov's fiction can be seen right up to Chekhov's death in 1904. Although Chekhov wrote many stories attacking Tolstoy's theory of non-resistance to evil (thereby dispelling once and for all the myth that Chekhov was morally neutral), still the Russian giant's shadow loomed over the writings of this sensitive and humane physician. Critics found Tolstoy's *The Power of Darkness* in "In the Ravine," and *Anna Karenina* in "The Lady with a Dog." Tolstoy may have been right when he admitted that Chekhov was a greater artist of fiction than he was, but Chekhov also may have been correct in stating that great artists, like Tolstoy, seize the reader and move him towards some great goal of society—an effect which Chekhov could only begin to achieve through indirection, subtlety, and buried humanitarianism.

9. Letters; *Sakhalin Island; The Shooting Party*

Since Chekhov has often been called one of the world's great letter writers, and since his letters open windows of understanding into the nature of his achievements as a literary and dramatic artist, it is profitable to trace what critics of his letter writing have said during the past century. Chekhov's plays puzzled early critics, and even his fiction was considered to be pessimistic by many early reviewers. The publication of his letters was a marked influence in getting a more sympathetic hearing for his plays, and in helping develop a more discriminating appreciation of his stories. Ultimately the function of his letters was to drive home the realization that this Russian writer was humane and moral through and through.

Leonid Grossman in 1914, quoted in Jackson (1967), shows how Chekhov's letters revealed his attitude towards Tolstoy. On the one hand he admired the art of *The Kreutzer Sonata* and *War and Peace*, but he excoriated Tolstoy's lack of medical knowledge. In no way could Prince Andrey in *War and Peace* smell of putrefaction, Chekhov said, adding, "I could have cured Prince Andrey of his malady." Yuri Eichenwald in 1915 called Chekhov's letters works of art, revealing not only the "beauty, modesty, and purity of Chekhov's spirit," but also his loneliness and private sorrows.[1]

Robert Birkmyre, reviewing a volume of Chekhov letters in 1919, said that Chekhov most closely resembled Heine and Burns—the motto of the letters was "Love one another." These letters, said Birkmyre, showed a personality far from being isolated from Russia's current intellectual problems. A shrewd and able critic, Chekhov gave many acute appraisals of other Russian writers. At times he would proscribe Russian critics for their pettiness, cruelty, and lack of sensitivity. He could also point out the limits of Zola's naturalism. For the artist, he said, the moral law is higher than the purely biological law, and so attempts to idealize sex perversion, for example, would inevitably leave readers with a final deep sense of dissatisfaction. Birkmyre concluded that Chekhov's era of stagnation was fortunate in having as an interpreter a man with such kindly understanding and keen intellect.[2]

Constance Garnett's translation of Chekhov's letters in 1920 evoked many favorable reviews in England and America. *The London Mercury* called the book a manual on the craft of short fiction,[3] and *The Spectator* found wisdom – rare, it said, among Russians – in Chekhov's comments on esthetics and philosophy.[4] One reviewer believed that Chekhov's credo of personal freedom clearly emanated from the letters.[5] Maurice Baring stated that the letters showed Chekhov's personal charm, his love of landscape, his faith in people, and "the quiet aura of goodness that surrounded him."[6] Edmund Gosse reported Chekhov's two motives to be "an insatiable curiosity about life, and an irresistible impulse to fix his observation in durable form."[7] Robert Lynd attacked previous critics who had called Chekhov gloomy. If there ever was a writer with a faith in the decency of man, it was Chekhov, Lynd asserted. Chekhov was seen as a compassionate doctor making his literary rounds in a sick world.[8] J. Middleton Murry said that the letters provided a prime opportunity to examine some of the "chief constituents of the perfect art" of "the only great modern artist in prose, a standard by which modern literary effort must be measured." Chekhov's greatness, for Murry, lay in "a rigorous intellectual and moral honesty that revealed a candor of soul and a pureness of heart."[9] George Sampson found the letters "a delight to read," being the spontaneous theorizing of an unbiased artist that brought the reader a little nearer to the heart of Chekhov's art.[10] Only Edward Garnett (1921), though he called Chekhov "a saint" and "a hero," demurred from granting Chekhov unique praise as a critic of his era; Garnett said that Chekhov was merely the spokesman for thousands of Russian intellectuals who had worked for a freer and more just social system.

American reviewers of Constance Garnett's translated letters were scarcely less laudatory than their British counterparts. Many critics commented on the spontaneous humor and levity found in the letters. One focused on the saneness of vision and the balanced outlook – an absence of "humbug" that preserved "a real flick of vitality" upon each page. He went on to say that the letters made a person feel "that he is in genuinely personal contact with a man about ten times more real than are most men."[11] John Mason Brown noticed that Chekhov's fearless and accurate appraisals of fellow writers' works were always constructive, "especially interesting because they are followed by his own solution of the problem. His continual plea was for simplicity."[12] Francis Hackett applauded Chekhov's distaste for magniloquence, and listed his two fundamental traits – he was thoroughly unaffected, and he has a profound belief in personal freedom and in the importance of individual persons.[13] Robert Morss Lovett said that the most important function of a writer's letters was to show how his life experiences became the substance of his art, and that in this regard Chekhov's letters were most revealing. Lovett said that a letter to Suvorin, for example, was indispensable for understanding *Ivanov*.[14] William Lyon Phelps contrasted Chekhov's letters, the work of "a splendidly healthy mind," with those of Dostoevsky, which aroused dislike that could only be overcome by recalling Dostoevsky's illness, courage, and genius.[15]

J. Middleton Murry, reviewing Gerhardi (1923), presented a detailed analysis of the "amazing letters" which are "simple and strange in a new way. They seem more natural than any letters we have ever read, yet unlike all others. They are informed by a new consciousness." Although they are simple, "we sense in that simplicity a complete knowledge of all the complexities with which the modern consciousness is laden. Chekhov has somehow passed beyond all this." Gerhardi is right—Chekhov is far in advance of Joyce and Proust. "By his side they are curious antiquarian survivals of a superseded past." Chekhov's simplicity undercuts "their illimitable intellectualisms."[16] Murry's wife, Katherine Mansfield, like Chekhov dying of tuberculosis, spent many of her last days reading Chekhov's final letters, terrible in their lack of hope, seeming to say, "I never had a real chance. Something has been all wrong."[17]

Reviewers continued to show their gratitude when Louis S. Friedland (1924) translated Chekhov's letters on literary topics. Several critics called the work "a useful reference book to the student of the drama and the short story,"[18] and another stated that these letters, not one of which was dull, showed the conscious side of Chekhov's art.[19] Johan Smertenko observed that the letters revealed Chekhov's personality, which was hidden in his objective stories and plays.[20] Leo Wiener chastised Friedland for the poor quality of his translations.[21]

Koteliansky (1925) brought out views by Chekhov's brother Michael and E. Zamyatin. Michael Chekhov stated that the letters revealed his brother's low opinion of the theater and of actors. Zamyatin noted that many letters referred to Chekhov's need for money, but usually stated in a typical half-joking manner.

D.S. Mirsky said that Koteliansky (1925) was a "needed" volume, containing all of the essential letters of the Russian six-volume edition.[22] One reviewer noted how Chekhov adapted each letter to the very "soul" of his correspondent,[23] and another named Chekhov as "one of the best letter writers in the world."[24] Iris Barry wondered how anyone seeing his love of mankind could call Chekhov gloomy, [25] and John Freeman called this book "a whole gospel of esthetic righteousness."[26] J.B. Priestley found an explanation why Chekhov's "enormous influence" was already apparent in the best short-story writers, in Chekhov's vivid imagination, exquisite capacity for significant detail, and evocation of atmosphere.[27] Leonard Woolf observed that not even the most captious critic could find anyone but "a character of extraordinary charm" behind these letters.[28] Another reviewer said that each page of the book revealed some aspect of Chekhov's "searching, compassionate genius": his practicality, spiritual insight, and utter truthfulness.[29]

American reviewers of Koteliansky (1925) continued to receive the letters warmly. Rosamond Gilder hailed them for their revelation of Chekhov's mind at work,[30] and Robert Littell found them disclosing the secret of Chekhov's art in his "marvelously representative selectivity and his supreme gift of anonymity."[31] Robert Morss Lovett, prizing the letters for Chekhov's "exposition and defense of his art," now ranked Chekhov with the Russian giants—Dostoevsky, Tolstoy, and Turgenev.[32] Calling Chekhov a definite part of contemporary American literary currents, Stuart Sherman defied "any intelligent reader to resist the fascination of his high spirits, delicious humor, artistic alertness, critical penetration, steady good sense, and sensitiveness to the ideas of his time."[33] The letters were not only excellent guides to the art of short-story writing, claimed Pitirim Sorokin, but were also indispensable in understanding Chekhov's achievement as a writer.[34] Jacob Zeitlin admired Chekhov's zest for life, and said that he had become acquainted with "the invigorating energy of a soul in love with truth and nobility."[35]

Chekhov's letters to his wife, translated by Constance Garnett, elicited further opinions in 1926. Some reviewers found them to be his most intimate and charming letters, especially those in which he acted as a gloom chaser for Olga. D.S. Mirsky demurred, saying that these commonplace letters would never have been published, except for the "strange infection in the air" of English Chekhovism.[36] The following year, however, Mirsky was willing to grant that Chekhov was Russia's third best letter writer, after Pushkin and Vladimir Solovyov.

In 1928 John Cournos reviewed a collection of Russian letters edited by N.K. Piksanov. Cournos noted Chekhov's dissatisfaction at not having written a satisfactory novel. Chekhov knew that a novel required more than a string of short-story episodes. In 1888 he confessed, "I haven't yet any political, religious, or philosophical outlook on life. I change my outlook monthly, so I shall have to limit myself to descriptions of how my heroes love, marry, beget children, and die." The absence of such an outlook, Cournos felt, accounts for Chekhov's success as a short-story writer—he had detachment and terseness to present a portrait without preaching.[37]

A review of hitherto-unpublished letters in 1931 confirmed that Chekhov had narrowly missed being blackballed by the Writers' Union for Mutual Assistance on the grounds that his story "Peasants" was a "reactionary" production. Noting that four volumes of recently discovered works by Chekhov had been published in 1930, the reviewer felt that year might be described as "the time of the second coming of Chekhov."[38]

In 1937 S.D. Balukhaty edited the Chekhov-Gorky correspondence. Toumanova (1937) observed that Chekhov loved to write letters, and so on his trip to Sakhalin he gave a full description of every changing scene. Of himself, he said that he looked so ragged that "even tramps squinted at him!" James T. Farrell in 1940 recommended to short-story writers that they read the letters of Chekhov and Dostoevsky, and the short stories of Chekhov, Joyce, and Maupassant.

Josephson (1948) admired Chekhov's extreme honesty, as revealed in his letters. Chekhov had a horror of anything resembling bombast, and he liked to make fun of himself in his correspondence. "He is so charmingly unaffected," said Josephson, "that to read his letters is to enter his study and sit down at ease to listen to him."

Hellman (1955) pointed out how Chekhov's letters charted his change and growth. For example, in 1890 he angrily defended himself when Vukol Lavrov, editor of *Russian Thought,* called him "a writer without principles." But in 1892 he told Suvorin that the trouble with modern Russian writers, including himself, was that "we have neither near nor remote aims," and that "he who wants nothing, hopes for nothing, and fears nothing cannot be an artist." Seemingly as Chekhov grew more secure he became more honest.

Ehrenburg (1962) judged Sophie Laffitte wrong to say, based on Chekhov's letters, that he was a profoundly indifferent person. His letters also said that he was lazy, had no talent, and that his life and writings were useless. "Such self-denigration was dictated by a remarkable humility," Ehrenburg said. Simmons (1962) noted that Chekhov's letters to Suvorin from 1897 to 1899 dealt with student unrest and the Dreyfus affair, and are fervent statements on behalf of freedom of conscience and freedom of the press, and in opposition to anti–Semitism.

Nils Ake Nilsson in 1968 made a detailed study of the style of Chekhov's letters. He found an increasing use of biblical and Church Slavonic expressions, foreign phrases, colloquialisms, neologisms, and slang. Displaying great lexical richness, the letters are the linguistic laboratory for his prose, Nilsson said.[39]

A new note was struck by Melchinger (1972), who said that his contemporaries feared Chekhov's sharp tongue. "The innumerable letters he wrote are full of vitriolic and pertinent comments. Each proves that he was not merely observing what was before him but also looking through and behind it." The letters are full of contradictions, Melchinger said. "They were not written for publication. They are expressions of his temperament, his state of mind, his fleeting thoughts, and his physical health. Above all, they are words addressed to particular persons. Chekhov had an uncommon sensitivity to people. He had a talent for human beings."

Simon Karlinsky, in Heim (1973), praised Constance Garnett's translations of Chekhov's letters, but severely criticized Friedland (1924) and Hellman (1955) for inaccurate renditions. In his collection, Heim eliminated trivial letters in favor of those giving a comprehensive picture of Chekhov's literary, social, and scientific views.

Yarmolinsky (1973) summarized the publication history of Chekhov's letters. In 1909 a collection of 325 letters appeared. Between 1912 and 1916 Chekhov's sister Masha edited nearly 1900 more. A few years later 900 more were published, including the collection to Olga Knipper in 1924. From 1948 to 1951 eight volumes (with 4200 items) were published as a part of the 20-volume collected works of Chekhov. During the 1950s and 1960s a two-volume edition of Chekhov's letters sold 1,500,000 copies in the U.S.S.R. Chekhov archives in Moscow contain 7000 letters addressed to him. The Soviet government has censored parts of Chekhov's letters, especially those containing crude expressions, "unpatriotic" references to Russia, and references to people like Vsevolod Meyerhold, who have been purged by the government. Gleb Struve has also analyzed the editorial tampering by the Russian government with Chekhov's letters.[40]

Insight into Chekhov as a man and as a writer can be found in Yarmolinsky (1973). Chekhov is seen as a man with irrepressible humor, strong family feeling, and an enthusiastic gusto for life, including foods. There is much agreement and disagreement with Suvorin. There are some contradictions; for example, this agnostic seldom ended a letter without invoking a heavenly blessing upon the addressee. His warm relationship with his wife is shown: "Few of his stories equal the pathos, veined with jocularity, of these pages." Inwardly, Chekhov was a free man, and "his honesty was equal to his humanity," said Yarmolinsky.

N.I. Gitovich in 1974 summarized Chekhov's epistolary career. E.A. Polotskaya that year furnished explanatory notes for Chekhov's letters written between 1875 and 1886.[41] Hingley (1976) discussed Soviet censorship of the letters. V.S. Pritchett, reviewing collections of letters in 1979, noted that Chekhov's comedy lay in the collision of solitudes, as he catches people acting out their inner lives.

Kirk (1981) recalled Chekhov's letter to Dmitry Grigorovich in 1886 thanking him for Grigorovich's praise of his talent: "Your letter struck me like lightning. I almost cried, I was overwhelmed by emotion. It astonished me, leaving a deep trace in my soul." "Never again," Kirk observed, "was Chekhov to write such an emotional and naked letter."

In 1983 L.D. Opulskaya edited the index to the Soviet edition of Chekhov's letters. The index includes references to Chekhov's works, his pseudonyms, his addressees, and the names mentioned in the letters. Kenneth A. Lantz in 1985 summarized the proof that Chekhov was no gloomy pessimist: "One need read only a few of his delightful letters to discover a very different Chekhov, a man of bubbling humor, gentle self-mockery, and immense charm."[42]

Sakhalin Island

Sakhalin, a bleak island between the Tatar Strait and the Sea of Okhotsk, was used as a governmental penal colony. In 1890 Chekhov read a number of books on criminal law, Russian prisons, Siberian penal colonies, and other scientific and travel books, and then traveled 6000 miles across Siberia to visit the Sakhalin penal colony. His three-month journey eastward took him through Perm, Omsk, Tomsk, Krasnoyarsk, Irkutsk, Chita, Blagoveshchensk, and Nikolaevsk. He went by carriage, boat, and train.

He spent three months on Sakhalin, interviewing all of the 10,000 prisoners and their families. The detailed records he kept were useful to him when he wrote *Sakhalin Island*, the history of his trip, in 1893. The return trip of nearly two months was relaxing. Suvorin tried to get him to return via the United States, but Chekhov vetoed the plan as too expensive and too dull. Instead he sailed home by way of Hong Kong, Singapore, Port Said, Constantinople, and Odessa. Crossing the Indian Ocean in hot, humid weather, he brashly jumped into the sea and swam around the boat, being picked up by a rope flung to him from the stern.

When asked why he made the trip, Chekhov's replies were indirect. He was depressed over the death of his brother Nikolai. He was tired of hearing critics call him morally neutral. He may have been escaping from a broken love relationship. Above all, he was bored—he was at a critical juncture in the development of his literary style, and he needed a breathing spot, a change of scenery, while he re-established his priorities and prepared himself for his future career.

Letters he wrote at this time, as recorded in Koteliansky (1925), show his current frame of mind. He told Suvorin that "the glorified sixties did nothing for the sick and the prisoners, and thus violated the chief commandment of Christian civilization." Questioned about his morality by his friend Jean Shcheglov, Chekhov replied that there was "only one morality, namely that which in olden times gave to us Jesus Christ, and now prevents us from stealing, insulting, and lying." Incensed at Russian travelers who accused the British of exploiting Asians, Chekhov answered, "I thought, yes, the English exploit the Chinese, the Sepoys, the Hindus, but for that they give them roads, water supplies, museums, Christianity – and you also exploit, but what do you give them?"

Critics were unanimous in asserting that *Sakhalin Island* proved conclusively Chekhov's deep humanitarian concerns. This view was expressed in an anthology of critical articles edited by V.I. Pokrovsky in 1907, as well as in Koteliansky (1925). The latter source quoted Chekhov's description of his book to Suvorin: "It should live a hundred years after me as a literary source and guide to all who are at work, or are interested in, the penitentiary system. The chapter on runaways and vagrants has turned out to be interesting and instructive." Mirsky (1927) called the book "an important historical document – remarkable for its thoroughness, objectivity, and impartiality."

Toumanova (1937) recalled the origin of the trip as related by Chekhov's brother Michael. One day, reading the penal code, Chekhov said that convicts are of public interest only during their trials, and then are completely forgotten. He immediately began to plan the trip, but no one took him seriously. Family and friends warned him of the risk to his health but on 9 March 1889 he told Suvorin that he had "Mania Sakhalinosa. Sakhalin is a place of unbearable sufferings. To such places we should go on a pilgrimage as Turks go to Mecca." He traveled with the credentials of a newspaper reporter. On Sakhalin he gave special attention to children as the innocent victims of someone else's crime. Although the trip exhausted his finances, as well as his body, he told Suvorin in 1894, "I am glad that these stiff prison overalls hang in my literary wardrobe."

Chekhov's friend Kornei Chukovsky (1945) was disappointed at the style of writing in Chekhov's book. It was an important scholarly work, Chukovsky conceded, but much weaker than anything else Chekhov ever wrote because it lacks Chekhov himself – his language, vivid images, and gentle personality. Here we have the scientist minus the poet, a grave lack.

Bruford (1948) remarked that the administrators of the penal colony were friendly and helpful to Chekhov. Chekhov was shocked to find whole villages where no one was legally married. Hingley (1950) points out that Chekhov was impatient writing "The Duel," because he wanted to write this book. He spent several years on it, including research in St. Petersburg to reinforce some of his findings. He wanted to produce an authoritative scientific work. Since he was unfamiliar with non-fiction, he struggled to arrive at the appropriate tone. Hingley feels he succeeded in making it both objective and "extremely readable, a shining example of what a research thesis can be."

Hingley thinks that the book achieved Chekhov's main purpose of informing the Russian people about the unpleasant facts of penal life. When it appeared it was widely discussed in St. Petersburg and Moscow, and "had considerable influence both in Russia and abroad." It amazingly not only passed the censorship but impressed the Department of Prison Administration, which sent an investigative team to Sakhalin that confirmed Chekhov's findings. Even though no sweeping prison reform resulted, Chekhov felt that at last he had repaid his "debt to medicine."

Magarshack (*Life*, 1952) felt that in this book Chekhov's medical training was a handicap, because it screened out his creative genius in the interests of "science." In letters to Suvorin Chekhov described his dilemma—he wanted an objective work, but he also wanted to move his readers. When he finally let himself go, he said, and described "what awful swine some of the officials were," he found the writing progressing rapidly.

Yarmolinsky (1954) called "Yegor's Story" in this book "a literary gem." Yegor's uncouth talk does not hide his immense hatred of the juggernaut of the state. Whether Yegor is guilty of murder is not disclosed, but his story reveals the cruel power of accident. Ermilov (1956) recalled Chekhov's statement that "not more than 25 or 30 years ago some Russians investigating Sakhalin accomplished remarkable feats, feats which incline one to worship man." Ermilov felt that Chekhov had finally found his "great goal" in life—adoption of a more humane penal code. He unified two aspects of his nature, the poetic and the scientific. He also struck a blow against autocracy, a society of exploiters. The more objective Chekhov was in his presentation, Ermilov said, the more effective was his indictment.

In an anthology of critical articles edited by K.I. Kniazeva and others in 1959, five of the articles dealt with the trip and this book.[43] Returning from Sakhalin, said Simmons (1962), Chekhov wrote that "God's world is good. It is only we who are bad. One must work, and to hell with everything else. The important thing is that we must be just, and all the rest will come as a matter of course." Chekhov hoped to teach medicine and use this book as his dissertation for the degree of Doctor of Medical Sciences, but he was turned down by the dean of the medical school. Chekhov's art in this book is based on careful selectivity, choosing items he knew would move readers. He turned dull passages from his sources into little gems.

In 1967 Luba and Michael Terpak brought out a new English translation of the book. Kenneth J. Atchity in 1968 stated that the book should not be considered simply a social document, for it is "literature in the making, the raw material of Chekhov's realism." Reading the book, he said, is like traveling with Dante through the Inferno.[44] Gilles (1968) said that Chekhov wrote a three-act play, *General Flirt*, ridiculing a high official on Sakhalin, but the manuscript is lost.

Laffitte (1971) recalled that 2700 miles of Chekhov's trip were by carriage. As he crossed Siberia, Chekhov wrote that "the lowliest of the deportees breathes more freely here than the greatest of generals in Russia." Chekhov's census of the Sakhalin residents was the first scientific census in Russia. In his book, Laffitte says, one discovers traces of anger, disgust, grief, and human tenderness. Stories growing out of the trip include "Gusev," "In Exile," "Murder," and "Peasant Women." One effect of his trip was to awaken his feeling of social protest; another effect was to rouse the poetic side of his nature, where he could dream, in his writing, about a better world.

In 1974 V.B. Kataev asserted that here Chekhov developed a new writing style, one that would lead a sensitive reader to action. Rayfield (1975) quoted Chekhov as saying that the book's weakness was its didactic intention. Chekhov was following the practice of American journalist George Kennan, whose accounts of Siberian exiles were underground literature in Russia at the time. Now Chekhov was finally admired by liberals who wanted governmental reform. Two results of the trip were his abandonment of romantic solutions to life's problems, and his discarding Tolstoy's theory of non-resistance to evil.

M.L. Semanova in 1976 made a study of the influence of the Sakhalin trip upon Chekhov's fiction.[45] Hingley (1976) said that this book stands with Dostoevsky's *The House of the Dead* and Tolstoy's *Resurrection* as the best of Russia's penological literature, and it exceeds those two works in being wholly factual. Chekhov deleted some material about kindly guards, fearing they might be punished if identified. The style of the book is "cool, light, objective, admirably controlled, free from pomposity and jargon." Reviews of the book helped create a pressure for prison reform. The public sent money, clothing, and books for the prisoners. At least one woman, after reading the book, devoted her life to welfare work on Sakhalin. This is one of the few works for which Chekhov claimed literary merit.

In 1977 E.A. Polotskaya studied how the Sakhalin trip influenced the writing of the story "Murder." Stanley E. Hyman in 1978 said that the book was "repetitious, too long, and full of pointless statistics," although he admitted that it showed many examples of human resilience and courage. M.L. Semanova that year made a study of the trip, the book, and criticism of the book.[46]

Tulloch (1980) states that Chekhov had a deep scientific commitment to life's improvement. Here he depicts two islands: the one he found, and the one as it should be. Joanne Troutman in 1981 said that Chekhov went to Sakhalin "to face in reality the most profound metaphor of his life, the prison," and to get the kind of release that neither medicine nor his writing could give him. His works are filled with various sorts of confinements, and with the unending quest for freedom.[47] In 1982 V.I. Kuleshov examined Chekhov's relationship toward naturalistic writers, and found some features of naturalism in this book.

McConkey (1984) points out that Chekhov liked both General Kononovich, the island commandant, and Baron Korf, governor-general of the entire region that included Sakhalin. The two leaders seemed determined to abolish chains and corporal punishment, and to help the "unfortunates" regain their full rights and liberties.

Despite its objectivity, Chekhov's book contains one indictment after another. He showed that infectious diseases were leading towards virtual genocide of the colony. Like his stories and plays, the book derives more from its "large structure" than from its story content or narrative movement. The last four chapters of the book, which were banned by the censors in the magazine publication, contain Chekhov's main points. The first of these chapters shows that the free population were all caught in a net of human indignity. The next chapter explores the morality of both the convicts and the settlers—everyone suffered spiritual paralysis. The following chapter indicates that everyone desires freedom so much that he tries to escape—the convicts by running away, and the officials by getting re-assigned. The final chapter contains Chekhov's specific recommendations for reform.

Upon his return to Moscow, Chekhov collected several thousand books for the Sakhalin schools. In 1903 flogging was eliminated on Sakhalin, and in 1904 the penal colony was discontinued there, perhaps because of the war with Japan. Chekhov felt that Sakhalin was too cold and non-arable to be a self-sustaining settlement. McConkey concludes: "Sakhalin gave Chekhov nothing he hadn't known all along. It proved the validity of his own intuitions. How strange that an impulse toward a freedom beyond one's self would grant mutuality with all other individuals!"

Troyat (1984) states that Chekhov joked that he had gathered so much material about Sakhalin that he would marry any girl capable of classifying it. He remarked that the usual literary squabbles seemed petty and pathetic after what he had seen on his trip.

Joseph L. Conrad, in Clyman (1985), recalls how Chekhov saw a doctor examine a convict to see how many more lashes he could stand. Not only prisoners but also guards and witnesses were coarsened by corporal punishment. Women, outnumbered four to one, seemed to be little more than purchasable property. Cohabitation between unmarried men and women was encouraged by both the administration and the clergy, in order to have children in the colony. The child bearing age for women seemed unusually high on Sakhalin, which Chekhov attributed to evolutionary causes—nature responded to the shortage of women and the adverse living conditions by keeping women fertile longer. Chekhov's literary talent appears in his depiction of the climate and the landscape, and also in his dramatized scenes with his interviewees. His picture of a wedding scene employs all of the literary tools of his best short stories. His compassion and art dramatize forgotten lives. For a change, his style is not indirect: "His straightforward criticism of governmental policies, specific individuals, and the administration of the colony as a whole are far different in style and temperament from his other literary works."

The Shooting Party (1894) (Drama on a Hunt)

The plot of Chekhov's only novel has an external "frame." A busy editor reluctantly agrees to read the mystery novel written by his friend Kamyshev, a former examining magistrate.

In the novel the narrator Zinovev, an examining magistrate, and his two friends, Count Alexey and the count's bailiff Urbenin, vie for the affections of beautiful young Olga, daughter of a forester. Urbenin wins out, and Zinovev is best man at the wedding. At the wedding dinner, Olga confesses her love for Zinovev, who wants Olga to elope with him, but she refuses. The count and Zinovev continue to court married Olga. Olga leaves Urbenin, alleging that he beat her, and begins living with the count. He soon tires of changeable Olga, so Zinovev has an affair with her. Olga is stabbed to death after a hunting party, and Urbenin is found with blood-stained hands. When a peasant who saw the murder is about to testify, his dead body is found. As examining magistrate, Zinovev questions all the suspects and concludes that Urbenin is guilty. This judgment is agreed to by the count, the public prosecutor, and ultimately the court, which gives Urbenin a sentence of 15 years of hard labor. After eight years Urbenin dies and the count, an alcoholic, is penniless.

In the final "frame," Kamyshev confesses to the editor that Zinovev was really the murderer. He stabbed Olga when she admitted, while in Zinovev's embrace, that had she not been married to Urbenin, she would have married the count.

Chekhov's first biographer, A.A. Izmailov, said that Chekhov spent a lot of time on this novel, experimenting with how to develop a style for serious fiction. Izmailov said that the editor of *News of the Day,* the newspaper in which the novel appeared serially, had Chekhov prune certain lyrical passages in order to put a greater stress on the melodrama.

A.E. Chamot made the first translation of this novel into English in 1926. In his introduction Chamot analyzed the novel, which he called Chekhov's "most ambitious effort, at least with regard to length and complexity of plot." It was written in the style of the sensational novels of the period, Chamot said, rather than in the episodic style of Chekhov's later works. Although the reader finds in it "occasional awkward blendings of conventional phraseology with snatches of brilliant impressionism, it already shows many of Chekhov's characteristics." Chekhov at that time had been reporting law cases for a daily paper. "The insight he obtained into the backwash of many a crime probably weighed on his mind until it found expression in the present work, which is perhaps the blackest indictment of Russian provincial law courts ever written." Chamot found the dramatic interest well sustained throughout the novel. There are, however, signs of inexperience in the plot construction. Instead of a lengthy canvas filled with many characters, as the masters of the novel give, "his style rather resembles that of the impressionists, who with a few bold strokes bring out the salient points. We find already short word-pictures of nature that give the necessary atmosphere, a few pregnant words that denote the mood, while deeds express character without lengthy analysis." Because it shows signs of Chekhov's increasing power in the perfection of his technique, it will always be "a precious document for every student of Chekhov," Chamot concluded.

Reviewers of Chamot's translation were somewhat less sanguine. One of them thought it "pleasant and amusing" that Chekhov should be playing the literary game of concealment in this murder-mystery novel, but found that it did not create in the reader "an attentiveness of spirit and a quickened sense of humor," as all his mature writings did.[48] Another critic noted that the coordination between Chekhov and the assumed author Kamyshev was not carried out skillfully.[49] The unusual device of identifying the narrator with the murderer was said by one reviewer to be a good method of revealing the murderer's falsity and cunning, but the characters seem not to be "living and fresh," and the work lacked interest and suspense.[50]

Hingley (1950) called the novel excellent light reading, albeit uneven as to quality, with parts reading like a parody. Hingley felt that Chekhov had used "an extremely ingenious and surprise device" to conceal the murderer's identity. Ralph E. Matlaw, in Eekman (1960), said that Chekhov gave the public what it likes—a mystery story, written with considerable technical competence. The clever beginning, "A husband has killed his wife," turns out to be a parrot talking. As usual in this genre, the first section contains the sensational material and the second part reports the investigation of the murder. The reader is tricked into condoning the conduct of the narrator by his lame excuses, until finally he is unmasked as the culprit. There is in this work some discussion of the novel as a literary form. Rare in Chekhov is the use of uneconomical dialogue. There is also a mechanical double plot, with two orgies, two storms, and two murders. When the narrator's memory lapses, the other characters reveal the narrator's defects. Although A.A. Izmailov praised the nature description, in fact it is generally "literary" and trite. Apparently the novel form was incongruent with Chekhov's "essentially miniaturist skills," Matlaw said.

Simmons (1962) simply called this work "a short crime novel which to some extent parodies this genre, so popular at the time." Lucas (1963) was less generous, calling the plot crude and improbable, the nature description "thin," and the characters neurotic and impulsive. It shows just how badly Chekhov could write on occasion, Lucas concluded.

John Hagan in 1965 defended the novel. Although it has many structural weaknesses, Hagan said, it shows impressive mastery of the melodramatic thriller. While studying the form, Chekhov was at the same time lampooning it. The narrative techniques and themes appear in a more refined form in his later works. It represents one of the earliest efforts to give a comprehensive literary portrait of Russian society, Hagan felt.[51] N.Y. Berkovsky in 1966 pointed out that the play *Platonov* owed some of its material to this novel.

Winner (1966) agreed that this was a burlesque of the popular murder mystery: "Surprise endings, preceded by elaborate complications, including misleading clues and false evidence, caricature the traditional devices of the genre." Kramer

(1970) felt that the effort was a failure. Although the reader assumes that he is reading a detective story, for over half the novel no crime has been committed. Later writers of murder mysteries, such as Agatha Christie, used this plot of the narrator being the murderer. But Chekhov's plot, says Kramer, is in conflict with his theme, and therefore he could not possibly have written either a successful detective story or a satisfactory novel attacking detective-story clichés, for "the two elements are mutually destructive."

L.I. Vukulov in 1974 stated that this was no parody, but a serious attempt by Chekhov to write the sort of serialized "newspaper novel" that was popular at the time. Rayfield (1975) was not as harsh as Kramer. The novel reflects much of Chekhov's reading, Rayfield said, and contains embryonically much of what he was to write. Begun as a parody of Émile Gaboriau's style, in which an elaborate plot ends in an unpredictable denouement, it becomes an ingenious detective story and at times a substantial psychological novel. Although many details are pure parody, "much of the highly melodramatic action is so vividly realized that it suspends disbelief." Furthermore, the novel represented a breakaway from the stranglehold of the editor, N.A. Leykin, who wanted Chekhov to write nothing but short comical vignettes.

Hingley (1976) doubted the worth of the novel. He called it a curio, one of the greatest anomalies in Chekhov's works. Chekhov wisely ceased writing this genre, seeing the failure of this work. Stowell, in Clyman (1985), reported that Emil Loteanu's film in 1977 was better than Chekhov's novel, which is long on parody and short on irony, and even the ironies are narrative rather than dramatic.

10. One-Act Plays

The Anniversary (1891) (The Jubilee)

Bank chairman Shipuchin is preparing his bank for a visit by the board of directors on the bank's fiftieth anniversary. Overworked Khirin, a clerk, tells Shipuchin to keep out women, or they will ruin the preparation. Mrs. Shipuchin enters, and bores Khirin with a long, irrelevant speech. Merchutkina, a confused wife of a retired civil servant, mistakenly thinks that the bank should pay her husband money owed him by the army medical department. To get rid of her, Shipuchin pays her the money and then tells Khirin, "Throw her out!" (alluding to Merchutkina) but Khirin by mistake tries to throw out Mrs. Shipuchin, who faints, just as the bank director enters. Shocked at what they see, they leave shortly thereafter.

Chekhov's last one-act comedy, this play was based upon his short story "A Helpless Creature" (1887). C.E. Bechhofer, in a note to his translation in 1916, said that, although this was Chekhov at his best, still Chekhov was more of a journalist than an artist, and thus "his work has no permanent importance."[1] A reviewer of Bechhofer's translation said that Chekhov gives here, as in his short stories, "the grey muddle of human life." Chekhov "insinuates the external interference of life into the worry of human beings. Here is the Chekhov of the short stories, but vitalized and intensified by association with the footlights."[2]

Worrall (1986) quotes a review by Yuri Yuzovsky of a 1935 Moscow production of the play, directed by Vsevolod Meyerhold. "The people in Chekhov's vaudeville are strange enough," said Yuzovsky. "In Meyerhold's production lunatics are on the loose. In Chekhov, these are just amusing people," but Meyerhold turns them into crackpots.

Magarshack (*Dramatist*, 1952) says that the only incident taken from "A Helpless Creature" is the persistent wife who wants to collect her husband's money in the wrong office. In spite of its broad comic elements, said Magarshack, it is more serious than Chekhov's other comic vaudeville pieces, in its satire of banking practices. Simmons (1962) concurs, saying that although its comedy is quite hilarious, "there is a dark undercurrent of savage satire against some of the practices of private banks." Hingley (1968) noted that the play's theme is the lack of communication, and that Chekhov revised the play many times.

The leading authority on Chekhov's one-act plays is Vera Gottlieb (1982). Gottlieb quotes Yuzovsky on the characters' humours or obsessions: Shipuchin has his "grandeur"; his wife, her eroticism; Khirin, his suspicion of women; and Merchutkina, her insistent demand for money. The irrelevant, says Gottlieb, mixes in with the relevant to form a scene of chaos and farce. The characters are a combination of stock, grotesque, and three-dimensional. Each character suffers because of his obsession: Khirin, who hates women, is given his dose of two "impossible" ones; Shipuchin, who wants to window-dress for the directors, has them come at exactly the wrong time; and Mrs. Shipuchin, who loves romance, is treated in anything but a romantic fashion. Prone to headaches, Shipuchin receives cause for a good one. Disliking muddles, Khirin is in the midst of a huge one. In Mrs. Shipuchin Chekhov parodies both romantic love and cheap stage presentations of it. In a bank, efficiency, formality, and proper conduct are expected—the reverse of these obtain here. The farce results from the clash between the pretentious and the comically inappropriate. The play is thus a satire on pretension, pettiness, and philistinism.

Master (1982) points out that Chekhov deleted a final fight scene in later versions of the play. He apparently was trying to avoid a sense of "closure," even as he did in his later serious plays. Merchutkina uses disconnected dialogue as an oblique reaction when she is told she is in the wrong office. Her responses are partially intentional; she will get her money, fair means or foul.

Senelick (1985) noted that this play was not performed until 1900, when Chekhov was already famous. The *Moscow News* called it "a strange play" that year. At its first performance in St. Petersburg in 1903 critics attacked it for its "crude vulgarity." By now critics could not forgive "serious" Chekhov for employing slapstick humor. The farce is heightened by the fact that the four main characters are to some extent despicable, and thus the audience is pleased to see them inconvenienced. Laurence Senelick, in Clyman (1985), reported that Evgeny Vakhtangov produced the play in 1920 at the Third Studio of the Moscow Art Theatre. He told the actors to play it as vaudeville, not comedy. "By cluttering the stage, reducing its space, he rendered the action caricatural and eccentric, forcing the players into unexpected and bizarre behavior." In this fashion, said Senelick, the play remained popular well into World War II.

Egri (1986) states that the title change from "A Helpless Creature" to *The Anniversary* indicates a shift from a funny incident to a satirical comedy. In the change, Shipuchin is made more pompous, but Merchutkina is shown somewhat more favorably. Now the conflict is sharper: Is it reasonable for the bank chairman to pay 45 rubles to bind the address he is about to give, while denying 25 rubles to a woman whose husband is ill and has been mistreated? Chekhov here satirizes the people for their ludicrous conduct, but at the same time attacks the system of which they are products.

The Bear (1888) (The Boor) (The Brute)

Mrs. Popov is in deep mourning for her husband, who died seven months previously. Her old servant Luka advises her to forget her husband, but she vows to defend his sacred memory (even though she admits that he had been untrue to her). Her neighbor Smirnov arrives, asking for the 1200 rubles owed him. Popov says he will have to wait several days, until her steward returns with the money. Smirnov says his taxes are due tomorrow—he will stay until paid. Popov tells Luka to throw out Smirnov, but Luka faints. Popov calls Smirnov a "bear"—insulted, he challenges her to a duel. She accepts, and goes out for pistols. Seeing her spunk, Smirnov decides that he loves her. When she returns, he gives her shooting lessons, and then confesses his love. She says "No—Yes" a dozen times—but finally accepts his proposal!

The Bear was not originally intended for the stage, but was published in *New Times* as a feuilleton, or light filler. Chekhov, however, had N.N. Solovzov, an actor at Korsh's Theater, in mind as Smirnov. A tall man with a loud voice, Solovzov produced the play at Korsh's, and subsequently acted the leading role hundreds of times. Chekhov enjoyed the first performance, but unfortunately the coffee pot exploded on stage and burned Miss Rybchinsky, who played Popov. "The coffee pot killed my bear," complained Chekhov while a substitute actress was being groomed as Popov. But the play continued to be popular. In 1889 Chekhov wrote that "a gypsy wouldn't earn so much with a live bear as I have done with a dead one. The beast has already brought me 500 rubles."[3]

At its first performance in London in 1911, as a curtain raiser to a movie, the play was well received, as it was at its first New York City production in 1914. Noting that the theater was "crowded to the doors," a reviewer said that *The Bear,* which was written to throw a sidelight upon fashionable life in Russia, provided "a little laughter after an evening devoted to teaching deep and gloomy lessons."[4] Hiram K. Moderwell that year called *The Bear* and *The Proposal* "two delightful one-act farces, filled with the most engaging fun, which up to the last line never dulls a bit. In them one feels the comic genius of *The Inspector General* alive again."[5]

The following year the Washington Square Players staged the play to an enthusiastic crowd. Samuel Eliot as Smirnov was said to have a thunderous voice and personality which "almost burst the poor little Bandbox Theater apart."[6] A Boston production that year was called "interesting and excellent of its kind. This fantastic trifle runs along as if impromptu; now and then a stroke of observation or a hint of character spices it."[7]

In 1916 the Washington Square Players again staged *The Bear* in New York. One reviewer thanked the troupe for this "rollicking farce," and for performing "intellectual European drama which otherwise would hardly be presented here."[8]

In 1920 in London S.R. Littlewood found it "quite an amusing little trifle," based, he said, on "the oldest story in the world," the couple having been seen previously as Shakespeare's Richard and Anne, as well as his Kate and Petruchio.[9]

M. Lykiardopolous found more fault with the production than with the play. Played rapidly, like a French bedroom farce, the play could not bring out its witty dialogue, he said.[10] In 1926 Francis Birrell called *The Bear* "a perfect divertisement in which the absurdity never palls for an instant."[11]

Magarshack (*Dramatist*, 1952) said that this play derives from the French vaudeville *Les Jirons de Cadillac* by Pierre Berton. Chekhov saw a Russian adaptation of the play, made by N.N. Solovzov, at Korsh's Theater. Called *Conquerors Are Above Criticism*, the play tells of the taming of a coarse but good-natured sea captain by a beautiful society woman. Chekhov liked Solovzov so much in the role that he created a Russian "bear" for him to play. The first performance in 1888 was so successful that the audience had to wait for applause breaks before saying their lines. All of the newspaper critics applauded the play except S. Vasiliev, drama critic of the *Moscow News*. At later performances Chekhov complained about the acting, saying that he and his sister could have played the roles better than the actors had. He might not have been jesting, for the Chekhov family loved to stage amateur theatricals.

Simmons (1962) recalled Chekhov saying that he had not written about a bear but about a milk cow, judging by the royalties his play brought him. Lucas (1963) remarked that "the humor of his farces seems often strangely clumsy compared with the delightful humor of his letters." Hingley (1968) found the play to be based upon misunderstanding and communication failure—Smirnov cannot really believe that Popov has no money in her house. Her clash with Smirnov gives Smirnov the opportunity to deliver some "splendid" tirades against women. In his farces, Chekhov often used women as the butt of his jokes. Had this been serious drama, this play would have destroyed the "cosy stereotype" that Chekhov automatically "loved people."

This is a variation of the time-worn theme of *The Widow of Ephesus* by Petronius, says Melchinger (1972). But Popov is mourning her untrue husband not out of respect for him but to shame him posthumously. Which person is the bear? asks Melchinger. Popov overawes Smirnov by her energy, resistance, and bravery. The only Chekhov play ever produced by the famous director Max Reinhardt was *The Bear*, in 1905. Hingley (1976) quoted Chekhov as saying that while writing a serious story like "The Steppe," it was relaxing to simultaneously work on a farce like *The Bear*.

Gottlieb (1982) states that Tolstoy roared with laughter in 1900 at a performance of *The Bear* and *The Wedding*. He told the actors that "after Gogol, we don't have such a brilliant, powerful humorist as Chekhov." Tolstoy explained that Chekhov's farces are good because they avoid the usual "French nonsensical surprises." But Gottlieb found Yuri Yuzovsky praising Popov for her "French irony," in Meyerhold's production in 1935. Popov, said Yuzovsky, hides her hypocrisy gracefully, so that it can be seen: "Here hypocrisy is playing with open cards, that is to say, revealing its method."

The two main characters are "excessive," said Gottlieb. Popov exaggerates her grief, for effect, and Smirnov insists on getting his money, despite her grief. Only Luka provides a sense of proportion. When Popov admits that her husband was untrue, it makes probable her desertion of her grief-stricken memory of him. Just as Popov's hypocrisy must be debunked, so Smirnov's machismo must be tamed. For a time the contrast is ludicrous — the greater his vulgarity, the more delicate her refinement. Their falling in love after such a wide chasm has opened between them constitutes a parody on the concept of romantic love. Ironically, when Popov stops behaving like a lady, Smirnov starts behaving like a gentleman. The duel is also a parody: Popov does not know how to use a gun, and even though her insults grow worse and worse, Smirnov refuses to duel her. Although no gun duel takes place, the two have been duelling all along. To show her how to hold the gun, he puts his arm around her — and love, naturally, cannot be denied. Although originally the censor thought the play was too coarse for the stage, he eventually approved it. The play is essentially a "comedy-joke, with a small cast, a brisk tempo, tension, a peculiar love triangle, amorous entertainment, farce, slapstick, and a happy ending." But the characters are three-dimensional, and the tension arises organically out of the characters. Much of the humor, says Gottlieb, comes from parody and irony.

Senelick (1985) finds the humor based upon the characters' lack of self-knowledge: Popov fancies herself a deep mourner, and Smirnov considers himself to be a woman hater. They are made comic by pretending to be more than they really are. Chekhov uses Popov's favorite pony Toby to signal the transfer of her affections from the pony to Smirnov. Some critics cavilled over the improbabilities, apparently forgetting that improbability is one of the root causes of comedy.

Dishonorable Tragedians and Leprous Dramatists (1884)

Worrall (1986) recounts the ridiculous plot: Tarnovsky, a dramatist, is trying to think up new ways to make the blood curdle. In a clap of thunder the impresario appears, demanding a new play. Charles XII of Sweden sentences Tarnovsky to prison for writing a play about him. Stella, the impresario's sister, makes love with a young count, and then escapes from prison. Charles XII orders virtue to triumph over vice.

Gottlieb (1982), who translated this "theatrical joke, " calls it a parody on melodrama and a brief satire on science-horror plays. Tarnovsky, whose head is a skull, is killed, but springs back to life. The impresario wants action, saying, "I shall not spare the gunpowder." Despite Tarnovsky's efforts, the impresario is not satisfied. Gottlieb finds in this *esprit* a satire on Suvorin for his pontifical manner of foretelling future events.

A Forced Declaration (1876)

Worrall summarizes the zany plot: Two lovers, fleeing from her irate husband, urge the cabman onward. He whips his horse, which drops dead. The husband, a count, catches up with the group, and rewards the cabman. "The driver declares that saving the count's honor is worth more than financial reward and is hoisted shoulder high by the appreciative crowd which has gathered." Gottlieb (1982) calls this a parody on melodrama and its stock situations. The count tells the cabby that the money is for buying a new horse. Chekhov was very much opposed to ill treatment of horses. But in his one-act plays he sometimes uses the very techniques that he parodies.

The Night Before the Trial (1895)

On the eve of his trial for bigamy and forgery, Zaitsev meets elderly Gusev (who, unknown to him, will be his prosecutor) and his young wife Zina. Zaitsev fondles his pistol, as if contemplating suicide. Bitten by bed bugs, Zina asks help from Zaitsev, who is masquerading as a doctor. Gusev asks Zaitsev to examine Zina's body, to determine whether she has been bitten badly. Zaitsev formulates for Zina a bogus prescription containing two drams of *sic transit* and an ounce of *gloria mundi.*

Hingley (1968) pointed out that this unfinished playlet was based upon Chekhov's story of the same name, written in 1886. In the short story Chekhov had used heavy badinage, like Charles Dickens at his worst. But since Chekhov excelled in writing comic dialogue, the play is much better than the story. If finished, this could have been an excellent one-act farce, Hingley believes. The denouement would have had the cuckold Gusev prosecuting the cuckolder Zaitsev.

Gottlieb (1982) reports that this, one of Chekhov's most overt parodies, was published posthumously. It uses stock characters and actions, and has a predictable ending. The stock characters are from the *commedia del l'arte.* A succession of misunderstandings arises from mistaken identity. Everything is excessive: Zaitsev's crimes, Zina's beauty, and Gusev's ugliness. Even the names are symbolic: Gusev means "goose" and Zaitsev means "hare." The Russian proverb states, "First catch your hare—then cook him." Zaitsev's character is a satire on pessimism. Falsity underlies the characters. The husband encourages the false doctor to examine his wife, and is thus practicing self-deceit. But the wife is not really ill, and Zaitsev writes a false prescription in pig Latin. Here Chekhov parodies parodies. The playlet shows Chekhov's familiarity with conventional comic techniques. It also shows that he was experimenting with cuckoldry, a theme he was to use in *The Three Sisters* and *Uncle Vanya.*

Senelick (1985) found this to be close to a French boulevard farce in its sexual emphasis. The tone is persistently vulgar, he feels, and the playlet uses burlesque gags. Zaitsev speaks endearingly to his pistol, he notes, as if it were his best friend.

On the Harmfulness of Tobacco (1886–1903) (Smoking Is Bad for You)

Ivan, whose wife runs a girls' boarding school, lectures against tobacco to obey his wife (although he admits that he smokes). His whole monologue is one digression after another: on insects, a tic in his right eye, his wife's school, her stinginess, his henpecked status, and his marriage-seeking daughter. To show his rebellion against being picked on, he takes off his coat and jumps on it. But his wife appears in the doorway, so he dons his coat, finishes his lecture, and walks off with dignity.

Wolcott Gibbs, reviewing a performance of the play in 1948, said that it "oscillates between comedy and pathos without really achieving either."[12] Magarshack (*Dramatist*, 1952) points out that Ivan's surname, Nyukhin, means "smelly." Chekhov told the actors of the Moscow Art Theatre that they must create their own characters, based on the playwright's cues, and when the two conceptions merged, a work of art resulted. Chekhov also told Meyerhold in 1900 that the way to play his characters was not to rush about the stage but to feel the part from within, to use not hands and feet so much as eyes and tone of voice. The six different versions of this monologue, written between 1886 and 1903, mirror Chekhov's change from direct-action drama to indirect-action.

Magarshack traces the changes made in three versions of the play. First, tobacco's harmfulness is stressed, and there are asides on Ivan's life. In the second version, tobacco is not mentioned much, and in the third not at all. In the first version the comedy grows out of a pedant lecturing on a topic unfamiliar to him. In the second version Ivan's "inner man" keeps popping out of its absurd shell. The third version dispenses entirely with cheap external effects and focuses wholly on Ivan's repressed life. As Ivan becomes more human, we feel more pathos for him. In the last part of the play, the appeal is universalized as Ivan searches for freedom.

Ermilov (1956) calls this a farce with tragic overtones. Ivan is identified with his worn coat. "The wretched threadbare waistcoat is his true physiognomy— hopelessly blurred. His wife is a very real presence, without ever stepping on stage. Here Chekhov blends comedy and tragedy.

The changed versions show Chekhov's dramatic evolution, Simmons (1962) agrees. He moves from relying on external comic effects to showing a subtle psychological analysis of Ivan's inner character. Ivan's true self discloses a fine man whose qualities are being destroyed by a domineering, selfish wife.

Hingley (1976) feels that despite constant improvement, the play "remained at all stages essentially what it had been at its inception: an amusing trifle." Hahn (1977), however, discovers more significance: "The sudden gesture of self-revelation, where a lifetime of frustration releases itself without premeditation, is a major development of lasting importance for Chekhov's art, a distinct departure from the manipulation of simple stereotypes in the earlier works." After comparing the varying versions, Brigitte Schultze in 1978 says that the final one is "tragic farce," the first work in the tradition of the Theater of the Absurd.[13]

Gottlieb (1982) states that when Ivan yearns to escape from his commonplace life, he is voicing Chekhov's perennial theme. Ivan's ludicrous search for self-respect resembles that of Pishchik in *The Cherry Orchard*. The audience, asked to respond to Ivan's plight as much as to his message, becomes at once participant and spectator. The play is a comedy of character. Ivan deviates so often into irrelevancies that soon they become the main action. Out of the stock henpecked husband Chekhov creates a three-dimensional character. Living exclusively in a woman's world, Ivan nonetheless does the womanly chores: cleans, shops, and walks his wife's dog. By teaching many subjects at his wife's school, he has helped her make a tidy profit. This play is the tragedy of the unappreciated little man.

Senelick (1985) reported that this monologue was written for the talented but alcoholic comedian L.I. Gradov-Sokolov. In the revisions, Chekhov replaced the pseudo-scientific jargon with clichés. As Ivan protests more against "husband abuse," the ridicule shifts more into pathos.

On the High Road (1884) (On the Highway)

Bortsov, a ruined landowner, is reduced to begging a drink from a bartender. He finally exchanges a gold medallion bearing his wife's picture for a drink. Kuzma, his former serf, enters the tavern and tells the crowd how Bortsov's wife Maria ruined him. Maria enters, sees Bortsov and tries to leave, but Merik, a tramp, swings an axe at her but fortunately misses. Merik recovers his composure and asks forgiveness for his act.

In the introduction to his translation of this play, Julius West (1915) said that one sees in it, in embryonic form, "the whole later method of Chekhov's plays—the deliberate contrast between two strong characters (Bortsov and Merik, in this case), the careful individualization of each person, the concealment of the catastrophe in the personality of the characters, and the creation of a distinctive group-atmosphere." It is definitely not a "dirty" play, as the censor alleged in 1884, since "Chekhov was incapable of writing a dirty play or story."

Reviewers of West's translation admired this play. A British critic praised the brilliant character drawing, adding that "there is charm in Chekhov's humor, in his delicate writing, and in the humanness of his characterization that should win him a wider audience."[14] An American reviewer also found "much vigorous and realistic characterization, and much dramatic quality," although he granted that it was crudely constructed, with a main incident that was highly improbable.[15]

This play is like Gorky's *The Lower Depths*, said S.R. Littlewood, except that

Chekhov "is betrayed into the most threadbare old melodramatic story of a long-lost, unfaithful, and well-to-do wife turning up accidentally."[16] M. Lykiardopolous stated that Chekhov never wanted this play published, thinking it "too vulgar a melodrama," with a "too exalted idealization" of the Russian peasant. Chekhov, it was alleged, received the plot from Gorky. Nonetheless, the play had been well received by the London audience.[17] Another reviewer found "here and there a tragic story peeping out and disappearing again, getting itself told in the end, but composed in the Chekhov manner, with no central point and no emphasis — a strange, ugly beautiful atmospheric effect."[18]

Although Chekhov's major plays were getting favorable reviews in 1929, this play suffered at the hands of critics of a New York production. One critic said that "its dark coincidence is not convincing,"[19] and Brooks Atkinson called it "a grim and turgid story. The actors play it with so much pungency that the maudlin theatricalism of an apprentice job is much less trying than it might easily be."[20]

Toumanova (1937) noticed that, after hearing of Bortsov's sad life, the crowd was eager to buy him drinks. Magarshack (*Dramatist*, 1952) reported that the play was adapted from Chekhov's story "In the Autumn" (1884). He kept the original dialogue, but enlarged the scope for the play. The new character Merik is introduced, who is not only a chorus figure but also a direct successor to Osip in Chekhov's play *Platonov* — a Robin Hood type of robber. Chekhov took the leading figure Bortsov from a shy alcoholic landowner named Zabelin that he knew. This is Chekhov's only naturalistic play, and the only one in which he attempted to portray common people.

Lucas (1963) finds the play "looking forward to the low-life scenes of Gorky." Hingley (1968) calls the play melodramatic, for Bortsov's woe is so exaggerated that "one would have to have a heart of stone not to laugh at his travails." But in its own way the play is well made, and has offered rich material to Russian character actors. Merik is an unusual character for Chekhov, since he had little contact with tramps. At the time, however, he was exploring all kinds of characters for many kinds of dramatic vehicles. Rayfield (1975) acknowledges this as melodrama, noting that the bartender returns the gold medallion when he hears of Bortsov's woes.

Gottlieb (1982) says that the censor's rejection came for two reasons: a landowner is shown as an alcoholic, and a man chases a woman, wielding an axe. From the story, Chekhov made three changes: he has a group of travelers at the inn; Merik becomes a central figure; and Maria returns to the inn. The censor accepted in the story something he would not accept in a play. In *Uncle Vanya*, Telegin is a refurbished Bortsov, a man who still has his pride and dignity. Had this been a comic play, Chekhov could have got away with the improbabilities: Maria's return, and Merik missing her when he tries to hit her with an axe. After this effort, Chekhov never again wrote a play unrelieved by humor.

Eisen (1982) says that, surprisingly, the story version was more subtle and more artistic, because the broad action in the play turns it into a melodrama. Master (1982) identifies this as "early" Chekhov, for Kuzma uses the story-telling technique to give the background exposition about Bortsov and Maria. The "later" Chekhov would have used indirect-action techniques to convey the information. Senelick (1985) said that Merik was introduced to give the play version more action. At the Moscow production in 1914, most critics called the play a melodrama, but one of them was ecstatic over Fedya as an archetype of Lopakhin in *The Cherry Orchard*.

The Proposal (1889) (The Marriage Proposal)

Lomov, a hypochondriac, visits neighbor Chubukov in order to propose to Chubukov's daughter Natalya. Not knowing the purpose of the visit, Natalya quarrels with Lomov over a strip of land between their estates. Lomov leaves in a huff. When Natalya hears that Lomov wants to propose, she calls him back. Now Lomov and Chubukov get into a quarrel over whose hunting dog is better. Natalya wants Lomov to propose, but Chubukov insults Lomov, who falls into a faint. Revived, he proposes, Natalya accepts, and the two "lovers" continue the quarrel about the hunting dogs.

Czar Alexander III was very complimentary about a brilliant performance of this play at his summer palace. Chekhov's brother Michael, in Koteliansky (1925), said that this amusing farce quickly became a favorite in provincial theaters, clubs, and private theatrical groups. It first appeared in *New Times*, indicating that Chekhov looked on it more as a literary work than as a stage vehicle.

One student of the one-act play felt that Chekhov's farces were "not necessarily conventional vaudeville material. They are forerunners of what gives promise of being a significant dramatic product in a not far-off future."[21] Hallie Flanagan described an experiment at Vassar College in which this play was performed three different ways in one evening, as realism, expressionism, and constructivism. First it was staged in a realistic manner, "for which it was obviously written," with the usual scenery, and with actors as characters. Then, in an experiment with the abstract, the actors wore masks, "expressing the eternal deadly struggle between man and his implacable enemy, woman. Played expressionistically, the farce comedy is tragedy at the core." Finally, in constructivism, the actors, wearing undifferentiated work suits, appear from within the audience. The setting is a playground, with a teeter-totter depicting life's ups and downs. "The rhythm of the play is that of a ball tossed back and forth. Behold, a contradiction: The actors have lost a whole world of costume and gained their souls." The audience preferred constructivism as capturing "the rhythm of our time. It is the age of skyscraper, radio, airplanes; it has freedom, boldness, sweep, crudity, power; it throws away both esthetics and decadence."[22]

At a Moscow Art Theatre production in London in 1931, a reviewer explained why this (and other Chekhov farces) were successful in arousing humor: British actors merely present an illusion, but Russian actors are also free to act in accordance with their deepest instincts.[23] When Meyerhold staged this play in Moscow in 1935, he used stage properties as symbols, A. Fevralsky explained: "The serviette which Lomov and Natalya tear to shreds symbolizes the subject of their embittered quarrel—the Volovy meadows. Lomov's relationship to the two hunting dogs is emphasized by the way he handles his top hat and his soft hat."[24]

A study of Chekhov's one-act plays in 1939 revealed that they have a place in the modern theater, for "they have a clear line, quick development, and sufficient variety to prevent an impression of being too short. The longer ones, such as *The Bear*, *The Proposal*, and *The Wedding*, might well be placed in the repertory of any one-act company. They would act well, and would certainly suggest new kinds of subtlety in the short farce."[25]

Magarshack (*Dramatist*, 1952) said that in this play Chekhov's technical hunting terms came from *The Diary of an Insignificant Man* by Yegot Driansky, a novelist and playwright. Hingley (1968) felt that Chekhov was here making fun of a feminine foible: an eagerness to get married at any cost, including taking such an undesirable mate as Lomov. When all else fails, Chekhov uses a fainting spell, as he did in this play. Chekhov said that he had written this "wretched, boring, vulgar little skit" for the provinces. In 1888 he told I.L. Leontiev, "Roll cigarettes out of it for all I care," but when Leontiev staged it in St. Petersburg it quickly became popular.

This is a situation comedy, assumed Melchinger (1972). The lovers are an odd couple—he is a hypochondriac and she is quarrelsome. Since Chubukov seems to dislike Lomov, why does he want him as a son-in-law? Improbability, far from being a drawback, is an asset in farce.

This is more farcical than all other Chekhov plays, says Gottlieb (1982). The plot here is not the proposal but all the impediments preventing it. In his one-act plays, Chekhov's characters are "rounded" by having apparently contradictory traits. Chubukov tells Natalya that Lomov is a dealer collecting goods (Lomov is seeking a marriage deal, and the "goods" are Natalya). Yuri Yuzovsky said that Meyerhold's production failed in 1935 because he interpreted Lomov as a victim of czarist oppression, and people began to pity him rather than laugh at his ridiculous behavior. The play's structure is a parody: Lomov twice comes to propose, Lomov and Natalya quarrel twice, and Chubukov interrupts them twice, each time making the argument worse. The "end" of the play signals the "continuation" of the quarrel. "By substituting misunderstanding and character for plot and intrigue, and introducing the convention of rival landowners, 'the proposal' becomes subsidiary to what, in effect, is closer to social satire," Gottlieb concludes.

Master (1982) remarks that Chekhov handles well the dialogue reflecting the loss of tempers. Senelick (1985) feels that Chekhov was good at depicting botched proposals. Here he shows that he "understood how to accelerate the basic misapprehensions into a barrage of insults, and how, after building to a climax, to reinvigorate the action by introducing a fresh contretemps."

Swan Song (1887)

Vasily, an aged, broken-down comic actor, returns to a darkened stage several hours after a benefit play in his honor has ended. Although he was given many curtain calls, no one saw him home. Drunk, he soliloquizes that he should go to church in his few remaining years. The prompter Nikita comes out in a long white coat, scaring Vasily. They reminisce about their lives. Vasily says, "I finally understand the audience. They will applaud my acting, but not permit their daughter to marry me, an actor. And so I became a buffoon instead of a man." He starts to quote lines from famous tragedies — Nikita helps him by filling in missed lines. For a moment Vasily feels that he has recovered his lost art and his lost youth.

Reviewing a translation in 1912, a critic said that although it is "a mere sketch and not wholly original in idea, it exhibits more of the true theatrical sense than either *Ivanov, The Sea Gull,* or *Uncle Vanya.*"[26] Henry T. Perry in 1939, speaking of this play, said that "for a moment, genius can annihilate time; in the long run, time will get its revenge and blot out the individual artist. This basic paradox runs through all of Chekhov's work and explains many of its superficial inconsistencies."[27]

Magarshack (*Dramatist,* 1952) noted that this play closely followed Chekhov's short story "Kalchas" (1886), and at its first performance in 1888 it had that name. Chekhov revised the play several times. It is a study of the conditions of the Russian theater at that time. Actors had no social standing, and many ended as drunkards. Stanislavsky did much to raise the social status of actors. Simmons (1962) reports that Chekhov said that he wrote the play in a little over an hour.

Hingley (1968) can scarcely believe that Chekhov, the master of understatement, wrote such a florid work. There is so much exaggeration, Hingley feels, that the effect is humorous, despite Chekhov's serious intent. Vasily's orgy of self-pity offers good material for a character actor, but would have been far more effective in Chekhov's later style, when restraint and indirection would have heightened the effect. Chekhov said that this play had no merit, but A.P. Lensky, the actor and producer, insisted on performing this role.

Mel Gussow, reviewing Morris Carnovsky in the lead role in 1972, said that "the whole play turns as Mr. Carnovsky moves skillfully from self-pity to self-mockery to dignity." The audience can believe him when he concludes that "where there's talent, there's no old age."[28] Rayfield (1975) stated that Chekhov wrote this play for actor V.N. Davydov, grateful for his performance in the lead role in Chekhov's *Ivanov.*

Gottlieb (1982) said that Chekhov often wrote about the role of the actor — is his a sacred art, or is he merely a puppet? This is an epiphany — Vasily is in a moment of self-recognition, having just performed the role of Kalchas the seer. Too late in life Vasily realizes what life might have been — a universal condition. Chekhov called this play "a dramatic study" rather than a vaudeville. A darkened stage is ominous: "Like all empty theaters it is peopled with both memories and echoes, waiting for something to happen." Vasily enters carrying a candle, nothing like the footlights when the crowd is here. To Vasily the audience is a black pit, about to swallow him. Chekhov here creates illusion by appearing to expose illusion, for after all, an audience *is* in the theater, watching *Swan Song*. Like Brecht, Chekhov makes an audience think. As in Beckett's plays, the actors and the audience alike are participants. The structure of the play combines monologue and false monologue. Nikita is so poor that he is forced to sleep in the theater—finally Vasily has found someone worse off than himself. But Nikita is sober and has no self-pity. He acts as a real-life prompter—Vasily reacts to him by telling him more of his life story. There is pathos as old Vasily speaks of his life, "The show is over. You can bring down the curtain." By exposing the sordid reality of the stage, Chekhov enables us to look beyond the illusory façade of the theater and into life itself.

Master (1982) observes that Vasily ignores Nikita's commands to go home, but instead "confesses" his sorrows and the reasons for them, a technique that Chekhov often used in later plays. This play has many "confessions," some self-motivated and others motivated from outside. The play also contains "stories," in which nothing secret or private is revealed. Some speeches begin as stories and end as confessions.

Senelick (1985) recalls that Vasily had been playing Kalchas, the soothsayer in Offenbach's comic opera *La Belle Hélène*. Thus, his short tunic and tights on 68-year-old legs make him look ridiculous as he declaims Hamlet, Lear, and Othello. The play permits a skilled character actor to have a field day, as had Dumas in his *Kean*. Vasily's surname Svetlovidov means "seeing the light." Vasily's ending is a "pocket enlightenment, a compressed version of the awareness that tragic heroes take five acts to achieve."

Tatyana Repina (1889)

Sobinin, a Lothario, is marrying Madame Olenin. Most of the action is a montage between the church ritual and the people's frivolous comments. A woman in black faints—Sobinin fears that the actress Tatyana Repina has taken poison over having been jilted by him. The crowd acts as a chorus, saying that he deserted Tatyana, just as the priest asks God to bless this holy matrimony. No longer able to resist his conscience, Sobinin deserts the marriage ceremony to have a mass for the dead said at the cemetery. The woman in black confesses that she too has taken poison, out of sympathy to Tatyana.

Chekhov wrote this as a continuation of Suvorin's four-act play of the same name, which tells of how Tatyana committed suicide on the stage while playing the role of Ivan the Terrible's wife, who was poisoned. Needing a French dictionary, Chekhov traded this continuation to Suvorin for one. He asked Suvorin not to show it to anyone, but Suvorin had a copy printed for each of them.

Soviet critic A.S. Dolinin in 1925 said that although Chekhov had Suvorin's play in mind, this is not a parody of it. This play can be seen as an experiment, presaging Chekhov's later plays.[29] Henry T. Perry, however, calling the play a parody of Suvorin's, said that it was "a macabre flight of Chekhov's poetic imagination."[30]

Hingley (1968) called this play a private joke between Chekhov and Suvorin. Here Chekhov is quite kind to women. A mixture of farce and tragedy, the play contains an element of despair, which was a recurring factor in Chekhov's own mood. At other times he had "fits of optimism." The tension he achieved between these two moods helped make him a great artist. N.A. Nikipelova in 1971, as quoted in Lantz (1985), compared Chekhov's play with Suvorin's. She found that Chekhov's version avoided clichés and put more emphasis on psychological motivation.

Gottlieb (1982) provides historical background on the plot. In 1881 E.P. Kadmina, playing the role of Ivan the Terrible's wife (who had committed suicide), during a performance of Alexander Ostrovsky's play *Vasilisa Melentieva,* took real poison at the time in the play required by her role. She had sent the lover who rejected her, plus his wealthy fiancée, tickets to watch the performance. Many plays, besides Suvorin's, had been written about this affair. Chekhov's continuation of Suvorin's play may have been a parody of it. E.S. Smirnova-Chikina in 1974 argued that in addition it parodies *Autour du Marriage,* a play by the French writer Gip (pseudonym of Countess Gabriele de-Martel-de-Janvil).

Chekhov's strong criticism of Suvorin's play, Gottlieb says, makes it unlikely that Chekhov's play was a compliment to Suvorin, as Hingley maintains. Chekhov helped to stage Suvorin's play at the Maly Theatre, thereby gaining insight into the play's weaknesses: stilted language, flat characters, and basic lack of artistic truth. Chekhov objected to the anti–Semitism in the character of Sonnenstein, and he saw no reason for Tatyana to constantly say "damned." Smirnova-Chikina said that Chekhov "laughs at the melodramatic content which had charmed Suvorin by giving it a silly outcome." Chekhov's play could never have been staged in czarist Russia because it depicts a church service. At the end, Chekhov uses melodrama to expose melodrama: the woman in black recommends that *everyone* should follow her practice and take poison. Chekhov uses Kuzma, the cathedral caretaker, as a kind of raisonneur or mouthpiece. Ironic and comic effects are achieved by interspersing church ritual with gossip and jokes by the people. "This play illustrates the thin dividing line in his work between parody, satire, and criticism," says Gottlieb.

John Raicu in 1983 studied Chekhov's use of church ritual in the play.[31] Senelick (1985) says Chekhov uses counterpoint between the ritual and the gossip. He also states that Suvorin's play prefigures Chekhov's *The Sea Gull:* the journalist Adashev is an early Trigorin, and Tatyana is a forerunner of Nina. Chekhov's play is not parody but pastiche, an early example of "the intricate interweaving of melodramatic pathos and crass diurnalism that was to become the trademark of Chekhov's later plays."

A Tragedian in Spite of Himself (1889) (A Tragic Role)

Tolkachov, returning from a shopping trip with all sorts of boxes in his arms, asks his friend Murashkin for a pistol—he can no longer stand being a flunkey for his family. After waiting in lines at the stores, he comes home to things like gnats and his wife's amateur theatricals. Murashkin seems sympathetic but, on leaving, asks Tolkachov to take his friend Olga a sewing machine, a canary in its cage, and several other items. Broken, Tolkachov chases his friend around the stage, shouting, "I want blood!"

One student of the one-act play called this "a cartoon of the comic supplement, liberally inflated by dialogue—a good example of the sort of humor admired by the average Russian. The final scene is the first dramatic situation. Complication, lying in ambush, has been present in advance of it. Development there is none. The dramatic situation *is* crisis and resolution." This is jokebook humor. "It is interesting, but not dramatically interesting. There is a head and a tail, but no body."[32]

Wolcott Gibbs also reacted unfavorably to a New York production in 1948: "If it could be cut down to about a third of its length, and equipped with a few bright lines, it might be fairly funny, but as it is, no."[33] Magarshack (*Dramatist*, 1952) noted that this is based on Chekhov's story "One of Many" (1887). In the revision Chekhov edited out things he thought improper for the stage, such as a scene with a child's coffin, and some bedroom talk between Tolkachov and his wife. The play was performed many times, and Chekhov was always fussy over who played Tolkachov. Hingley (1968) observed that this was written for the actor K.A. Varlamov. When Tolkachov's eloquent tirade is lost on his best friend, the stage is set for one of Chekhov's best comic endings.

Gottlieb (1982) says that Tolkachov's reaction to being a henpecked husband is excessive and thus comic. The play is universal—Chekhov would say that most of us are "more likely to be 'martyrs' to lampshades, petticoats, and gnats than to abstract ideas or dramatic actions." When tired Tolkachov finally gets home from his shopping tour, his wife suggests that they go to a dance. All of the action occurs during a summer heat wave. Tolkachov's monologue gives not only self-exposition but exposure of a whole way of life. As in many of Chekhov's works, we see tragedy in the petty and the banal, but that is also comical, says Gottlieb.

Senelick (1985) says that the mélange of things that Tolkachov is supposed to buy is surrealistic. This, plus the detailed comparison of married life to Jewish slavery in Egypt and the Spanish Inquisition, "creates a manic impression of an ordinary middle-class existence as Bosch's hell." In this work, says Senelick, Chekhov moves halfway from Gogol to the absurd comedy of Jarry and Ionesco.

The Wedding (1889) (The Marriage)

Nunin has promised to bring a general to the wedding banquet of Aplombov and Dashenko, to give "class" to the occasion. But the best Nunin can do is show up with a long-winded sea captain, who prates endlessly in sea jargon. Considering himself no more than a hired hand, the sea captain leaves in a huff. Since Nunin has kept the money allotted for the general, he has the band strike up some music to hide his guilt.

Magarshack (*Dramatist*, 1952) points out that the Chekhov family in 1885 lived in a Moscow apartment, beneath a room rented out for wedding parties. While the real celebrants were wining and dining upstairs, Chekhov and his family and friends would stage a mock wedding party of their own. This playlet was based on three of Chekhov's stories: "The Marriage Season" (1881), "A Marriage of Convenience" (1884), and "A Wedding with a General" (1884). Here, however, Chekhov used over ten characters, compared to the two or three characters of his previous vaudeville skits.

Noting that Chekhov's reputation "stands very high among a small body of British intellectuals," a reviewer of this play in 1917 called it "a deliberately over-charged picture of manners." He found it amusing, but added that comedy based upon stock characters has limited appeal.[34] A later production evoked the comment that the play was "a satirical romp with a tinge of sadness in the ending,"[35] and "a pitiful little farce" which has to be played in an exaggerated "non–Chekhovian" fashion in order to please a non–Russian audience.[36] Another reviewer observed that by careful pruning and emotion control, this production had reached "a concert pitch, without which a Chekhov play is impossible on the stage."[37]

In 1920 Evgeny Vakhtangov used music to help define the characters, said Laurence Senelick, in Clyman (1985). At first, the characters were grotesques caught up in a manic quadrille; at the end, their dreams shattered, they sat and listened to very sad music. Ruben Simonov (in 1960) discussed in detail this Vakhtangov production.[38] Nikolai Gorchakov recalled, in Worrall (1986), that Vakhtangov believed that Chekhov's characters acted like puppets. "It is one of the possible interpretations of the real theatrical significance of Chekhov's plays," Vakhtangov felt.

A film made of this play provided "an unexpectedly diverting program" in 1945 to William Whitebait. "Can one imagine," he asked, "a more pompous ninny than this bridegroom, who must be bribed with furniture and linen, and have a general at his wedding? A lively sense of caricature bounces us through the festivities. The surprise is the hired 'general,' no general at all but an honest old tar who makes an exit of genuine dignity."[39] A live performance in 1948 in New York gave Wolcott Gibbs "a few moments of effective, if rather primitive, comedy, but the rest is just confusion and noise."[40]

Ermilov (1956) saw the play as a satire on middle-class snobbery. The bride's mother is more concerned over what happened to the 25-ruble fee than that the old sailor has been dishonored. Hingley (1968) comments that the obtuseness of the sea captain in realizing that he is there simply to add "dignity" to the occasion is an improbability that heightens the comedy. Aplombov says, "As a man of honor, I'll make my bride wish she'd never been born" (because the promised dowry never arrived)—but what kind of honor is that? The characters are intentionally stupid and greedy; they are humorous, as if slaves to their humours. For a change Chekhov portrays the men as more stupid than the women.

Mel Gussow, reviewing a production in 1972, found this more a vignette than a play, with more noise than humor.[41] Melchinger (1972) noticed that Chekhov built the characters on real-life Taganrog counterparts, where Greeks like Aplombov were a part of the rising middle class.

Gottlieb (1982) called this play "frightening," because of its atmosphere, mood, characters, and especially the play's milieu. She recalls how in 1969 Ruben Simonov contrasted two plays dealing with a general at a wedding: Dostoevsky's *A Nasty Joke* is cruel and sarcastic, whereas Chekhov's play has a subtle, and at times a bitter, humor. Zhigalov, the doubter, says that the electric light will not work. The Greek Dymba speaks a kind of pig–Russian dialect. With a theme of banality, this play is a cross between a farce and a comedy of manners.

Master (1982) notes that in this play Chekhov has moved away from the direct confrontation and melodrama of *The Bear* and *The Proposal*. Here we see the beginning of Chekhov's disconnected dialogue in the oblique reactions of the bride's mother, who blithely continues to set the table when asked about the dowry.

Here, says Senelick (1985), Chekhov "subjects the lower middle-class to the merciless derision of a Daumier." He emphasizes the comic gap between a character's pretensions and reality in "a masterful exhibition of the dissolution of social convention: Every pretense kept up by one character is demolished by another."

Summary—One-Act Plays

According to the critics, Chekhov's one-act plays served several important purposes in his development as a major dramatist. For one thing, they established his nature as that of a fun-loving, not a gloomy, person. For another, they gave him practice at converting stock characters into three-dimensional ones. They also permitted him to express social criticism within the context of an acceptable format. Above all, these short plays gave Chekhov experience with plots, characters, and themes that, strained through his sensitivity into his characteristic indirect-action format, appeared later in plays of subtlety, refinement, and purpose.

The Anniversary showed how misunderstanding produces misfortune. *The Bear*, perhaps Chekhov's most popular play in any format, might be called the untaming of the shrew. *Dishonorable Tragedians and Leprous Dramatists* and *A Forced Declaration* gave Chekhov a chance to use parody to sharpen his sense of humor and to find an avenue to escape banality. Although *The Night Before the Trial* was not very original, it showed that Chekhov was familiar with a broad range of comic techniques. *On the Harmfulness of Tobacco* and *Swan Song* are monologues that begin as satire but, because of Chekhov's gentle touch, end as pathos. *On the High Road*, Chekhov's only serious one-act play, was condemned as melodrama, although some critics found in it prototypes of characters in Chekhov's later serious plays.

Popular throughout the decades, *The Proposal* was seen by some critics as more than a farce, as a deep insight into some aspects of universal human nature. *Tatyana Repina*, a private joke between Chekhov and Suvorin, abounded in parodies of diverse kinds. *A Tragedian in Spite of Himself* exhibits at once the farce and the tragedy of everyday life. *The Wedding*, like many of Chekhov's vaudevilles, satirizes a social class for hypocrisy and affectation. Although most of his one-act plays use the direct-action approach, their themes and characters were stepping stones toward the great drama of the mature Chekhov.

11. *Platonov; Ivanov; The Wood Demon*

Three early full-length plays by Chekhov show the gradual steps he climbed as a dramatic craftsman. They exhibit a wide variety of themes, dramatic techniques, and attitudes towards the theater. Each of the plays merits study, to some extent as a separate dramatic vehicle but probably to a greater extent as a way-station towards some of the finest dramatic art of the past century.

Platonov (1881) (also called *A Country Scandal; Don Juan in the Russian Manner; A Play Without a Title; Wild Honey)*

Handsome schoolmaster Platonov loves not only his wife Sasha but at times three other women: landowner Anna, her daughter-in-law Sofia, and Maria, a young intellectual scientist. Osip, a violent horse-thief employed by Anna, out of jealousy vows to kill Platonov for having an affair with Anna. Trying to commit suicide on a railroad track, Sasha is saved by Osip. Sofia wants to elope with Platonov. In a scuffle, Osip stabs Platonov in the arm. Sasha unsuccessfully attempts suicide by eating matches. Maria openly declares her love for Platonov. Frustrated, Sofia shoots and kills Platonov.

In 1929 N.K. Piksanov studied horse thieves in four of Chekhov's works, including *Platonov.* Piksanov believed that Chekhov created these characters as a contrast to his more melancholy and inactive characters.[1]

In 1930 John Cournos made the first English translation of this play. This, plus Chekhov's rapid rise in general popularity, was the occasion of a spate of reviews assessing the quality of this play. Grace Anshutz found it "a gay and tragic play." Its faults were "long bracketed speeches, the manipulation of unimportant scenes, and the multiplicity of roles." Although structurally blemished, the play is worth reading, Anshutz said, for the "amazingly alive characters," the strong emotions, the lifelike conversation, and the "amplification of life."[2]

Lyle Donaghy said that one must wait until the end of the play to find out whether Platonov is a clever villain or a clever fool. This is due partly to the fact that the male characters are boring and the four women all mediocre, but more importantly it is a flaw in the way the characters are revealed: "Chekhov soon learned to give dramatic poise to subtler Platonovs."[3] Walter Prichard Eaton called it "unexpected good fortune" to have another play by "the great naturalist, Chekhov." It deals with the same theme as that in *The Cherry Orchard*, "but here the story has never been pulled into stage compass and given the unerring direction which so subtly marks Chekhov's later drama."[4] O.W. Firkins found the play "close enough to the normal Chekhov to attract his admirers, yet far enough way from him to interest, and perhaps propitiate, his critics." Although Chekhov here is too wordy, in his central character he created his best character, except for Firs and Lyubov in *The Cherry Orchard*. "In its mixture of profligacy, limpness, and whimsicality, in its self-deriding yet not insincere pathos, this seems to me a portraiture of an original and high validity," said Firkins.[5]

Arthur Hood found little value in "a series of scenes that resemble the bacchanalia of savages rather than a house party of civilized persons."[6] T.S. Matthews said that, despite the verbosity and too much action, the character insights made Chekhov "a never failing delight."[7] Alexander Nazaroff thought the central theme, showing a weakness in character, was well handled, but there was too much material for one play, and the characters' entrances and exits were handled clumsily.[8] One critic called it an imperfect blend, with too much comedy at first and too much tragedy at the end.[9] Another said merely that "no one but warm hearted, skeptical Chekhov could have written it."[10]

Soviet critic S. Danilov in 1948 said that the play enables us to see embryos of future Chekhov characters. Platonov grows into Ivanov, and the theme of aristocratic decay appears in *The Cherry Orchard*. "But intrinsically the play lacks artistic merit," Danilov felt, being weak in its structure and relying on external melodrama: "Chekhov is here entirely under the influence of prevailing theatrical clichés and of the 'problem' drama of the popular Russian theater of his time."[11]

Magarshack (*Dramatist*, 1952) feels that Danilov was too harsh on Chekhov, since this was an early unfinished work that Chekhov did not want published. It was remarkable, said Magarshack, that a man of 21 could have "appraised the whole social fabric of his times and passed judgment upon it." Osip, the honest thief, contrasts with the wealthy hypocrites who conceal their type of stealing. Platonov, the superfluous man, speaks his mind freely, and although what he says is often true, it is his frankness that offends people. The four women who love him are well realized: Anna is lustful, Sofia wishes to reform him, Sasha is the longsuffering wife, and Maria is so proud that she seeks his arrest for mistreating her. Chebutykin in *The Three Sisters* derives from Dr. Triletsky in *Platonov*. This play, which uses pauses and poetic irony, set Chekhov on the road as a reformer in dramatic technique.

A reviewer of Basil Ashmore's adaptation, called *Don Juan in the Russian Manner*, in 1953 noted that Platonov is not shot in this version but dies of illness. He wanted to see this version staged, "particularly because it is full of the direct, cynical comment that in Chekhov's later plays tends to get lost in self-pitying performances by the actors."[12]

In 1954 Thomas Eekman studied this play and its place in Chekhov's dramaturgy. E. Kannak in 1956 examined the revisions that Chekhov made to the play. In 1957 Anne-Marie Bon made comparisons between Platonov and Ivanov, noting that both characters are seeking redemption.[13] Bruford (1957) said that although the play is too long and too complicated, it already shows Chekhov's bitter-sweet flavor, plus his preference for characters under the stress of unfulfilled desires. Platonov's only refuge from the women who pursue him is suicide – he is "a kind of Werther in reverse."

Alex Szogyi's adaptation, called *A Country Scandal*, was reviewed in 1960 by Brooks Atkinson, who approved the pruning of the text and the fact that Platonov dies a natural death. Atkinson felt that Chekhov lovers would appreciate the picture Chekhov gave of "the spiritual misery of the garrulous upper classes" in this "fresh and foolish comedy."[14] Lucas (1963) sees this play as a burlesque melodrama – chaotic, unconvincing, and tedious – and valuable chiefly in showing how much of Chekhov's genius was the result of hard work.

N.Y. Berkovsky in 1966 showed that this play grew out of Chekhov's stories "A Lady" and "An Unnecessary Victory" and *The Shooting Party*.[15] Valency (1966) stated that "Platonov speaks not only for the lost generation of the 1880s but for all those who periodically find it possible to rationalize their ineptitude in terms of a tragic sense of the world's absurdity. If he speaks badly, it is because Chekhov did not as yet know how to make him speak well."

Hingley (1967) calls this the most Dostoevskian of Chekhov's works. It is wordy, has lots of action, and the plot, as in Dostoevsky, is a web of financial and amorous complexities. Also, the characters, under extreme emotional pressure, oscillate between love and hate. Platonov discovers that fornication is unpleasant. This play is far less facetious than the comic sketches that Chekhov was then writing. The loss of the family home had bothered Chekhov ever since Selivanov, their lodger in Taganrog, tricked the Chekhov family into allowing him to buy their home. As in *Ivanov*, a single protagonist dominates the play. But seeing that this experiment in overstatement failed, Chekhov changed and instead became the most laconic of the great Russian prose writers.

Kenneth Tynan in 1967 said that *Platonov* is "proof of Chekhov's genius." The central figure "must be regarded as one of the great comic creations of the last hundred years." The characters have "the Chekhovian habit of taking calamities lightly and trivialities tragically." This play of Russian country life "makes a singular impression," Tynan declared.[16] Gilles (1968) was unconvinced, finding the play wordy, unfocused, disorganized, and in places unbelievable. Helen Muchnic in 1971 labeled the play "an intellectual farce" that parodies the superfluous man.[17]

Melchinger (1972) found the play "an encyclopedia of Russian life." He said that most of Act I can be eliminated, because it is wordy exposition. Rayfield (1975) agrees that *Platonov* is the forerunner of Chekhov's mature drama, having a country estate, oppressive atmosphere, seemingly irrelevant dialogue, and eerie symbolism.

The strongest parts of the play are its setting, stage effects, and stage properties. Chekhov had the habit, said Rayfield, of writing comedies out of tragic material.

Hingley (1976) noted that a curtailed version of the play had stage productions in at least four countries between 1928 and 1960. Unusual for Chekhov, in this play there is too much action and too much talk. Hingley (1977) observed that the play had two attempted suicides, two attempted murders (one successful), and a lynching. Peter Egri in 1978 showed how Chekhov linked together several short stories to form this play.[18]

Nicholas Moravcevich, in Barricelli (1981), commented that all four women in the play are seen primarily in terms of their love interest in Platonov, and hence are quite flat as characters. Master (1982) indicates that the opening chess game merely provides realism, whereas the lotto game in *The Sea Gull* is used symbolically. Here Chekhov uses story telling as an expository device; in later plays he uses the "confession." He also uses third-person responses ("Why did he do this to me?") in a search for a way to represent thoughts and indirect action.

Reviewing Michael Frayn's free adaptation of this play as *Wild Honey* in London in 1984, Frank Rich called *Platonov* "one of the most problematic scripts ever written by a major playwright," and Frayn's adaptation "an uneven but impressively well-shaped amalgam of clever Frayn and undeveloped Chekhov."[19]

Senelick (1985) recounted the history of the play's composition. While in school in Taganrog Chekhov wrote a play called *Without Patrimony*. In Moscow he revised it, but it was still too long. He gave it to the famous actress Maria Yermolova, but she rejected it, and so he tore up the manuscript. His brother Michael kept a copy, which was published in 1923. The title refers to the loss of their estates by the main characters. Osip is like Platonov's shadow—when he recognizes the resemblance he gives up his intent to murder Platonov. Egri (1986) shows how Chekhov linked short story elements into this plot. The "undramatic" action of the play is due to Platonov's vacillation. He searches in each of his love affairs for an aspect of his disintegrated ego, but the fragments can provide him no unity. His agony has a tragicomic hue, because he is a drifting, rather than a preying, Don Juan.

The New York production of *Wild Honey* elicited further reviews. Benedict Nightingale recalled the praise of the London critics in 1984, when the *Times* had said that this play was "Chekhov as he might have been." He said that Michael Frayn had eliminated the awkwardness and wordiness of Chekhov's play. Frayn believes that the characters in this play are well drawn, particularly Platonov and Anna. Frayn likes Chekhov's "wonderful double vision, his ability to be effortlessly inside people and yet coolly watching them from the outside at the same time." Nightingale calls Platonov "a peculiarly Russian combination of Hamlet and Don Juan." The railroad, he notes, is used symbolically as a power which, misused, can be destructive. So too with Platonov's personality—he releases emotional powers that he cannot control, and they destroy him.[20]

Mel Gussow reported that in *Wild Honey* Frayn had "reduced the melodrama, trimmed the verbosity, and made the chaos seem more comic." The result is a play as stageworthy as *Ivanov*. Sergey in this play is but a step away from Uncle Vanya, Gussow feels. Frayn makes Platonov a victim of the train. "The Frayn finale, neither homicide nor fright, is more dramatic as well as more symbolic. Platonov is less a manipulator than a victim of circumstance."[21] Brendan Gill, amazed at seeing a full-scale locomotive on the stage, says that the hero of the play is the locomotive. Platonov, in "flagrant display of charm and energy," used "every trick of his trade to keep from being upstaged by an iron horse."[22]

Ivanov (1887)

Ivanov, 35, member of the Council of Peasant Affairs, is bored with his wife Anna, and would rather visit his neighbors the Lebedievs, whose daughter Sasha, 20, interests him. Young Dr. Lvov chides Ivanov for ignoring his sick wife. Anna catches Ivanov embracing Sasha, who wants to elope to America with him. Lebediev offers to secretly lend Ivanov the money he owes them, since Mrs. Lebediev wants the loan repaid. A year later, with Anna dead of tuberculosis, Ivan plans to marry Sasha, over the objections of her parents. Ivanov then calls off the match, saying that he is a bad influence on everyone. Agreeing that Ivanov has become strangely melancholy, Sasha is nonetheless determined to marry him. Lvov denounces Ivanov as a scoundrel for the way he treated Anna. Sasha exposes Lvov as a hypocrite who has tried to make love to her and to Anna. Frustrated and disillusioned, Ivanov says, "My youthful strength has returned," and he kills himself with a revolver.

Fyodor Korsh, Moscow theater owner, pestered Chekhov for a play, and so he wrote the first draft of *Ivanov* in ten days. At its first performance in November 1887 there was much excitement, with both cheering and booing. Chekhov said that "the praises lavished on it somewhat cheered me up," although Peter Kicheyev in the *Moscow Gazette* called it "impudently cynical and immoral rubbish." Chekhov felt that the actors were misinterpreting their roles. Sasha, he explained, loved Ivanov not for himself but for the challenge of helping raise a fallen man. He said that Ivanov had two crucial monologues: one in Act III, "which should be sung," and the other at the end of the play, "which should be read savagely." He denied that the actor N.N. Solovzov had made some revisions in the play. He told his brother Alexander that "the plot of *Ivanov* is complicated but not stupid. My whole energy is expended on a few powerful scenes—the rest is insignificant filler. The acts are quiet and peaceful, but at the end of each act I give the spectator a punch in the nose!"

Chekhov told Suvorin that if he and others could not understand why Ivanov appeared attractive to the other characters, he had failed as a playwright. Ivanov was a tired liberal, he said, who had been frustrated so often in his attempts at reform that now he is beaten by life. But he should be honored for his former high ideals. A Moscow critic in 1889, however, questioned Ivanov's character: How could a supposedly good man treat his wife so meanly, and fall in love again shortly after her death? P.A. Andreyevsky, theater critic for *The Kievan Word*, said in 1889 that no other contemporary play had created such a sensation.

Chekhov's brother Michael, in Koteliansky (1925), described the changes made in the play for the St. Petersburg production in 1889. Written in haste and given insufficient rehearsals in Moscow, the play needed radical alterations. Chekhov, sorry it had been approved by the theatrical committee, said, "I realize how badly it was made. The last act is astonishingly bad. I made a new Sasha, radically changed Act IV, and got so tired out that I came to hate my play." Since he was helping Suvorin revise *Tatyana Repina*, Chekhov got help from him in revising *Ivanov*.

At the St. Petersburg production most critics praised the play, Nikolai Leskov calling it "a wise play, revealing great dramatic talent." The leftist critics, like Vladimir Korolenko, N.K. Mikhailovsky, and Gleb Struve, were less favorable, stating that the play lacked meaning and showed no tendentiousness. Paul Milyukov found no action in the play, "and the principal character presents an impossible combination of contradictions, leaving the reader hopelessly bewildered."[23] Mikhailovsky in 1897 chided Chekhov for "idealizing the absence of ideals," but forgave him as a victim of his milieu.

Long (1902) admitted that the play was stageworthy, but added that "in Chekhov's drama his peculiar genius is obscured, the subjective element becomes apparent, and there is no compensating element of ingenuity of plot or delineation of character." Andrey Bely in 1904 called it Chekhov's weakest play, revealing the nightmarish aspects of a recent era. Shestov (1905) said that this play showed Chekhov to be "a poet of hopelessness." D.N. Ovsianiko-Kulikovsky in 1909 called the play a picture of the inability of the intelligentsia to bridge the gap between their high ideals and the poverty of the materialistic culture of the 1880s.[24]

A reviewer of Marian Fell's translation in 1912 found no merit in the play. The hero, he said, is "a spineless, contemptible driveller whose incessant bewailings of his own worthlessness—which is indisputable—soon become direfully monotonous."[25] Another reviewer took an opposite stance: *Ivanov* was "a very powerful and sinister play upon the theme of temperament," and Chekhov's "fresh" dialogue made the language interesting and suggestive.[26] Neith Boyce added that "the background is so rich, each personality is so suggestive, the details so vital, that one has the impression not only of a firm design, but of an endless interplay of inter-relations, and of that individual isolation that we all feel."[27]

M.V. Trofimov in 1916 analyzed the play at length, calling Chekhov "an original exponent of the new realistic tendency in modern drama."[28] Katherine Mansfield said that this play was Chekhov's determined effort to put an end, once and for all, to the depiction of the melancholy and frustrated superfluous man of Russian literature.[29] Gerhardi (1923) said that the theme of the play is that human nature is too subtle and elusive to permit facile pigeonholing of it.

The Moscow Art Theatre productions in New York in 1923 brought out varying reactions. One critic found it melancholy and tragic, yet brimming with life. Its strength comes not so much from its plot as from "the ill-assorted mob that passes through the play."[30] Another reviewer said that one need not understand Russian to revel in the play's perfection, for "it is written in the international language of genius." Its high point is "a gorgeous second act, a miracle of caricatured human beings living, not acting, before us."[31] But another reviewer felt that not even such an outstanding actor as V.I. Kachalov could keep up interest in the gradual disintegration of Ivanov's character.[32]

A Chicago reviewer recommended this play, "a symbol of the Slav ego in the throes and tortures of self-analysis."[33] Another found this to be "a fretful, poetic, bitterly graphic study in melancholia, with over 17 carefully sketched characters."[34] Kenneth Macgowan said that Chekhov's plays "become life subtly sifted through the intelligence of an uncommon artist, retaining, as no other plays do, the effect of rambling reality and high drama."[35] Leo Wiener recalled the play's first performance in Moscow, when the audience almost came to blows discussing the play. For a long time the one copy of the play was in great demand, for many people wished to read it.[36]

A bevy of critics greeted a London production in 1925. Calling Chekhov "the laureate of futility," E.A. Baughan said that this "strange, repulsive, and yet tremendously interesting play" was more theatrical than *The Cherry Orchard.*[37] This is a composition in the unheroic, said Ivor Brown, and the huge cast of secondary characters amuse us as "lively bundles of what the Elizabethans called 'humours'."[38] J.T. Grein, however, felt that Chekhov lacked technical skill, and "his method often suggests his vision very incompletely. His humor is ironic and saturated with a distrust of life."[39]

Calling Chekhov "the Russian Sean O'Casey," one critic said that the audience was deeply interested even when bewildered.[40] Another praised the vivid depictions of secondary characters, but added that the hero's suicide was "very welcome."[41] A third was grateful to see the excellent characterization of these "born self-revealers," although he felt that irresponsible people like Ivanov are poor choices to convey the will-conflict of drama.[42]

Chekhov's biggest fan, however, was revealed as Desmond MacCarthy. He found Ivanov broken by the immense load he carried: his failed reforms, his bankruptcy, and his loss of love for his wife. The comedy MacCarthy found in "the fact, so true to life, that the private perplexities of the soul are also the concern of people who conspicuously leave that element entirely out of consideration in judging people."[43]

S.D. Balukhaty in 1927 said *Ivanov* represents Chekhov's effort to incorporate contemporary dramatic practices in his own way.[44] Toumanova (1937) reported that many of Chekhov's contemporaries saw Ivanov as themselves—persons lacking willpower, and feeling guilty because of their worthlessness. Bruford (1948) indicated that when Ivanov failed to find the reason for his failure outside himself, the resulting self-indictment led to his collapse. Fen (1951) found a sensitive person destroyed through lack of intellectual companionship and cooperation from other idealists – his milieu was far too miasmic. Magarshack (*Life*, 1952) reported that a student in St. Petersburg committed suicide after seeing the 1889 production.

Magarshack (*Dramatist*, 1952) stated that in the original version, Ivanov died of heart failure after being insulted by Lvov. Magarshack felt that *Ivanov* is a great advance over *Platonov*, for it is compact, its characters are alive, and they avoid extreme self-exhibitionism. By straining to end each act with "a strong curtain," Chekhov sacrificed some realism. In 1889 the *St. Petersburg Gazette* explained "the enormous success, a success rare on our stage" as due to "its accomplished dialogue, its vital truth, its characters taken straight from life, and its far from conventional plot." Another critic praised Chekhov for capturing the current mood, being "among those creative artists who know how to depict the inner physiognomy of an age." The unfavorable notices said that the play had too many scenes, too much talk, and too little action. Some were brave enough to state that its social implications were not justified from a medical viewpoint.

Alexei Diky in 1954 said that despite its defects, *Ivanov* was a very important play, for it condemned a society that had no room for a man of high ideals. M.N. Stroeva in 1955 agreed with Diky, after finding Ivanov a complex character full of contradictions.[45]

Ermilov (1956) said that "Ivanov's suicide symbolized the bankruptcy of the various liberal tendencies rife in the eighties." When Suvorin said that the play's message was that one should stop tilting at windmills in life, Chekhov sharply retorted, "You say there can be nothing more contemptible than our liberal opposition. What about those who do not belong to the opposition? Are they any better? The mother of all Russian ills is crass ignorance, and it is especially characteristic of all parties."

Bruford (1957) found Chekhov daring, in several ways. He dared to use an unconventional hero, and he bravely created an atmosphere of boredom by using sights and sounds to orchestrate the dialogue. Each character gives a new side of Ivanov, while at the same time revealing himself. Ivanov is neither as bad as Lvov thinks he is, or as good as Sasha believes him to be. Elisaveta Fen, looking at *Ivanov* from the standpoint of a translator, felt that it expressed Chekhov's own "discouragement and disgust at having to struggle against so much inertia or downright dishonesty in his environment."[46]

A.P. Skaftymov in 1958 found the play based upon "involuntary guilt": Ivanov did not consciously hurt other people. V.E. Khalizev in 1959 showed how this play grew out of a number of similar plays by lesser known playwrights of that period.[47] Saunders (1960) felt that Chekhov's theme, that Russia had no place for a man of brains and talent, was too subtle for drama.

Charles B. Timmer, in Eekman (1960), explained the play in the light of the bizarre. Ivanov fights the bizarre, and ultimately becomes its victim. Lvov does not admit the existence of the bizarre, but Lebediev accepts the bizarre as an intrinsic part of life. As in Shakespeare, it is Lebediev, the "fool," who gives the best advice: If you and Sasha are in love, get married—if not, part. The fool has not only naïvete but a confidence which all of the horrors of the world cannot shake. It is Chekhov's confidence in the regenerating powers of life, the voice that will be heard "200 years from now."

Slonim (1961) noted that this play's use of intervals, pauses, and disconnected dialogue was not made clear until the Moscow Art Theatre production in 1904. Corrigan (1962) finds in the play the "strong curtains" of the "well made" play. Simmons (1962) said that in Chekhov's revision of the play he wanted to make it clear that Ivanov had arrived at a dead end—even Sasha's love had only lowered himself in his own eyes. Lucas (1963) believed that Sasha was like Chaucer's Wife of Bath: If she can reform Ivanov, it will be a tribute to her power. Why, asks Lucas, does so much of Chekhov's strength lie in depicting weaklings like Ivanov? Partly, he answers, because he was trying to cure himself, or more likely his brothers, of similar afflictions. Also, Chekhov told Suvorin that "only indifferent characters are capable of seeing things clearly."

Meanwhile a critical war was raging among Soviet critics over this play. Nemirovich-Danchenko's 1904 lecture was reprinted, characterizing Ivanov as disillusioned after perceiving the failure of the reforms of the 1860s. L.A. Malyugin in 1960 said that V.V. Ermilov seriously underestimated the importance of *Ivanov*, and then Malyugin refuted the alleged weaknesses found by G.P. Berdnikov. Ermilov defended his position in 1961 by quoting Chekhov on weaknesses he found in the play. In 1964 V.E. Khalizev supported Ermilov, stating that the play lacked a solid ideological foundation, and that Chekhov was warning against reconciling oneself to injustice.[48]

In 1966 John Gielgud adapted *Ivanov* and then directed the production and played the leading role. He called Ivanov an aging Hamlet but with no thought of revenge. He found four scenes of the play exquisitely contrasted, like the movements in a musical composition, "with the exact progression of a born dramatist."[49] Reviewing the play, Stanley Kauffmann said that "the turning point in the history of apathy in drama is Chekhov." In all of his plays, but particularly in *Ivanov*, apathy is the theme. This makes Chekhov very modern, said Kauffmann, in fact, a close bedfellow of Beckett, Ionesco, and Pinter.[50] Wilfred Sheed doubted, however, that Americans had the same "melancholy fascination with neurasthenia and paralysis of the will used by Russian writers."[51] *Variety* found the play "generally absorbing, but in time repetitious," even though "much of the dialogue is pungent, even soul-searching."[52]

Valency (1966) recalls how Chekhov told A.N. Pleshcheyev that revising a play was as hard as turning a soldier's old trousers into a dress coat. Fiction was his legal wife, he added, but the theater was "a noisy, impertinent mistress." After the St. Petersburg performance he left quickly, partly out of modesty and partly out of shame, saying, "It is a play put together like a pudding, with a ludicrous climax and a desperate end. The ballroom scenes in Act II are childish. The comic

characters Borkin, Shabelsky, and Madame Lebediev are stock caricatures."
Valency feels that, like Platonov, Ivanov suffers from an indisposition of the soul.
He has unconscious qualms that perhaps he married Anna for her money. When
he perceives his coming marriage to Sasha as also mercenary, he loses faith in
himself. To depict his inner anguish was an ambitious chore. "No one had
attempted anything so complex before on the Russian stage. Ivanov is the first of
that remarkable gallery of portraits which Chekhov created. The fact that his
character was not quite realized at this time made it likely that it would be reworked
until it came completely to life." The character reappeared two years later as Laevsky in "The Duel." Chekhov at the time was still primarily a fiction writer, and he
became a great playwright only when he abandoned the "rules" of the "well made"
play as practiced by Eugene Scribe.

Hingley (1967) found outspoken social satire in the play. Its lesson is the
danger of making facile moral judgments. Chekhov felt that Ivanov was not a
superfluous man, because he derives from life rather than from literature, and he
blames himself rather than society for his plight. But Hingley felt that he nevertheless had many of the traits of the superfluous man.

Jackson (1967) disagreed with Leon Shestov on whether the play illustrated
Chekhov's destructive tendencies. Jackson quoted A. Skaftymov on Chekhov's use
of boring conversation to show the spiritual emptiness surrounding Ivanov and
Sasha. He also noted that G. Berdnikov had identified the plot as centrifugal, with
the movement away from the central action. Gilles (1968) called *Ivanov* Chekhov's
only effort toward a realistic, active, and popular serious play. Chekhov's theme is
that the idealist's disillusion is really only a kind of romantic self-indulgence.

In 1969 Joseph S.M. Lau noted how Ts'ao Yu's play *Peking Man* (1940)
resembled *Ivanov* in dramatic technique, both plays dealing with the superfluous
man.[53] Arnold B. McMillin (1969) found that all of the elements of conflict in the
play are present from the start: "The tragedy is not of conflict between individuals
but of attrition—the hero is destroyed from within."

Kramer (1970), after observing Chekhov's difficulty in depicting Ivanov
through the various revisions of the play, stated that Chekhov did a much better
job with this kind of character in his tale "A Dreary Story." Speirs (1971) says that
it took Chekhov a long time to find out how quick an audience can be in its
responses. The good parts of *Ivanov* come when Chekhov has the characters talk
as people do in real life.

Melchinger (1972) pointed out that Ivanov had been brave enough to marry
a Jewess. "The anti–Semitic background for the play must be taken seriously; the
young Chekhov had witnessed the deportation of 20,000 Jews from Moscow." Shotton, in Fennell (1973), stated that Chekhov failed in his attempt to get the audience
to reject the didactic ethical practice of contemporary Russian drama, and to prefer
the ineffectual though natural Ivanov to the conventional but hypocritical Lvov.

In 1973 Herta Schmidt employed a structuralist approach of the Prague
Linguistic Circle to *Ivanov*, and found that it was an extreme variant of the drama

of situation. The following year I.U. Tverdokhlebov studied the creative history of the play, using a newly discovered copy of the corrections Chekhov made after the first performance.[54]

Rayfield (1975) called this the best Russian play since Alexander Ostrovsky's best plays of the 1850s. It has a terse, tense texture, with a total integration of every detail. Anna resembles Ophelia; she is the only woman ever to die in a Chekhov play. This play has a lyricism stronger than in any other Chekhov play.

Hingley (1976) says that this play, a better one than *The Sea Gull*, established Chekhov as a serious dramatist. The hissing at the first production was due to the performance—some actors were drunk. The play has a devastating anti–Tolstoyan moral: Do not moralize! Chekhov here may have been castigating the priggishness of his own nature. This highly didactic play has the theme, Do not be didactic. The play is a triumph of craftsmanship. "The scenes are well put together; the dialogue is subtle and lively; and the background is suitably light, and throws the somber elements of the main drama into effective relief."

Benedict Nightingale, reviewing a Royal Shakespeare Company production in 1976, observed that Anglo-Saxons have difficulty getting subjective enough to capture what Chekhov called "the purely Russian" extremes of frenzy and lassitude found in the play, which is a clinical study of spiritual menopause.[55] Hahn (1977) found genuine insight into Ivanov's portrayal of self-disgust, but felt that most characters do not come to life, and most theatrical effects are trite and obvious. Hingley (1977) said that although the play has a conventional structure based upon rising suspense in each act, its technique is sound, using, for example, a light background to introduce several minor comic characters.

In 1977 T.K. Shakh-Azizova examined the play as an example of "Russian Hamletism," saying that although Chekhov could not explain the phenomenon, he always sought for its causes in the objective conditions of life. Peter Egri in 1978 showed how Chekhov linked short stories to form this play, and said that Eugene O'Neill also employed this Chekhovian technique in his plays.[56]

A group of Moscow actors, critics, directors, and dramatists discussed this play in 1980. Playwright Alexei Arbuzov preferred the Royal Shakespeare Company production to that of the Moscow Art Theatre, because the RSC made Ivanov more interesting by showing the cause of his breakdown. Sergei Desnitsky, an MAT producer, explained that Oleg Efremov, the MAT director, had to overcome the lead actor's lack of faith in the play and in the character of Ivanov. Efremov built his reading of the play on the idea of the evening of life as a sunset. Producer Anatoly Efros said that Ivanov shows all the despair of "Ward No. 6"—he is authentic, making a journey into an inferno. Drama critic Konstantin Rudnitsky called Efremov's production excellent: He captured Chekhov's repetitions, which are those of life and which bring out life's tragedy. Mark Zakharov, who produced *Ivanov* at the Lenin Komsomol Theatre, said that people call this play dreary but in reality Chekhov is rejecting everything that is decayed, that has outlived its time.[57]

Tulloch (1980) described the medical background of the play. In 1887 the

Russian psychiatrist I.P. Merzheyevsky gave the first significant Russian lectures on mental health. He adapted Benedict Morel's degeneration theory to Russian conditions.

Besides the usual European decadent factors (alcohol, higher education, sexual abnormality, and bad working conditions), Russia had "intellectual frustration" caused by the unfulfilled promises following Alexander II's reforms. As a follower of Merzheyevsky, Chekhov created Ivanov as just such a frustrated intellectual. Chekhov modestly admitted a lack of dramatic talent, but said that in Ivanov he had presented a new type of Russian who needed to be studied and understood. Ivanov is not just another superfluous man, said Tulloch, but he is an inauthentic hero, one unable to come to grips with his problem.

Kirk (1981) states that Dr. Lvov is a caricature of characters popular in the liberal populist plays of Chekhov's period. Lvov's aggressive honesty is a parody of what Soviet critic G.P. Berdnikov calls Ivanov's "subjective honesty," which permits Ivanov to judge himself with more insight than Lvov has. Chekhov was proud when Fyodor Korsh had not found a single technical error in the play, but that simply showed that Chekhov had written a conventional play.

Master (1982) differs with Tulloch, feeling he has ignored the historical perspective of Ivanov as being in the tradition of Russian superfluous men. As one looks at Ivanov's successive relationships with characters, one finds the action switching from direct to oblique encounter, and then come unasked-for "confessions"—revelations of what is bothering a character. This play thus marks a step towards the "reaction drama" (rather than the "action drama") created by the mature Chekhov.

Senelick (1985) states that Ivanov's suffering comes from his awareness of his own wasted potential. Chekhov's problems were to keep the audience from idealizing Ivanov's pessimism, while also keeping Ivanov from looking as immoral as Lvov says he is. The backbone of the play is gossip. Although Chekhov kept revising the play until 1901, "he never managed to eliminate the mannerisms of boulevard drama that vitiated the subtlety of his concept." Soviet critic A.R. Kugel called Ivanov's suicide "a sacrifice made by Chekhov's soul to the god of theatrical gimmickry." In this play Chekhov had begun to learn the secret of dramatic atmosphere, and he worked carefully to use setting to enhance it. Ivanov's public suicide fits in with his continual self-dramatization; he is always comparing himself to literary characters, but none of them adequately expresses his complexity.

Egri (1986) states that in this play Chekhov did a better job of unifying the short-story elements than he did in *Platonov*, and thus he achieves a clearer and more moving dramatic structure. But Chekhov himself seemed undecided whether Ivanov was a hero or a villain, and therefore the result he obtained is melodrama.

The Wood Demon (1889)

Worrall (1986) recounts the plot: Serebryakov, a retired professor, and his young wife Elena have moved from the city to live with George Voynitsky, his first wife's brother, and Sonya, her daughter. Wealthy Dr. Krushchov ("the wood demon") is a pessimistic ecologist. He and landowner Zheltukhin are both fond of Sonya. George used to admire Serebryakov, but now finds him egotistical and boring. When Serebryakov announces that he is going to sell the family estate, George goes into a rage and commits suicide. Elena, beautiful but aloof, asks a neighbor, Dyadin, to elope with her, but he refuses. As the play ends, a forest fire is burning. Sonya accepts Krushchov's proposal, and Julia, Zheltukhin's sister, will marry Fyodor Orlovsky, a neighbor.

Koteliansky (1925) contains letters by Chekhov describing this play. Chekhov calls the professor "a disgusting selfish fellow who brings despondency and gloom to all those near him." Krushchov sees the utter reliance of mankind upon forests. Chekhov was satisfied with his play: "Positively new characters come through; there is not a single footman, widow, or comic relief character in the play." Chekhov's brother Michael said that the play was written in 12 days, but Chekhov's letters indicate that the writing stretched from May until October.

Reviewing S.S. Koteliansky's translation of *The Wood Demon* in 1926, D.S. Mirsky pronounced it better than its successor, *Uncle Vanya*. "If Chekhov is to be worshipped, he may just as well also be studied," Mirsky said, and *The Wood Demon* was "a distinctly valuable addition to the material available in English for such a study."[58] Another reviewer preferred *Uncle Vanya*, but found "flashes of deep pity and understanding" in the earlier play. He longed to see *The Wood Demon* staged, for "it is a nobler and more amusing play than all but a few that are produced in England and Russia."[59] Still another reviewer found Krushchov "a beautiful human soul, the nearest approach to Alyoska Karamazov that Chekhov could create."[60]

In a study of Chekhov's dramaturgy in 1927, S.D. Balukhaty applauded *The Wood Demon* as a new departure for Chekhov in plot making and dramatic structure.[61] Toumanova (1937) quoted Chekhov's reaction to his play: "I am surprised that such strange things come from my pen." At an amateur production in Surrey in 1938 A.V. Cookman found "occasional flashes of Chekhov's compassion and understanding," and felt it was interesting to see characters who were forerunners of those in *Uncle Vanya*.[62]

Bruford (1948) observed that the characters seemed to assume the responsibility for their own tragic plights. Elena says, "The world is going to ruin not through thieves but because of the latent hostility of open hatred between decent people." Eric Bentley in 1949 compared *The Wood Demon* and *Uncle Vanya*, finding in the latter more "grace," that is, "the least possible number of movements over some definite action."[63] Hingley (1950) stated that nearly all of Chekhov's contemporaries attacked the play as a mechanical presentation of a humdrum person.

They said it would have been better as a novel. Chekhov, however, was feeling his way towards a new approach to drama.

Magarshack (*Life*, 1952) recalls that Chekhov told Suvorin that he was trying to write a "literary" play, since the theater, run by businessmen, was being ruined. While working on the play, Chekhov called it "a lyrical comedy" or a "comedy-novel," the vague terms indicating that in his own mind he was groping for the identity of such a genre. The play was rejected by the Literary and Dramatic Committee, of which D.V. Grigorovich was chairman, on the ground that it was no play but a story written in dialogue. Thus came Chekhov's final break with Grigorovich, whom he resented for always boasting of having "discovered" him. Concerning the play, Chekhov's mind was divided: He was preaching Tolstoy's doctrine of non-resistance to evil, but his instinct told him that a dramatist's job is not to preach but to present life as it is. After his Sakhalin trip convinced him that Tolstoy's theory would not work, Chekhov refused to allow *The Wood Demon* to be published or performed.

Magarshack (*Dramatist*, 1952) called this play a morality on Tolstoyan lines, in which vice is converted to virtue. While trying to write a play of indirect-action, Chekhov unconsciously slipped back into a romantic play with all of its crudities. When he discovered how to master the indirect-action play, he transformed the crude melodrama of *The Wood Demon* into a stage masterpiece, *Uncle Vanya*. Alexander Lensky, producer at the Maly Theatre, rejected *The Wood Demon* as totally unfit for the stage. Grigorovich spread the rumor that Serebryakov was modeled after Suvorin, but Chekhov angrily denied it. The characters eat, drink, talk, and make love, but they do not come to life. There is no scene in which the characters seem to be independent of the play. Their entrances and exits are unmotivated. Coincidences abound, and the *deus ex machina* is used. Nemirovich-Danchenko said that the chief weakness of the play was its obscure plot. At its first performance the only critics who liked it were Dmitry Merezhkovsky and A.I. Urusov.

Saunders (1960) recounts the poor casting of the first performance. The thin young hero looked ridiculous trying to get his arms around the stout middle-aged actress who played Sonya. Also, at the end "the glow of the forest fire was so intense that it caused the audience to laugh." Embarrassed, Chekhov once again vowed to give up writing for the theater. After seeing the Moscow Art Theatre production in 1960, however, Thomas G. Winner felt that the play was stageworthy, and had perhaps been underestimated all along.[64]

Simmons (1962) said that despite its preachment, the play is a movement toward the indirect-action drama of Chekhov's mature period. Although the play is melodramatic, confused, and tiresome, said Lucas (1963), dramatic tastes are so subjective that A.I. Urusov told Chekhov in 1899 that *Uncle Vanya* had spoiled *The Wood Demon*.

Hingley (1964) felt that Krushchov was Chekhov's unsuccessful attempt to create a "positive" hero. Valency (1966) said that Chekhov wrote the play for the actor N.N. Solovzov, who staged the first performance. "The second act was magnificent, but on the whole the play was a perfectly conventional piece of dramatic rubbish," the sort of thing that was usually a success on the Moscow stage. Chekhov liked the theme: Russian wastefulness. Thinking that their resources were endless, the Russians wasted forests, soil, people, and talent. This play was intended to be a comedy of manners. The characters revealed themselves through awkward soliloquies, unlike real life, where people try to use speech to conceal their inmost thoughts. Later Chekhov learned to write subtle dialogue to portray such thoughts. The general consensus was that the play's ending was improbable.

Jackson (1967) quoted Soviet critic A.P. Skaftymov that the the play bemoans the lack of attention that people show one another. "It attacks preconceived labels and stereotypes which prompt one to judge people without any real basis," Jackson said. Fernald (1968) analyzed the love match of Sonya and Krushchov. Sonya is extremely earnest and naïve, and Krushchov, despite his sympathetic nature, is unaware of his effect upon other people. The scene between them has this structure: Sonya expectantly probes his feelings of her; his ambivalence creates suspense; adventure enters, as Sonya suggests love; recognition comes that love really exists; consummation is shown in the form of a lovers' quarrel.

Chudakov (1971) recalled the comments of early critics. N.P. Kicheyev in 1890 complained of the many "aimless episodes." That year Ivan Ivanov said it was a mistake to dramatize humdrum life, "for the more the work of art contains ideas and facts which are rich in content, the better the work." Ordinary conversations bore us, whether at home or on the stage, Ivanov said, "and there's no need to go to the theater and sit through four acts of 'comedy' to hear ten times how people inquire after the health of some stranger." Krushchov, said Chudakov, may be the first hero in Russian literature whose purpose in life is the preservation of nature.

Speirs (1971) found the play shapeless, a dreary succession of squabbles, followed by an occasional reconciliation. Halfway through, Chekhov recognized the lack of coherence, and so the final scenes are more compact. In 1972 Ian Matley reported on Chekhov's conservation interests, as seen in *The Wood Demon* and *Uncle Vanya*. He also listed a number of scientists and scholars who influenced Chekhov's ecological concerns.[65]

Melchinger (1972) used *The Wood Demon* as an example that Tolstoy's influence on Chekhov was not necessarily a good one. Chekhov's subtitle, *Scenes from Country Life*, indicates that he did not regard the finished work as a comedy. Melchinger said that George's suicide was motivated largely by his frustrated love for Elena. Pitcher (1973) felt that the characters were one-dimensional but that the dialogue had Chekhov's typical spontaneity. In Act II, weather and offstage sounds heighten the psychological effect. But in Act III the play falls apart: In an apparent effort to get more action, Chekhov piles up one melodramatic situation after another. In the trumped-up ending Zheltukhin (whose name means "jaundice") receives poetic justice—he is left without a mate, apt treatment for having spread slanderous lies about George and Elena having had an affair.

Shotton, in Fennell (1973), believes that most of the characters represent a degenerate scale of values. Krushchov voices Chekhov's dislike of pigeon-holing people: "When they don't understand me, they stick a label on me, thereby blaming me for something in themselves." The play fails because the inner world of the protagonist is without movement. To atone for this, Chekhov invented a melodramatic plot of purely external events.

Rayfield (1975) calls the play a regression, saying it lacks the compassion and biting wit of *Uncle Vanya*. He attributes the failure to the fact that it was begun as a joint venture with Suvorin, and it contained material that Chekhov was saving for a novel that he planned to write.

Hingley (1976) said that Chekhov's practice was to overpraise his poor works, like *The Wood Demon*, but modestly downplay his masterpieces. Later he was far too hard on this play, however. It is "eminently stageable," as proved by good productions by the British Actors' Company in 1973 and 1974. Hingley (1977) notes that when Chekhov has Krushchov exhibit conventional morality, he does not make it convincing.

In 1981 G.P. Berdnikov discussed the role of *The Wood Demon* in the development of Chekhov's dramaturgy.[66] Kirk (1981) said that the kindest early review came from the journal *The Actor*, which said in 1890 that Chekhov undoubtedly had more talent than this play revealed, attributing the play's failure to the haste with which it had been written.

Barricelli (1981) voiced the views of Simon Karlinsky and Nicholas Moravcevich. Karlinsky labeled it Chekhov's most tendential play, "the one that most concretely embodies his innermost ideas about life, society, and nature." To keep Krushchov from seeming too good to be true, Chekhov made him a prude. He treats Elena rudely, although she is the only one who appreciates his conservationism. Chekhov uses bird symbolism: Elena and Sonya are likened to caged birds, the professor to a horned owl, and Krushchov vows to grow the wings of a free eagle. Alexei Pleshcheyev called Krushchov's action unmotivated and contradictory: "He loves the forest, but treats humans in a far from human way." Dmitry Grigorovich called the play an unsuccessful imitation of Dostoevsky, "halfway between *The Possessed* and the Karamazovs." Suvorin failed to notice the ecological thrust of the play. Moravcevich observed that in this play the female characters are much more richly delineated than in *Platonov* and *Ivanov*.

Laurence Senelick, in Clyman (1985), reported on Yuri Zavadsky's Moscow production of the play in 1960. The hero was treated sympathetically, "but his distance from the others, who ate continuously, rendered him ludicrous."

Senelick (1985) calls the play a comedy of unrequited love and universal hatreds. To answer charges that he was a pessimist, Chekhov postulates Tolstoy's doctrine of universal love as the solution to humanity's problems. For progress in a society, good people must cast aside narrow distrust. "Do not call me a Tolstoyan or a democrat," Krushchov pleads. "Try to find the human being in me first." When the characters accept this view, a happy ending ensues. A slave to his message, Chekhov uses improbabilities: overheard conversations, a conveniently discovered diary, and speedy conversions. But he cleverly had Elena play the pre-duel aria from *Evgeny Onegin* as Act III starts, presaging the coming violence.

Finding George's diary, Krushchov sees how wrong he was to blame Elena as a flirt, Senelick continues. Krushchov's epiphany of self-revelation summarizes the play's meaning: If people like the professor and me are heroes, there is a shortage of them in modern Russia. Chekhov achieved the "staging of real life" that he sought, but the play failed because of its contrived ending, its tendentiousness, and its manipulated psychology. Its ideology, however, Chekhov maintained throughout his life: Honesty in human relations will cure far more social ills than will any doctrinaire program.

12. *The Sea Gull* (1896)

Act I—Young Treplev is staging his futuristic play. Amidst sulphur fumes, it describes the World Soul reigning 200,000 years from now, having conquered Satan, the principle of matter. The actors, his friends, do such a poor job that he calls off the performance. He loves Nina, but her head has been turned by the novelist Trigorin. Treplev's mother, Arkadina, is a former actress, and is now in love with Trigorin. Sorin, Arkadina's brother, owns the estate where the action occurs. Masha Shamraev, daughter of Sorin's steward, loves Treplev, and in turn is loved by Medvedenko, a schoolmaster. Dr. Dorn is having an affair with Masha's mother, Polina. This, then, is clearly a play of displaced love.

Act II—Everyone seems bored by the static life. Treplev puts a dead sea gull at Nina's feet, saying, "Soon I shall kill myself in the same way." He is depressed over the failure of his play, and by Nina's coldness towards him. Trigorin tells Nina how lonely it is to be a famous writer—all he cares about is taking notes for his next book. Nina shows Trigorin the dead sea gull. He invents a short-story plot for her: A girl, as free and happy as a sea gull, is destroyed by a man who has nothing better to do.

Act III—Despondent over Treplev's coldness, Masha will marry Medvedenko. Nina gives Trigorin a medallion engraved "If ever my life can be of use to you, come and take it." In offstage action, Treplev shoots himself in the head, but the wound is superficial. He quarrels with Arkadina over her living openly with Trigorin. Trigorin, slightly drunk, raves about Nina. Arkadina and Trigorin quarrel, then make up and decide to go together to Moscow. Trigorin plans for a secret rendezvous with Nina in Moscow.

Act IV—Two years have elapsed. Masha congratulates Treplev on his success as a writer. Treplev tells Dorn the story of Nina: She ran off with Trigorin and had a child by him. The baby died; Trigorin tired of her and left her. At first, she did well as an actress, but now she has become homesick and is grotesque. Considering her immoral, her father will not let her return home. The whole company plays a game of lotto. Treplev forgives Trigorin for seducing Nina. Treplev says he now understands that literature is not a matter of new or old forms—"a person should write what springs freely from his soul." Nina admits that she still loves Trigorin. Treplev tells Nina that he still loves her. "You've found your path," he says, "but

I'm still floating in a chaos of dreams." Shown a stuffed sea gull, Trigorin does not remember having seen it before. A shot is heard. Dorn takes Trigorin aside and tells him: "Get Arkadina away somehow. Treplev has just shot himself."

In November 1895 Chekhov wrote Suvorin: "I've finished the play. I began it *forte* and finished it *pianissimo*, against all the rules of dramatic art. It came out like a story. Reading it, I became once more convinced that I am not a playwright at all." Theater owner Fyodor Korsh said of the play, "It isn't dramatic. The main character shoots himself behind the scenes, without having given a farewell speech!" A play with new dramatic technique needed a sympathetic producer, but E.P. Karpov, director at the Alexandrinsky Theatre in St. Petersburg in 1896, was used to nothing but the "well made" plays of Victorien Sardou and the younger Dumas. From their poor performances at rehearsals, Chekhov could see that the actors did not understand what he was trying to do in the play.

The first performance of *The Sea Gull* on 17 October 1896 was a fiasco. It was a benefit performance for the buxom comic actress E.I. Levkeyeva, and her fans expected a farce to be staged. During Nina's monologue in Treplev's playlet laughter broke out, and hisses and boos followed. It was one of the greatest failures in Russian stage history.

Chekhov heard fans in the foyer ask, "Why does the management allow plays like this to be performed?" He wrote to his brother Michael that "the play has fallen flat. There was oppressive bewilderment in the theater. The players acted abominably. The moral of it is that one ought not to write plays." The following five performances, however, were better acted and better received.

Simmons (1962) provides a review of the critical reaction to this first performance. A.R. Kugel said, "In all of this, there is too much realistic detail for symbolism; for realism, there is too much symbolistic nonsense." Selivanov, writing for the liberal *News*, called the play "absurd," adding that no great writer would ever write such trash. The *Petersburg Leaflet*, after asking "What is the point of this decadence?" went on to call the play "badly conceived and unskillfully put together; its contents are very improbable, or better, there are no contents. Every act reeks with despairing, dull, false people." I.I. Yasinsky in the *Bourse News* said that the play was "confused and wild." "This sea gull," said Yasinsky, "is a goose."

N.A. Leykin told Chekhov how critics unfavorable to him had congregated after Act I, and did their best to provoke the offensive behavior of the Levkeyeva fans. The *Theatergoer* in November 1896 said that at least half of the playgoers that first night were "the worst enemies of Mr. Chekhov. They were out to settle personal accounts." The critic in the *Week* wondered "what evil could Chekhov have done, whom had he offended, to deserve the evil suddenly heaped upon him?"

The lotto game in Act IV baffled critics. A.A. Sokolov wrote a parody in 1896 in which ten artists, "having nothing to do, played a game of lotto and left." I. Alexandrovsky was exasperated when the play came to Kiev. While spectators waited anxiously to see what had happened to the main characters, he said, a group of other persons calmly played lotto, as if nothing mattered.

Following that dreadful first night, some positive reviews began to appear. Leykin and I.N. Potapenko praised the play, and A.F. Koni, a prominent lawyer, wrote to Chekhov, "This is life itself on the stage, with its tragic alliances, eloquent abstractions, and silent sufferings. And how wonderful is the conclusion! But scarcely anyone has understood its concealed irony." The irony was that "fragile" Nina was not the pathetic sea gull, but rather the would-be strong Treplev. Chekhov told Koni that he had more faith in him "than in all the critics put together."

Vladimir Nemirovich-Danchenko, who along with Konstantin Stanislavsky founded the Moscow Art Theatre (MAT) in 1898, asked Chekhov for permission to stage *The Sea Gull*, saying that it was playing all over the country; why not put it on in Moscow? "The enthusiastic reviews in the Kharkov and Odessa newspapers are quite unprecedented," Danchenko said.

At the first MAT rehearsals Stanislavsky said that the play, being unsuited for the theater, would fail, but Danchenko insisted on going ahead. Stanislavsky, who then worked hard on the play, later (1924) described his feeling at the time: "After my first acquaintance with *The Sea Gull* I did not understand the essence, the beauty of his play. When I directed the play I still did not understand it. But some of the inner threads of the play attracted me. Apparently there are many ways to hidden riches into the soul of the play."

Stanislavsky interpreted the play as a romantic melodrama. Chekhov protested that he made Trigorin too elegant and too formal. Some critics disliked Stanislavsky's mannerisms and his elaborate stage effects. A.I. Urusov, after calling the lighting "phony and unnatural," wrote that "Moscow has positively fallen in love with *The Sea Gull*; at moments it seemed that life itself was speaking from the stage."

Much has been written about how Chekhov and the MAT mutually saved each other. *The Sea Gull* was an outstanding success in the MAT production in 1898, and a symbol of a sea gull adorns the MAT curtain to this day. Before his death Chekhov became a shareholder in the MAT.

Since Chekhov had missed the successful MAT production in 1898 (being ill in Yalta), he was given a private performance on 1 May 1899. He disliked the performance, saying that Nina sobbed all the time, even in Act IV where her strength is revealed, and Stanislavsky made Trigorin look as if he were paralyzed. Not all critics received the play favorably. Evgeny Solovyev in 1900 called it "a strange symbolic play without a beginning or ending." But Leonid Andreyev applauded Chekhov's "panpsychology," meaning the technique of having every little nuance in the play contribute to the overall effect.

When the play was finally staged successfully in St. Petersburg in 1902, Sergei Diaghilev's *World of Art* said that the performance proved that "as a dramatist Chekhov has become a classic." Yuri Eichenwald joined the yea-sayers in 1904, calling Treplev (along with Trofimov of *The Cherry Orchard* and Vershinin of *The Three Sisters*) "aristocrats of the spirit who incarnate the best quality of mankind, the ability to thirst spiritually."

More charitable towards Chekhov's drama than towards his fiction was Leon Shestov (1905). It was an original concept to use chance as a determining factor in the play, said Shestov, since it is such a factor also in life. Here Chekhov captured the true artist's attitude towards life—he is slave to his art as if under a hypnotic trance. Trigorin confesses that he cannot escape from his plots. The speech of some characters is intentionally monotonous, betraying their dull personalities. Shestov said that young people like Treplev and Nina typically speak of a new life but hardly ever get there.

In the United States Chekhov's drama had to undergo a similar trial by ordeal by the critics. Leo Wiener in 1903 said that all of the characters of this Russian pessimist "seemed to be fit subjects for the psychiatrist, especially in *The Sea Gull* and *The Three Sisters*, in which there is not one redeeming person, and where the very language of the actors is nothing but a series of semi-articulated hysterical ejaculations."[1]

The first performance of a Chekhov play in the United States was *The Sea Gull*, staged by a company directed by Paul Orlenev, a Moscow actor who led a touring company that was raising money to establish a Russian national theater. The performance, in Russian, took place at a Russian Lyceum on East Third Street in New York City on 22 December 1905. One reviewer commended the "supple, intense effort" obtained by the actors who used restraint to express the play's deep emotions.[2] Christian Brinton said that this play by "the gentle, ironical painter of the intellectuals" made a profound impression on the public, awakening them to "a pathetic consciousness of their weakness and lack of will." He contrasted theatergoers in Russia and in America, where the theater is a place for diversion or escape from boredom. In Russia literature has a vital role to play, he said, and "not until most of the country's wrongs are righted will fiction or the drama settle down to a trivial dilettanteism."[3]

Chicago critics welcomed the Orlenev troupe. One reviewer was so impressed by the "perfect performance" of this "grim sort of comedy" that he proudly announced a return of the Orlenev company scheduled for later that year.[4] Another called *The Sea Gull* "a curious gallery of brilliant, insecure egotists rapturously absorbed in making themselves miserable. All were drawn with exquisite verity, and over the whole representation rested an indefinable somber, wistful charm."[5]

The Sea Gull was also the first Chekhov play to be performed in Great Britain. On 2 November 1909 George Calderon directed his own translation of the play at the Royalty Theatre in Glasgow. One reviewer said the audience was puzzled to see an innocent young girl ruined in a "comedy." But the play had "remarkable character contrasts, and is full of interesting commentaries on life and art—a drama of realism which ought to be seen by every serious student of the stage."[6] Another critic called it "a most enjoyable intellectual experience, a picture which results from a thousand minute, carefully calculated touches. The futility of life is seen, but the whole is illumined by comedy, and the humanity of the play is so warm and appealing that it somehow touches and interests more than it depresses."[7]

Maurice Baring in 1910 made a detailed analysis of *The Sea Gull.* By showing the conflict between mother and son, and between Treplev's generation and Trigorin's, this was the play by Chekhov that most resembled conventional Western drama, Baring stated. Arkadina's character was drawn with great subtlety, her real love for her son being just as plain as "her absolute inability to appreciate his talent and cleverness. Equally subtle was Trigorin, an egotist presented with no tinge of ill-nature or malice." This was the most dramatically effective of Chekhov's plays, Baring felt.[8]

The importance of George Calderon's introduction to his *Two Plays by Tchekhof* (1912) has already been mentioned. Calderon showed that the first two acts of *The Sea Gull* were largely atmospheric, and the last two contained the main action. Whereas Act I builds "an atmosphere of rustic quietude," in Act II "a squall of nerves is brewing." The characters have a remote comedic point of view which enables them to envision their misfortune without malice. Thus Sorin, who has missed out on most of life's joys, spends most of his time laughing, and Masha cannot help dancing a few solo steps when Treplev played a waltz celebrating his love for Nina. Although the sea gull symbol was too obvious in the play, at least it was used more artfully than Ibsen's symbols, Calderon felt.

Reviewers welcomed Calderon's translations. One mentioned "Chekhov's remarkable gentleness towards his bankrupt individuals,"[9] and another found the play "interesting but baffling," portraying "life with all its unexpected turns, its trivialities, and its baffling denouements."[10]

Reviewing the first production of *The Sea Gull* in London, several critics mentioned that the play demands ensemble acting that the English company had not achieved.[11] One critic felt that the author must have had "a strange outlook" in order to show so many "pairs of frustrated lovers."[12] Huntly Carter believed that Chekhov had created a new form of drama, in which the audience forgets the theater and concentrates on the play. Chekhov's strengths were his symbolism and lyrical dialogue, Carter said, while his weaknesses were an uninspiring plot and the use of asides and soliloquies.[13]

Ashley Dukes in 1913 said that "the weakness of Chekhov's strikingly original technique is that his characterization depends so much more upon what the characters say than upon what they do. The conversation is always extraordinarily good," but unfortunately Chekhov lacks a sense of theater.[14]

Barrett Clark agreed with Dukes, asking how a play can be built by just having characters tell us their thoughts. Chekhov nearly succeeds, Clark said, "but his plays fall short of perfection through too great insistence upon character in the abstract."[15] Calling Chekhov "a modern Turgenev," Emma Goldman said that this play reveals the triumph of an idealist who would rather die than surrender his ideals.[16]

A number of American reviewers, reacting to *The Sea Gull* as staged by the Washington Square Players in New York, said that the characterization was excellent, but the play was too gloomy for an American audience.[17] One wondered how a person could "take seriously the neurasthenic maunderings which in this play are paraded in the guise of dramatic complications."[18] Another, after saying that "a little common sense would wipe out all the complications," agreed that the play holds one's interest throughout, with "no little humor and considerable insight into character."[19] Philip Littell went further, saying that, after this realistic picture of Russian boredom, it would be hard to return to the "unreality" of a typical American play. Chekhov, amused by the people he pities, shows us that life is not only absurd but also deeply moving, Littell averred. But since "a Chekhov play gets its unity in your mood," the audience must concentrate with something more than the usual half-hearted effort.[20]

At each performance of *The Sea Gull*, one critic seemed to chastise the others for their obtuseness. In 1919 at the London Art Theatre presentation the "chastiser" was "J.S." in the *Athenaeum*. First of all, he gave extracts of all their views. William Archer in the *Star* had professed an inability to "recognize and place" the Russian characters. The *Daily Mail* called the play an unconscious burlesque of modern monotony and gloom. The *Daily News* had said that drama cannot be made of such negative natures as these. The critic in the *Daily Telegraph* labeled it "a superfluous spectacle of unredeemed gloom and pessimism," and the London correspondent of the *Manchester Guardian* found it insincere and full of irrelevancies. Sydney Carroll of the *Sunday Times* said that the play presented "a coterie of neuropaths, all adept at making themselves unhappy." In explaining the inadequacy of all these views, "J.S." pointed out that the play had "an infinitely careful balancing of values and building up of details" which had been blunted in this production.[21]

Gilbert Cannan likewise marveled that a dramatic masterpiece like *The Sea Gull* could survive such fumbling by actors who did not understand their lines. Even so, their speeches and actions went thrillingly "down to the center of their being, revealing their passions." The play's incidents were soul events not expressed in external action, but indicated by seemingly irrelevant gestures.[22] A list of many of these subtle devices was provided by the former secretary of the MAT, who also showed how errors in the costumes, setting, and staging of the play made it seem incoherent to an English audience.[23]

Storm Jameson in 1920 said that the play's message is that it is not failure to continually struggle for a better life, whether one achieves the goal or not. Chekhov goes beyond Gorky and Tolstoy, Jameson said, in realizing there is no solution to the problem of life, but his art is not strong enough to carry him through the despair brought on by this realization. Chekhov is thus a great artist but not a great dramatist. Even so, his plays lie on the threshold of the future, Jameson opined.[24]

Arnold Bennett in 1923 said that *The Sea Gull* was not being performed in England, probably because it was far inferior to *The Cherry Orchard*: "There are too many prominent women in it, the interest is too diffused, and the heroine is not salient enough."[25] Gerhardi (1923) gave an example of Chekhov's effective use of disconnected dialogue in *The Sea Gull*. When Shamraev tells the story of the church cantor who sang "Bravo, Silva!" one octave lower than the famous basso Silva, underpaid Medvedenko can only respond, "And what is the pay of a church cantor?"

In his autobiography Stanislavsky (1924) recalled the partnership between the MAT and Chekhov. "I now realize," he said, "that Treplev's play must be taken seriously, for it is the theater of the future." Treplev's theatrical rules are important for all actors to follow. The tragedy is that his mother, an actress, knows this to be so, but cannot admit it out of jealousy and pride. Stanislavsky said that the progressively longer time intervals between the acts bear out Chekhov's intent of the "increasingly more serious results that stem from Treplev's playlet in Act I."

That year Leo Wiener asserted that it was *The Sea Gull* that saved the MAT in 1898, not the other way around. The play had been popular from Kiev to Astrakhan before Danchenko convinced Stanislavsky that it should be staged in Moscow, Wiener claimed.[26]

At a London production in 1925 some reviewers saw the play as an unusual blend of pathos and comedy,[27] and others as a portrait of feckless upper-class Russians.[28] Francis Birrell lauded "this magnificent play," having "not only the wit, the sadness, and the beauty, but that marvelous loose construction which gives Chekhov's plays that enormous sense of reality."[29] Desmond MacCarthy recommended that everyone who likes to study human personality and dramatic technique should see this "beautiful study in human nature, penetrating, detached, and compassionate."[30]

The year 1929 marked the apogee of the reception of Chekhov's drama in England and the United States. *The Sea Gull* alone saw three London and two New York productions that year. A reviewer of the London Art Theatre production remarked on Nina's growth from a naïve girl to a worn woman of the world,[31] and others marveled at how scores of seeming "irrelevancies" were necessary to achieve the overall effect.[32] A critic said that the play, though Chekhov's weakest, preached "Great are the dangers of excessive sensibility," and concluded that "of course a bad play by Chekhov is better than a good play by almost anyone else."[33] Chekhov was clearly superior to G.B. Shaw in characterization, one reviewer insisted, for "his characters are not intellectual types presenting different points of view on current topics, like the members of a debating society, but living people who feel joy and sorrow, hope and despair, and all the mercurial alternations of mood which real men and women know."[34]

Later that year, at the Fortune Theatre in London, there were reviewers praising the blend of irony with sympathy,[35] and others decrying the lack of humor in the production.[36] Herbert Farjeon, after calling it "one of the most beautiful plays in the world," said that "in the hierarchy of genius Chekhov's place lies somewhere between Shakespeare and Shaw."[37]

At Leo Bulgakov's production in New York City one critic felt that *The Sea Gull* "lacks the accented note of resurrection necessary to give it completion and full universality,"[38] while others said that the play was not only about art but about "the blind ineffectuality of life, and the tragic gap between desire and attainment."[39] No wonder that Communist Russia distrusts Chekhov," said Joseph Wood Krutch, "for he is the end of an era of which he is at once the most graceful apologist and the most damning critic." Here Chekhov casts a spell creating "an experience as preciously fragile as any which the theater has to offer."[40]

Reviewers of the production of Eva LeGallienne's Civic Repertory Company were somewhat divided on the merits of the play. Three of them felt that *The Sea Gull* suffered from a declining spiritual tempo,[41] while two praised its picture of pre-revolutionary Russia.[42] When Brooks Atkinson said that "to report that it is the quintessence of human life on earth is to exaggerate hardly at all," at least one other critic seems to have agreed with him.[43] The production led Stark Young to observe that "for our American dramatists Chekhov affords the closest great influence to be had, for his realism has the same world as our realism, the only world our art knows for the present. What Chekhov can give us is plain: more delicacy of perception, more deeply interwoven themes, more poignancy, sincerity, and truth of intention."[44]

To cap Chekhov's greatest year in the Western world, E.H. Carr summarized Chekhov's ranking 25 years after his death. Carr noted how far critical opinion had changed, from its original apathy and hostility to its nearly excessive current encomium. In *The Sea Gull*, said Carr, Chekhov both employs symbolism and parodies its use, as he evolved an esthetic ethic which, new to Russia, divorced literature from political reform or other tendentiousness. "Economy of effort, emotional restraint, perfection of form, ethical objectivity—this is the note which Chekhov imported into Russian literature," Carr believed. More than anyone else, "Chekhov saw the triviality of life's tragedies." When the current furor over Chekhov has subsided, Carr predicted, "Chekhov's place will be secure among the classics of the second rank."[45]

In 1936 Danchenko in his autobiography described in detail the first performance by the MAT of *The Sea Gull*. Theodore Komisarjevsky, a disciple of Stanislavsky, staged the play in London that year. Several critics objected to the slow pacing of the production,[46] and one attacked the characterization, saying that "a sane man in a Chekhov ménage is as curious as an Esquimo in the tropics."[47]

Ashley Dukes, who in 1913 said that "Chekhov was by no means a great dramatist," now reversed himself. After praising the main characters in the play Dukes called Chekhov "the most popular of international dramatists," for having achieved "the supreme expression of dramatic naturalism as an art form."[48] A number of reviewers agreed with the critic for the *Times*, who said that this "supreme masterpiece of the theatre" gave "a terrible insight into human weaknesses."[49] Desmond MacCarthy, after asserting that a superior work of art needs to embody "a suggestion of desirable life," found it in the mood of Chekhov, "in the infection which we catch from the spirit of the whole play, in the delicate, truthful, humorous compassionate frame of mind of one who observed human nature, understood, and forgave."[50]

Toumanova (1937) said that, to protest against theatrical conventions, Chekhov evolved an original dramatic structure while portraying the rapid alternations of human moods. In 1938 S.S. Balukhaty published a study of the play which included Stanislavsky's text, notes, and production score. That year A.I. Roskin gave a detailed explanation of the reasons for the failure of the initial production in 1896.[51]

Probably the most famous of all American productions of *The Sea Gull* was the one by Alfred Lunt and Lynn Fontanne in 1938. Stark Young, whose translation was used, criticized previous translations for making Chekhov appear gloomy, and for missing the slight variations, repetitions, and juxtapositions which subtly enrich the play's texture.[52]

Several reviewers could not recommend the production, feeling that Fontanne displayed a shallow Arkadina.[53] One alleged that this "museum piece of the theater creaks in its construction."[54] Others, however, considered Chekhov to be one of the few modern dramatists who know the magic of the unspoken word.[55] Some critics thought of the play as an excellent study of human growth and decline.[56] Richard Watts Jr. said that Chekhov had "poured forth the bitterness of his soul with such eloquence, compassion, and almost comic sadness that the play becomes beautiful, not futile; not pathologically morbid but richly understanding; not childish in its misery but magnificent in its pity."[57]

Chicago reviewers also welcomed the play, one saying that Chekhov poetically synthesized "dream-stuff" into life's realities,[58] and another calling the battle between Treplev and Arkadina "one of the peak moments of the theatrical season."[59] Henry T. Perry that year called the movement of the play circular rather than linear. The dialogue moves on two levels at the same time, one the casual talk of everyday life "and the other a deeper, more intense, and less clearly defined realm of inner illumination. At the end the contrast between these two planes of experience is so violent that one is shocked into admitting the paradoxical nature of the universe as it appeared to Chekhov."[60]

Two American critics in 1945, asserting that *The Sea Gull* is neither comedy nor tragedy, said that Chekhov maintained an esthetic distance from his characters so that the audience will adopt an attitude of "wise pity" towards them.[61] N.E. Efros in 1946 discussed the play's inception, various productions, and its reception by critics and the public.[62] Bruford (1948) said that the effect of Treplev's playlet is to show the pettiness of human life contrasted with the beauty of nature.

Avilov (1950) recounted the nature of her relationship with Chekhov. In the introduction, David Magarshack says that Nina is based on no actual person, but was "a completely realized individual portrait of a strongminded girl." Perhaps Chekhov was revealing his love for Avilov, Magarshack stated, when he insisted that she see the special performance put on for him by the MAT in 1899. Avilov recounted the stories of the medallions with engravings that figured in the lives and works of Chekhov and Avilov.

Magarshack (*Dramatist*, 1952) pointed out that Chekhov drew upon three of his stories in writing *The Sea Gull.* "A Dreary Story" gave him the Nina plot; "The Wolf" provided Trigorin's description of a writer capturing the moon's reflection; and "The Neighbors" contained the idea, from Lydia Avilov, of engraving the page number of a literary work upon a pendant. In a letter Chekhov described his sadness at seeing a woodcock shot by Isaac Levitan. The Potapenko-Mizinova affair was part of the plot. Levitan's attempted suicide triggered Chekhov to try to put all of these things into one play. Nikolai Efros was wrong to say that Levitan had killed a sea gull—he had wounded a woodcock, and then asked Chekhov to kill it. After Suvorin criticized Chekhov for Trigorin's resemblance to Potapenko, Chekhov spent three months revising the play. It was Potapenko who got the censor to approve the play. For the published version in *Russian Thought* in 1896, Chekhov restored the censor's cuts and made many other changes. He made further revisions to the play in 1897 and 1901.

This play is "a complete synthesis of theme and character," Magarshack said, which creates an illusion of real life. Although there are many love triangles, none is decisive. Chekhov remarked, "To me, Nina's part is everything in the play." The sea gull symbolized the destruction of beauty by those who do not appreciate it. What destroyed Treplev was his mother-fixation. His whole aim in life is to convince her that he is a genius, but she calls him "a Kiev artisan." Treplev hates Trigorin for two reasons: his love of Arkadina, and of Nina. Trigorin is not a great writer because he has "no iron in his blood"—the courage to write what he feels. Dorn, one of Chekhov's most endearing doctors, has a passion for humanity. The only well balanced character in the play, Dorn relieves the nervous tension found in the other characters. "Masha, like her mother, sees the whole aim of her life as being the mistress of the man she loves." Masha's life is empty—people who have nothing to live for are doomed to a life of constant unhappiness. This is the play's leit-motif.

Reviewing Magarshack's book, Brooks Atkinson recalled Chekhov's complaint that Stanislavsky had ruined his plays by turning them from comedies into tragedies. Chekhov saw a "better life" coming soon. The horrors of Stalinism, Atkinson complained, had turned comedies like *The Sea Gull* back into tragedies, "despite Chekhov's more cheerful intention."[63]

Reviewing a New York production in 1954, Atkinson called Chekhov "the writer with the most profound insight. He is for all times and all places because he goes to the roots of life."[64] John Beaufort called the production good in humor and in the tragic aspects of misdirected love, but lacking the required ensemble acting and sub-surface tension.[65] Also that year John Gassner named Chekhov "Sophocles of modern Europe," able to keep his poise even while dealing with life's harshest realities. In dramatic technique he focused on a group rather than on an individual, and he created a "poetry of environment" by subtly shifting the mood.[66]

Ermilov (1956) stated that Lydia Mizinova's unhappy love life (first with Chekhov and then with Potapenko) was the source of the plot. This play was Chekhov's most personal work, in which he disclosed the difficult life of the artist.

Treplev's suicide came when he realized how far Nina had outstripped him as an artist. Although he has sympathy for characters like Masha, Treplev, and Trigorin, Chekhov cannot quite forgive their weaknesses. Masha's love, lacking a deep purpose, turns beauty into ugliness. The 1896 failure of *The Sea Gull* led directly to the onset of Chekhov's fatal illness, Ermilov believed.

Also in 1956 Thomas G. Winner traced the effect of *Hamlet* upon *The Sea Gull*. The early play serves as "an ironic commentary on Treplev's pretensions" and also heightens the tension in Chekhov's play.[67] Bruford (1957) said that although the play seems to be naturalistic, its effect is profoundly lyrical. Bruford feels that Chekhov preferred to show unhappy love in his plays because happy love, lacking in tension, is undramatic. Each act has a dominant character: I–Treplev, II–Trigorin, III–Nina, and IV–all themes clash and are reconciled. As in Greek tragedy, the final tragic act, Treplev's suicide, occurs offstage.

In 1958 Alvin B. Kernan asserted that this play was Chekhov's own search for an adequate dramatic format. Each character possesses a different theory of drama. T.A. Stroud that year studied the influence of *Hamlet* upon *The Sea Gull*. V.E. Khalizev in 1959 showed the links between *The Sea Gull* and previous Russian drama. The following year L.A. Malyugin argued that Ermilov overestimated Dorn's importance, and Robert Tracy recalled George Calderon's work as a Chekhov translator, director, and critic.[68]

Eekman (1960) quoted Soviet critic A.N. Roskin that some lines from *Hamlet* are used as one of the leitmotifs of *The Sea Gull*. Ehrenburg (1962) reported that when the French writer Jean-Richard Bloch saw *The Sea Gull* in Paris in 1939 he said that Chekhov's characters resembled those of Louis Aragon, Andre Malraux, and François Mauriac–in other words, Chekhov's characters are universal. Chekhov built them out of a complex mixture of many persons that he knew. They are "an amalgam of observation, personal experience, knowledge of life, conjecture, and imagination."

Simmons (1962) felt that Trigorin resembled Chekhov more than Potapenko, because of his manner of writing and his ideas about art. Even more, in Simmons's opinion, Dorn reflects Chekhov's views that there is no beauty without seriousness, and that every work of art must embody a clear idea. Chekhov shared many of Stanislavsky's views concerning the modern theater's weaknesses: it had melodrama and false pathos, and the declamation of the acting made the play seem unnatural. When the cast of the MAT congratulated Chekhov after the successful production in 1898, Chekhov "to the depths of his being felt that he had been morally and artistically resurrected."

At a performance of the play in New York in 1962, Howard Taubman said that the cast, in modern dress, transformed Chekhov's portrait of decaying czarist Russia into "what looks like a troubled house party of middle-class Americans." But paradoxically the more Russian Chekhov's characters remain, "the more readily other people can see themselves mirrored in them."[69]

Lucas (1963) opined that the subtitle of this play could well be *The Egotists*.

Stanislavsky, said Lucas, did well in getting the cast to take infinite pains with their roles so as to produce an ensemble effect, but he overdid the emphasis on stage business and stage effects. Jim W. Miller in 1964 pointed out that Stark Young's novel *River House* used an ending very similar to Act IV of *The Sea Gull*.[70]

After studying *The Sea Gull* and a number of Chekhov's stories, V.N. Ilin stated in 1964 that these works showed "an irrefutable Christian argument in favor of the existence of God." L.A. Malyugin that year reviewed the stage history of the play, and Martin Nag argued that *The Wild Duck* by Ibsen did influence Chekhov's symbolism in this play. In 1965 Christine Edwards showed Chekhov's contributions to the MAT productions of his plays, and Nicholas Volkov studied the use of themes from *Hamlet* in *The Sea Gull*.[71]

Dorothy Seyler that year disagreed with Martin Nag, stating that in *The Sea Gull* Chekhov was satirizing symbolism, Ibsen, and especially *The Wild Duck*.[72] Valency (1966), on the other hand, agreed with Nag that Chekhov's debt to Ibsen was very great. *The Sea Gull*, said Valency, was an expiatory offering to Lydia Mizinova. Chekhov's comedy lacks the objectivity of classical drama, for Chekhov is sympathetic towards his characters. The weaknesses of Chekhov's play are the clumsy exposition, Nina's unmotivated return in Act IV, and the fact that Act IV is an epilogue. When Chekhov eliminated the usual "stage rubbish"—big roles, heated tirades, displays of passion, climaxes, and strong exits—he found the MAT moving in the same direction, having learned from the Meiningen Players that in order for a play to have unity, a single will should govern it. The problem arose when Stanislavsky, who wanted to govern as director and who liked exaggeration, clashed with Chekhov, wishing to govern as author and craving simplicity.

Winner (1966) saw *The Sea Gull* as an inverted *Hamlet*, with Treplev as Hamlet, Arkadina as Gertrude, and Nina as Ophelia. But Treplev turns out to be only a pseudo–Hamlet, Winner believes, for he fails due to his own mediocrity rather than a tragic flaw. L.P. Grossman in 1967 studied Lydia Mizinova as the prototype for Nina. Julius Mrosik that year, after tracing Chekhov's use of the symbolic sea gull, concluded that the major influence came from Ibsen.[73] Hingley (1967) found a clumsy use of the sea gull as a symbol, and said that the play's somber tone did much to establish Chekhov's reputation as a pessimist.

Jackson (1967) disagreed with Leon Shestov's assessment of Chekhov as a "poet of despair," pointing out that Chekhov cannot be equated with his characters, for in describing them he maintains an esthetic distance from them. Although A.V. Lunacharsky said that the characters flounder about, waiting for something to happen, in actuality Chekhov here "views man's interaction with reality as one which contains a creative potential." Treplev's playlet, depicting the struggle against Satan, is repeated in Treplev's struggle against his mother's sinful lust. The big issue of the play is, how does one struggle against fate? Treplev is overcome, and dies; Nina struggles successfully to endure.

Fernald (1968) noted that sound effects, especially music, are very important in this play. They reinforce characters, build atmosphere, heighten suspense, and provide leitmotifs that unify the play.

Gilles (1968) believes that the play shows life's duality: The disparity between our aspirations and reality is frightening. Chekhov goes beneath surface realism, "to open the doors of one's most secret self, the self of unbearable contradictions, the star chamber of conscience," where we condemn ourselves for failing to be what we would like to be. The disquieted spectator feels himself to be the accomplice of these characters who resemble himself. Such "poetry" can even revive one's own thwarted ambitions, at least for an evening.

Williams (1968) pointed out that Stanislavsky's detailed production score enabled the MAT to carry out Chekhov's intent, for Chekhov's text was rather sparse. In 1969 Konstantin Rudnitsky discussed productions of the play by both the MAT and Vsevolod Meyerhold. Paul Gromov in 1970 showed Chekhov's influence on Stanislavsky and Meyerhold, and argued that Treplev's playlet contained philosophical ideas of Vladimir Solovyov, influencing both Chekhov and Meyerhold.

N. Ulianov that year said that Chekhov was "a mystic by nature," and that Treplev's ideas in the playlet were Chekhov's. To prove his point, Ulianov showed mystical and supernatural elements present throughout Chekhov's writings. In 1971 N.A. Kovarsky stated that Chekhov's heroes sometimes belong in different genres. For example, in this play Trigorin is a comic hero and Treplev a tragic one.[74]

Jacob Adler in 1970 showed parallels between *The Sea Gull, Hamlet,* and *The Wild Duck.* Just as *The Wild Duck* provides a critique of *Hamlet,* so does *The Sea Gull* provide a critique of *The Wild Duck.*[75] Burton Kendle that year said that the characters' repeated requests for horses express their subconscious desire to escape their forbidding environment. Nina, he points out, is the only one to use her horses.[76] Chudakov (1971) shows that Chekhov, in his fairness, shows not only two conflicting views on writing (those of Treplev and Trigorin) but he also has even these characters question their own basic premises about writing.

Speirs (1971) says that here Chekhov is trying to educate his audience into a new attitude towards drama, but he deals with too many themes at one time. He is not only answering Tolstoy's question "What is art?" but is also showing the relationship between art and life. Treplev's playlet is pretentious and vapid. Chekhov does a good job presenting the Treplev-Nina-Trigorin love triangle but a poor job resolving it. Act IV is "a smokescreen to cover up the fact that his play had fizzled out." We are left in the dark about Nina's ultimate outcome, in her life and in her art. The collaboration between authors and actors is one of the many "teasing problems" presented in the play. Soon enough Chekhov and the MAT were acting out this problem in real life. "Chekhov gradually discovered that one way to prevent overstatement on the stage was to understate everything in the text," Speirs said.

Styan (1971) says that although each character is engaged in a lonely struggle, he reveals himself only in social groups, and hence this play is "the first great experiment on the modern stage which demands orchestrated symphonic acting." Stanislavsky said that developing his production score was like scoring for an orchestra. Silent reading cannot bring out the notes – only a stage performance can. The audience needs to find the universal statement contained in the individual lines. "Treplev's sea gull in Act II is part victim, part tribute, and part threat," Styan feels. Masha's addiction to snuff and brandy is her rebellion in search of a greater stimulant than Medvedenko. Treplev is an anti-hero used to point up the selfish indifference of those about him. Dorn serves as the *raisonneur*. Treplev's playlet is a parody of French poetic symbolism and German romantic drama, thus showing the direction that new forms of drama should not take. "A play-within-a-play has the effect of sharpening the meaning and reality of the play which is its context."

In Act II, says Styan, Dorn hums the song "Tell her, my flowers," a "sly criticism of the whole love-sick pack, all sick of self-love." Nina has more courage than Treplev: She abandons her tyrant father but he cannot abandon his tyrant mother. Had the play ended with Act III, it would have seemed like a "well made" play by Scribe or Sardou. Of the lotto game, Arkadina says it is the same old game they played as children – so too the love triangles endlessly repeat themselves. Arkadina says she has not had time to read her son's works, but she has time to play lotto. Ironically, Trigorin even wins the lotto game.

James M. Curtis in 1972 argued that Chekhov's use of juxtaposition in this play shows him to be a modernist; he juxtaposes both themes and motifs.[77] Magarshack (1972) states the play's main theme: A writer will lose his way if he lacks a clear purpose, and then his talent proves to be his doom. Nietzsche was very popular at this time, and Nina raves about him, but Chekhov thought him to be a passing craze, "spectacular rather than convincing." Dorn is the only person who realizes that Treplev is a better writer than Trigorin. When Treplev realizes he can never have Nina, he is left alone on the stage, tearing up his manuscript. This is a symbolic suicide, for if a writer cannot express himself, he has lost his purpose in living.

Pitcher (1973) shows that Chekhov makes the minor characters memorable by such devices as speech idiosyncrasies, references to their jobs, and showing their prevailing interests. Some of the unconventional stage techniques that Chekhov experimented with in this play proved to be blind alleys: use of autobiographical material, an exotic natural setting, the recurring symbol, and the use of as many as four main characters. The two main subjects of the play, art and talent, were important in czarist Russia because literature and drama were felt to have both spiritual and political force, since they were areas in which some opposition to the government could be expressed.

Nina survives, says Pitcher, because she is spiritually healthier than the other three main characters. Talent destroys them, but "such talents as she has are not flawed by any personal defects." In this way she was like Chekhov himself. Current MAT productions of this play involve a virtual rewriting of Act IV. One reason this play is dated is that literature and drama no longer appear to be powerful spiritual forces capable of regenerating mankind, Pitcher feels.

Keith Sagar in 1973 disagreed with Dorothy Seyler: Chekhov uses symbolism

seriously, like Ibsen, to escape naturalism, Sagar believes. The lake and the sea
gull act as a symbolic pair—the lake seems a prison to those dwelling on its shore,
but the sea gull represents freedom, giving Nina wings to escape from the lake.
Shotton, in Fennell (1973), states that Chekhov finds a better criterion for judging
artists than the usual ones of talent, genius, technique, or worldly success. Instead,
Chekhov suggests the distinction between a positive and a negative personality.
Arkadina and Trigorin are self-centered, and Treplev is full of inner weakness; only
Nina achieves a perfect awareness of herself and her destiny.

Y.K. Avdeyev in 1973 cast doubt about the influence of Lydia Mizinova on this
play. In 1974 Richard Gilman said that, beginning with this play, Chekhov's drama
stated that life's most crucial moments can be its least dramatic ones. That year
Simon Karlinsky compared the dominating mother figures in *The Sea Gull* and in
Innokenty Annensky's play *Thamyras the Cythara Player*. Also in 1974 James
MacAulay discussed Bernard Sznycer's method of translating *The Sea Gull*, and
M.F. Murianov traced the symbolic sea gull to such sources as a poem by Vladimir
Shuf and the writings of Nietzsche and Vladimir Solovyov. Bernard Sznycer that
year explained his method of translating this play.[78]

In January of 1975 John Gruen analyzed the reasons for the avant-garde
rediscovery of *The Sea Gull*, since three productions of it were being given that
season in New York City, and a national television production of the play was
scheduled for that month. Joseph Chaikin, directing one of the New York productions, called the play "humanizing to work on—a play both timeless and re-
juvenating." André Gregory, director of another production, said that this play mirrors the contemporary search for new forms of theater.[79]

Rayfield (1975) found an importance in Treplev's playlet as a demonstration
of Chekhov's lyrical and mystical love of nature. It was, Rayfield avers, a serious
attempt to find new forms for art. "The neo–Platonic idea of all creation reverting
to the spiritual state of the World Soul and then fighting the spirit of evil is one of
the main themes of Russian symbolism." Rayfield discovered literary influences
upon *The Sea Gull* in Shakespeare, Maupassant, and Ibsen. One of the first great
modern plays, says Rayfield, it made Chekhov a progenitor of modern European
drama.

In 1975 W. Gareth Jones called the lotto game of Act IV a second play-within-a-
play, one which showed that the new forms of symbolic drama could succeed if
handled skillfully. V.B. Kataev in 1976 showed Chekhov's use of Hamlet mythology
in this play, and V.I. Kuleshov (and others) edited an anthology containing discussions of productions of the play, including a filmed version. That year A.P.
Kuzicheva revealed that Treplev's playlet and other devices in the play involve the
spectators by giving them a mirror that reflects their lives. Also in 1976 Eleanor
Rowe listed the Hamlet motifs in the play, and K.L. Rudnitsky reviewed Stanislavsky's productions of the play.[80]

Brahms (1976) regretfully reported that the only one of the four main
characters "who is certain to survive, and indeed thrive, is the morally and

artistically indefensible Trigorin, who has been the ruin of them all." Hingley (1976) quoted Potapenko as saying that Chekhov personally held the same views on the concept of the World Soul as those contained in Treplev's playlet.

Bristow (1977) expressed the views of Vsevolod Meyerhold and Thomas G. Winner. Meyerhold said that the secret of Chekhov's mood lies in the rhythm of his language. Out of love for him the MAT actors worked hard to learn to master that rhythm. Winner pointed out parallels between *Hamlet* and *The Sea Gull*, including the Oedipal elements and the reversals involving the main characters.

Ellen Chances, in Debreczeny (1977), asserted that the sea gull is not a serious symbol but a "stuffed bird," standing for the stripping away of the many layers of artificiality. Chekhov himself laughed at the image, saying that a sea gull is a scavenger bird. Arkadina, after reading a passage from Maupassant in which women are described as chasing after famous authors, acts out the role in her pursuit of Trigorin. Hahn (1977) found the play "over-ambitious and marred by intense self-consciousness. There is still not the sense, as there is in the later plays, of a situation developing with its own momentum. The resolution of the drama depends on changes in the characters which we have simply to take on trust."

Laurence Senelick in 1977 examined the theatrical background of the play. In 1978 Virginia Scott studied the generation gap, finding the sea gull a rich image, standing for freedom and creativitiy, as well as for "Treplev's desire to murder his faithless Nina, and the younger generation's scavenging on the leavings of the older." That year Zoya Yurieff reported on the influence of the play upon Andrey Bely's unfinished mystery play *He Who Has Come*.[81]

In 1980 Walter Kerr scolded Andrey Serban for a production in which he allowed his "players to lapse back into the slow and moody languors of stock Chekhov," forgetting his earlier vision that "farce and heartbreak can be the closest of friends."[82] At a Canadian production that year Henry Popkin praised Maggie Smith for her portrayal of Arkadina: "Her lover, her son, her brother and the others constitute an audience that she plays upon more effectively than upon the theater audience."[83]

In 1980 A.G. Golovacheva delineated Turgenev's influence upon the play, seen both in *Rudin* and in *A Month in the Country*. Z.S. Paperny that year published a lengthy study of the play's genesis, structure, and stage history, and A. Colin Wright discussed translating the play for a performance in Canada. In 1981 Steve Giles asserted that Chekhov's plays pushed drama to its limits, and A.G. Golovacheva examined the links between the monologue in Treplev's playlet and Chekhov's other writings at that time. In comparing Chekhov and Shakespeare that year, Victor Shklovsky said that both playwrights could write simply about life's complexities.[84]

Barricelli (1981) presented views on the play by Michael Heim, Jerome H. Katsell, Sonia Kovitz, Nicholas Moravcevich, Louis Pedrotti, Richard D. Risso, and Laurence Senelick. Heim observed character pairing: The Masha-Medvedenko duo parallel, and to some extent parody, the Nina-Treplev pair. The same relationship exists between the Polina-Dorn and the Arkadina-Trigorin duos. In the latter pairing, both women are possessive mistresses and both men are weak-willed lovers. "This layered effect gives the play increased depth of characterization." Thus, no one character can stand out without upsetting the balance. Katsell showed the similarities between this play and Maupassant's *Sur l'eau*. Both focus on the themes of art and freedom. In Maupassant people are trapped by life; in *The Sea Gull*, by their own emotional immaturity. Both works depict attempts to escape responsible living through vanity, superficiality, and monotonous work. Chekhov is not nearly as pessimistic as Maupassant, for he feels that art can help humans achieve love and recognition. Nina (whose last name means "beyond the river") can succeed because she has confronted death and rejected it.

Kovitz sees Treplev's suicide as the premature conclusion to the playlet. If Satan is "the misery of the world which alone drives man inward," then Treplev falls by the wayside long before God can reveal Himself. Treplev fears the shadow side of his personality, which contains "demonic chaos, the union of opposites, the act of creation." Treplev abdicates his personality by projecting his soul's powers onto Nina: "He relies on her pressure to bring him psychic wholeness and life." But in him the opposites never join. He remains the eternal youth, terrified at being the one human being that he is. Humiliated at losing both Nina and his playlet, he kills the sea gull as a symbolic suicide.

Moravcevich feels that Arkadina's self-concern is no sign of anti-feminism in Chekhov, as alleged by Virginia Llewellyn Smith. As a matter of fact, he says, "no hard evidence exists in this female characterization for any justifiable suspicion of his misogyny in the realm of drama." Pedrotti thinks that Dorn reflects Chekhov's own disappointment in the daily humdrum treatment of patients, having expected more soul-satisfying rewards from an artistic and creative medical practice.

Risso studied the use in the play of irony, as seen in the disparity between what a character anticipates and what he gets. It is ironic that each character pursues something that he cannot have because of the other characters' pursuits. Treplev wants acceptance from Arkadina, who wants Trigorin's love, but Trigorin wants a successful literary career. Senelick sees Maeterlinck's influence at work in the play, especially in the setting: "The doors and windows take on specific meaning as apertures to another world." The lotto game seems like a deliberate imitation of Maeterlinckian stasis.

Kirk (1981) noted that in this play flowers, like youthful dreams, are destined to be either destroyed by insensitivity or neglected through indifference. Nabokov (1981) observed that even though Chekhov was flaunting dramatic traditions, he was still confined by them, so "despite his authentic genius he did not create the perfect masterpiece." Future dramatists should imitate his effort to be original but not his particular dramatic techniques, for they were peculiar to this type of drama. He does not handle women's dialogue well, and he sometimes employs improbabilities. When Chekhov escapes "the obligatory scene" his technique is weakest. But he recovers in an excellent scene between Nina and Treplev in Act

IV. The ending is remarkable—Arkadina must have had a premonition based upon Treplev's previous attempted suicide. Since a doctor reports the catastrophe, we know that Treplev has already had a doctor's service. The suicide is thus unexpected but probable, fulfilling Aristotle's dictum.

Carol Strongin, however, raises the challenging suggestion that Treplev may not have killed himself. This may simply be another grandiose gesture on his part. He missed a serious wound previously, and since he seems to be a born failure at whatever he does, he probably botches his suicide attempt again.[85]

Eisen (1982) points out how Chekhov uses "gapping" in this play. Many important actions occur in plot gaps, testing the audience's shrewdness of observation and power of inference. The lotto game is symbolic of life: Treplev is interrupted seven times during the game (showing that life will not give him the peace of mind for concentration), and Trigorin wins (the game of lotto and Nina's love). They portray emotional relationships similarly, and both find hope even while acknowledging the worst about human nature. The violent displays in their mother-son confrontations illustrate hope merging from deep despair.[86]

Symbolism was discussed by Peter Holland and Leigh Woods in Redmond (1982). Holland felt that the awkward use of the sea gull as a symbol derives more from the characters than from Chekhov. A dead bird is an awkward prop, as John Gielgud discovered when the audience laughed at his Treplev in 1925. Stanislavsky had Nina stroke the head of the dead bird, but the effect was ludicrous. Woods believed that the meaning of the sea gull is vague. It stands variously for love, death, creativity, freedom, and innocence—such shifting around destroys its usefulness. Later, in *The Cherry Orchard*, Chekhov showed how a symbol can be worked artistically into the total fabric of a play.

In 1982 Leslie Epstein wrote a novel, *Regina*, in which a middle-aged former actress returns to the stage to star in her former vehicle, *The Sea Gull*. There are numerous parallels between the play and the novel, said George Stade in reviewing the novel.[87] M. Dmitrevskaya in 1983 reviewed a Leningrad production of *The Sea Gull* which stressed the pain that total dedication to art can bring. Clara Hollosi that year showed the difference between Nina as played in 1896 and in the MAT production of 1898.[88] Praising the sets but panning the acting, Edith Oliver wondered if *The Sea Gull*, Chekhov's most fragile play, could really be indestructible, as the performance she was reviewing seemed to indicate.[89]

Peace (1983) pointed out that the use of a rat to symbolize Trigorin comes from Maupassant's *Sur l'eau*. In Treplev's playlet the lake seems to stand for art, for it reflects both the past and the future. Significantly, when Treplev plays "She loves me, she loves me not" with flowers, he is referring not to Nina but to his mother. All the women in the play seem drawn towards Dorn. Shamraev's story of the rural chorister who outshines the famous basso Silva implies that an unknown writer like Treplev may some day outdo the famous writer Trigorin.

Clyman (1985) gave further views on the play from Laurence Senelick and J.L. Styan. Senelick reviewed recent Soviet productions of the play. In 1966 Anatoly

Efros brought out two themes: uncompromising youth facing adult reality, and the incompatibility of talent with fakery. Boris Livanov experimented with the Hamlet elements in the MAT production in 1969. In 1970 Oleg Efremov, by downplaying love at the expense of art, "confused the motivation in several cases." In 1984 Rumanian director Lucian Pintilie innovated in staging the play in Minneapolis. The play opened with the final moments of Act IV and then returned to Act I. "This circular structure was enhanced by a set of giant mylar screens that threw back reflections on the narcissistic characters. The central visual metaphor was Treplev's platform stage, always on view, its back to the audience, suggesting a motif of life as performance." Styan showed how the play used an ever-increasing penetration into Treplev's privacy: Act I is in Sorin's garden; Act II is outside Arkadina's house; Act III is inside her house; and Act IV is laid in Treplev's study.

Senelick (1985) stated that Chekhov's intent was not to write a cheap romance but a serious play on the role of art and literature. He wanted multiple heroes and multiple conflicts, but Stanislavsky tried to reduce the play to a single-line plot. There are many predecessors in Russian literature of Nina, the victimized young girl. In Act IV Dorn describes a mystical crowd experience he had in Genoa, when he felt that he had merged with the World Soul, just as Treplev had depicted in his playlet. Egri (1986) observed that Edmund's poetic pantheism in O'Neill's *A Long Day's Journey into Night* has many parallels in *The Sea Gull*.

13. *Uncle Vanya* (1897)

Act I – Ivan (Vanya) Voynitsky, brother of deceased Vera, the first wife of retired professor Serebryakov, resents the return of the professor and his new young wife Elena to live on the estate owned by Vanya's mother. Vanya says that the professor lectured on art for 25 years without knowing anything about the subject. Vanya tells beautiful Elena that she need not be faithful to her husband. Dr. Astrov orates on the need to conserve forests. Elena says that just as people destroy forests, so do they destroy one another through mistreatment. Elena tells Vanya that Sonya, the professor's daughter by Vera, is in love with Astrov. Vanya confesses loving Elena, but she rebuffs him.

Act II – The professor is bored and boring, as he idles about the house. Sonya begs Vanya to stop drinking and to get Astrov to stop also. Astrov tells Sonya that he could fall in love with Elena. Sonya, who loves Astrov, feels inferior because of her lack of beauty. She and Elena heal a breach in their friendship, and now confide in each other. They would like to play music together, but the professor forbids it.

Act III – Elena tells Astrov that Sonya loves him, but he responds by making love to Elena. Just as he kisses her, Vanya enters. Elena plans to leave the estate immediately. The professor announces his plan: The family estate will be sold, and he will buy a villa in Finland. Vanya is furious, since the estate was supposed to go to Sonya, and he had worked for years to pay off its mortgage. Sonya reminds her father how she and Vanya copied manuscripts for him, while he was writing articles. Vanya says to the professor, "You are my bitterest enemy!" The professor tells Vanya to leave the house. Vanya fires two pistol shots at the professor, but misses both times.

Act IV – Astrov insists that Vanya return his bottle of morphine. Astrov admits that modern life is mean, but in 200 years life will be wonderful. Parting, Elena confesses that she loved Astrov somewhat, but felt that she had to be true to her husband. Astrov, bitter, says that she and her husband have ruined everyone's life. Nonetheless, he and Elena embrace before she leaves. The professor forgives Vanya, as he and Elena leave for Kharkov. Astrov leaves; he may return for a visit the following winter. Sonya consoles Vanya: "I have faith. After death all evil will be drowned in mercy. Wait, Uncle Vanya, we shall rest."

Chekhov worked for several years on revising *The Wood Demon* into the new play *Uncle Vanya.* He submitted it to the Maly Theatre, Moscow's oldest and most prestigious theater. The professors on the theater committee considered it indecorous to have a professor shot at, and returned it to Chekhov for revisions. V.A. Telyakovsky, administrator of the Moscow imperial theaters, took Chekhov's side. He said that the play was very good, and that he would approve it over the committee's protest. Chekhov, however, was glad to have an excuse to give the play to Danchenko for the MAT.

In December 1898 Chekhov wrote Gorky: "I wrote *Uncle Vanya* long, long ago. I have never seen it on the stage. Of late years they have been giving it frequently on the provincial stages, perhaps because I have published a collection of my plays." The play had thus been performed many times before the MAT premiere on 26 October 1899.

During rehearsals mild-mannered Chekhov was surprisingly frank in his criticism of the actors, especially the female ones. The actors kidded him as "the actress inspector." In Yalta for his health, Chekhov missed the opening performance in Moscow. Telegrams assured him that there had been much applause, but he knew from the beginning that the play enjoyed only middling success.

Chekhov felt that in rehearsal Stanislavsky had overstressed Astrov's love for Elena. Olga Knipper, who had played Elena, confessed that she had acted poorly. Chekhov modestly admitted that the play had many defects. In time, however, the play became a fixture in the MAT repertoire.

Perceptive critics like Ignatov said that although there is little action in the play, unity of mood replaces unity of action. Perhaps because of the success of *The Sea Gull,* most critics were favorable to *Uncle Vanya.* In 1899 Maxim Gorky saw a performance of *Uncle Vanya* in Nizhny Novgorod and said he had wept "like a peasant woman" seeing a play in which "the sawteeth run directly across one's heart. It is a totally new formula in the theater, a hammer with which you strike the empty heads of the public." But Gorky was perplexed. He wrote to Chekhov: "You have enormous talent. But what nail do you hope to drive in with such blows? In this play you treat mankind with fiendish coldness."

Gorky moderated his views when he heard that Chekhov was threatening to stop writing plays. "People," he said, "say that *Uncle Vanya* and *The Sea Gull* are dramas of a completely new kind, in which realism is elevated to become a symbol that unites inspiration with depth of thought. Plays by other playwrights do not divert mankind from reality, do not drive it towards philosophical meditation as yours do. You are a mighty genius." In January 1900 Gorky said of *Uncle Vanya:* "I don't consider it a pearl, but I do think it has more content than others see. The content is rich and symbolic, and the form makes it completely original, incomparable."

Tolstoy was unconvinced. He asked, "Where is the drama? It doesn't go anywhere." His feeling was that the technique had overcome the theme. In place of a tragic situation, Chekhov had substituted guitars and crickets. The proper conduct for Astrov and Vanya, he said, would be to each find a peasant woman for easy lovemaking, and leave Elena for her husband.

Tolstoy reluctantly admitted to Danchenko that there were "brilliant spots" in the play. Nikolai Engelgardt in 1900 said that, like Chekhov, Tolstoy was torn between the stale old theater and the new one. Tolstoy told Engelgardt that he was captivated by the play's subtle psychology and by the faithfulness of its illusion of life.

In March 1901 newspaper critics were hostile at the St. Petersburg performance. Conservative critics linked the revolutionary approach to drama by the MAT with the growing student rebellions. A.I. Bogdanovich, however, paid great tribute to the MAT, saying that texts which looked boring became moving stage vehicles in their hands. The critic Chenko said that the many images which were extraneous to the plot nevertheless did contribute to the overall mood of the play.

A proponent of stage naturalism, Sergey Glagol in 1902 said that the constant fluctuation between comedy and tragedy left the playgoer confused. But he had to admit that the play was nonetheless interesting, perhaps because of its hidden symbolic action. In 1904, when Vera Komisarjevskaya opened a theater which lasted two seasons, *Uncle Vanya* and *The Sea Gull* were two of her standard plays.

Shestov (1905) called *Uncle Vanya* the last play in which Chekhov protests. Regretting his wasted life, Vanya fights back, but his protest is more inward than external. Although Chekhov could not be an idealist, said Shestov, he was uncomfortable with scientific materialism because of its cold inhumanity.

Dmitry Merezhkovsky was less kind. In 1907 he professed to be "horrified at the vulgarity" of *Uncle Vanya*. He resented Chekhov's materialism and rejection of Christian values, and his "spiritual bumming." He said, "I have come to hate the Moscow Art Theatre, and Chekhov too."

Translations of Chekhov's plays by George Calderon and Marian Fell in 1912 led to a harsh reception by American reviewers. One said that these depressing plays were attracting "a new cult, on their merry way to nowhere, the cult of the ignoble."[1] Another called this "drama of the crudest order. *Uncle Vanya* is packed with petty or morbid detail, and even if it is photographically truthful, it is not any more artistic or instructive than it is entertaining."[2] Still another granted Chekhov's good characterization, detailed naturalism, and able sense of humor, but insisted that the plays were "invertebrate and episodical in form," that they dealt with dull and selfish characters, and that the plots were conventional and uninteresting.[3]

The poet Vladimir Mayakovsky continued the attack. In 1914 he said, "We don't need Uncle Vanyas flopping on divans—we have uncles like that at home." But he granted Chekhov's ability to get the maximum dramatic intensity out of seemingly "gray" words. He called Chekhov "a liberator of the word, a precursor of the futurists," in finding deep meaning in simple words and phrases.

The London Stage Society put on the first English production of *Uncle Vanya* in 1914 to a chorus of mixed reviews. There were those who said that the lack of conflict among these apathetic characters could never please an English audience.[4] Others called it a beautiful study of stagnation, but "shuddered to think how a drama of inferior technique would have handled the subject."[5]

But *Uncle Vanya* already had its supporters in England. H.W. Massingham said that in Sonya Chekhov had created "a rare person – the complete moral heroine, a person full of helpfulness, inspiration, and redemption."[6] One reviewer called the play "rich in subtle suggestion," presenting characters that, despite their apathy, were "undeniably human. They are the genuine blend of good and bad, weakness and strength, that we all are, and if they are failures, it is less from any fault of theirs than from bad luck."[7]

Desmond MacCarthy called *Uncle Vanya* "an unforgettably good play. It is a real tragedy, with the flatness and poignancy of life itself." A student of Turgenev, Chekhov excels in creating the beauty undergirding disillusionment. His motto might well be: "Desolation is a delicate thing."[8]

The following year an American reviewer said that "no art of the stage is more concealed than Chekhov's." Where else, he asked, could one get so imperceptible a feeling of time's passage as in Act II of *Uncle Vanya*, or the momentous feeling of departure as found in Act IV? "When nothing is new in plays but their subjects," he added, "they grow stale in a few months, but when a dramatist has talent and technique mastery enough to make us share his fresh and complex emotions, his play may stay modern for years."[9]

Theodore Komisarjevsky, a former director at the Moscow State Theatre, directed the Stage Society production of *Uncle Vanya* in London in 1921. One impressionistic critic said, "I am as sure that this play of castigation is a masterpiece as I am that I shall never know exactly what it means."[10] Others admired the play's "strange, morbid beauty," which creates a poignancy by revealing characters in greater depth than any playwright since Shakespeare.[11] Comparisons with the plays of G.B. Shaw were inevitable. One reviewer preferred Chekhov's implicit humor to Shaw's superficial cleverness,[12] but another, after conceding that Chekhov "subtly suggests a social value in the frail beauty of his characters' uselessness," chose Shaw because of his firmer and more ironic humor.[13]

Desmond MacCarthy felt that Chekhov had achieved what no one else had ever attempted, to stage what in other plays happens between the acts. "You hear the dull machinery of everyday life creaking in its customary groove. This experience is novel and indescribably moving when it is presented on the stage with discretion."[14] Another critic mused that the British were too much like the Russians to find this sort of play comfortable, for Chekhov "takes the lid off" and reveals us for what we are – a revelation both rare and disconcerting. "Moreover, if he can convey his story of loves and hates and the travail of the human soul in such frail vessels, he has something extra that the grandeur of Racine cannot give us."[15]

Speaking in favor of the establishment of a British national theater, W.J. Turner in 1923 said that its purpose would be to produce effects like the recent *Uncle Vanya* production, at the end of which he could only grope blindly for his hat – if anyone had spoken to him, he would have burst into tears, he said. The crowd, who prefer *Kiki,* can keep their popular theater, "but to play down to the masses in the hope of slowly educating them is sheer lunacy," for the masses themselves have sound enough instincts to despise such efforts.[16]

In 1924 C. Nabokoff summarized Chekhov's dama as based upon the concepts of irony and pity. One of his greatest characters was Astrov, Nabokoff said, and the final act of *Uncle Vanya* was Chekhov's dramatic masterpiece.[17]

That year, when the MAT toured the United States, reviewers were quite enthusiastic, especially considering that the plays were performed in Russian. "After long detours of flowery dialogue and graceful gesture," said one critic, "intense impassioned climaxes are reached."[18] The characters may seem puppets, said another, "but their foibles, vanities, and passionate unrequited loves never failed to grip the interest of the unusually discriminating audience."[19] Several critics marvelled at the acting, unable to believe that these were the same persons who had performed *Ivanov.*[20] One went so far as to say that it took a troupe of acting geniuses to keep interest in this dull play, a story of "the unresolved problems of unimportant neurotics."[21]

The time was ripe for Stanislavsky to publish his autobiography. In it he recalled Chekhov's effect upon MAT productions. At first the MAT considered Vanya a rustic overseer in boots and cap. "Read the play!" Chekhov ordered, and then the players found that Vanya was fashionable and up-to-date. "Soon we came to see Chekhov's point in the play," Stanislavsky said. "Real achievers, like Astrov and Vanya, must tear down giftless posers like the professor."[22]

There were few negative comments by critics at a London production in 1926. A number of reviewers commended Chekhov for being able to discern the universal in the ordinary.[23] Another stated that "in less than a quarter of a century Chekhov has been more acclimatized than Ibsen has ever been."[24] Still another found that Chekhov makes us more aware of human beings than we have ever before been: "His people are extraordinarily open and direct. They reveal themselves without seeming to know it. If we can bring ourselves to accept them, we will understand not only them but also their unhappy country."[25]

John Shand said that "who sneers at Uncle Vanya sneers at all those whose sense of life is stronger than their power to grasp it," a vast number of people. Shand showed that the main characters of the play led productive lives. Astrov is a dedicated doctor and conservationist; Vanya has been an efficient manager of the estate; and Sonya has looked after the house, meanwhile cheering everyone she meets. Their lives have been far more useful than that of the professor.[26]

Horace Shipp said that, above all, *Uncle Vanya* causes the audience to reflect on the meaning and purpose of life. The sensitive playgoer cannot help asking himself, What are my values in life and what ought they to be? Instead of giving us a predigested formula, Chekhov accurately describes the process of value formation, giving us the clearest possible insight into human character and motives. The presentation is so accurate that "we cannot but be exalted to his godlike plane" as we contemplate the fate of his characters. This great art thus performs its true cathartic function. "During these moments we exist in complete understanding sympathy with the great movements of human life. The artist has fulfilled his task."[27]

At an MAT production in London in 1928 one critic said that this is the way that Chekhov ought to be acted, "not as something remote and solemn, but as something very simple, human, and vivid."[28] Another noted the play's "wonderfully detailed realism, with each character being a complete and vivid human being."[29] "The moods of *Uncle Vanya* are no doubt too close to everyday matters to provoke rash comment," was one response; "the intelligence and kindliness of Astrov are brought out in a hundred little gestures, and the hard, honest cynicism of the man shines through him with painful clarity."[30]

At a New York production in 1929 Alison Smith applauded the blend of irony with compassion, helping the playgoer achieve that detachment that Chekhov felt necessary if one was to see life in a clear perspective.[31] Brooks Atkinson judged that *Uncle Vanya* was not one of Chekhov's best plays, either in plot or structure, but that it gave one a direct look into the hearts of the characters, a rare, if somewhat upsetting, theatrical experience.[32]

The most spectacular staging of *Uncle Vanya* in America occurred in New York in 1930 under the inspired direction of Jed Harris. It was one of the rare occasions when the boxoffice and the critics united to hail a masterpiece. Robert Littell set the pace, calling *Uncle Vanya* Chekhov's best play, Chekhov's drama the best of the century, and this production the best Chekhov that America had yet seen. Littell said that an American company could achieve such great success with a foreign play only because the characters are universal.[33] Americans have finally discovered that Russians are not gloomy and incomprehensible people, Littell added, and are learning to find behind the strange names and fleeting moods "something so human and true as to pass all boundaries, leap over prejudices, and recognize that as an artist and a creator of human characters, Chekhov is the first of all modern dramatists."[34]

Littell saved special words of praise for Lillian Gish in the role of Elena, as did several other reviewers.[35] One who praised Miss Gish ascribed Chekhov's unique stage mastery to his profound sympathy and complete understanding.[36] "In fact," said another critic, "if ever we saw a materialization in human form of an intangible quality, it is Miss Gish as the virginal young wife of the egotistical professor."[37] Stark Young agreed that "the line and movement of that frail figure and delicate, honest spirit are unforgettable."[38]

Several reviewers were pleasantly shocked by the candor of the characters.[39] One, after lauding the outstanding direction, called the play "a comedy of the soul, a play of fundamentally strong characters, tried to their utmost depths, and found capable of whatever sacrifices are demanded of them."[40]

"Chekhov continues among us as a conqueror," announced John Hutchens. "What distinguishes Mr. Harris's production is simply the greater vitality that he has induced from an endless succession of subtleties. It has the scintillant flashes that make the Chekhov plays comedies in a wide, sardonic sense. Despair pervades *Uncle Vanya* but compassion illuminates it."[41]

This time even George Jean Nathan joined the accolades. "Unaccustomed as I am to public superlatives," he wrote, "I nominated Mr. Harris's presentation as the most satisfying and the most intelligent production of a Russian play made on the English-speaking stage in the period of my critical incumbency." Harris got playgoers versed on the characters and their interrelationships within 15 minutes, Nathan said. Chekhov's bitter humor destroys the gloomy atmosphere, as "Chekhov reaches into his characters and fondly strokes their hearts and then, with willful irony, gives them a playful but painful pinch. It is a comedy of carefully directed inflection and tone rather than a comedy of line or antic."[42]

Disagreeing with Nathan that there was sufficient humor to alleviate the gloom, two Chicago critics deviated from the general consensus. One said that Slavic peoples could not understand the attitude of Robert Louis Stevenson when he said, "We must all fail in life. Our business is to continue to fail in good spirits."[43]

Years later Jed Harris recalled this happy time. Production costs of $9,900 had been paid off in ten days, and eventually some 200,000 people saw the production. To avoid "star" problems, Harris had looked past Paul Muni and Edward G. Robinson to cast Walter Connolly as Vanya and Osgood Perkins as Astrov. The play proved its lasting merit, Harris said, because it is grounded in the fundamental aspects of universal human nature.[44]

The translation used in this production was by Rose Caylor. In his review of the translation, one critic pointed to the Jed Harris production as proof of its efficacy. He felt that she had achieved her goal: "To keep the marvelous dramatic nuances of the broken dialogue, and to maintain the comedy which never is quite absent even from the gravest scenes."[45]

Universality was also noted in a London production in 1937. "These people are as typical of Reading as of Russia," proclaimed Henry Adler.[46] "One could transfer the setting almost without change to anywhere in County Cork or Galway," added Derek Verschoyle.[47] Several reviewers found unintentional burlesque, as when Vanya shoots at the professor and misses.[48] When the characters talk, "what divine inconsequence, what ruthless self-analysis," reported one critic, who said that two conclusions stemmed from the play: No wonder the Russian revolution came, and these characters, "despite their social inadequacy, seem to make the best play material in the world."[49]

Desmond MacCarthy remarked that "there is a difference between these characters and ourselves, but it is not wholly in our favor: They do not keep up a conventional façade of self-respect—they admit to being the childish creatures they are, and we are."[50] Dorothy L. Sayers differed with MacCarthy in his interpretation of Astrov: "Astrov is not a man who has lost his soul and looks like it, but one who has lost his driving power and does not look like it. His tragi-comedy is that he still has his moments of believing in himself." The mingling of the tragic and the absurd, found in *Uncle Vanya*, also lies at the base of Shakespeare's appeal, Sayers said.[51]

Toumanova (1937) felt that this play showed Chekhov's growth as a dramatist. It has a strange tension, out of proportion to the trivial life depicted. Henry T. Perry in 1939 traced the influence of Turgenev's *A Month in the Country* upon this play. Both are comedies of thwarted love, but Chekhov goes beyond romance to examine the philosophy of work as his unifying theme. Astrov is the antithesis of Vanya—he drinks regularly, to recapture the dreams of his youth, but Vanya takes to drink only during his temporary loss of ideals.[52]

A wartime production of *Uncle Vanya* in London in 1943 led one reviewer to note the paucity of good male actors.[53] Most critics agreed that the production properly had more sympathy than contempt for the characters.[54] Whether the play, or life, is comic or tragic depends upon one's point of view, said Herbert Farjeon. "But a great artist may rise above a point of view, and if one half of an audience laughs while the other cries, both may be paying tribute to a masterpiece."[55]

The chief critical gain from this production was the opportunity it gave Ashley Dukes to do penance for his early castigation of Chekhov. This "marvelous play" by "a universal poet of the theater" had never been better directed, said Dukes. "How did Shaw ever suppose he had written a Chekhovian drama in *Heartbreak House*? Who could mistake the self-revelation of these characters for talk, or fail to become absorbed in the unfolding drama of their personal relations? The reasonable critique of Chekhov is that he is a dramatist to end dramatists—his supreme naturalism, conceived as an art form, makes all other lifelikeness on the stage look wooden or obsolete." Dukes went on to show that *Uncle Vanya* had the traditional elements of exposition, development, climax, and denouement, but done in so natural a manner that one observed life rather than drama as the play unfolds.[56]

The critical consensus at the Old Vic production in London in 1945, which had Ralph Richardson as Vanya and Laurence Olivier as Astrov, was that the good acting was insufficient to carry the play's dramatic message.[57] Dido Milroy found here "Chekhov's unique blend of compassion and impartiality."[58] Herbert Farjeon said that Chekhov reminds us "that without a sense of the unattainable there can be no beauty, for beauty itself is but a desire."[59] James Redfern said that "Chekhov is the first to present on the stage the ordinary human being in his full sensibility and as Western civilization and Christianity have hammered him into shape."[60]

When the Old Vic Company came to the United States the critical reception was no better. There was general agreement that the needed ensemble effect had not been attained.[61] Wolcott Gibbs went so far as to call it "a deliberate and wicked parody of all Russian drama."[62] Euphemia Wyatt traced the blame to a play of intimacy being staged in a theater of large size and with poor acoustics.[63] John Mason Brown laid the blame at Chekhov's feet, saying that although the characters' faults are fascinating, they do not win our affections as do the faults of the characters in *The Cherry Orchard* and *The Three Sisters*.[64]

The lone dissenter, Joseph Wood Krutch, discovered not only an ensemble effect but a performance which "made the play seem much richer, more meaningful, and more interesting than I had thought it was. Chekhov did not see his characters exactly as they saw themselves." He writes realistically about people "whose inveterate romanticism is one of their most prominent characteristics," and the result is bound to be humor that is both sympathetic and mocking.[65]

In 1949 Eric Bentley showed how Chekhov revised *The Wood Demon* in making *Uncle Vanya*. First he eliminated four characters. Then he made the actions of the new characters consistent. *The Wood Demon* was a farce spiced with melodrama. Chekhov now employs restraint or what he calls grace: "When one spends the least possible movements to produce an effect, that is grace." The paradox is that playwrights like O'Neill try to depict passion but end up being superficial; Chekhov pretends to show us only the surface, but he is deeply passionate. "No modern playwright has presented elemental passions more truly. At a time when Chekhov is valued for his finer shades, it is worth stressing his simplicity and strength, his depth and intensity." The final scene of the play presents a stage picture "such as drama has seldom known since Shakespeare."[66]

Magarshack (*Dramatist*, 1952) also discussed the conversion of *The Wood Demon* into *Uncle Vanya*. Chekhov mended his errors: He had mishandled the messenger element, and the chorus effect had been submerged in irrelevant detail. Most important of all, the vital reversal was missing, producing a very unconvincing ending. To make the Vanya-professor clash the main action, Chekhov now played down the role of Astrov as a conservationist. Telegin becomes not only a chorus figure but a foil for the professor, for he is full of mercy and unselfishness. Just as Elena stands for physical beauty, Sonya is made to represent spiritual beauty. It never occurs to Sonya to resent Elena for having turned Astrov away from her. The new play's principal theme is not frustration but courage mingled with hope. *Uncle Vanya* is a better play than *The Sea Gull*, largely because here Chekhov made better use of reversal.

In 1955 Louis Kronenberger stated that *Uncle Vanya* has a "more life-sized sense of truth" than do *The Cherry Orchard* and *The Three Sisters*. It has more direct emotion, showing the irritations and resentments of ordinary life. Chekhov's method is a dangerous one, requiring good actors and directors. His plays work best when sentimentalized, for his fluidity can very easily become sheer formlessness.[67]

David Ross drew critical praise for his 1956 production in New York City. Walter Kerr said that Ross had captured Chekhov's "wild strain of fatuous anguish and comic despair."[68] Brooks Atkinson noted how the main characters are transformed by their experiences: "personalities clash, destinies are settled, lives are destroyed."[69] Stark Young, whose translation was used, explained how to translate Chekhov. His supposed gloominess, Young said, is actually patient good temper and kindly wit. He uses repetitions knowingly, since "the sequence of speeches is part of the whole idea of dramatic movement."[70]

Milton Esterow described how this company made a film of the play during the stage run. The actors, including Franchot Tone as president of the film company, shuttled daily between the film studio in Queens and the Fourth Street Theatre. "Not a single word of the play was changed," said scenarist Marion Parsonnet. "Chekhov was a master screen writer—the play just cries for the motion-picture technique. As we see it, it's a kind of Chaplin story in which the human tragedy is personified by pretty broad comedy, by the ridiculousness of it all."[71]

Ermilov (1956) said that the main theme of the play, the destruction of beauty, is struck at the start of the play. Music, the subtext of Chekhov's plays, is forbidden by the professor, who is determined to stamp out joy. Thus, says Ermilov, even un-sounded music is integral to the plot, and not merely ornamental. Vanya is the sym-bol of many people who have sacrificed their lives in service to others, while the professor stands for those who do not deserve the sacrifice. Astrov exhibits two types of love: false, for Elena, whom he calls a parasite; true, for Russia, since he works hard to save the forests. Act IV indicates how each character, with crushed hopes, will adjust to an undesired fate. Vanya says, "Work!" Sonya advises, "Have faith!" and Astrov starts drinking again. Chekhovian action has little external change but profound inner change.

Bruford (1957) points out that in Act III, when Elena asks Astrov if he loves Sonya, she is really testing to see whether Astrov loves her. In 1958 Philip Bordinat wrote that the play's tight structure becomes clear as one realizes that there are many protagonists in the play. That year V.Y. Lakshin made a detailed comparison of the play with Tolstoy's play *A Living Corpse*. In 1960 L.A. Malyugin argued that Ermilov minimized the social content of *Uncle Vanya*.[72]

Nils Ake Nilsson, in Eekman (1960), recalled that Chekhov told Stanislavsky that when Astrov whistles, he is showing his fight against inner despair. Corrigan (1962) reveals Chekhov's effective use of disconnected dialogue, which provides realism, humor, and pathos. As the professor forbids the playing of music, a watch-man's voice is heard outside, reinforcing the idea that the professor is a censor or "watchman" over every nook and cranny of the lives of the other characters.

A.P. Shtein in 1962 located the source of the characters' unhappiness in exter-nal actions beyond the control of the other characters. Michel Saint-Denis in 1963 evaluated recent productions of the play. He felt that the MAT was turning Chekhov into a "bourgeois." Laurence Olivier's anti-naturalist staging in 1962 "gave a more intense reality to the expression of the characters and thus to the meaning of the play." But Olivier's approach also eliminated that "life of things" so important in the play.[73]

Lucas (1963) said that Chekhov was a good doctor in drama, that is, he was sensitive about not harming his characters but objective in diagnosing their weaknesses. He recalled Gorky saying that the actors in the 39th performance of the play still wept as they played their roles. But Tolstoy was wrong—what Vanya wanted was not Elena's body but her heart. Through Vanya, Chekhov was attacking critics, for whom he had little use. Vanya tells the professor that in all of his criticism he has merely told intelligent people what they already know, and stupid people what they do not care to hear.

Hingley (1964) discussed the changes that Chekhov made from *The Wood Demon*. Astrov, Elena, and the professor are all nastier but more convincing than their early counterparts. Much of the early humor, however, is lost. The theatrical committee of the Maly Theatre rejected *Uncle Vanya* on these grounds: The play is too long; Elena is too dreary to be interesting and her passionate outburst in Act III is unmotivated; and Vanya's change in attitude toward the professor is unmotivated.

Valency (1966) noted that Elena's excessive beauty brings to a previously contented group of people an indefinable sense of lost opportunities. Because Chekhov had no precommitment to explain life, "he was able to see and exhibit what few dramatic writers before him had seen or exhibited." If, as some critics say, the play has "no meaning," it does, like music or a painting, evoke a mood: Why does beauty make us sad, or why does life give us a sense of waste? "In Chekhov's world, to live is to suffer, and those suffer least who are least vital." His favorite characters have a sudden burst of desire but with a tragic lack of energy. Vanya has double motivation, against Astrov for making love to Elena, and against the professor, for being a parasite. When he finds Elena in Astrov's arms, he springs into action against the professor, rather than against his old friend Astrov. In traditional drama, when a worm turns it becomes a higher creature. But for realistic Chekhov Vanya's turning is ludicrous, and so "the worm remains a worm." Because Chekhov felt that people do not change, his later plays lack a reversal. Like *The Sea Gull*, *Uncle Vanya* depicts the generation gap: Vanya is an older Treplev, and the professor an older Trigorin. Like Chekhov, Astrov was a meliorist rather than a perfectionist — the world may never be perfect, but we should try to improve the quality of life around us.

In 1967 Kenneth Tynan, in Worrall (1986), praised the acting of Olivier as Astrov and Michael Redgrave as Vanya. Tynan speaks of the missed opportunities portrayed in Chekhov's plays, a constantly nagging "if only," which gives his plays their abiding power.

McMillin (1969) says that unlike Pushkin, Turgenev, and Goncharov, Chekhov does not show us the vigorous, positive heroine as a foil to the superfluous man. McMillin believed that "Chekhov was not, as some critics suggested, destroying drama, but rather expanding its scope by discarding what was unnecessary for the faithful representation of human emotions and problems. The larger themes emerge naturally from among the banal everyday conversations." Laffitte (1971) observed that Chekhov's poetic effect often comes from phrasing in triads — three phrases or clauses in parallel — stemming no doubt from his childhood experience as a chorister, where the Orthodox Church service modulates in three tones.

Speirs (1971) notes what happened when Chekhov put the best scenes, language and all, from *The Wood Demon* into *Uncle Vanya*. "Identical dialogues have completely different meanings in each play." Vanya and Elena are big improvements over their forerunners. "He was a man who could not submit to an artistic failure." Speirs agrees with Tolstoy, however, that Chekhov should have shown in *Uncle Vanya* signs of previous goodness in Astrov and Vanya. This play is merely a technical exercise carefully planned and executed, but for the first time Chekhov achieved a good final act. In Act IV the surprises come "in small details which we immediately feel we ought to have foreseen."

Styan (1971) said that this play is a documentary, containing social history. Chekhov depicts the problems of absentee landlordism and the bankruptcy of the intelligentsia, and he refuses to romanticize the peasant class. *Uncle Vanya* not only completed 19th century naturalistic drama but also started the 20th century movement towards "many major sub–Chekhovian comedies like *Heartbreak House, Juno and the Paycock, The Iceman Cometh,* and *The Glass Menagerie."* Discarding the trumped-up ending of *The Wood Demon,* "anticlimax and the denial of expectations become a finely tempered technique by which the audience's sense of truth to life is fostered." The professor is very much like Belikov, the teacher of Greek in Chekhov's story "The Man in a Case." Both characters always wrap themselves up, as if trying to sanitize themselves from contact with reality. As Sonya describes to Elena reasons why she likes Astrov, Elena sees reason to like him herself. Irony is seen in these two characters: Beautiful Elena (lacking love) is unhappy, but plain-looking Sonya (out of her love for Astrov) is quite happy. Sonya jokingly calls Elena "a witch," and she is, because of her beauty.

In Act IV, after the professor and Elena have left, "everyone is a hundred years older for the summer visit, and yet everyone is unchanged." J.J. Moran has summarized those who interpret Sonya's final optimism literally (H.W.L. Dana, Vladimir Ermilov, John Gassner, Phyllis Hartnoll, David Magarshack, André Maurois, Ernest Simmons, Stanislavsky, M.N. Stroyeva, and Raymond Williams) and those who do not (Eric Bentley, W.H. Bruford, Robert Brustein, Rose Caylor, Ilya Ehrenburg, Elisaveta Fen, Francis Fergusson, William Gerhardi, Maxim Gorky, F.L. Lucas, Henry Popkin, Michel Saint-Denis, O.M. Sayler, Leon Shestov, B.O. States, and Nina Toumanova). In other words, the literalists think Sonya's optimism is real and productive, and the non-literalists do not. Sonya's final impassioned speech has been set to music by Rachmaninov.

Magarshack (1972) finds in the play two chief themes: The selfish idealist Vanya realizes that he has been worshipping a false idol in the professor, and the unselfish idealist Astrov hopes that future generations will benefit from the forests that he has helped to preserve. The two themes do not coalesce, nor do they lead inevitably to the denouement. Since the characters are static, the audience does not participate in the dramatic action. Like her namesake, Helen of Troy, Elena is a passive destroyer, "a predator too indolent to be unfaithful to her old husband." Ian M. Matley in 1972 discussed Chekhov's concern with conservation as seen in *The Wood Demon* and *Uncle Vanya.*[74] Melchinger (1972) interprets the old nurse Marina as the personification of Mother Russia. She remains calm and helpful through every crisis, and as the play ends she is knitting a stocking.

Pitcher (1975) states that in building *Uncle Vanya*, Chekhov replaced a play of action with one of emotion. The overt moralizing is gone, and cynical Uncle George becomes hardworking Uncle Vanya. His name shows Astrov ("starry") to be an idealist. Tolstoy said that one felt no sympathy for characters like Vanya and Astrov, because they had always been either mediocre or evil. But Tolstoy errs in overlooking the fact that by Chekhov's conceiving his characters on an emotional plane, they become universalized. Astrov calls Elena "a beautiful fluffy marten," but martens are predators. Catharsis in this play comes from Sonya's religious faith, Vanya's philosophy of work, and the admiration we feel for the courage and endurance of the characters who suffer. Astrov gave the play's theme in Act II: "I'm fond of life as a whole, but this petty provincial Russian life I can't stand." Pitcher feels that "Chekhov, like Telegin, harbored a stubborn underlying belief that there was no reason why men should not live in peace and harmony."

Shotton, in Fennell (1973), notes that Astrov, despite his good qualities, cannot appreciate or respond to Sonya's pure love. As in *The Three Sisters*, here "contentment is the perdition of the soul, and unhappiness the key to its salvation." Rayfield (1975) praises the rocklike religious faith of the nurse Marina, which contrasts with the idleness and vacillation of the ruling class.

Brahms (1976) mentions that Telegin, deserted by his wife because of his pockmarked face, finds contentment caring for her children by another man. She, however, loses both her beauty and her lover. Little wonder that Elena avoids a love liaison. Stanislavsky said: "Read Chekhov in the kitchen of life and you will find in him nothing but the simple plot, but take him where art soars and you will feel the eternal longings of man for happiness."

Few writers have ever accomplished such a satisfactory revision of an earlier work as Chekhov did with *Uncle Vanya*, said Hingley (1976). "Everything which had been too clear-cut in the earlier play becomes enchantingly indefinite in its successor." Here we enter a world of drama that never existed before Chekhov. Climax, romance, and everything "dramatic" is discarded, in "a world with its own laws, dimensions, and brands of humor."

Bristow (1977) reprinted earlier essays by Eric Bentley and Charles B. Timmer. Bentley's essay was described above. Timmer explains Astrov's bizarre (and seemingly irrelevant) remark about the map of Africa in Act IV: Everyone is trying to delay the final moment of parting, and they are all grateful even for this "irrelevancy." Edgar L. Frost, commenting in 1977 on the effort to escape from time's ravages by the characters, remarks that Astrov in Act IV dreams of a utopia where happiness is secure even from the erosion of time.[75]

Hahn (1977) calls time one of Chekhov's protagonists. Here we feel time's preciousness and thus the tragedy of wasted lives. Chekhov's "emotional realism," in which he captures the sub-surface shifts of emotions, places him way ahead of Ibsen in this regard. Chekhov has a greater range of important characters in any one play, and unlike Ibsen he is not chained to one prevailing idea or symbol.

O.E. Mandelshtam in 1977 asserted that chance seemed to be the governing factor in the play. In 1978 Ieva Vitins argued that the emotional ties between Vanya and the women in his life render him incapable of leading an independent life.[76] Clayton A. Hubbs in 1979, assuming that repetition is one of Chekhov's major themes, showed how this play used "repeated non-action" structurally.[77]

There are many similarities between Chekhov and Astrov, said Tulloch (1980). They both believed that a better social environment produced better people, but that not all change is improvement. Chekhov's words while planting trees at Yalta sound like Astrov's, as do his hopes that in 200 years life on earth will be very beautiful.

Barricelli (1981) contains comments on *Uncle Vanya* by Philip Bordinat, Sonia Kovitz, Nicholas Moravcevich, Nils Ake Nilsson, Richard D. Risso, Laurence Senelick, and Ieva Vitins. Bordinat showed that the professor's plan to sell the estate would harm all of the other characters. Kovitz remarks that Chekhov's characters usually end up defeated: "Chekhov arranges the destruction of each character's personal happiness for the same reason that God gives Job into Satan's power—to find out who he is." At the end, "does Sonya see only a delusionary light in the distance? Her vision is neither imagined nor desired, but felt within. In the moment of embracing with love her own and Uncle Vanya's despair, she herself is the light."

Moravcevich believes that Elena's inner strength is seen in her determined struggle "not to allow the devastating effects of her beauty upon others also to change her view of herself." She knows herself to be more of a spectator than a participant in life, and her strength lies in her willingness to accept herself as she is. Nilsson discussed Vladimir Mayakovsky's view of Chekhov as "a liberator of the word." Risso demonstrates how comic elements ironically contrast with the play's dominant theme of frustration. Senelick recalled the views of Russian critics Sergey Glagol and Dmitry Merezhkovsky.

Vitins finds Vanya so bound by emotional ties to his mother and his dead sister Vera that his masculinity has been repressed. True to Vera's memory, he feels that the professor violated his love for Vera by marrying Elena, and thus he no longer need be loyal to the professor. Now his warlike nature can emerge (Voynitsky comes from *voyna*, "war"). In Vera ("faith") Vanya recognized spiritual beauty, but Elena (Helen) upsets him with her physical beauty. Professor Serebryakov ("silver") was flashy as a young scholar but now appears tarnished and dull. Sonya (Sophia, or "wisdom") becomes the leading feminine character in the family. She opts for clarity of vision, even if "the truth hurts." She becomes Vanya's surrogate wife, mother, and sister. Chekhov had other male characters whose emotional lives had fixated: Treplev had a mother attachment, Andrey a sister attachment, and Gaev a sister attachment. Vitins finds a parallel of these sister attachments in Chekhov's devotion to his sister Maria.

Kirk (1981) shows how Chekhov uses space confinement in this play. In Act IV, for example, all avenues of escape from Vanya's room are blocked. Eisen (1982) quotes Kathleen George that Chekhov deliberately used two leave-taking scenes at the close of the play, the first one intentionally long and dull so as "to provide an echo for the more poignant subsequent scene." Reviewing a National Theatre production in 1982, Richard Findlater found the characters de-romanticized until the performance oversimplified some of the play's emotional complexities.[78]

Master (1982) quotes Avram Derman that such a strong pact grows between Chekhov and a sensitive playgoer that the latter is like a "co-author." Master shows Bordinat analyzing the play in terms of Samuel Selden's "fighting triad": the principal force, the opposing force, and the deciding agent being the overpowering quality of the wasteland. But this approach will not work, says Master, because the interaction in Chekhov's plays is often oblique, and the characters are often motivated more by reaction than by action.

Redmond (1982) gives the views of Peter Holland and Laurence Senelick. Holland shows the symbolic role played by the weather. Senelick recalled George Calderon's point that Chekhov's symbols stand not only for values in the play but also for generalizations about life itself. In this play the storm not only reflects the character's moods but in a larger sense depicts life as a storm, with conflicts that must be faced.

Peace (1983) notes that in Act I the way a character takes tea indicates his basic personality. The tea drinking connotes idleness, when what is needed is work. Act endings, through mood or theme, set the stage for the beginnings of the next acts.

At Andrey Serban's production in New York in 1983, Benedict Nightingale quailed. Why use a mammoth stage with walkways leading in every direction, he asked, in a claustrophobic play in which characters get on each other's nerves? Nightingale preferred Serban's earlier, braver Chekhov productions. True to life, Chekhov shows his women as the product of what their men want them to be, but a veiled protest lies beneath the presentation. For "the one badge he might have worn with pride was that of feminism—not of course the hard, narrow variety, but the sort that seeks to release and expand."[79]

Edith Oliver also found this production eccentric, although perhaps saved by the fact that the key role of Astrov was in the competent hands of actor F. Murray Abraham.[80] The Russian magazine *Teatr* in 1983 published the comments of director Georgy Tovstonogov made during rehearsals of his 1982 production.

Clyman (1985) printed the views of Laurence Senelick and J.L. Styan. Senelick quoted Vladimir Mayakovsky's comments on the play, and noted that after 1917, Chekhov was in disfavor with the Soviets for a number of years. Styan observed that all eight main characters are in a master/slave relationship. The masters are the professor, with his prestige, and Elena, with her beauty. Those who have succumbed to the dead hand of routine are Maria, Marina, and Telegin. The ones still unreconciled to their new servile status—Astrov, Sonya, and Vanya—are the principal objects of focus in the play.

Senelick (1985) identifies four sets of doublets in the characters. Where the professor "sponges" on everyone, Telegin is altruistic. Marina understands human behavior but Maria does not. Whereas Sonya works, Elena manipulates. Of the two disillusioned crackpots, Astrov is a cynic but Vanya an idealist. As the action moves inward, the feeling of oppression mounts: Soon Vanya has no personal living space that has not been violated. Time also acts as a pressure. For a change, Chekhov uses a compact timespan, with the play representing a period of only 36 hours.

Egri (1986) states that Chekhov's skill in unifying short-story elements results in an effective climax in Act III. His extremely economical exposition enables him to portray a society ripe for a change but as yet unable to renew itself. At the same time he goes dynamically beyond the passivity of naturalism and impressionism. There are many similarities between *Uncle Vanya* and Eugene O'Neill's *A Touch of the Poet:* Both are not only tragicomedies but play identical roles in the historical merger of comedy and tragedy, and both plays employ an overpowering climax. The parting kiss of Astrov and Elena depicts the "might have been" sadness used often by O'Neill in *A Long Day's Journey into Night*.

14. *The Three Sisters* (1901)

Act I — Irina Prozorov is celebrating her twentieth birthday. Her sister Olga, 28, a high school teacher, recalls the death of their father, a retired general, a year ago. Their sister Masha, 24, is married to Kulygin, a dull teacher. Baron Tusenbach, an army lieutenant, says "a vast healing storm is gathering — we shall work in another 25 or 30 years." Lt. Col. Vershinin, the new battery commander, says that in 200 years life on earth will be unspeakably beautiful. Andrey, brother to the girls, is engaged to Natasha, a poor local girl. Tusenbach tries to make love with Irina but she spurns him.

Act II — Several years have elapsed. Andrey has married Natasha, and given up hope of becoming a professor. Natasha moves Irina into Olga's room in order to have a room for her little Bobik. Captain Solyony vies with Tusenbach in courting Irina. Vershinin, disgusted with his wife because she keeps taking poison, courts Masha. Natasha keeps company with Protopopov, the universally disliked head of the district board. The sisters yearn to go to Moscow where they feel they can find happiness.

Act III — Vershinin brings his family to the Prozorov home, to escape a town fire. Natasha abuses the aged maid Anfisa, but Olga defends her. Captain Chebutykin, a doctor, is drunk, remorseful over having lost a woman patient. Andrey mortgages the estate to cover a large gambling debt. Natasha now controls all of the Prozorov finances. Masha makes love with Vershinin, who announces the brigade's departure. Irina consents to marry Tusenbach, who is now a civilian.

Act IV — Olga, now headmistress, lives at the high school. Irina is happy, for tomorrow is her wedding day. Tusenbach, about to duel Solyony, now appreciates every little beauty in life. Vershinin, leaving town, embraces tearful Masha. Kulygin sees the embrace but forgives Masha. Natasha has decided to cut down all the fir and maple trees. Chebutykin tells Irina that Solyony has killed Tusenbach in the duel. Masha says, "We must begin our lives all over again." Irina states, "Some day we will know all the answers. Now we must work." Olga replies, "We shall soon be gone forever, but our sufferings will turn into joy for those who live after us. Happiness and peace will come on earth."

Saunders (1960) says that the idea for this play dates back to 1883, when Chekhov spent a holiday at Voskressensk, where his brother Ivan was tutor to the three children of Col. B.I. Maevsky. Chekhov watched love affairs develop between village girls and the army officers, and noted the sad partings when the army unit moved out. Also, in 1888 Chekhov rented a house on the Lintvarev estate on the Psyol River near Sumy. He was fascinated by the three Lintvarev sisters, who were intellectual, charming, and high-minded. Two of the women were doctors, and the eldest was blind from a brain tumor.

In 1900 Chekhov said that the paper *News of the Day* felt that the play's title was inappropriate, but he refused to change it. In November 1900 he wrote to the actress Vera Komisarjevskaya, "The play turned out to be dreary, long, and awkward; it has four heroines and a spirit more gloomy than gloom itself. The hostile press in Moscow made fun of it by pretending to publish telegrams announcing its progress: 'First act written,' etc."

At their first reading the MAT actors said, "This is not a play, but only a scheme; there are no roles but only hints." At the first performance on 31 January 1901, there were 12 curtain-calls after Act I but only a half-hearted one after Act IV, Stanislavsky said. Danchenko and others reported a somewhat more favorable reception. The critic Chenko said that all of the play's irrelevancies were used to convey the profoundly pessimistic mood of the author.

At first, Russian critics were puzzled at why the sisters did not go to Moscow—they were wealthy, and nothing kept them from the move. Later, however, they explained the characters' seeming lack of motivation as the feature of a new dramatic method. I.N. Ignatov in 1901 said that to the sisters Moscow was not a city but "a symbol of a distant resplendent ideal to which suffering souls yearningly direct their thoughts." A critic in *Niva* in 1901 said that "Moscow is an illusion, a mirage—to the traveler in a hopeless wilderness it is a vision of a better life."[1]

Chekhov was pleased to see that *The Russian Veteran* in 1901 applauded the play, finding no fault with the military allusions. He took a personal hand in coaching actors and advising Stanislavsky about stage effects. In September 1901 the play, as staged by the MAT, received generally favorable notices. The *Daily News* described the "whole series of rapturous ovations" given Chekhov. The critic in *Russian Word* praised Chekhov's effects in rehearsing the actors, something that Stanislavsky as director naturally resented. In his later reminiscences, Stanislavsky admitted that he felt awkward in Chekhov's presence. Awed by Chekhov's prestige, Stanislavsky overreacted at first, missing the simplicity that Chekhov wanted in his characters.[2]

The negative attack on the play was led by Suvorin's *New Times*, for by now Chekhov and Suvorin had quarreled over the Dreyfus affair and other matters. Valery Bryusov said that to overcome boredom, these provincial people "diversify life by their malignant gossip, vodka, cards, and quarrels. The women deceive their husbands and the men lie. The actors torment each other. All loathe themselves, and know that there is no way to extricate themselves from their position."[3] Tolstoy remarked, "I could not make myself read this play. What is it all for? Modern dramatists have lost their way. Instead of telling us the whole of a man's life, drama must place him in such a situation, tie such a knot that when it is untied, the whole man is made clear."[4]

A.I. Bogdanovich in 1901 summarized the play's weaknesses: There was no action, and the characters were more allegorical than real. But he admitted that in the MAT performance the characters came alive and the audience was completely enthralled. V.M. Lavrov agreed, telling Chekhov, "When you read it, it seems an excellent literary work, but when it's interpreted on the stage things emerge brightly with merciless inevitability." In 1901 Chekhov stated that "Kondakov, the academician, writes me that he attended a performance of *The Three Sisters*, and his enthusiasm is indescribable. Today I had a long telegram from the actor N.N. Solovzov about a performance of *The Three Sisters* in Kiev, an enormous, desperate success."[5]

In 1902 even the conservative critics in St. Petersburg praised the play, and the Society of Dramatic Writers awarded Chekhov the Griboyedov Prize for it. Leonid Andreyev, warned that the play was very depressing, said that he felt drawn into intimacy with persons having a deep yearning for life. With this amount of frustration, one could see that something was bound to explode, he said.

A.V. Lunacharsky in 1903 said that if the play is a satire on weak-willed characters it was too subtle to be effective. He also urged Chekhov to create a positive forceful hero who could "show us the the seeds of a new life." In 1906 I.F. Annensky made a detailed study of the major characters and their interrelationships. Zinaida Gippius in 1908 castigated the play's pessimism. Chekhov's love of life, she said, "stiffens in the clutch of the devil, who must be glad to win back such a choice tidbit for his beloved Death." Gippius believed that Chekhov was too much of a naturalist ever to ascend to the spiritual plane of symbolism.

Kornei Chukovsky, on the other hand, felt that Chekhov's knack of finding beauty in ordinary events brought his readers closer to God than do most pious tracts. *The Three Sisters* shows Christian virtue at work, Chukovsky said, for "it not only evokes sympathy for the downtrodden and suffering but makes them an image of beauty."[6]

Although he admitted that *The Three Sisters* was the most melancholy of Chekhov's plays, Maurice Baring in 1910 said that the departure scene of Act IV was the most poignant one he had seen. In his opinion Chekhov's plays were "a thousand times more interesting to see on the stage than they are to read." The reason for this is that Chekhov followed Goethe's advice: "Everything in a play should be symbolical, and should lead to something else." If Chekhov's plays seem gloomy, it is because they represent the last hour before the dawn. "His note is not a note of despair, but of invincible trust in the coming day," said Baring.[7]

Ashley Dukes in 1911 said that "*The Three Sisters,* if unrelieved, would be intolerable. It is relieved by its note of revolt, its distinctive dialogue, and its plea that comfort and civilization alone can give no dignity to existence." For Chekhov, said Dukes, individuality was the highest value.[8]

In 1914 Vladimir Mayakovsky wrote about "the two Chekhovs." The first one was the voice of twilight Russia. But the second one, the one that appealed to the poet, was "the king of the Word," the harbinger of futurism. Chekhov's language in *The Three Sisters* was seen as revolutionary. As examples Mayakovsky cited the love tunes hummed between Masha and Vershinin, and Chebutykin's refrain: ta-ra-ra-boom-de-ay.

In his introduction to his translation of Chekhov's plays Julius West (1915) remarked that *"The Three Sisters* is said to act better than any other Chekhov play, and should surprise an English audience exceedingly." West believed that the drama of inaction, showing the tragedy of everyday life, was just as overwhelming as that of Lear and Othello.

Gertrude Besse King, in reviewing West's translation, showed the obstacle that Chekhov had set for himself in his drama. "He must raise interest in a play whose main theme is dreary monotony, force one to like the most futilely ineffective group ever gathered on the stage, make harmony out of the clashing confusion of three plots, and after emphasizing empty loneliness and discontent in every character, send the audience home artistically reconciled with life." But through Chekhov's subtle magic, "you feel as though you were intimately acquainted with a very likeable lot of individuals. Instead of having your sympathy divided between abstract right and wrong, it is bestowed on all these very human persons." For, like us, they take themselves and their petty defects so seriously that we are led to a philosophic awareness of how easily we get discouraged, of what small barriers keep us from happiness. The catharsis has been imperceptibly achieved.[9]

Another reviewer of West's translation reacted quite differently. He called *The Three Sisters* "suggestive of a collection of casual notes for an uncompleted novel of realistic impressionism." Unfit for the theater, its value is as the diagnosis of a Russian national malady. One could have only "an almost exclusively literary and ethnical interest in Chekhov's plays, because of their loose, haphazard construction, constant reiteration, excess of trivial talk and incident, and monotonous drabness."[10]

Hamilton Fyfe continued the attack in 1917. The men winning Russia's battles in the war were not like Vershinin and the other officers in *The Three Sisters*. Nor were the valiant workers on the home front the Prozorov sisters. "As an interpreter of the Russian character," Fyfe said, "Chekhov is out-of-date."[11]

Chekhov's defenders, however, were waiting in the wings. Harley Granville Barker, recalling an MAT production of the play, said that he had never realized that such perfection could be achieved in the theater. "The most telling stage picture I have ever seen," he said, "was that final moment in the play."[12] Arthur Ruhl had also seen that production, which he called "one of my most vivid theatrical impressions." The sensation was "not so much of getting into a play as of getting into Russia." One found something which will "deepen and make more rich and understandable the life we are living."[13]

A friend of Chekhov's, the writer N. Teleshov, called him a prophet. Teleshov recalled Chekhov almost using Vershinin's words in saying that "in a few years the autocracy will be gone."[14] In 1919 Nikolai Efros described the MAT production of *The Three Sisters* given in 1901.

The London Art Theatre production of *The Three Sisters* in 1920 was the play's first British performance. So thoroughly had Chekhov's fiction prepared the way that there was only one adverse critic, who said that "Nothing happens. We are not interested in the characters. We neither like them nor sympathize with them."[15] Many who were critical of the production nevertheless praised the play.[16] One who found "something cantankerous and stifling about a play like this" went on to admit that "Chekhov has the supreme art of making his nerveless creatures live."[17] Frank Swinnerton said this was a "crude and puzzling" production of a play which is "beautifully ordered and full of contrast and essential reality. Chekhov is the nearest thing in literature to a symphonic composer."[18]

One reviewer said that the play revealed "the gradual, undramatic tragedy of time — time the coarsener, the destroyer."[19] Desmond MacCarthy asked, What does Bernard Shaw know about heartbreak? Here, he said, one finds that "infinite pity for weak-winged aspiration" depicted in George Gissing's *Odd Women*.[20] W.J. Turner admitted that *The Three Sisters* was not Chekhov's best play but found it nonetheless better than Shaw's *Candida* and *Pygmalion,* and the *Medea* of Euripides. Turner said that "the poetry, the creative power of Chekhov, infuses the whole conception of the play. It is extraordinarily imaginative. You feel that this is what goes on inside millions of us, all the years of our lives."[21]

In 1922 Oliver Sayler explained the "spiritualized realism" that was achieved in an MAT production of a Chekhov play. The most important part of the technique consisted of a deliberate restraint, an understatement which caused the spectator to complete the emotional circuit. Abhorring exaggeration, Chekhov had decided to interpret life through its nuances. There was a cumulative power about Chekhov's simple but subtle technique that made it overpowering by the final act. To illustrate his point, Sayler pointed to the three love-duets between Masha and Vershinin.[22]

Gerhardi (1923) noticed Chekhov's use of leitmotifs to accompany each main character. He also commented on Chekhov's understanding of social psychology: Solyony is a sensible person with only one other person present, but in a crowd he becomes either silly or a bully. Gerhardi said that the sisters would have been better off being stupid, for their delicate sensitivity tortures them. Chekhov seemed to be a progressive, Gerhardi opined, for Vershinin's speeches sound like the optimism of Mr. Huss in H.G. Wells's *The Undying Fire.*

S. Hoare in 1923 said that, just as he has abolished plot in the short story, so has Chekhov shelved action in the drama. "To convey the sense of beauty inherent in all of life takes great, universal art. *The Three Sisters* is not only a drama of self-inhibition, or it would fail of universality. He has created the emotional stasis: Life seems fixed in a moment of significance."[23]

The first American production of *The Three Sisters* was performed in New York in Russian by the MAT in 1923. The critics were effulgent in their praise of the acting.[24] John Corbin, however, found this "static" drama frustrating: "In this Slavic

world there is neither the will to live valiantly nor the genius that snatches spiritual
triumph out of worldly loss. The technical problem of presenting the heart history
of three women in three hours is well nigh insoluble. Chekhov's plays leave English-
speaking peoples cold, and perhaps inclined to resentment."[25] The Chicago critics
agreed with Corbin, one calling the play "a drab document of futility and
discontent—a chronicle of gray, paltry lives, beating feebly at the barriers which
surround them, but with no will to break out. It proceeds in desultory fashion,
beginning nowhere and getting nowhere."[26]

     The tour of the MAT was nevertheless very successful. One reviewer said that
"when the curtain fell upon the performance of *The Three Sisters* Saturday night,
one of the most remarkable demonstrations in the history of the American theatre
was staged by the capacity audience." After 12 curtain calls, Stanislavsky spoke to
the audience in French. When this failed to satisfy the crowd, Stanislavsky came
out and addressed them in Russian. When he finished, the applause lasted for
nearly half an hour.[27]

     America was ready to read Stanislavsky's autobiography, published in 1924.
Stanislavsky explained that "the men of Chekhov do not bathe in their own sorrow.
Just the opposite. They, like Chekhov himself, seek life, joy, laughter, courage. The
men and women of Chekhov want to live. It is not their fault that Russian life kills
all initiative."

     Theodore Komisarjevsky directed *The Three Sisters* in London in 1926. E.A.
Baughan was the lone dissenting critic, calling the play "too diffuse—its shades of
humor and pathos make it a bewildering pattern."[28] Although some found fault with
the acting, all praised the vividness and originality of the characterization.[29] One
reviewer objected to anachronisms in the staging,[30] but another found "things of
delicate beauty, not merely the scenes between the sisters in Act III, but also certain
subtle strokes in the character of the doctor and in the speech of Kulygin to Masha
near the end."[31]

     Ivor Brown found a play "as sadly beautiful as autumn itself yet graced with
springtime flash of merriment. It has given at least one spectator the kind of
pleasure for which he has waited through many a sad evening of disenchantment
with the magic that a theatre should possess."[32] John Shand agreed that "this production approaches so near to perfection that I never hope to see a better one."
Chekhov's only match in the theater was Shakespeare. "Something of divinity
hedges round about Chekhov as it also encircles Shakespeare. Chekhov shows us
no mysteries, only the great mystery of life itself, and he mirrors every mood and
passion of mankind in a crystal-clear vocabulary. His ineffable toleration is of the
kind which passes understanding."[33]

     Also in 1926 Eva LeGallienne organized her Civic Repertory Theatre, which
staged *The Three Sisters* that year in New York. Several critics said that the play's
dullness exceeded its "wistful beauty."[34] Most, however, felt that the play throbbed
with the pulse of life itself.[35] Brooks Atkinson found the play "drenched in humanity. It illuminates the uncertainties of human existence, the inadequacy of human

forces."[36] John Mason Brown discovered action "as poignant as any that the present day theatre has offered. Under the guise of outward realism, Chekhov transcends reality, and sublimates the petty trifles of a drawing room until they soar to a throbbing and revelatory beauty."[37] Walter Prichard Eaton said that those who called this play dull revealed "a palate made abnormal by sensationalism." Chekhov had so mastered realism that he "takes us bit by bit into the very lives of a family, a community, a nation, until all sense of the theatre melts away."[38]

S.D. Balukhaty in 1927 stated that in this play Chekhov made new advances in the art of creating character through dialogue. Discussing plotless drama that year, Stark Young said that *"The Three Sisters* is theater, as experience has proved, but the idea is most expressed through character and atmosphere. What the people in it do not do constitutes a kind of negative plot that counts more than anything else in our impression of the play."[39]

In 1929 Komisarjevsky again produced this play in London. Several critics caviled at the production,[40] but more felt that it captured Chekhov's twin themes of hope for the future and despair in the present.[41] Ivor Brown called the play "the loveliest of its type," and found Chekhov's genius in his giving "a lyric quality to a universal tale." Herbert Farjeon said, "My pen is ashamed to expose its bankruptcy in thanks for this work of supreme loveliness"—the sisters remain "living mysteries" because of their unexplored depths.[43] Desmond MacCarthy accounted for the play's excellence by recalling two terms used by George Calderon in 1912: centrifugal plot and disconnected dialogue.[44]

The American playwright George Kelly at this time called *The Three Sisters* "the finest play I have ever seen," largely because it freed itself from a rigid plot formula.[45] In 1930 several former actresses from the MAT staged this play for the American Laboratory Theatre in New York. Critics agreed that through understatement and deep simplicity, the play portrayed life's frustration slipping past imperceptibly.[46]

By now having directed many successful Chekhov plays, Komisarjevsky in 1930 explained his technique, an offshoot of that used by Stanislavsky. Stanislavsky's method, which he called "psychic naturalism," had been used previously by the theorists of the French classical theater. First the actor must discover beneath the play's lines what feelings prompted the author to write them, and then recall his own feelings in similar circumstances and substitute them for those of the author. Stanislavsky found that the inner life of Chekhov's characters is intimately connected with the sounds around them, and that these sounds must harmonize with the feelings of the actors. "The big success of my production of *The Three Sisters* in London," said Komisarjevsky, "was largely due to the fact that I evolved the way to convey Chekhov's inner meaning, and made the rhythm of the 'music' of the play blend with the rhythm of the movements of the actors, giving the necessary accents with the lighting and other outer 'effects.' If this synthesis had not been completely harmonious, the play might have seemed meaningless, as it did during rehearsals to the majority of the actors."[47]

London critics were harsh on Henry Cass for his Old Vic production of *The Three Sisters* in 1935. Apparently missing Komisarjevsky, reviewers found too little humor and too much despair in the production.[48] Ivor Brown was even led to the "irreverent" comparison of the sisters to the groups of girls' trios who "moaned their blues" into radio microphones. Was a part of Chekhov's success due to the fact that the young people of this generation, bred on postwar disillusion and depression frustration, were particularly responsive to Chekhov's compassionate studies of defeatism, Brown asked.[49]

Toumanova (1937) recalled that Beethoven called his Pastorale Symphony (No. 6) "more emotion than picture." This play had a similar structure, she felt, for it was built upon leitmotifs and lyrical fluidity. Chekhov's accurate picture of the defunct aristocracy, wrote this former Russian princess, presaged "the coming storms and the dawning new age," as borne out by the revolution of 1905. Toumanova also recalled a parody of this play, by Victor Burenin, an editor at *New Times*, called *Nine Sisters and Not Even One Fiancé!*

Michel Saint-Denis directed *The Three Sisters* so well in 1938 in London that he almost made playgoers forget Komisarjevsky. One reviewer demurred, finding too slow a pace and too much self-pity.[50] Most, however, concurred with Ivor Brown that Saint-Denis had achieved wonders with "an all-star cast in a no-star play."[51]

One reviewer stated that "no dramatist in the world has ever equalled Chekhov in his ability to catch these wavering emotional situations in passing, and unerringly draw their fullest essence from them."[52] Henry Adler thought that only Shakespeare could compare with Chekhov.[53] Finding an affinity between Chekhov's plays and the great impressionist paintings, Ashley Dukes said that "our stage stands still while these works dating from 1900 develop."[54] Lionel Hale doubted that he would ever see this production of *The Three Sisters* surpassed, for Saint-Denis knew his characters thoroughly: "He can play with exquisite modulations on their fits of temper, their childish kindnesses, their self-tormenting talk, so that sudden laughter shakes out of our eyes the tears that have been gathering."[55]

Chekhov's former friend Paul Shishkoff in 1938 alleged that his family was the basis for *The Three Sisters*. Shishkoff's father was an army doctor, and his mother and her two sisters were daughters of a general. Neighbors always called the women "the three sisters." Shishkoff told Chekhov about an army duel he had witnessed. Shishkoff believed that his father's garrison life at Batum was the background for Chekhov's play.[56]

Anita Block in 1939 said that Chekhov's profound influence on the contemporary theater was due to more than his subtle technique and his catalog of characters. "For his subject matter and underlying social philosophy transcend character portrayals and technical achievements as completely as do Ibsen's." His major plays are the most damning indictment of pre-revolutionary Russia. "A revolutionary by indirection," Chekhov condemned the intelligentsia, except for those who express his own social vision: Vershinin, Tusenbach, and Irina.[57] Noting that in Act I they are unwed but in Act IV Andrey and Natasha have three children, Henry T. Perry found in "the procession of the years a sort of epic quality, which unrolls with a wanton prodigality of splendor, as dazzling as it is confusing."[58]

Most critics agreed that the New York production by the Surry Players in 1939 failed to capture the needed ensemble effect.[59] This is the most difficult Chekhov play to produce, explained Grenville Vernon. As in life, apparent irrelevancies keep interrupting this impressionistic play. "What is hinted at is often what is important. It is the color, the diapasonic undertow which is the secret of Chekhov's genius. Chekhov must be produced in the manner of a mosaic. Each line, each bit of business, must be fitted in so that, incomprehensible as it may seem at first, the final result is crystal clear." Failing to do this, the result here is "that what is deep often becomes trivial and sometimes even absurd."[60]

Reviewing a Dublin production in 1940, Gabriel Fallon, after conceding Chekhov's "immense talent, poetry, and unique originality," said that "he leads us through a catharsis of smiling tears to a dangerous sympathy for his abnormal creations." Since, however, Chekhov's name was now used to describe the highest art of contemporary drama, Fallon said, it would be good to see more of his plays so as to have a fuller view.[61]

Soviet critic N.A. Gorchakov described an MAT production of *The Three Sisters* in 1940, directed by Danchenko. This performance showed the sisters strong and confident, sure of a better future. Gorchakov called them "a magnificent type of Russian womanhood, with its suffering, self-renunciation, and moral strength." A.I. Roskin also welcomed the optimistic tone of this production, although he felt that the four love triangles made the play resemble a novel.

In his translation of *The Three Sisters* published in 1941, Stark Young explained Chekhov's wit. Previous translations had made Chekhov appear gloomy, Young said, but this whole play is conceived by "a witty doctor who sees what human life is and how tragic it can be but who nevertheless keeps a certain easy sense of humor, a poignant smiling observation and scope."[62]

The most spectacular staging of *The Three Sisters* in the United States took place in New York in 1942. Casting for the play made American theatrical history. Judith Anderson played Olga, Katherine Cornell was Masha, and Gertrude Musgrove was Irina. Ruth Gordon played Natasha, Dennis King was Vershinin, and Edmund Gwenn was Chebutykin. The director was Guthrie McClintic. For once a Chekhov play was a box-office hit on Broadway.[63]

Wartime newspaper critics were sharply divided about the play. Howard Barnes, Lewis Nichols, and Burton Rascoe found it badly outdated. John Anderson, Louis Kronenberger, and Richard Lockridge said that its vivid characterization made it one of the best plays of the season. Burns Mantle found himself "of a mind halfway through the play to head a movement to raise the money to send the Prozorov girls to Moscow with single-trip tickets and a prayer that they and their unhappy friends will henceforth stay out of my play-going life."[64]

Other reviewers found the play dated,[65] Mary McCarthy adding that, morally speaking, these unfortunate people are all a little hollow, and their dreams of nobility and hard work have in them an element of pretense."[66] The majority of the periodical reviewers called the production very good, if not what the outstanding cast had promised it might be.[67]

By no means was the play outdated, argued Rosamond Gilder. It would always be timely, "both because Chekhov knew the human heart with all its aspirations, fears, and frustrations, and because he could present them in a unique and imperishable theatre form. This rich and complex theatre fills the stage with abundant life and seems by its validity and implications to stretch beyond the ordinary bonds of dramatic expression."[68]

Joseph Wood Krutch, after confessing that "there is a real sense in which Chekhov, like most modern writers, is minor," found the ensemble performance for which the other reviewers had sought in vain. Trite comments that the plot had no action were false—even in outward action the play had more things occurring than another classic like *Othello*. "Chekhov's inversion of the normal method of story-telling" was most appropriate for this collection of idlers and dreamers, since it best brought out his peculiar brand of sympathetic criticism.[69]

Describing his technique, Guthrie McClintic called *The Three Sisters* "a director's dream. Chekhov leaves his play to the director and actor to interpret." The characters are real and universal, with not only common strengths and weaknesses but "an abounding faith in our ultimate destiny." McClintic said his "three sisters" had received a congratulatory telegram from their counterparts in the current MAT cast. He said he had received many letters from American soldiers and sailors who were "keenly appreciative" of the chance to see this great play.[70]

Another director's notes on staging *The Three Sisters* were now shared with American playgoers. The death of Danchenko in 1944 led the assistant director of the MAT to send America a ten-page telegram outlining Danchenko's advice to his actors for the 1940 production. The great Russian director said that "the most essential feature of this play is its musicality. Every act of Chekhov's plays has its own musical design. To use everyday language in Chekhov's plays would be wrong. His text is elevated and poetical. In its structure and resonance it is perhaps most closely akin to Pushkin. Even the characters who reflect the seamy, vulgar side of life are profoundly musical."[71]

Chekhov was now seen as a bridge between New York and Moscow. "In a vast confusion of conflicting thoughts and ideas," said Nina Toumanova, "humanity at the crossroads gazes toward the tantalizing Moscow that haunted the imagination of the three sisters."[72] The *New York Times* was ready with a reason for this. Aside from Chekhov's great influence upon American and British writers, it was noted that "the problems of Taganrog resemble those of Main Street." While the United States eagerly awaited diplomatic camaraderie that would secure world peace and reconstruction, she was described as feeling that "Chekhov remains a gracious ambassador of the people of Russia."[73]

In 1944 Soviet critic D.I. Zaslavsky argued that throughout Chekhov's works one finds the quest for a better life such as Vershinin proposes.[74] Helen Muchnic in 1947 noted the irony Chekhov used in calling his villainess Natasha, for she is the converse of Tolstoy's domesticated Natasha in *War and Peace*.[75]

Magarshack (*Dramatist*, 1952) said that this play deals with "the inmost mysteries of man's soul, the purpose of man's existence, and the ultimate values of life." Solyony is "the typical fascist: He exalts his own neurosis to an article of faith." He tells Irina: "I shall tolerate no rivals. I swear to you that I shall kill my rival." Chebutykin is always reading a newspaper, a practice that Chekhov considered a waste of time. He could have stopped the duel by telling Irina about it, but he says, "One baron more or less in the world—what difference does it make?" Masha, an accomplished pianist, has not played in years because her husband fears his headmaster might disapprove of her playing a public concert. Of the many love triangles, the only real one involves Masha. Vershinin tells the sisters, "You won't notice Moscow when you live there." When they finally realize this, they know they will have to face reality—this is the play's message.

A.N. Gribov in 1954 said that Vladimir Ermilov is wrong: Chebutykin is not a villain but has been deeply wounded in the past. Louis Kronenberger the next year called *The Three Sisters* the best play in modern drama, partly because the sisters refuse to let themselves be beaten inwardly. M.N. Stroeva in 1955 said that Danchenko's production stressed three truths: social, theatrical, and truth to life. He also had the sisters more passive in accepting their fate than had Stanislavsky.[76]

David Ross produced *The Three Sisters* in New York in 1955. Brooks Atkinson said that the play expressed Chekhov's impatience with "the inability to take action, the flimsiness of illusions, and the triumph of bourgeois callousness over gentility."[77] Judith Crist said that the excellent cast "made it not only bearable but brought many moments of tragic intensity and intended comedy."[78] Calling it the best ensemble performance of Chekhov that he had seen, Maurice Zolotow said it had "a sense of the grotesque that is the essence of Chekhov's comedy."[79]

Ermilov (1956) found the comedy in the disparity between the sisters' bold dreams and timid actions. He said that to Chekhov, any event can be seen to have both comic and tragic aspects. Bruford (1957) found this play more universal than *The Sea Gull* or *Uncle Vanya*, because its themes apply to everyone: the freshness of youth, the fading memory of childhood, lovable family ties, and the role of one's vocation. Opening the play with a birthday party allows all the characters to be quickly introduced. At the play's close, the fading band music signifies the continual departure of happiness.

In 1958 L.A. Plotkin compared the styles of Chekhov and Turgenev, especially studying parallels between this play and Turgenev's story "The Duellist." At a 1959 production of the play by David Ross, Brooks Atkinson saw it as a composite of Chekhov himself—his artistic nature mirrored the sensitivity of the sisters, but his medical background kept him objective enough not to sentimentalize the representation.[80]

N.Y. Berkovsky in 1960 said that this play reveals the secret of all of Chekhov's works—it is not the characters who are ill but "the interests represented through those characters." Also that year A.R. Vladimirskaya showed the editorial revisions that Chekhov made to the play.[81]

Eekman (1960) contained views on the play by Nils Ake Nilsson and Charles B. Timmer. Nilsson noted Chekhov's use of intonation to convey meaning. Chekhov told Olga Knipper not to look sad while playing Masha, for "people who have long borne grief only whistle or become absorbed in thought." Timmer felt that Chekhov's use of bizarre elements in the play approaches the technique of the Theater of the Absurd. When Chebutykin reads that Balzac was married in Berdichev, an ugly Russian border town, it tells the sisters that happiness can be found in *any* town, given the proper mind set.

Corrigan (1962) shows how Chekhov uses disconnected dialogue in this play. Several times when the sisters yearn for Moscow, other characters in other conversations laugh, or say "This is nonsense." Simmons (1962) said that "the subtle interaction of symbol and reality creates an atmosphere of unusual psychological density. The inner action is made more meaningful through the seemingly disconnected dialogue. The illusion of happiness is the main theme. As in the conclusion to *Uncle Vanya*, Chekhov distills from frustration and failure a renewed faith in life."

Lucas (1963) states that most tragedies tell of terrible things that happen, but here the tragedy is terrible because of the things which do not happen. This play uses far more pauses than any other Chekhov play: 66 to 44 for *Uncle Vanya*, the play with the second highest number of pauses.

Lee Strasberg directed an Actors Studio production of *The Three Sisters* in New York in 1964. Judith Crist said that the variety of acting styles and the diversity of moods vitiated the cumulative impact of the play.[82] Howard Taubman praised the production for avoiding self-pity, and for showing the sisters as "a chorus affirming the promise of the future and the regenerative powers of work."[83] In their London production, however, George C. Scott became so angry at what he considered to be Strasberg's ineptitude that he threatened him with bodily injury, and Kim Stanley, who played Masha, left both the Actors Studio and the legitimate stage, never to return.[84]

Hingley (1964) recalled that Chekhov did not want to burlesque the military, since he felt that they played an important function by bringing culture to the provinces. After an absence of 40 years, the MAT returned to perform *The Three Sisters* in 1965 in New York. Howard Taubman reported that the sisters were "individualized yet indivisible," and that the MAT's "radiant art argues the case for creative repertory theater with irresistible eloquence."[85]

In 1965 F.W. Dupee showed how this play anticipated the Theater of the Absurd, and L.A. Malyugin discussed a 1964 Soviet film version of the play. E.S. Kalmanovsky in 1966 accounted for the play's abiding interest both in the Soviet Union and abroad as being due to the characters' honesty and creativity.[86]

Valency (1966) recalled the play's similarity to Chekhov's story "On Official

Duty" (1899), where Lyzhin meets the beautiful and cultivated Von Taunitz sisters. Lyzhin's faith is also that of Vershinin, Tusenbach, and Irina: "Everything is the result of a universal idea; everything has one soul, one aim." Life seems fragmented to most people, but to Lyzhin these fragments, in Chekhov's words, "were seen to be parts of a single organism, marvelous and rational, by one who thought of his own life as part of that universal whole." This play is not only Chekhov's best, but through its polyphonic structure is "the flower of impressionism in drama." No other play, says Valency, "has conveyed more subtly the sense of the transitory nature of human life, the sadness and beauty of the passing moment." The play is a high point in the drama of characterization, but the roles are difficult to act because Chekhov is dealing with the inner life of the characters. Maurice Maeterlinck's influence can be seen, in the atmosphere, lyricism, symbolism, the inner life, and the representation of the drama of everyday life. Chekhov is more than an impressionist: "To understand him, it is important to add to the sense of episode, the sense of process, and after that, the all-enveloping doubt." Chekhov's own ambiguity is portrayed in two characters: He had Vershinin's faith in the future, but Chebutykin's doubt that life shows progress.

Jackson (1967) agrees with Ilya Ehrenburg that Chekhov's message lies not in any teaching but in his art, which recognizes the permanence of man despite the ups and downs of his culture. Jackson felt that Danchenko erred in considering Chekhov's characters as puppets controlled by fate. Stanislavsky not only better carried out Chekhov's intent, but also reflected the Russian intellectuals' hope for a better day, on the eve of the first Russian revolution. Gilles (1968) recalled Chekhov's changing attitude towards this play. At first he considered it a failure, but later he said "I'm amazed to have written such a thing."

Herbert Muller in 1968 asserted that this play is a tragedy for a democracy, since its characters are really every man. George Tovstonogov that year explained that in his 1965 production the characters bore most of the responsibility for their failures.

Randall Jarrell, in his notes to his translation in 1969, said that an essential part of the play is its assertion about the meaningfulness of life. That year Bernard de Bear Nicol edited a discussion of naturalist and absurdist elements in the play. One view said that Chekhov's extreme naturalism led him into a growing awareness of life's absurdity. A second view argued that calling him an absurdist waters down the force of his observations on people and "weakens the potential of his poetic achievement."[87]

At a New York production by the American National Theatre Association in 1969 Stanley Kauffmann commented that it is easy to make a Chekhov play look good, for "the moody lighting, the Victorian clutter, the picturesque groupings, all are accessible even to a modest directing talent."[88] McMillin (1969) observed that the characters who extol work are those who have never experienced it. When Irina does start working, she quickly becomes disillusioned with her job.

Brinley Rhys in 1970 discussed the difficulty of translating Chekhov's plays,

especially *The Three Sisters.* In 1971 Witold Kosny examined the literary quotations
used in the play, and Barbara Paul called the play "Five Sisters," saying that Andrey and Chebutykin are intimately involved in the play's pattern.[89]

Laffitte (1971) recalls Suvorin's comment: "What petty characters when we
wanted tragic ones." The play is a long inner dialogue between Chekhov and his
wife. Separated from Olga Knipper, Chekhov converted his loneliness into this play.
"No poet has ever depicted so effectively the different forms of separation that lie
in wait for lovers." Speirs (1971) called Tusenbach both the most original thinker
and the most isolated person in the play, which is "Chekhov's blackest work of art.
It shows the hell people bring about through cowardice and mental weakness."

Styan (1971) states that this play is the most frequently acted play in Russian
theatrical history. Here Chekhov does what he did in many of his short stories—set
hope ironically against reality. Natasha would be the villainess "were it not for the
fact that her narrowness of spirit makes her the most satirically comic character.
She is symptomatic of those little pressures of destructive self-interest present
everywhere, part of the cruel nature of life which fragile people like the sisters are
unable to withstand." "The audience finds Natasha's vulgarity so familiar that it is
laughable." Each sister has her own time orientation: Olga, past; Masha, present;
Irina, future. Styan sees Vershinin as a comic character, but admits that the great
directors—Stanislavsky, Komisarjevsky, and Saint-Denis—all played him as a
romantic character.

Every line that Kulygin speaks, says Styan, is a gem of comic precision: "His
self-satisfaction is his moral and intellectual death." Natasha walks around carrying
a candle, like Lady Macbeth. Styan feels that Chekhov would not be so naïve as
to think that any new society would not have overly sensitive people, unrequited
love, poor marriages, or unrealized potential. "This is a play about time," says
Styan. "The sisters represent people searching for answers they will never have
because they are asking the wrong questions. Chekhov is too gentle to have them
appear stupid. Is this a play of hope? Rather, a play of resignation and endurance."

Penelope Curtis in 1972 said that the play deals with "the mystery of personal
and psychic freedom" and "the communal nature of human reality." Beverly Hahn
that year called it "the finest of modern plays," with "a deep organic and poetic
unity." Joyce Carol Oates, on the other hand, said that this was an absurdist play,
and that Chekhov was less conventional than most absurdist playwrights. Most of
them build to a climax, but not Chekhov. The birthday party, which should be
happy, is elegiac—an absurdist theme. Instead of action, we get talk. Instead of
truth, we get false rhetoric. The nonsequiturs of the disconnected dialogue show
further disintegration. Chekhov's plots are meaningless—nobody cares about them.
They are not what the plays are about. In both Chekhov and Samuel Beckett, "the
less tangible the means of salvation, the greater the urgency for salvation."[90]

Magarshack (1972) feels that here Chekhov has widened his dramatic scope.
He uses more characters than previously, and he divides the stage into parts, with

small conversation groups in each part. There are literary references in the play. Masha quotes lines from Pushkin which give a hint as to her character. Solyony cites a passage from a Krylov fable about a bear hugging someone to death; this could apply both to him and to Protopopov. Andrey's long soliloquy in Act IV is really Chekhov condemning provincial society: Vulgar parents extinguish the divine spark in their children.

Melchinger (1972) reported a Prague production in 1967 in which director Otomar Krejca ordered the characters about against their will, creating a state of inner tension of the sort that Chekhov was depicting. This was, said Melchinger, "so far the richest example of a revision of the Chekhov theater." Soviet critic Maya Turovskaya praised a Moscow production directed by Anatoly Efros, saying that the ending should not be sentimental and melodramatic, but rather farcelike, since the sisters are really ludicrous.

Pitcher (1973) noted how sophisticated Chekhov's use of dialogue had become—words not only reveal feelings but now also mask them. Natasha's victory is hollow, Pitcher feels, for the sisters will never surrender their spiritual freedom, and even Andrey is defeated only outwardly. The sisters can be so dignified in adversity because they have each other, and harmony can mitigate personal distress. Today's world has the same problems as those the sisters faced, Pitcher believes. "The main difference between our world and Chekhov's is that these problems have acquired a far more agonizing relevance today than they had in his day."

Shotton, in Fennell (1973), describes the sisters. "Tempered by experience, liberated from illusion, they now look hopefully towards the future and see their short lives as only part of a greater pattern, which they can accept, if not comprehend. The superb balance between their misfortunes and the positive shift in consciousness produced thereby makes it the most excellent of his plays." Contemporary audiences and critics, unprepared for such theatrical subtlety, tended to reject the play.

William Babula in 1975 noted the constant use of clocks and watches as an indication that time is really in charge of life.[91] Rayfield (1975) defines the theme as the destruction of beauty by philistinism. The characters are eccentric, not comic. The play's lyricism keeps it a drama rather than a comedy. The play has a longer time span and a greater variety in setting than Chekhov's other plays. Symbols are used well: the migratory birds suggest that man is not at home on this planet, and the trees, standing for new life, are going to be chopped down.

At a performance at the Brooklyn Academy of Music in 1977, Tovah Feldshuh, who played Irina, said, "The play is really about the struggle against banality and toward endurance." Director Frank Dunlop called Chekhov's dramatic technique "pointillism," for it uses delicate strokes, like impressionistic painting.[92]

Bristow (1977) has articles on *The Three Sisters* by Robert Brustein and Georgy Tovstonogov. Brustein says that Chekhov expresses his revolt by criticizing the real world as he presents it. Beneath the calm surface are depths charged with dissent.

From Aksinya in his story "In the Ravine" Chekhov got Natasha, "the most malevolent character he ever created." She keeps limiting the Prozorov living space until finally she has dispossessed them. Never sated, now she will cut down the garden trees. The fire in Act III symbolizes the conflagration destroying the Prozorovs. "Despite the bleakness of his vision," says Brustein, "Chekhov possesses a deeper humanity than any other modern dramatist. No one has been able to write of him without the most profound love," and he remains his own most positive character. "Coupling sweetness of temper with toughness of mind, Chekhov makes his work an extraordinary compound of morality and reality, rebellion and acceptance, irony and sympathy. There are more powerful modern dramatists, but none more warm and generous, and none who bring the drama to a higher realization of its human role."

Tovstonogov described his 1965 production of the play. People must take the responsibility for their conduct, Chekhov is saying, for we are more than the product of our environment. Chekhov was directing his art against what he called "the slave in man." To achieve a cinematic effect, this production used a revolving stage and small moving platforms, in order to present the action from different angles. As the army departs in the final scene, the band music switches from a martial beat to a funeral dirge. "Verisimilitude is not worth much today," said Tovstonogov. "If Chekhov is not played with the idea of finding out what lies behind the externals, all of the theatre's efforts will be fruitless. Chekhov was ahead of his time, and so productions of his plays must look to the future rather than to the past."

Hahn (1977) calls this play "the consummate product of Chekhov's art." Chebutykin reflects time's corrosive influence, as well as the supreme wastage of people's energies, affections, and talents. Although the ending of the play is sad, "to Chekhov no fate is complete this side of death."

Hingley (1977) found supreme irony in Natasha's self-indictment when she tells the aged servant that "there's no room for misfits in this house." "Even if love always proves a failure," says Hingley, "ordinary affection does not, and it is there in plenty in this play." Nicholas Moravcevich, in Debreczeny (1977), says the play's one obligatory scene is that in which Irina realizes that the sisters will never escape from the provinciality of a small town.

Declaring that the MAT's productions obscured the very elements that make Chekhov a modern dramatist, Ingrid Dlugosch in 1977 stated that this play has many absurdist features. Howard Moss that year found that time was the main factor in the play—the characters would like to recover the past. Thomas R. Whitaker, describing the characters, quoted the philosopher Josiah Royce, who said that most human problems grow out of people's inattention to their relationship to God and to other people. Herta Schmidt in 1978 developed a vocabulary for the structural study of plays, and then applied it to *The Three Sisters*.[93]

Clardy (1980) says that this play best expresses Chekhov's feelings about "the superfluous man." Because they have not found a meaningful role to play in society, the Prozorovs are superfluous, and Andrey even becomes manic-depressive. While the village burns, he, like Nero, fiddles. But in his manic moods, Andrey conveys the message of great hope for the future.

Stowell (1980) said that *The Three Sisters* and *The Cherry Orchard* laid the foundation for the Theater of the Absurd. As an impressionist, Chekhov experimented with different senses of time. Each character has not only clock time but his own subjective time scheme. The audience is aware of both clock time and "play time." "Chekhov's vaunted moods are often the product of his temporal patterns. Those complex patterns emerge to form a gestalt." This gestalt, or sense of the whole, must be captured in a Chekhov play or all is lost, for he has neither Shakespeare's rich imagery nor Ibsen's social problems as a focus. So in a Chekhov play everyone needs to get involved: actor, director, stage designer, and audience. Chekhov's daring juxtapositions—comedy/tragedy, dream/reality, action/stasis, hero/villain—make it hard on an audience, but if they participate, they get an impressionistic gestalt effect that no one else gives.

Tulloch (1980) believed that the sisters embody different stages of a typical Chekhov heroine, from transfigured desire of love and work, through dreary marriage and seduction, to the stagnation of life without a vocation. They spoke foreign languages well, but in Perm only Russian is spoken. Tulloch differed with Styan, saying that the ending is not pessimistic. "Styan," says Tulloch, "misses the fact that Vershinin is the mechanism of change in the play. Styan completely destroys the structure of the play. The crucial dual impact and the polarizing function of Vershinin and Natasha is lost."

Normand Berlin in 1981 said that Samuel Beckett is Chekhov's heir, and that his *Waiting for Godot* echoes the sisters' "waiting for Moscow." Chekhov's determinism is seen in the theme of death, which pervades the play. Chekhov mingles the surface and the subsurface, and combines them with an ironic perspective. Since a balance of tragedy and comedy would confuse the playgoer, he tips the balance clearly towards tragedy. Clayton A. Hubbs in 1981 stated that the "main tension in the play is between profane ritual and lost myth." Chekhov sounds contemporary to playgoers accustomed to the despair of existential literature and the humor of the Theater of the Absurd.[94] Kirk (1981) noted that the only characters in the play who do not reflect on life's meaning are the shallow "power grabbers," Natasha and Protopopov.

Barricelli (1981) provides views on this play by Eugene Bristow, Simon Karlinsky, Sonia Kovitz, Karl D. Kramer, Nicholas Moravcevich, Richard D. Risso, and Laurence Senelick. Bristow discovered countless triads in the play: three sets, character groups of three, love triangles, and he mentions N.N. Sretensky's linguistic analysis—three subjects, verbs, and predicates, and three adverbial modifiers. In Tusenbach's farewell to Irina there are many sets of triads which develop contrapuntal elaborations on the theme of unrequited love. The phrase "It doesn't matter," used over thirty times, dominates the play, which is concerned with the meaning of existence. Karlinsky said that Chekhov used symbolism to achieve conservationist goals: The birds represent freedom and escape; the trees stand for good values that should be maintained; and the huntsman callously kills (in this case, even a human being!). As in many of Chekhov's works, here is "an expression of longing for a decent, natural, unpolluted life, a life that mankind cannot achieve if it continues to exterminate other living beings, destroy forests, and abuse the planet that we all share." Although largely ignored by his contemporaries, Chekhov and his warning strike us today as "genuinely visionary and deeply prophetic."

Kovitz feels that, in Chekhov, reality turns into a mirror: "By frustrating our desires and forcing us to a halt, it plunges us into the hell of our own nature." Chekhov constantly goads us to question the characters' moral and spiritual integrity, thus thrusting us into what Kierkegaard calls "the cleansing baptism of irony." This irony enables a person to retain his balance while facing life's frustrations. Kramer sees the play's main action as the response by each character to love. Andrey's love is inauthentic, since he is seeking an illusory escape from life. Chebutykin once loved Mrs. Prozorov, and when he breaks her clock he may unconsciously be trying to destroy time itself, that which separates him from his former lover. Since he cannot love, Solyony turns friendly situations into hostile ones. Vershinin woos Masha by his poetic predictions of the future. Tusenbach, happy in love, is killed, for love cannot exist in this time and place. The play moves from naïve faith to a more solidly rooted ability to endure. Also, at the beginning the sisters are separated but by the end they are united.

Moravcevich surprisingly finds Natasha not to be deliberately mean or vulgar: "The raw vitality and assertiveness behind her vulgar manners and selfish schemes are not artificial at all; they are the wellspring of her superior strength." Risso locates several ironies in the play, chief of which is the disparity between what the sisters want and what they get. Also, the sisters laud work, but have been reared to avoid it. Senelick recounted how Zinaida Gippius castigated Chekhov's pessimism as a relapse into the control of Satan.

Eisen (1982) finds an ominous overtone in the mention of Balzac's marriage. He had courted his bride for 18 years, he was now terminally ill, and he died within five months. Master (1982) says that this play is in Chekhov's "reactive mode," that is, most characters are reacting rather than acting. "Reactive sequences can encompass many activities: confessing, recollecting, complaining, speechifying, to name a few." Bernard Beckerman says that a play's movement depends on how the dramatist handles causation, repetition, and emphasis. Chekhov tends to play down causation, and use repetition to gain emphasis. Redmond (1982) presents the view of Leigh Woods, who studies the play's symbolism. The sisters wear the colors of blue, black, and white, each appropriate for her personality. Chekhov synthesizes symbolism into his realism—the frantic effort to speak foreign languages symbolizes a lack of communication in Russian.

Peace (1983) notes that characters are individualized by the way they present birthday gifts. When Masha quotes the lines from Pushkin about a green oak with a golden chain, all the audience knew the next two lines: "Day and night a learned tomcat goes round and round about that chain." The tomcat, Kulygin, always supervised Masha's actions very closely. Since he always quoted Latin phrases, Masha conjugated the Latin verb "to love" to him, parodying his cold, pedantic notion of love. There are many elements of classical drama in *The Three Sisters:* unity of place; a chorus; classical restraint; violent action occurs offstage; and a sense of fate haunts the sisters. The name "Prozorov" suggests "the ability to see into the future." There is the evoked presence of the dead and the absent: the girls' parents, Vershinin's wife, Kulygin's headmaster, and Protopopov.

Denis Bablet in 1982 edited detailed materials dealing with Otomar Krejca's production of the play in 1981. Z.S. Paperny that year said that the play is a good example of Chekhov's belief that people must be told the frank truth about themselves if they are ever to improve their conduct. M.N. Stroeva described a new production of the play by Yuri Liubimov in Moscow. Quite different from the MAT tradition, this production abandoned much of Chekhov's lyricism, and stressed the threat of war facing the characters. In 1983 Victor Emeljanow described Komisarjevsky's successful direction of Chekhov's plays in London in 1926, and Marina Majdalany came to Natasha's defense. Natasha, she felt, was displaced from her social class, considered inferior by her sisters-in-law, and has an unresponsive husband. Many of her undesirable actions can be understood as an effort to overcome her feeling of social and cultural inferiority.[95]

In 1984 Mel Gussow found that Zelda Fichandler's direction and Randall Jarrell's translation helped the Arena Stage in Washington bring out the play's "sagacity and lyricism."[96] Troyat (1984) showed how Chekhov drew upon his life experiences in developing the play's plot.

Clyman (1985) provided the views of Martin Esslin, Harvey Pitcher, Donald Rayfield, Laurence Senelick, and J.L. Styan. Esslin said that "the death of tragedy derives from the loss of moral certainties." Thus, modern people no longer adopt the heroic stance of assuming full responsibility for their actions. "Chekhov was the first to cast his drama in this mode of tragicomic ambivalence. The three sisters' inability to get to Moscow, the ruination of Andrey's talents, the death of Tusenbach—all are prime examples of socially determined inevitabilities." Pitcher noted how Chekhov employs in this play some of his early journalistic techniques. Rayfield found "shades of *Macbeth* in *The Three Sisters*, where Solyony stalks his victim and vainly perfumes his hands, like Lady Macbeth."

Senelick reviewed the recent stage history of the play. Georgy Tovstonogov used stage islands jutting out into the theater, giving the audience the effect of movie close-ups. "The tone was epic, emphasizing the wind of history blowing through the characters' lives." Anatoly Efros explained the characters' motivation in terms of sex. Yuri Liubimov began the play by sliding open a wall of the theater to reveal a military band on a city street. When the wall was closed, its mirrored surface reflected the audience—the sisters' plight is *ours!* Styan noted that *The Three Sisters* and *The Cherry Orchard* both have nearly fifty offstage characters.

Senelick (1985) quoted Randall Jarrell as saying that Chekhov's technique here is like a painting by Edouard Vuillard: Just as Vuillard mingles seemingly unrelated objects, so Chekhov employs apparently random speech habits, mannerisms, and personal traits to build a unified character. The Rumanian critic Jovan Hristic said that the Prozorov girls are "true spiritual sisters of Hedda Gabler, who corrupt everything around them by dint of thinking themselves superior." At some point, says Senelick, each of the sisters is as callous as Natasha. The Prozorovs stagnate not because of their environment, but because "they have established nothing of value to give meaning to their existence. Wastefulness is seen in the military: a peacetime army seems a needless expense." Also, idle soldiers get into trouble, making illicit love or fighting over nothing. Great irony is seen at the end of the play. Olga keeps saying "If only we knew!" but Chebutykin's simple ditty had lyrics known to everyone in the audience: "I'm sitting on a curbstone bitterly crying, because I don't know much."

Michael Frayn, in his translation of the play, said in 1986 that Vershinin does not represent Chekhov's vision of the future. "The whole structure of the play," Frayn feels, "is designed to undercut Vershinin."[97] Vincent Canby that year described *Hannah and Her Sisters,* "Woody Allen's best film to date," as the story of three loving but often wrongheaded Manhattan sisters. Canby felt that the movie "invokes Chekhov, the master-of-theater whom the film maker most admires. Like Chekhov, Allen discovers a muted kind of glory in characters who slide between farce and tragedy."[98]

15. *The Cherry Orchard* (1904)

Act I—Liubov Ranevsky returns from Paris to her estate. With her are her daughter Anya, 17, and Anya's trick-playing governess Charlotta. They are greeted by Varya, 24, Liubov's adopted daughter; Gaev, Liubov's brother; and Lopakhin, a wealthy neighbor, who recalls Liubov's kindness to him as a youth. It is May, and the estate will be sold for indebtedness in August, unless funds can be raised. Lopakhin will lend Liubov 50,000 rubles, if she will permit the estate to be divided into lots for summer homes. Trofimov, a perpetual student and Anya's boyfriend, enters, and Liubov recalls that he was tutor to her seven-year-old son Grisha when he drowned six years ago, one month after Liubov's husband died of alcoholism. There are several plans to save the estate: Gaev will try to secure a loan; Liubov will talk further to Lopakhin; and Anya will visit her wealthy great-aunt, a countess in Yaroslavl.

Act II—The maid Dunyasha is being courted by Yasha, Liubov's new valet, and by Epikhodov, called "Twenty-two Misfortunes" because of his bad luck. Lopakhin tries to get the Ranevskys to be more business-minded. Liubov confesses that she squandered her fortune on her unfaithful lover in France. Lopakhin and Varya are in love, but Trofimov considers Lopakhin to be an insensitive materialist. Varya dislikes Trofimov as Anya's suitor, since he seems to be an impractical idealist. Firs, the aged valet, longs for "the good old days" before the serfs were emancipated. Liubov gives gold to a drunken beggar. Trofimov is glad the estate will be sold, for he says that every leaf in the cherry orchard tells of a serf's complaints.

Act III—It is August, and the estate is being sold to meet mortgage payments. Gaev is attending the sale, hopeful that the money from the great-aunt will suffice for the payments. At the mansion a farewell party is underway, even though there are not funds to pay the orchestra. Charlotta performs card tricks and sleight-of-hand. Liubov and Trofimov quarrel, then make up and dance together. Varya scolds Epikhodov for breaking a pool cue. When he retorts, she swings a stick at him, and almost accidentally hits Lopakhin as he enters the room. Lopakhin triumphantly mentions that he has bought the estate. Varya throws down the house keys in disgust. Seeing Liubov's sorrow, Lopakhin is remorseful and wishes that "this miserable disjointed life could somehow be changed." Anya comforts her mother, promising that together they will build a new happy life.

Act IV—When the peasants come to bid farewell to the Ranevskys, Liubov gives them a generous gift. She will now live in Paris on the money from the great-aunt. Anya will accompany her and attend school. Gaev has a job as a bank clerk. Lopakhin offers Trofimov some money but he refuses to accept it, for he now works as a translator. Lopakhin hires Epikhodov to work for him, and promises to find a new position for Charlotta. Liubov is worried about the health of Firs, but is told that he is in the hospital. An eccentric neighbor, Pishchik, reports that a valuable mineral deposit has been discovered on his estate, and so he pays off his debts to Liubov and Lopakhin. The Ranevskys and their entourage depart. Firs has been left alone in the deserted house. Axe strokes are heard outside, as the cherry orchard is being cut down.

As a boy, Chekhov found it devastating when his Taganrog home was sold to pay off its mortgage. Several of his short stories employ this theme. His original intention was to write a four-act farce. He wrote to Olga Knipper in 1903 that Alexander Schoenberg, the assistant producer at the MAT, would not like the play because "the whole play will be merry and frivolous. He will say I have become shallow." While writing the play he told a student, "I don't want people to weep over my plays. I want to tell people honestly, 'Look at yourselves. See how badly and boringly you live!' When they do they will surely create a better life for themselves. I will not see it, but I know it will be entirely different from what we have now."

He told Olga Knipper that Act II was as boring as a cobweb, but he still felt that there was something new about his play. He told Stanislavsky that "Lopakhin came out not bad at all, although I don't want to judge, because generally in reading plays I understand very little." He warned Danchenko that the direction "through tears" meant merely a facial expression, not actual weeping.

Stanislavsky in 1903 was a director in his father's factory, and perhaps wanted to play Gaev (rather than Lopakhin, as Chekhov requested) in order to expiate for the damage done by businessmen to the landed gentry. Stanislavsky said that the prototype for Charlotta was an English governess on his father's estate, who loved to play pranks. She would nimbly leap upon Chekhov's shoulders, doff his cap, and greet passersby with a "Goot mornink!" She and Chekhov teased each other constantly.

In November 1903 Chekhov was angry that Danchenko had not yet read the play to the MAT actors. "We begin with misunderstandings and we shall end with them," he told Olga. "Such, it seems, is the fate of my play." He wanted Olga to play Charlotta and Stanislavsky to play Lopakhin, but when they played Liubov and Gaev, the center of interest shifted away from Lopakhin and toward the Ranevskys, against his original intent. The MAT got Chekhov to shorten Act II. It originally had a lyrical scene between Firs and Charlotta at the end, but it was eliminated because Stanislavsky thought that it would then be too hard to pick up the action at the beginning of Act III.

The first performance on 17 January 1904 was a gala occasion, celebrating

Chekhov's 25th anniversary as a writer. Many speeches were given, and the play seemed favorably received. As usual, Chekhov was embarrassed by the attention he received. Danchenko said that it took some time before the critics appreciated the play. To them Lopakhin seemed too good to be a Russian merchant, and Trofimov too weak to be an adequate representative of the coming generation.

F.D. Batyuskhov admired Chekhov's faith in the future, as seen in this play. Andrey Bely found it inferior to *The Three Sisters*, but still felt that "the instances of reality are scrutinized so closely in this play that one falls through them into a concurrent stream of eternity." He called the party in Act III a *danse macabre*, in which "the masks of terror are dancing rapturously." Valery Bryusov admitted that Chekhov had portrayed the landed gentry well, but found the plot trite and noted that both Dumas and Scribe had previously used parties to contrast with the mood of the main action.[1]

Y.I. Eichenwald called the play "a festival of art," a delicate elegy having subtle characterization. Z.N. Gippius, however, recommended that the MAT stop staging Chekhov's decadent plays.[2] A.V. Lunacharsky found the play "unbearably sad, showing man's helplessness before life." Vsevolod Meyerhold said that the play was abstract, like a symphony by Tchaikovsky, and that in the party scene "there is something Maeterlinckian, terrifying." Act III he called "a nightmarish dance of puppets in a farce," and said that the contrapuntal sense of imminent doom was "a fateful beginning in Chekhov's new mystical drama."

M. Nevedomsky was intrigued by the characters, who were at once living persons and yet abstract symbols of their personality types. He liked Chekhov's use of symbolism, particularly as it was used to depict the status of modern art. As expected, the disparaging critic in *New Times* said that there was more life in such inanimate objects as trees and bookcases than in the characters. The only American notice of the play called it a character study of Russian middle-class life by the "thoughtful, gentle pessimist, Chekhov."[3]

Angry at drama critic N.Y. Efros, Chekhov called him a "noxious animal" for garbling the plot summary, and for calling Lopakhin "a vulgar S.O.B.," when Chekhov had portrayed him as subtle and sensitive. As Hingley (1976) observes, Chekhov was touchy: He rebuked Danchenko for comparing Anya to Irina of *The Three Sisters*, and he even criticized Stanislavsky's calling him "a genius."

Chekhov complained in April 1904 that his play was being advertised as a drama rather than as a comedy. He accused Danchenko and Stanislavsky of finding things in the play that were not there: "They both haven't read my play attentively even once," he remarked. "It's no longer my play. Except for two or three parts, nothing in it is mine. I describe ordinary life, not despondency. They make me into a crybaby or a bore. This is beginning to make me angry." After becoming depressed at seeing a poor production of the play in Yalta, however, he was cheered to receive telegrams from Danchenko and Stanislavsky telling of the play's big success at an MAT production in St. Petersburg.

Chekhov's friend Ivan Bunin remarked that the cherry orchard must be a symbolic one, for nowhere in Russia are cherry trees grown by themselves, and the trees are unattractive with puny blossoms, not having the beauty of Chekhov's trees. Meyerhold told Chekhov that his plays were so original that European dramatists could learn from him. Meyerhold felt that the MAT had erred in playing Act III as boredom when what it really represents is indifference. He also felt that Stanislavsky had ruined the pathos for Liubov and her plight through too great an emphasis upon background tricks and mood music.

In 1906 A.S. Glinka observed that here Chekhov used a much sharper contrast between the real and the ideal than in his previous work, and Tikhon Polner said that Chekhov was portraying a whole society doomed to destruction, but with the hope of a better future order.[4] Professor Max Mandell of Yale, in the introduction to his translation of the play in 1908, said that "Russian critics have agreed that Chekhov is the most original writer Russia has ever produced." Mandell said that in place of the usual Russian gloom, one would find here "a new bright page, full of hope for a better future."[5]

In 1910 D.N. Ovsianiko-Kulikovsky placed the play in its context of Russian literature, stating that it sums up many portrayals of the decline of serf-owning Russia. Gaev and Liubov are seen as "superfluous people," but Lopakhin suggests a new, vigorous force in the rising merchant class.[6] The following year Maurice Baring praised the play's structure, in which seemingly casual remarks carefully contributed to the play's theme. For the first time, Baring said, he had seen a dramatic rendering of the atmosphere of an arrival and a departure.[7]

The first performance of *The Cherry Orchard* in London was the Stage Society production in 1911. Most critics agreed that, however accurate its portrait of Russian life might be, it "was not a play," since the plot was actionless, and the characters dull or grotesque.[8] J.T. Grein agreed that it was not original, since it derived from Ibsen and Gerhardt Hauptmann, but he found it valuable because it had vivid characterization and it introduced a person to modern Russian thought.[9] H.W. Massingham liked the play, finding "Chekhov's irony at its roots a sad and profound sentiment."[10] Arnold Bennett said that Chekhov's daring naturalism marked another step in the evolution of drama. The characters were no more strange than the average members of the Stage Society, but "people never properly look at people; they remain blind to the facts."[11] John Palmer called it "a great play," a supreme comedy which had a mysteriously cumulative effect upon the playgoer. The apparent aimlessness of construction reinforced perfectly the feckless characters. "Every piece of irrelevance is relevant to the dramatic impression of irrelevance," he said.[12]

Marion Fell (1912) in the introduction to her translation of Chekhov's plays, said that Chekhov painted the inevitable tragedy of Russian existence in the 1880s, but that *The Cherry Orchard* heralds a new epoch, when the people's burdens would be lifted. George Calderon, reviewing two volumes of Chekhov's works in Russian, noted that Chekhov had influenced Gorky and even Tolstoy. He called *The Cherry Orchard* "a picture of the nothingness of hope in all countries and all ages," and said it would never be out-of-date as long as human desires were unrequited.[13] Reviewers of Calderon's own translations of Chekhov's plays that year concluded that though there were occasional flashes of humor and pathos in these plays, they were poor dramatic vehicles, with no plot action and flabby characters.[14]

W.L. Courtney, however, said that the modern age needed a new drama, and that there was no better playwright than Chekhov to show the way, for he not only employed delicate artistry but also, like life, combined comedy and tragedy in a new kind of realism.[15] Storm Jameson called Chekhov "not a great dramatist but a great artist." Jameson placed *The Cherry Orchard* with the philosophy of Henri Bergson and with the scattered art theaters of Europe, as a part of the revolt against the philosophy of determinism, which had done much to ruin Ibsen's drama. The final scene of this play was unique, in the opinion of Jameson: "So subtle is the blending of speech and action that gradually the mind sweeps beyond them, seeing beneath these broken lines the movement and purpose of humanity."[16]

An American reviewer struck an entirely different note, saying that the play had neither plot nor character. Its only possible value to a dramatist would be to illustrate "the antithesis of dramatic method. Surely the rankest American amateur would be suspected of softening of the cerebrum should he seriously submit such soufflé to the producing manager."[17]

Another American had seen a MAT production of the play, however, and she had felt tremendously moved in some mysterious way. "The actions of the people," she said, "are not isolated episodes, but carry you to what they have done, and to what they will do long after the curtain has fallen."[18] Another critic said that people erred in evaluating Chekhov's plays according to Aristotle's canons. *The Cherry Orchard* was no more regular than *Hamlet;* what mattered was not whether rules were obeyed but whether a pleasing esthetic object had been created, as certainly was true in these two plays.[19]

But the critical battle had just begun. Homer Woodbridge in 1917 called the play "pure affectation," and said that there had never been a duller play, unless it was *The Three Sisters.*[20] That year, while defending the Little Theatre movement, Professor Brander Matthews, one of America's experts on drama, declared that "one *College Widow* is worth a dozen *Cherry Orchards.*"[21]

When the London Art Theatre produced *The Cherry Orchard* in 1920, the critics again differed widely in their reactions. Most of the newspaper critics panned the play, calling it silly, tedious, boring, amateurish, or just what one might expect from a nation of Bolsheviks. Incensed, J. Middleton Murry wanted to concoct a time-capsule of their views "and drop it into literary London in 1930, when *The Cherry Orchard* will have become a classic."[22]

The periodical critics were doing their best to make it a classic. Even those who decried the production probably agreed with Sydney Carroll, who said that "to take these undone humanities and make them ring with reality and excite us through them with love of our fellows is possible only to a genius. He excels Dickens in fidelity to life, and compares with him in creative exaltation, sympathy with human suffering, and good-natured insight into the follies of human beings."[23] W.T. Turner could find only Shakespeare to equal the author of "this great play—great in its construction, its wonderful variety and vividness of portraiture, its imaginative sweep, its depth of compassion, its humor, and its lyricism."[24]

An unofficial Chekhov cult was being organized under the leadership of Katherine Mansfield. "Until a play like *The Cherry Orchard,*" she said, "so intimate, so real, so beautiful is felt to be as near and dear to a cultivated British audience as it is to a Russian, there is not much to be done with English drama."[25] Frank Swinnerton found Chekhov's secret to be utter avoidance of the cynical and the sentimental, in a play full of "beauty, understanding, and a comprehension of the naïve egoism of all people."[26] Virginia Woolf declared that "there is nothing in English literature in the least like *The Cherry Orchard.*" The play overcame all amateurism in the staging. "Chekhov," she said, "has shed over us a luminous vapor in which life appears as it is, transparent to the depths. We feel our way among submerged but recognizable emotions." She felt, she said, like a piano resonating after a masterful concerto has played up and down its keys.[27]

Those who had seen MAT productions fanned the sacred flame. Harley Granville Barker said that the play was like the libretto of a great musical work. He compared the quiescent acting of Liubov at the end of Act III to the pause between crescendos in a symphony.[28] Kenneth Macgowan felt that Chekhov's technique had exhausted realism and gone on into expressionism to produce a "realism of the spirit," something rarely achieved in the theater.[29]

All critics praised the ensemble acting of the MAT when it toured the United States in 1924. They appreciated the scenery, stage pictures, and humor of *The Cherry Orchard,* even though it was performed in Russian.[30] Heywood Broun, saying that Chekhov spoke a universal language, confessed that "there were moments in which we were moved more profoundly than ever before in the theatre."[31] After decrying the lack of physical action, John Corbin admitted that the play induces "a perfectly original mood, peoples a world with characters each of whom is a clear-cut personality, yet is an integral part of the whole." Corbin felt that Chekhov had Turgenev's poetic sensibility, with more than Turgenev's humor and sympathy in characterization.[32]

"Chekhov's plays," said Stark Young, "carry realism to an honest and spiritual depth and candor, and to a relentless, poignant perfection and truth." Young found only in Shakespeare such "tragic excitement, pathetic beauty, and baffling logic of emotion" as he found here. Chekhov put together ordinary remarks and actions in such a way that they "suddenly fused into a revelation of the very soul of that moment of life. As is true of Shakespeare's plays, the whole of *The Cherry Orchard* remains suspended in one's experience, an infectious mystery of human living."[33] Edmund Wilson experienced a set of values seldom found in the theater: "the beauty and poignancy of an atmosphere, an idea, a person, a moment, are put before us without anything which we recognize as theatrical, but with the brightness of the highest art. The charm of the Russian gentry, even in decay, is somehow put upon the stage in such a way that their futility is never dreary, but moving, and their ineptitude is touched with the tragedy of all human failure."[34]

Gerhardi (1923) liked Trofimov's reply when Gaev asks, "Why work so hard—you'll die all the same?" Trofimov answers, "Who knows? Man may have 100 senses, of which only five die at one's death!" Gerhardi says this implies a gradation of consciousness in a universe perhaps dormant but not dead. Stanislavsky (1924) reported that he was surprised to see the Soviets permit a production of *The Cherry Orchard* on the eve of the October 1917 revolution, since the ruling class are depicted with sympathetic understanding. Ivor Brown in 1925 recalled seeing an MAT production in Paris in which "futility itself took on the mask of loveliness."[35]

James B. Fagan directed the first commercial run of a Chekhov play in London in 1925. A.E. Wilson doubted that the general public would ever care for the "splendid gloom" of *The Cherry Orchard*,[36] but the majority of the critics praised the play for its interesting characters, novel dialogue, and beautiful stage pictures.[37] James Agate called this one of the world's great plays, with characters so vivid that even the man in the street would enjoy the play.[38] Ashley Dukes, now a Chekhov convert, said that the characters "form a picture of true humanity, which is better than local color." Dukes found Chekhov's chief quality to be "a deep affection for his characters, a tenderness so fine that no base motive can live beside it."[39]

The following year Theodore Komisarjevsky staged the play. One reviewer feared that "before long, if the Chekhov vogue continues, his plays will be in danger of becoming set-pieces," when playgoers look mainly for minute details rather than submitting themselves to the play's effect.[40] Several critics found the production too farcical, one saying that "Chekhov's reputation in this country is not yet secure. The most solid element in *The Cherry Orchard* is its pathos, and therefore it is dangerous to overstress its comedy."[41]

In 1927 S.D. Balukhaty said that Chekhov used comic elements in the play as a type of renewal. A subtle type of action is achieved through the use of disconnected dialogue, with devices of interruption, severance, and recurrence of themes. Mirsky (1927) stated that judged by his own standards, Chekhov's plays are perfect works of art, but his standards cannot be accepted as the normal canons of dramatic art. His technique is so precarious that "no play written by an imitator of Chekhov is above contempt."

When Fagan brought his version of *The Cherry Orchard* to New York in 1928, Brooks Atkinson noted an absence of the spirit of the play, for behind Chekhov's lines "burned the fires of an all-embracing sympathy, and an understanding of character almost preternatural."[42]

Reviewers praised the acting of the Group de Prague of the MAT in London in 1928.[43] Ivor Brown said the play's theme was one "with which we ourselves are pitifully suffering. Lopakhin is abroad in the land and the axe rings out in our orchards. Scratch these people, and you find English men and women underneath."[44]

Alla Nazimova as Liubov drew much critical approval when Eva LeGallienne and her Civic Repertory Theatre staged the play in New York that year.[45] Joseph Wood Krutch said that instead of going to the theater, Chekhov made the theater come to him. There is art in every line of Chekhov's casual technique: "out of delicacy laid ceaselessly upon delicacy comes strength. His insight spares no one, and yet no one is really wounded. He is merciless in his exposure of every character, and yet every one of them finds mercy."[46]

The fourth production of *The Cherry Orchard* that year was staged by the Yiddish Art Theatre, directed by Leo Bulgakov. Reviewing the performance Brooks Atkinson said that the play mirrors the whole course of life. It is "the very ecstasy of 'stating the problem correctly,' and it is the problem that has no end."[47]

Elton (1929) felt that Chekhov's dramatic achievement lay in "his peculiar strain of poetic musing, accompanied by a symbol or a refrain, in this case the orchard itself." Elton quoted from one of Chekhov's notebooks: "In the next world, I should like to be able to think about our present life—'There were some lovely visions in it.'" Soviet critic A.P. Kugel that year said that Chekhov's characters are childish, living on the boundary between the real and the mystical. In this play, Kugel said, Chekhov smiles sadly but ironically at the vanity of life.

Harley Granville Barker in 1930 observed that Chekhov could take a trite plot, as in *The Cherry Orchard*, and by constantly relating vivid characters to it, evolve a fluid form that gave life to the play.[48] That year J.B. Priestley said that this play "could conjure beauty out of life. Here was life in all of its richness, its pathos and humor, its terror and beauty." Character and atmosphere, the qualities that make serious theater satisfying, said Priestley, are found in this play and in *Hamlet*.[49]

Anna Miller in 1931 recalled how Chekhov drew much of his inspiration from the MAT actors: "Artem, the unrivalled actor of very old men, was to become Chekhov's original for Chebutykin and Firs, and Moskvin's sublime fooling at an informal gathering gave the hint for Epikhodov."[50] Francis Fergusson in 1933 noted the influence of *The Cherry Orchard* upon Susan Glaspell's *Alison's House* and Paul Green's *House of Connelly*.[51]

When Eva LeGallienne revived *The Cherry Orchard* in 1933, critics applauded her as Varya, Alla Nazimova as Liubov, and Josephine Hutchinson as Anya.[52] Cy Caldwell said that "this wonderful old drama dealing with pathetic illusion, vain hope, frustrated endeavor, and general incompetence is a perfect allegorical expression of the meaning of our American political administration of the past few years."[53]

John Mason Brown tried to explain why the play never aged. In his characterization, Chekhov realized that "each person is his own acutest problem. He knew men and women far too well and loved them far too deeply to iron out their complexities and turn them into shadowless heroes and villains." The roles are challenging to actors, for "they have secrets they reveal only to those with the courage, intellect, and persistence to ferret them out. Always they leave room for growth. No wonder the members of the MAT could act his plays with pleasure for

20 years, or that Chekhov has occupied a place in the contemporary theatre that no other dramatist has filled."[54]

That year in London Tyrone Guthrie directed a production of *The Cherry Orchard*, the first Russian play to be put on at the Old Vic Theatre. Most of the critics liked the acting of Charles Laughton as Lopakhin, Athene Seyler as Liubov, and Leon Quartermaine as Gaev.[55] Several, however, felt that Guthrie lost the ensemble effect by overstressing the comic element.[56] One reviewer commented that "of all playwrights Chekhov approaches nearest to the Shakespearean insight into the mind of humanity. Like Shakespeare he is a master of the common touch. The least of his creatures share some thought, some habit, common to humanity."[57]

Desmond MacCarthy called this the best English production of *The Cherry Orchard*, for it captured the delicate timing and changes of tone essential in interpreting Chekhov's dialogue. MacCarthy liked the way Laughton brought out "Lopakhin's muddled inconsistent attitude towards the Ranevskys. He admires Liubov very much, and would love to save her from herself. Her fecklessness exasperates him, but on the other hand he feels an almost superstitious admiration for her sublimely silly indifference."[58]

Elizabeth Drew in 1937 called the play "a new type of social comedy," with little plot but with great emphasis upon grouping, lighting, and tone. Implicit irony growing out of character contrast replaces the old irony of situation. An Irish version of *The Cherry Orchard*, said Drew, was Denis Johnston's *The Moon in the Yellow River*.[59] Toumanova (1937) said that the Ranevskys were ready to embrace the whole universe, but suffer from the paralyzing neurasthenia that afflicted the intellectuals of that period.

In 1938 Stark Young lampooned G.B. Shaw for saying that his *Heartbreak House* was "an English *Cherry Orchard.*" It was absurd for Shaw, who exploited his characters to make "straw men" for pet theories to think that he was using Chekhov's technique, Young said. "Chekhov sees his people as rooted in something," and in their inner honesty that are their own harshest critics, a far cry from the poseurs and egotists created by Shaw.[60] Henry T. Perry, however, after calling Chekhov Russia's greatest writer of comic drama, ranked *The Cherry Orchard* below Gogol's *The Inspector General* because Gogol avoided the trace of world-weariness evident in Chekhov's play.[61]

Tyrone Guthrie directed an Old Vic production of the play in 1941. Most critics praised individual acting performances more than the play's overall effect.[62] Alan Dent, however, felt that this was one of the best productions of the play he had seen, although admitting that Charles Laughton as Epikhodov in 1926 had set the high-water mark for that role.[63]

In 1943 Francis Fergusson noted the similarity between the techniques of Henry James and Chekhov. Each employs a series of social occasions to throw light on the central theme.[64] That year Danchenko published his recollection of the MAT's staging of the play. Ivor Spector then observed the contrast between *The Cherry Orchard* and Margaret Mitchell's *Gone with the Wind:* "Tara meant to

Scarlett what the cherry orchard meant to Liubov. Both women faced the loss of their property to men who from their viewpoint were upstarts. Scarlett was ready to sell herself to a man she did not love in order to save Tara. Liubov remained an aristocrat to the end."[65]

The best-known production of *The Cherry Orchard* in the United States was produced by Eva LeGallienne and Margaret Webster in 1944 in New York. The newspaper critics were generally laudatory. Howard Barnes in the *Herald Tribune* called the play "a profound and pertinent commentary on mortal existence." John Chapman of the *Daily News* named it "the most profound of the hundreds of plays written about 'the mortgage'." Robert Garland in the *Journal-American* said it was "one of the most heart-breaking and most skillfully contrived modern comedies." However, Louis Kronenberger in *PM* decried the lack of fusion of comedy and pathos in this production. Ward Morehouse in the *Sun* called Chekhov "a spokesman for the little people, with their frailties and futilities." Lewis Nichols of the *Times* said that this production would be hard to beat in future years. Burton Rascoe in the *World-Telegram* called it "entertainment of the first order – witty, comical, satirical, pathetic, and realistic, and not a depressing study in Russian pessimism." Finally, Wilella Waldorf in the *Post* cast a negative vote, being "hardly prepared for the clumsy slapstick" she had seen.[66]

For a change, the periodical critics were less satisfied than their newspaper counterparts. Some disliked the production,[67] and others found fault with the play. One reviewer said that time's passage revealed that the play had "more aura than substance,"[68] and another said that the Russian revolution made the play obsolete.[69] Elizabeth Jordan joined Stark Young who called the production "an entirely honorable venture," in pointing out ways in which the acting could have been better.[70] Euphemia Wyatt said that this was more than a great Russian play – "it belongs in an international treasure house. Social progress may level temporarily the amenities of graceful living but true beauty has its roots deep in the ground of spiritual truth. Orchards will blossom again, not perhaps for Liubov but for Firs' children."[71]

This production occasioned an epistolary exchange between two great ladies of the theater. On 23 January 1944 Margaret Webster published an "open letter to Chekhov." You and Shakespeare, she said, must have a "Yalta Mermaid" rendezvous in the empyrean, for as enormously different as your techniques are, they both are aimed at holding audiences – making them laugh, cry, and above all, care. *The Cherry Orchard* is still popular in the theater because no other play since it was written proclaims so forcefully man's faith in man. It will always hold audiences, until some Wellsian future day when our hopes become actualities.[72]

Olga Knipper-Chekhov replied with an open letter to Margaret Webster, in which she said, "Evidently Chekhov's stories and plays can move the American reader and theatergoer. I remember the responsive attitude of your audiences twenty years ago when the MAT performed his plays. You were right to say that the principal content of his plays is a belief in the better future which will dawn for mankind no matter what sufferings some generations have to endure on the way to happiness for all. I look forward to attending your productions when the alliance of great countries is crowned with victory over Hitlerite barbarity, and when cooperation and friendly relations between our peoples are still further strengthened and flourish in the soil of culture and creative work. Let us believe, as Chekhov believed, that the brighter day of triumph for democratic mankind is not far off."[73]

Bruford (1948) pointed out how, under the leadership of Count Witte, Russia industrialized rapidly from 1892 to 1903. Chekhov reflects the change, replacing the crass merchants of "Three Years" with a sensitive Lopakhin eight years later. Francis Fergusson made a detailed study of *The Cherry Orchard* in 1949. He found that the play, "a theater-poem of the suffering of change," possessed many classical elements. Act I was the prologue, Act II the agon (or conflict), Act III the suffering and the reversal, and Act IV the epiphany. The "moment" depicted by the play, said Fergusson, corresponds to the Sophoclean chorus. "Because Chekhov says so little he reveals so much." The world we divine behind the cherry orchard is one we know well. "We may recognize its main elements in a cocktail party in Connecticut or Westchester." If Chekhov's dramatic range is somewhat limited, Fergusson felt, at least it is thoroughly sound. "He reduced dramatic art to is ancient root, from which new growths are possible."[74]

Charles W. Meister in 1950 showed that G.B. Shaw had little knowledge of Chekhov's dramatic technique, but that Clifford Odets echoed *The Cherry Orchard* in his play *Awake and Sing!*[75] Magarshack (*Dramatist*, 1952) explained that Chekhov took several themes from *Platonov* for *The Cherry Orchard*, for example, the theme of work. The spendthrift Nikolai of the early play became Yasha in *The Cherry Orchard*, which conforms to Aristotle's definition of comedy as "an imitation of characters of a lower type who are not bad in themselves but whose faults are ludicrous." Stanislavsky did not understand that a comic character (such as Quixote or Falstaff) can arouse sympathy. Here Chekhov employs comic reversal— the man trying to save the estate for the Ranevskys ends up buying it for himself.

When Lopakhin bleats through the door at Varya, says Magarshack, he is not making love but unconsciously calling the Ranevskys "sheep." He would never have bought the estate except that a rich merchant had already outbid Gaev. The sound of the breaking string is Chekhov's requiem for the disjointed lives of the Ranevskys. G.B. Shaw errs in saying that, lacking faith in the future, Chekhov exploited the Ranevskys for their charm. Chekhov was not a fatalist about future hope, and the only exploitation is by misguided producers who do not understand Chekhov's works.

In 1953 Charles W. Meister summarized English and American criticism of Chekhov, including *The Cherry Orchard*.[76] Jean-Louis Barrault in 1954 interpreted the play as a study of time's passage: Gaev is the past, Lopakhin the present, and Trofimov the future. G.A. Bialy that year called the play a new phase in Chekhov's dramatic development, in which groups of characters, rather than individuals, serve as the protagonist. In 1955 M.D. Sosnitskaya analyzed each act, pointing out the unity of form and content in the play.[77]

Ermilov (1956) quoted with approval Gorky's statement that the Ranevskys were parasites who deserved their fall from power. The plebeian Chekhov would have never had anything but hostile feelings towards the aristocracy, Ermilov stated. Bruford (1957) said that the play is more a comedy of manners than a comedy of character. He found a core of humanity in even the most ridiculous clowns in the play, saying that "the apparently nonsensical conveys a sense of the unanalyzable strangeness of life, together with a Russian warmth of human feeling for 'the soul'."

In 1958 Irving Deer showed that the disconnected dialogue conveyed the characters' inner conflicts and doubts. N. Bryllion Fagin revealed the influence of this play upon the drama of Paul Green, Lillian Hellman, Joshua Logan, Clifford Odets, Tennessee Williams, and Thomas Wolfe. David Gerould suggested using this play in a general humanities course because it has "one of the most perfect comic plots ever created." Jacqueline Latham observed that most productions of the play ignored its comic elements. Norman Silverstein conceived of the play as a mixture of farce and pathos. A.P. Skaftymov stated that the complications in the plot come from contradictions in life itself. John Kelson in 1959 found three levels in the play: the literal; the allegorical, with each character representing an element of Russian society; and the mythical, or the seasonal cycle, with Liubov symbolizing the continuing life-giving power of nature.[78]

Nils Ake Nilsson, in Eekman (1960), reported 175 stage directions on how lines are to be spoken. Nilsson showed that in the disconnected dialogue, it is not the words but the intonation that reveals character. James R. Brandon in 1960 took a middle position between those calling Chekhov a writer of melancholia and those considering him an absurdist. He cited the MAT production of 1959 to illustrate the middle view. A.I. Reviakin in 1960 prepared a teacher's guide with many helpful analytical and critical notes. A.R. Vladimirskaya studied changes made by Chekhov to Act II during the MAT's rehearsals for its first performance in 1904.[79]

Jean-Louis Barrault in 1961 said that *The Cherry Orchard* is the most universal of Chekhov's plays, since everyone is subject to the corrosive influence of time. The structure of the play is musical, with themes being started, fading away, and then returning. One must not confuse the action with the plot, Barrault warns. Though short on plot, the play is taut with action throughout. French actors, used to plot movement, have trouble picking up Chekhov's action. Barrault called Chekhov a true artist, one who does not prostitute his art to preach a particular message.[80]

David Ross received unfavorable reviews for his New York production of *The Cherry Orchard* in 1962. Walter Kerr said that the production "came apart at the seams," perhaps because the actors and the director took too much for granted.[81] Michael Smith found the theater itself hopeless, with bad sight lines and no definite demarcation between the actors and the audience.[82] Robert Brustein in 1962 noted that like *The Three Sisters*, this play deals with the collapse of a cultural elite, but this time does so from a comic-ironic point of view. Although Chekhov is the gentlest and most dispassionate of modern dramatists, beneath the surface of his plays lie depths of moral fervor and revolt.[83]

Corrigan (1962) notes the irony when Trofimov tells Liubov to "look the truth straight in the face." Gaev's famous speech to the bookcase reveals the angle from which Gaev views himself, an important thing for an audience to know. Simmons (1962) states that Chekhov "saw no contradiction in the development of serious themes through comic situations." He refused to judge idlers, alcoholics, theorists, and self-indulgent people. He felt them to be comic, condemning themselves by their actions but arousing compassion by their failure to see themselves as others see them. This is true of most of the characters in this play, Simmons feels.

In 1962 Allen Lewis analyzed the play as "a comedy of frustration," finding it difficult to perform because the characters are complex, not one-sided as are most comic characters. Michael J. Mendelsohn in 1963 traced the influence of *The Cherry Orchard* on Shaw's *Heartbreak House* in the plotlessness, the disconnected dialogue, the overall dreamlike tone, and the theme of the failure of a way of life.[84] Lucas (1963) calls the play a tragic farce, in which the unity of action is lost under the diversity of themes. The carefully studied confusion reminded Lucas of a ballet. This is the most popular play in the Soviet Union, after Gorky's *The Lower Depths*. Lucas sees the "real remoteness" of Shaw in thinking that his *Heartbreak House* was Chekhovian—it is no more like *The Cherry Orchard* than Hogarth is like Watteau.

Goldstone (1965) carried the views of Leonid Andreyev, Robert W. Corrigan, Irving Deer, N.E. Efros, and Jacqueline Latham. Andreyev said that Chekhov animated everything that he touched, and so the cast of characters should include objects and sound effects. Even time becomes an actor in his plays. His disconnected dialogue is really not disconnected, for it refers to objects, sound effects, and even to time itself. Corrigan feels that Chekhov carried dramatic realism to its completion; he showed that the mask (persona) people wear is not real, but just a stance. One function of the mask is to provide esthetic distance, lest we identify too deeply with the suffering characters. They are more concerned with how something is said than what is said: Epikhodov tells Varya, "I beg you to express yourself with delicacy." Deer reminds us that speech is action. Thus, Lopakhin, in his long monologue in Act I, reveals an internal conflict which is at the core of the play. When characters daydream, they are either escaping from their problems or reaffirming their aims—these are actions. Efros said that Chekhov added a new dimension to Russian dramatic realism: half-feelings. He creates an atmosphere out of half-tones. Latham recalls Dorothy Sayers stating of the play that "in its blackest moments it is inevitably doomed to the comic gesture." Liubov and Gaev engage in self-deception, which is more comic than tragic. Lopakhin, a slave to his watch, cannot even make love. In this play "Chekhov achieves a very rare blend of sympathetic and judicial comedy. Chekhov criticizes his characters both in their relation to the material world and in their relation to each other." The audience, seeing themselves on stage, can never quite assume a superior position.

Guthrie (1965), speaking as an actor, director, and translator of Chekhov, questions whether an author is always the best judge of what he has written. Stanislavsky and Danchenko were not only intelligent men but more experienced in the theater than Chekhov, and thus entitled to their interpretations of Chekhov's plays. Translations from the the Russian cannot be literal, because the Russian language and Russian acting are more emotional than their American counterparts. Leonid Kipnis, in Guthrie (1965), says that in *The Cherry Orchard*, Chekhov is at his most mature, "a wonderful mixture of realism and irony." It is understood by everyone in the world. The MAT alone has given over 1400 performances of the play, and it has been produced in many countries, including, China, Japan, Iceland, and Turkey.

Popkin (1965) said that "Chekhov's characters are extremely steadfast in fighting off entirely justifiable morbidity." But "in Chekhov, even the boldest optimistic generalizations are qualified by the ironic atmosphere that pervades the universe." Ronald Hingley, in Popkin (1965), pointed out that the censor changed Trofimov's "You owned living souls" to "Your orchard is tormented by painful visions of things that happened long ago."

Howard Taubman marveled at how an outstanding actor of the MAT was willing to perform (and brilliantly, at that) as the tramp in the play when it was given in New York in 1965. This was a sign to Taubman of the value of a permanent repertory theater.[85] Karl S. Guthke in 1966 said that this play embraced not only tragedy and comedy but also all the middle ground between those genres. It is the tragicomedy of the play that appealed to Thomas Mann, Guthke averred.[86]

That year G. Leman-Abrikosov suggested that I.P. Belonkonsky's *Rural Impressions* provided a source for *The Cherry Orchard*.[87] Valency (1966) says that the structure of all of Chekhov's major plays is the same: an arrival, a sojourn, and a departure. A dying man with little religous faith, Chekhov found life absurd. This sense of life's absurdity, on all levels from the individual to the cosmic, gives *The Cherry Orchard* its unique place in modern social drama. Its theme is universal: people who cannot change with change are lost. The sound of the breaking string means this: The chord connecting man with his father on earth and his Father in heaven has snapped—there is a breakdown of communication of man with man and man with God. This elicits a mournful strain, because now people are eternally lonely.

Jackson identified a theme with each act: Act I—Liubov; Act II—Lopakhin; Act III—sale of the estate; Act IV—Firs. Gilles (1968) observed that, paradoxically, because the play has "no action," it is full of suspense. The peaks of action are replaced by successive impediments set up against the unleashing of action. Finally we want inaction, realizing that is the only way to save the cherry orchard. J.L. Styan in 1968 found Chekhov to be the first writer of " dark comedy." Tragedy underlies everyday life, and a surface gaiety covers over a deep *Weltschmerz*. In Act IV "the structure of change and decay is welded into a firm whole, because its parts are drawn together here, and because the sympathies of the audience are under careful restraint and control."[88]

Hostile reviews greeted Eva LeGallienne in her production of the play in New York in 1968. Clive Barnes said that "although she had done more than anyone else for Chekhov in America, this production does not have the air of life about it."[89] Martin Gottfried found the production dull and boring, with "not the slightest sense of ensemble work."[90]

In 1969 A.G. Cross noted that Turgenev also used the sound of a breaking string, in "Bezhin Meadow" and "The Nymphs." Walter Kerr believed that the MAT productions of the play did not sufficiently stress its comic aspect. V.E. Khalizev stated that none of the major characters, including Lopakhin, seemed worthy of operating the orchard. Bernard de Bear Nicol edited a discussion of naturalist and absurdist elements in the play. Konstantin Rudnitsky described Meyerhold's productions of the play. In 1971 Bernard Beckerman, arguing that dramatic criticism should describe what is happening among the characters, said that this play shows the hand of a major dramatist in its manner of "shaping human relationships into provocative, unresolved actions."[91]

Speirs (1971) feels that this play fulfills Tolstoy's requirement that "the aim of an artist is to make people love life." Chekhov's natural dialogue, more accurate than any in 19th century English literature, comes from Tolstoy. Act I resembles any of Nikolai Rostov's homecomings in Chekhov's favorite novel, *War and Peace*.

Styan (1971) calls *The Cherry Orchard* the best naturalistic play in modern drama, a "plotless play with too many plots." Chekhov employs "undercutting"— reversing a current of feeling, muting a climax, contradicting one statement by another—to show that truth is relative. Ambivalence is a keynote of comedy. Michel Saint-Denis said that Chekhovian comedy achieved the perfect dialectical balance, neither condoning nor condemning. Despite her buffoonery, Charlotta is the most sane person in the play. Servants are given an important status in the play, because the same forces are at work at their level as at the master's level. Influenced somewhat by the symbolists, Chekhov here assimilated their techniques "in his own gentle, anti-didactic symbolism." Henry Popkin found communist directors accepting Trofimov's oratory as a sign of the coming revolution, even at the Slovenian National Theater in Ljubljana.

Styan enjoys the luxurious irony of lazy Trofimov preaching on work to industrious Lopakhin. Gaev's paean to nature "Thou dost give life and dost destroy," although humorous, was one of Chekhov's deepest beliefs, and so he laughs at himself through his characters. Trofimov's desire to "break with the past" is an error—"breaking with the past does not expiate it; rather, it only destroys some of the living tissues of the present." Like the Elizabethans, Chekhov uses a double-stage setting: The real audience is aware of a stage audience looking through an upstage frame. On the forestage a character can voice his inmost thoughts in a lower voice, and we hear of doubts and anxieties, but in the distant ballroom there is never a care. The set provides for ironic juxtapositions of sights and sounds, as life's tragicomedy proceeds. The leaders of the grand march are Charlotta and Pishchik, a comic duo. Chekhov's "parody of a majestic ball is amazingly detailed." Another unlikely pair is Pishchik and Trofimov discussing finances. Charlotta plays a game of auctioning off a rug—but the real auction is taking place. Chekhov's art ties together life's crazy quilt of humor and pathos.

The servant level has the same split as the master level: Firs, dressed in formal livery, yearns for "the good old days," but Yasha, in latest Parisian styles, sasses back his master, says Styan. Gaev is more upset over Yasha playing at his billiard table than at Lopakhin's purchase of the estate. The set in Act IV returns to that of Act I, demonstrating life's cycle. Some of the play's comic scenes resemble those of an absurdist like Pirandello. Maurice Valency says that the real reason that Lopakhin refuses to marry Varya is that he secretly loves Liubov.

In 1972 Penelope Curtis called this "the most determinist of Chekhov's plays" because its characters refuse to acknowledge time's passage. Ronald Gaskell, on the other hand, says that *The Cherry Orchard* is notable for its feeling of the reality of time in its passage. Christina Scheibitz that year said that in his mature drama Chekhov does not permit the audience to identify with his characters but instead forces them to be active as critical observers.[92]

Edward Mabley said that the play has much action, but that the events are insignificant and unrelated to the major plot concern.[93] Magarshack (1972) pointed out farcical elements involving Varya, with her stick and her umbrella, and Trofimov, with his galoshes. Melchinger (1972) said that Meyerhold, feeling that Stanislavsky had made Act III too sentimental, demanded a hard, cold attitude in his productions, "the projection of a nightmare." In one production Stanislavsky brought a real troika with horses onto the stage. When Meyerhold spoke of the symbolism and mysticism of the play, he was referring to its anti-realistic element, the "rhythmic movement" of the play as a whole.

Beverly Hahn interpreted the play as an ironic pastoral drama. V.Y. Lakshin studied the final revisions that Chekhov made after the first rehearsals.[94] Pitcher (1973) said that although Chekhov called Act II "boring and monotonous," it was "the most intriguing individual act Chekhov ever wrote, for it widens the play's emotional horizons." The sound of the breaking string is a characterizing device: Each person interprets it so as to reveal what is on his mind. Trofimov is more individualized than Vershinin but without Vershinin's "generalizing dimension, thereby making considerably less impact." After Liubov and Trofimov quarrel, they dance together. "The reconciliation is effected so quickly because she understands that he was only trying to help, just as he understands that her words were an overflowing of emotion and not directed at him personally."

Pitcher says that in Act IV Chekhov quickly dismantles the emotional network that he has so carefully created. The characters depart in inverse order of their love of the estate. "Chekhov's technique of emotional shorthand is so highly developed that it is necessary for him to only touch the right emotional nerve in the audience very briefly to trigger a deep response." The mysterious sound at the end of the play completes the emotional distancing, providing a cosmic perspective on the littleness of mankind and its petty affairs. "Individual human lives may end, but the emotional interrelatedness of human beings remains constant."

In 1973 Laurence Senelick showed the technique Chekhov used as Anya described Liubov's life in Paris. "This deft construction of an entire picture by accumulating a number of miniscule and seemingly unrelated details makes Chekhov the Seurat of stagecraft," Senelick said. As in pointillism, the viewer must step back, and then the isolated elements form a picture. Approaching Chekhov, one needs the perspective of objectivity, and then one discovers the unifying quality infused through his plays.[95]

Shotton, in Fennell (1973), found three planes, or levels, in the play: farce, tragedy, and the deepest plane, where we react not to what is happening to the characters but to what this action tells us about their inner worlds and their qualities as persons. Strangely, at this deep level *The Three Sisters* is seen as Chekhov's most optimistic play and *The Cherry Orchard* as the most pessimistic, for the former has an optimistic inner climax but in *The Cherry Orchard* the tragicomic external wrappings conceal a somber inner truth. In *The Cherry Orchard* no character changes for the better, as the Prozorov sisters had. "Liubov symbolizes the whole of her disinherited class, dancing with engaging insouciance around its own funeral pyre into extinction." As Meyerhold observed, in *The Cherry Orchard* the hero, which is opposition to vulgarity, is never seen on stage. As Chekhov's dramatic technique improved, "the quantity and intricacy of love relationships decreased." His contribution was to unite symbolism and impressionism with his naturalism so as to give his world both unity and meaning. "His greatest contribution to literature as a means by which we may better understand ourselves is his exposure of the many ways in which the external human world – appearance, words, posture – conceals its inner reality. The blend of ironic skepticism with dogged realism gives Chekhov's work its peculiar flavor."

Rayfield (1975) notes that this play reworks Chekhov's story "A Visit to Friends" (1898), in which the mistress of the mansion tries to get the hero to marry her daughter in order to save the estate from being sold. The play lacks both death and romantic love, and is a comedy because its characters cannot or will not understand what is happening to them. In Act III the poem "The Sinning Woman" by A.K. Tolstoy was a notorious one in which a courtesan boasts that she can seduce anyone, even Christ. When Christ appears, she is overcome with repentance. Here it is a sign of a guest's tactlessness towards his hostess. Chekhov's symbolism in this play influenced subsequent Russian symbolists.

In 1977 a previously unpublished article by Valery Bryusov appeared, calling this play a dead end for future Russian drama. Also, V.B. Kataev surveyed Russian literature before Chekhov for works dealing with the decline of the gentry, as

possible forerunners of *The Cherry Orchard*. M.L. Semanova that year studied
Chekhov's use of time in this play. In 1977 Walter Reed found the play to be neither
comedy nor tragedy, but a greater type of play which discloses reality beneath artificial surfaces.[96] Edgar L. Frost in 1977 said that the reason Gaev and Liubov
do nothing is an effort to make time, their enemy, stand still for them.[97]

Hahn (1977) says that *The Cherry Orchard* is a classical comedy. The lack of
will in Gaev and Liubov comes from a complex sense of guilt and self-degradation.
The sound of the snapping string symbolizes the passing of a social order. Chekhov
knew both Shakespeare and classical French comedy. This play belongs to the
same genre as *The Winter's Tale*, in that both contain unfulfilled tragedies. What
is lost at the end of *The Cherry Orchard* is what already had been lost at the beginning. This play also fits into the mode of early pastoral comedy. Since she feels that
she really does not deserve the estate, Liubov sees it as an act of penance to surrender it. Trofimov is the externalized figure of Liubov's own conscience. Act II
is pure pastoral, in which Charlotta itemizes, rather than feels, her sorrows, thereby
giving classical restraint to the picture of cultural decay. The act has a processional
structure—three groups of people, in turn, come to converse by the abandoned
shrine. Through her magic, Charlotta demonstrates the ability to will the world as
she wants it—a direct foil to Liubov. Charlotta may even, for justice's sake,
perversely will the loss of the estate.

Nicholas Moravcevich, in Bristow (1977), said that impressionism was
Chekhov's great contribution to drama. Examples are the outdoor sounds, the outdoor scenes even in interiors, and the centrifugal plot, in which the characters do
not care what is happening to them. Impressionism helped Chekhov avoid didacticism. "Only the impressionist technique could have provided his drama with that
structural quality in which the microcosm of apparently haphazard detail could successfully suggest the macrocosm of the larger reality of life." The obligatory scene
is discussed by Moravcevich in Debreczeny (1977). Since Chekhov's theme was not
the sale of the estate but the effect of the sale upon the characters, he did well to
omit the obligatory scene (the sale), "since in this type of construction its actual
enactment on stage would only destroy the imaginative subtlety of the whole." Also,
in tracing the effect upon the characters, every scene becomes equally obligatory,
Moravcevich felt.

A spectacular and controversial staging of the play in New York by Andrey Serban in 1977 evoked many critical comments. Richard Eder found that Serban, with
links to Antonin Artaud, Peter Brook and Jerzy Grotowski, gave "physical expression to primal forces, the archetypes beneath the characters' motivations."[98] Walter
Kerr called it "a daring, alternately vulgar and delicate, perverse, funny, deeply
original and visually stunning event. The comedy," Kerr said, "ranges from the
hilariously plausible to the frantically forced."[99] Jack Kroll called *The Cherry Orchard* "arguably the greatest play of the 20th century," and said that over this production hung "a rare sense of adventure, an air of freshness and rediscovery."[100]
Lally Weymouth recalled Brendan Gill saying that Serban is "on occasion

gratuitously vulgar" and that John Simon had called the production "a total betrayal of Chekhov's simplicity," but that Irene Worth, who played Liubov, believed that Serban brought out both the play's farce and its political protest.[101]

In 1978 Gerhard Ressel studied the role that dialogue plays in the overall structure of the play. Also, Herta Schmidt linked Chekhov with August Strindberg as playwrights who use space to show their characters' limitations. In 1979 Stephen L. Baehr surveyed the use of the name "Firs" in Russian literature, finding that Chekhov probably chose it because of its pastoral association with "Thyrsis." Jean-Pierre Barricelli said that *The Cherry Orchard* is "a drama of death," and the sound of the breaking string evokes a mood of regret for the passage of time. E.A. Polotskaya that year studied the reception of the play among spectators, readers, producers, and critics.[102]

Clardy (1980) pointed out the similarity to the decaying aristocracy in America's South. In *The Cherry Orchard,* serfdom had ruined the capacity of all of the characters to adapt to change. Stowell (1980) calls the play an unsurpassed work of modern impressionism. No other drama uses so many pauses and silences; each pause is filled by the audience, which thereby becomes a participant in the play. Here Chekhov makes space (the nursery), suggest time (the past), and time (the destruction of the future) suggest space (the cherry orchard). Chekhov's later plays all are about change, one of the keynotes of impressionism. He also juxtaposes stasis and motion; everything around the characters changes, but not the characters themselves. "The ambivalence of juxtaposition defines the basic character of the play, its sense of purposelessness and inertia. Lost in a directionless present, the characters search for the unreachable past and future." Liubov's reverie about her lost childhood is a perfect example of Chekhov's impressionism: She contrasts spring's white warmth with winter's cold darkness; she makes the past live in the present; and she finds change and changelessness in the same moment.

Tulloch (1980) says that most critics err in seeing Lopakhin as a villain. As a matter of fact, "he is the only one who understands this decaying orchard." He sees that the old way of life must go in order to prepare for the new way. Trofimov speaks a language of fatalistic Darwinism, to disguise the Marxist content from the censor, but for Chekhov both these value systems were part of the same "inauthentic" paradigm. "In a play of ritualized action and withdrawal, it is Lopakhin alone who is mobile, both socially and dramatically. It is around Lopakhin that the action moves." Like Lopakhin, Chekhov was upwardly mobile from serfdom, and thus he could portray Lopakhin sympathetically.

Barricelli (1981) contains views on *The Cherry Orchard* by Jean-Pierre Barricelli, Sonia Kovitz, Nils Ake Nilsson, Richard D. Risso, and Laurence Senelick. Barricelli said that since Chekhov saw life as paradoxical, he had used counterpoint to depict life's ambiguity in drama. Barricelli agrees with Aimée Alexandre, who called *The Cherry Orchard* the drama of death, "the disappearance of a past with all its good and bad." The breaking string, an important symbol in the play, is

Atropos snipping the final thread of life. Chekhov used the sound effect as a motif of unhappiness, its most prevalent use in European folklore. If a musician's string snaps, it is an evil portent. In folklore this often signifies death. When it is first heard in the play Gaev has just said that Nature unites within herself life and death. Gaev says the sound might have been a heron (an omen of good) but Trofimov thinks it might have been an owl (an omen of evil). White, the predominant color in the play, is also ambiguous, for it can stand for both eternity and for lifelessness. No one in the play is any happier, despite all the music that is played. The breaking string heard at the play's end is not "emotional distancing," as Harvey Pitcher suggested. It is more emphatic than a pistol shot, for it reaches into spiritual realms too. In folklore it unites the light and dark of creation, and that is its meaning here.

Kovitz comments that when Trofimov says that "all Russia is our garden" Simone Weil would agree, for she said that "we all have to be catholic, that is to say, not bound to any created thing, unless it be to creation in its totality." Nilsson alleges that Chekhov created a new poetic language for the theater by deviating from traditional syntax, using pauses, disconnected dialogue, nonverbal signs, and constant changes in the tonality and rhythm of the play. Risso observes that Gaev despises Lopakhin, who has the qualities that Gaev falsely ascribes to himself. Senelick reviewed the interpretations of previous critics concerning the meaning of the play.

Mel Gussow, commenting on Peter Brook's production of the play in Paris in 1981, noted the starkly simple setting which returned the play to the words of Chekhov. "The evening was comic without being farcical, and it was immensely human – an authentic ensemble piece," in Gussow's words.[103]

Kirk (1981) said that the play, having a melancholy fatalism, is comedy only in Henri Bergson's broad definition. Chekhov takes what is normally tragic – human isolation, time's erosion, and the certainty of death – and shows the comic side. "Only a great artist such as Chekhov could succeed in portraying the comic aspects of metaphysical questions which have been plaguing man for centuries," Kirk said. John Quintus showed the influence of this play on Tennessee Williams' *A Streetcar Named Desire*. Not only is the theme of two plays the common one of loss, but there are also similarities in some characters and in the use of music. E.M. Sakharova in 1982 showed Chekhov's influence on Alexander Blok, stating that in "The Song of Fate" Blok continued the themes of *The Cherry Orchard.* [104]

Eisen (1982) discussed the functions of "static" Act II. In this centrifugal plot, the act broadens concern beyond the characters – life now seems as disorganized to us as it does to the characters. The act widens the implications of the loss of the estate: The servants and neighbors will suffer too. Finally, the act clinches basic character traits: The Ranevskys cannot act but Lopakhin can and will. Master (1982) quoted Alexander Reviakin, who contrasted the self-reflective monologues of the "forward-looking" characters (Anya and Trofimov). During the course of the play, the characters learn to react. By the end, they can both act and react, making this Chekhov's most masterful work.

Bitsilli (1983) recalls that Meyerhold assumed that Chekhov's plays were symbolist works, and should be so staged. Bitsilli feels that he may have understood Chekhov's plays better than Chekhov himself did. Jane Kramer, reporting on Peter Brook's production in Paris, said that the French language seemed better than English or German for capturing the rhythms, nuances, and delicate syntactical structures of Chekhov's Russian.[105]

Peace (1983) calls Gaev "a comic shadow for the childlike and naïvely romantic aspects of Liubov." The comic secondary characters (Epikhodov, Pishchik, and Charlotta) perform a vital function. As conductors of ridicule, they draw laughter away from Liubov, keeping her from becoming a ludicrous figure. While *The Cherry Orchard* was in rehearsal, Gorky told Chekhov, "Now I am convinced that your next play will be a revolutionary one." But Chekhov was jousting with Gorky's "semi-mystical philosophy of God-building" in this play. Ironically, when Trofimov says that Russia is calling for great men, it is Epikhodov who responds! In each successive act, the cherry orchard recedes farther into oblivion. As in N.A. Dobrolyubov's essay "What Is Oblomovism?" here too the trees symbolize serfdom. Pishchik's absurdity derives from Gogol. Axe strokes are heard at the end of the play—the axe was the traditional weapon of peasant rebellion. Though very Russian, Chekhov writes for a worldwide audience, "to whom they speak of problems, relationships, and values which are eternal, and thus his appeal is universal."

Troyat (1984) stated that what makes this play a masterpiece is its unique mix—a tragic theme enacted by comic characters. Since the audience likes the characters, they want nothing to happen, realizing that if things do happen, the cherry orchard will be sold.

Harvey Pitcher, in Clyman (1985), noted the return of young "Antosha Chekhonte" (Chekhov's early alias) in *The Cherry Orchard*. Pishchik (meaning "squeaker") is a name from the comic sketch "Visiting Cards" (1886). Pishchik calls himself "an old horse," and his appetite and personality are horselike. His father joked that the family descended from the horse that Caligula made into a senator!

Senelick (1985) summarized the views of previous critics on this play. He feels that Chekhov's mastery can be seen in the way he blends impressionism with theatricality. Here, he says, Chekhov achieved a new dramatic form, "the amalgam of a symbolist outlook with the appurtenances of social comedy." Egri (1986) asserts that the oppositon between illusion and reality is not only a theme but a governing principle in both this play and in Eugene O'Neill's *A Long Day's Journey Into Night*. Egri finds many similarities in the two plays. Both synthesize interior monologue with dramatic monologue. Both get great significance out of ordinary sentences, and both discover that happiness may precipitate pain. Just as fog is the leitmotif in O'Neill's play, so is the cherry orchard in Chekhov's drama. Chekhovian traits multiply in O'Neill's more mature drama. Besides O'Neill, other American playwrights influenced by Chekhov include Edward Albee, Arthur Miller, Clifford Odets, Thornton Wilder, and Tennessee Williams, says Egri.

16. High Points in Chekhov Criticism

Critical Highlights: Chekhov as a Short-Story Writer

Chapter 1 summarized the main features of Chekhov's fictional technique, and described how Russian, British, and American critics have reacted to Chekhov's short stories. It remains for us to highlight some of the outstanding contributions to the criticism of Chekhov's fiction, as revealed above in Chapter 2 through Chapter 8.

The critical consensus is that Chekhov had keen insight into human nature, coupled with the ability to portray a vast array of character types with ingenuous but penetrating art. It is not surprising, therefore, that the critics found that the largest number of his distinctive stories were studies in human personality and character.

Beginning with "A Chameleon" (1884), Kramer (1970) made a detailed analysis of Chekhov's "chameleons," that is, spineless people who change their approaches to persons according to whether they outrank them or not in the social scale. Kramer pointed out that since this is a condition particularly prevalent in a rigidly hierarchical society, Chekhov uses chameleons of many kinds in his stories.

Sensitive and skilled, Chekhov uses his fictional art to protest against the bullying process. Hahn (1977) called "Agafya" (1886) an excellent picture of Agafya's complex feelings concerning a wife's responsibilities. As she leaves her lover for her husband, Agafya cuts a bright green trail through the grass, epitomizing her fearful subjugation to her husband's stern authority, while granting her lover "an enviable masculine immunity." Agafya finds herself trapped between two different forms of masculine domination.

Characterization of the professor in "A Dreary Story" (1889) attracted significant comments from Rayfield (1975) and Hahn (1977). Rayfield named the story Chekhov's best, considered from the standpoint of form. He contrasted it with Tolstoy's "The Death of Ivan Ilyich," where Tolstoy's moral preaching seems wooden next to Chekhov's ironic elegy of life. Chekhov tells "a remarkably modern confession story which lays bare existential absurdity," with a vision of life "too complete to be enlarged." Hahn stated that Chekhov replaces Tolstoy's incipient sarcasm with a series of tones ranging from nostalgia through regret to irritation. In Chekhov's hands a better portrait is given not only of a person's unpreparedness to face death, but also the fate of mankind's highest ideals during the declining years of a person's life. Hahn finds the professor "morally superior, braver, and more in control" than Ivan. The professor is discouraged to discover that art entails social and moral responsibility. As he uncovers his emptiness, he struggles to preserve his human dignity. Since most people go through this inner struggle, the story has a lasting significance, Hahn states.

Hingley (1970) notes that Matvey, in "Peasant Women" (1891), discredits himself in a masterpiece of ironic characterization, as his self-congratulatory narration exposes his basically unkind nature. Chekhov had such deep faith in human nature, Hingley feels, that he devoted much of the story to castigating human vices rather than portraying positive character types, confident that readers would avoid unseemly conduct after seeing it portrayed so vividly.

In "Anna on the Neck" (1895), Winner (1966) saw Chekhov using numerous linguistic devices to show character. Labial consonants, suggesting lip smacking, bring out the gluttony of Modest. Alliterative linkages emphasize the contrast between the older husband and the young wife, in whom Winner sees many traits of Anna Karenina.

Robert Lynd in 1916 said that Chekhov depicted common people better than anyone else in literature. In "Ariadne" (1895) the protagonist is seen from the perspective of the disgusted rather than the enamored lover. Ariadne's beauty is dwarfed by her greed. Simmons (1962) adds that Ariadne, "one of the most cruelly dissected Becky Sharp types in Chekhov's fiction," uses men for her own purpose. Even her shred of conscience merely designs schemes for her own advancement. "Affectation and pretense are the loose ornament of her conversation," Simmons says.

The Russian emigré, D.S. Mirsky (1927), a critic with few words of praise for Chekhov, said that finally in Poloznev, the hero of "My Life" (1896), Chekhov had created an exemplary man, whose delicate nature was "haloed by continuous defeat." Poloznev's story is "his Purgatorio, a true poem of immense symbolical pregnancy." Shaking off the "lullaby" effect of his usual endings, Chekhov here presents an Everyman figure of universal significance, in Mirsky's opinion.

The most famous critical reaction to "The Darling" (1898) was that by Tolstoy, who said that Chekhov began with the intent of ridiculing a spineless woman, but his sympathetic understanding took control of his genius and made Olga into a warm and loving person. Chekhov's guiding poetic angel, said Tolstoy, caused him to end up blessing the person he had originally planned to condemn.

Soviet critic Avram Derman in 1929 found terseness to be Chekhov's most characteristic trait. In "Ionych" (1898) Derman detected a laconic beginning and ending, a rapid development of theme, and the selection of crucial details to depict the change in the protagonist. For example, where early Ionych did not even own a horse, by the end he rides in a troika driven by a liveried servant.

Reacting to "The Bishop" (1902), Rayfield (1975) noted the agnostic Chekhov's skill at rendering the church atmosphere. Approaching death, the bishop finds his past more meaningful than his present. His fever causes hallucinations which merge with Holy Week themes. The moonlight reminds him of Christ's agony in Gethsemane. After evoking a chaotic assemblage of sensations and memories, Chekhov resolves "their discord into a harmonious set of images." As death approaches, Church Slavonic replaces Russian in his language. His last moments are particularly rewarding, for as he relives his childhood, he has finally discarded his mitre, and he can be accepted simply as a person by everyone, including his mother. Wilks (1982) finds a dreamlike quality permeating this "perfect work of art." The bishop's delirium provides a long-awaited catharsis of peace of mind and spiritual illumination. Wilks notes Chekhov's use of counterpoint: Dying on Easter Eve, the bishop is soon forgotten, but after Christ's death and resurrection, He will always be remembered.

Chekhov's last story, "The Betrothed" (1903), evoked penetrating comments from Winner (1966), Rayfield (1975), and Stowell (1980). Winner said that the three main parts of the story progressively portrayed Nadya's increasing realization of the inadequacy of her milieu. The story's theme is embodied through the interplay of elements of beauty and vulgarity. Chekhov employs a musical counterpoint of these two motifs, which clash with growing intensity. He holds many plot incidents static in order to set off the profound change occurring within Nadya.

Rayfield finds here Chekhov's most vigorous affirmation of life. The garden stands for life just as the house epitomizes sterility. Like Sasha, Chekhov refused to provide facile answers to life's problems. Instead, he "broke down the extraneous structures of thought on which his characters and scenes might easily have been superimposed." He evolves as an artist by withdrawing as a philosopher, Rayfield says. "He takes away the lies that are outside us and leaves us with the truth that is in us."

Stowell calls "The Betrothed" Chekhov's most misunderstood story. Critics are eager to write their own versions of Nadya's continuing life rather than seeing her as caught, as we all are, in life's evanescent flux. Nadya's dilemma is time: She wants future change, but she wishes to avoid surrendering the good things of the past. Chekhov's final philosophy of change is this—it is exhilarating but constricting, static and dynamic, timeless and temporal, but above all, impressionistic. Nadya's impressions never crystallize, and so she does not know whether it is she or her environment which is changing: "She remains in the swirl of relativisitic flux to the end."

Some of Chekhov's short stories show such acute psychological analysis that they have been used as paradigms in psychology textbooks. Chekhov is seen as a doctor, not merely of the body, but of the mind and soul. Hahn (1977) found it remarkable that at the age of 26 Chekhov, in "Misfortune" (1886), was already writing with authority about "the collision between conscience and instinct in the sexual life," describing "the romantic overtones of feminine sexual desire," and portraying "the self-delusion by which women in particular avoid recognizing sexual impulses in themselves."

Bruford (1957) sees "The Name-Day Party" (1888) as a study of the clash between educated people of contradictory views. Obviously Olga is being mistreated, but what really bothers her inwardly is that she feels that her own insincerity is worse than her husband's. She differs from a character in Kafka or in existentialist literature in that she remembers the formerly well-ordered society of her youth.

"The Black Monk" (1894) was included in Edward J. O'Brien's collection of the 15 best short stories in the world in 1928. O'Brien said that in the story Chekhov achieved, like Emily Brontë or Dostoevsky, "nothing less than a synthesis of the spiritual life of our time. Here all temptations are encountered, all sins committed, all hope for the future abandoned; but life makes its final affirmation from the brink of the grave."

Winner (1966) says that in Chekhov's symbolism, the black monk is Kovrin's frustrated goal, a projection of his repressed ego. Not only mystics but also artists and scientists are visualized as persons apart from common humanity. Setting and music are employed to enrich the moods of the characters. Like Henry James, said Winner, Chekhov here presents a complex portrait of a person's inner life. Hingley (1978) sees Kovrin as rebelling against Tanya's domestication of him, for he fears it will rob him of his personality. To him, even death is preferable to trivialization. As in "Ward No. 6," Chekhov cleverly places his very sane protest into the mouth of a supposed lunatic.

"Three Years" (1895) has also been called a profound psychological study. Speirs (1971) observes that Chekhov, the democrat, understands "small people," but Tolstoy, the count, does not. Tolstoy wants to educate the peasants towards a preconceived good life, whereas Chekhov wants them educated in order to develop their individuality. In this story Laptev hates to meet his brother, for he sees his own weaknesses reflected in him. A coward, Laptev brings out the reader's innate cowardice. His deep fear that he will be "merely an average man" dissolves when he finally realizes that there is no such person.

Second in importance to stories of character in Chekhov's catalog are those built around a theme. Stowell (1980) calls "Grisha" (1886) Chekhov's best children's story, for here he captures the raw, naïve perception of a child. Grisha's movements through space coincide with the expansion of his awareness. He ends up being confused, for the adult world has "so many mamas, papas, and aunts that one does not know whom to run to."

In a rare Chekhovian journey into the world of political intrigue, "An Anonymous Story" (1893) was seen by Kramer (1970) as being similar to Turgenev's *On the Eve*. Kramer identifies nearly farce-like effects, as if this were a story of mistaken identity; Zinaida's efforts to aid the revolutionary cause dissolve as her male companions constantly fail her. Kramer finds art in the way Chekhov unifies the several story lines, dealing with revolution, love, and relationships.

Rayfield (1975) calls "The Student" (1894) a parable about how art can overcome despair. All of the setting details are carefully mirrored in the story of Peter's denial of Christ. In a flash the student realizes that each day is a part of eternity. Chekhov's style reflects the change from despair to spiritual epiphany, for at first the syntax is harsh and terse, but towards the end it grows rich and gentle.

James T. Farrell in 1937, reacting to "A Woman's Kingdom" (1894), said that it demonstrated that a short story need not confine itself to creating a single unified effect. In speaking of social relationships within czarist Russia, Farrell says, the story is "a cross-section of many phases of that life. One gets from it impressions of class relationships, of characters, of moods." Chekhov's stories are thus seen as confounding rigid critical standards, for they are "like doors of understanding and awareness opening outward into an entire world."

In a critique of the same story, Hahn (1977) showed how Chekhov's tale differed from D.H. Lawrence's *The Lost Girl*, which has a similar plot. Overcome by her primal sex urge, Lawrence's Alvina really is not experiencing inner conflict. But Chekhov gives both inner and external reasons why Anna finds it hard to submit to Pimenov. Tempering her primal passion are her background, education, and cultural tradition, as well as the restraint which is a part of her personality. Studying human isolation and class dynamics, the story is similar to *The Three Sisters*. Like the play, the story has a four-part structure, in this case moving from night to morning to evening to night, with the mood of the story showing a parallel movement from loneliness to hope and back to loneliness.

One of the stories attracting the most attention from critics is "The Lady with a Dog" (1899). Smith (1973) sees Anna as the symbol of the ideal love which Chekhov could imagine but not embody in his life. The banal plot is saved, Smith judges, by Chekhov's artistry, which maintains a precarious balance between the prosaic and the poetic, meanwhile achieving vivid characterization through the use of half-tones. Gurov, a type of Everyman, has a fate similar to his author's: Real love had come to him too late in life, thus denying him total happiness.

Hahn (1977) notes that this story depicts the conversion of desire into love. Anna's unconscious portrait of herself as "a classical Magdalen" expresses a genuine shame and humility in her which makes her more attractive not only to Gurov but also to the reader. The slow rhythms of the prose narrating the Yalta sequences shift to a crisp, nervous pace when the scene shifts to Moscow. The story's dramatic structure focuses on Gurov, Anna, and their relationship. Like a play, it has four parts, each reflecting a different aspect of the love affair. Had it been a novel, details about his wife and her husband would have raised moral considerations that would have marred the esthetic effect. As the tryst encounters difficulties, Chekhov shows it through "a whole sequence of images of hardness, constriction, and enclosure." A tribute to the worth of human love, the story manifests such mellowness that few other Chekhov stories achieve "so lingering and lyrical an effect of tone," Hahn feels.

Stowell (1980) observes how Anna grows from being an anonymous "lady with a dog" to a person of such intensity as to change Gurov's whole attitude towards women. Chekhov uses the technique of impressionism to surround each thought and feeling with "the opacity of ambiguity and change." Love, says Stowell, is "the perfect impressionistic subject, because it is so responsive to change, so evanescent, and so dependent upon the subjective perceptions of both lovers." Time is a kaleidoscope in this four-part romance. The first part merely suggests its languid passing, while the second depicts the oppressive atmosphere of timelessness. Then comes the winter grayness of loss, and finally the lovers drift towards an ambiguous future, in what Stowell calls Chekhov's finest impressionist achievement.

"The unexpected little turns and light touches," says Nabokov (1981) of this story, "place Chekhov, above all Russian writers of fiction, on the level of Gogol and Tolstoy." Ignoring the traditional plot requirements of a crisis, a climax, and a denouement, Chekhov nonetheless gave us what Nabokov called "one of the greatest stories ever written." Typical features of Chekhov's fictional technique are seen here: The expository narrative employs a natural style. There is rich and exact characterization. Instead of a message there is a structure based on "waves of shades of mood." The story has no more ending than life has, causing the reader to project for himself the conclusion his logic justifies or his fancy desires.

Few of Chekhov's stories evoked as much critical comment as did "The Steppe" (1888). Many critics, finding little plot, considered the steppe itself to be the protagonist of the story. The setting is evoked so vividly as to produce an atmospheric effect. Brewster and Burrell (1924) noted how Chekhov, through the use of amazingly precise images, piled mood upon mood until exactly the sought-after impression is achieved. They found Chekhov and Mark Twain alike "in their spiritual outlook on the essential tragedy of man's loneliness." One saw life through the lens of exaggerated humor, while the other used the lens of tranquil realism. "Under more propitious conditions," they concluded, "Twain might have been as great an artist as Chekhov."

Winner (1966) notes that the picaresque structure of "The Steppe" is based upon the things that happen to a traveler. The central figure, Egorushka, is as lonely as nature, with which he is identified. Winner sees Gogol's influence at work here, but Chekhov replaces Gogol's biting satire with his own poetic observation and reflection. Winner's insights into the story reflect the perspective of the structuralist Roland Barthes. For example, Egorushka stops by a lonely grave which seems "audibly silent." This is what a structuralist would call a "high-cost" phrase, since it violates traditional categories of association. Winner delineates the connotation: Nature itself seems to want to cry out in protest of the neglected graves.

Several of Chekhov's stories brought forth praise for their use of the technique of impressionism. Savely Senderovich, in Debreczeny (1977), found that Chekhov achieved brilliant impressionistic effects in "On the Road" (1886) by constant shifts in points-of-view. Chekhov employs a whole mosaic of impressions which reflect the widower Grigory's life of sudden change and chaos. Just as an impressionistic painter captures beauty's evanescence by breaking it into a series of discrete images, so Chekhov renders spiritual beauty by a kindred prose-poetic technique.

Once the reader perceives Chekhov's method, says Senderovich, he realizes that the story is not so much about love as it is about faith, reaching its climax in the singing of the Christmas carol.

Stowell (1980) examines the impressionistic technique used in the story "In the Cart" (1897). As the schoolteacher Marya waits for a train to pass, Chekhov fragments and dissolves the material landscape as Monet or Turner might have done. Stowell lists the elements of impressionism he finds in the scene: "visual perspective, motion and stasis, harmony of feeling, formlessness of colors and shapes, random and isolated detail, and the pervading reflection of light at a particular time of day." Stowell feels that Chekhov's whole career seemed to be pointed towards this passage, for the impressionistic epiphany combines dream and reality, past, present, and future, and subject and object into "an atmospheric moment of presentness." Having moved in the cart, Marya is caused to stop, and the stasis, following the motion, gives her pause to reflect upon her problems, integrate her impressions, and chart a future course for her life.

In sum, critics found Chekhov's fictional style to be natural, terse, and economical but suggestive. The precise diction uses occasional apt figures of speech. Interest is aroused not by unusual plots but by unexpected insight into character or novel handling of the thought content. Every stroke fits into an exquisite mosaic, and nothing extraneous is inserted. The seeming irrelevancies are seen, at the proper esthetic distance, to be an impressionistic rendering that forms a beautiful picture. The themes almost always deal with some aspect of human dignity and its violation or realization. His vivid and appropriate settings are sometimes so intense as to constitute an atmospheric aura where stories develop. Most critics agree that in his unique combination of varied gifts, Chekhov represents one of the most seminal influences upon the short story as a literary genre.

Critical Highlights: Chekhov as a Dramatist

A summary of the main features of Chekhov's dramatic technique is given in Chapter 1, as well as a description of how Russian, British, and American critics have reacted to his plays. Useful now should be a review of the highlights of the criticism of his drama, as contained above in Chapter 10 through Chapter 15.

Chekhov's one-act plays have often been called among the best short farces ever written. Analyzing the sources of humor in *The Anniversary* (1891), Gottlieb (1982) found a satire on pretension, and parodies of both banking practices and romantic love. Each character is tortured by his "humour" or excessive obsession. A pleasant union of incongruity with realism, of irrelevant and relevant, produces mistaken identity that evokes chaos and farce.

In *The Night Before the Trial* (1895), Gottlieb discovered stock characters stemming from the *commedia del l'arte*. Here everything is excessive as well as artificial: the lawyer's gullibility, the wife's illness, and Zaitsev's deceitfulness. The humor is so broad that Gottlieb feels that Chekhov is parodying parodies. Brigitte

Schultze in 1978 said that this "tragic farce" was the first play in the tradition of the Theater of the Absurd.

Gottlieb says that *Swan Song* (1887) has the universal theme of what life might have been like under other circumstances. Like Brecht, Chekhov makes the audience think, says Gottlieb. And like Beckett, Chekhov forces the audience to become participants in the drama. This play combines monologue and false monologue. By exposing the sordid reality of the theater, Chekhov enables us to look beyond its illusory façade into life itself. Master (1982) observes that in this play Chekhov blends "confessions" with "stories," thus preparing for their use in his more mature drama.

Senelick (1985) saw *Tatyana Repina* (1889) as not parody but pastiche, a forerunner of "the intricate interweaving of melodramatic pathos and crass diurnalism" that occurs in the later plays. Speaking of *A Tragedian in Spite of Himself* (1889), Senelick says that Tolkachov's shopping list is a surrealistic mélange. The comparison of married life to the Spanish Inquisition turns ordinary middle-class life into a manic impression of Bosch's hell. Here, says Senelick, Chekhov moves halfway from Gogol's grotesque to the absurd comedy of Jarry and Ionesco.

The tones of Chekhov's one-act plays range from the slapstick of *The Anniversary* to the pathos of *On the High Road*. As Chekhov was learning to master his craft, he sharpened his technique for building plots, using or avoiding stock characters, creating dialogue, and mingling relevancy with irrelevancy—all devices helpful to him in his mature phase. His instinctive eye for a comic situation would make him a master of modern television's sitcoms.

Kenneth Tynan in 1967 called *Platonov* "proof of Chekhov's genius." The hero he regarded as "one of the great comic creations of the last hundred years." Tynan found the play making a singular impression through characters who have "the Chekhovian habit of taking calamities lightly and trivialities tragically." Michael Frayn, who has adapted this play into a modern version, in 1986 admired Chekhov's "wonderful double vision" in creating characters like Platonov and Anna. Chekhov, said Frayn, could effortlessly get inside of his characters, and at the same time coolly evaluate them from an external perspective.

In 1889 the *St. Petersburg Gazette* praised *Ivanov* for "its accomplished dialogue, its vital truth, its characters taken straight from life, and its far from conventional plot." Bruford (1957) admired Chekhov's daring in this play. The hero is unique, and is revealed by each character illuminating a different aspect of his personality. Ivanov is neither as evil as Dr. Lvov describes him nor as good as Sasha would have him to be. Minor characters are interesting in themselves, as well as serving as reflectors of the play's main theme. Bruford feels that Chekhov pioneered in creating an atmosphere of boredom by using sights and sounds to orchestrate the dialogue.

Hingley (1976) went so far as to call *Ivanov* a better play than *The Sea Gull.* He said that *Ivanov* contained the anti–Tolstoy moral: Do not moralize. It is a highly didactic play with this theme: Do not be didactic. Hingley sees *Ivanov* as a triumph of craftsmanship: "The scenes are well put together, the dialogue is subtle and lively," and the suitably light background "throws the sombre elements of the main drama into effective relief."

The critical insights of George Calderon (1912), Chekhov's greatest dramatic critic, were described in Chapter 1. Calderon noted Chekhov's creation of atmosphere, such as in Acts I and II of *The Sea Gull*, so that when the plot seems static often atmospheric effects are contributing importantly, in a non-plot fashion, to the overall effect. Calderon mentioned that Chekhov endowed his characters with a remote comedic point-of-view which enabled them to bear their misfortunes without malice. Seeing this, the viewer experiences a similar catharsis, finding it easier to place his own troubles into a more acceptable perspective.

Reviewing a performance of *The Sea Gull* in 1929, Stark Young said that Chekhov was the best possible influence on modern American playwrights, for what he could give them was "more delicacy of perception, more deeply interwoven themes, more subtlety of feeling, more poignancy, sincerity, and truth of intention." E.H. Carr that year said that in *The Sea Gull* Chekhov evolved a new esthetic ethic for Russian literature, divorcing it from political reform or other tendential preachment. "More than anyone else," said Carr, "Chekhov saw the triviality of life's tragedies." His dramatic technique incorporated "economy of effort, emotional restraint, perfection of form, and ethical objectivity."

The director John Fernald in 1968 commented that sound effects, especially the use of music, are important in *The Sea Gull*. They reinforce character, build atmosphere, heighten suspense, and unify the play through recurring leitmotifs. Fernald advocated sentimental music following Treplev's playlet, for sentimentality is romance with the reality omitted. That year Daniel Gilles analyzed the psychology of the play, a study in the disparity between what we are and what we aspire to be. Chekhov penetrates beneath surface realism, to "open the doors of one's secret self, the self of unbearable contradictions, the star chamber of conscience," where we condemn ourselves for falling short of our aspirations. The sensitive playgoer feels himself to be an accomplice of stage persons so much like himself. Such "poetry," said Gilles, could even revive one's thwarted ambitions, at least for one evening.

Michael Heim, in Barricelli (1981), pointed out a number of character pairings in *The Sea Gull*. The Masha-Medvedenko duo parallel, and also somewhat parody, the Nina-Treplev pair. Similarly, the Polina-Dorn pair reflect the Arkadina-Trigorin duo. "This layered effect gives the play increased depth of characterization," says Heim, and a balance is achieved in which no one character can stand out.

Sonia Kovitz, also in Barricelli (1981), provided a Jungian interpretation of the characters. She interpreted Treplev's suicide as a premature conclusion to his playlet. Satan is "the misery of the world which alone drives man inward," and Treplev succumbs before God can reveal Himself. Treplev fears the shadow side of his nature, which contains "demonic chaos, the union of opposites, and the act of creation." Treplev abandons his self when he projects his soul's powers onto

Nina, relying on her very presence to bring him psychic wholeness and happiness. But Treplev never arrives at individuation, the union of opposites within him, and so he remains fixated as an emotional adolescent, terrified to accept himself as the only human being he can possibly be. When both his art and his lover are deprived him, he kills the sea gull in a preliminary symbolic suicide.

Eisen (1982) showed how Chekhov employed "gapping" in *The Sea Gull*. A number of important events occur in the gaps in the action, testing the audience's acuity of observation and power of inference. The lotto game in the play symbolizes life. Treplev is constantly interrupted during the game, showing that life deprives him of the peace of mind needed for his art, but Trigorin, as usual, wins (not only the game of lotto but also Nina's love).

In 1926 Horace Shipp said that *Uncle Vanya* causes the sensitive playgoer to reflect on the meaning and purpose of life. Instead of furnishing the audience with a predigested formula of values, Chekhov accurately describes the process of value formation, giving the playgoers the clearest possible insight into human character and motivation. The presentation is so artful that "we cannot but be exalted to his godlike plane" as we contemplate the fate of his characters. We thus experience the catharsis of great art: "During these moments we exist in complete understanding and sympathy with the great movements of human life."

Dorothy L. Sayers in 1937 said that the mingling of the tragic and the absurd that was found in *Uncle Vanya* also lay at the heart of Shakespeare's drama. Eric Bentley in 1949 remarked on the improvements made as *The Wood Demon* became *Uncle Vanya*. Chekhov eliminated the farce and the melodrama, and wrote *Uncle Vanya* with restraint and "grace," or economy of movement. Paradoxically, said Bentley, playwrights like Eugene O'Neill try to depict passion but end up being superficial, but Chekhov, who pretends to show us merely the surface, is deeply passionate. "No modern playwright has presented elemental passion more truly," Bentley said.

Critics may discover fine shades of meaning in Chekhov's drama but one should never overlook his "simplicity and strength, his depth and intensity." The final scene of *Uncle Vanya* was a stage picture "such as the drama has seldom known since Shakespeare," in Bentley's opinion.

Lucas (1963) noted how Chekhov, through Vanya, attacked critics, who to Chekhov were little more than parasites. Vanya tells the professor that for 25 years he has done nothing but regurgitate other people's ideas about such nonsense as realism and naturalism. All you do, says Vanya, is tell intelligent people what they already know, and stupid people what they are not interested to hear. Speirs (1971) welcomed Chekhov finally achieving a good final act, in *Uncle Vanya*. Elsewhere Speirs had been disappointed, but here the surprises come "in small details which we immediately feel we ought to have foreseen."

Styan (1971) said that *Uncle Vanya* not only marked the culmination of 19th century naturalistic drama but also began the 20th century movement towards "many major sub–Chekhovian comedies like *Heartbreak House, Juno and the*

Paycock, The Iceman Cometh, and *The Glass Menagerie.*" After Chekhov discarded the trumped-up ending of *The Wood Demon,* "anticlimax and the denial of expectations become a finely tempered technique by which the audience's sense of truth to life is fostered." After the departure scene in Act IV, "everyone is a hundred years older for the summer visit, and yet everyone is unchanged."

Hahn (1977) says that time is a protagonist in *Uncle Vanya.* Feeling time's preciousness, the playgoer views the tragedy of wasted lives. Chekhov's "emotional realism," enabling him to capture the sub-surface shifts of emotions, places him much ahead of Ibsen in this regard. Chekhov not only creates a wider range of characters in any one play than Ibsen does, but he is also not chained to one prevailing idea or symbol, as was the Norwegian master.

In 1914 the poet Vladimir Mayakovsky said that Chekhov's revolutionary use of disconnected dialogue in *The Three Sisters* made him a futurist, "king of the Word." Gertrude Besse King in 1915 explained how Chekhov achieved catharsis in *The Three Sisters.* Instead of the playgoer dividing his sympathy between abstract symbols of right and wrong, he comes to feel very familiar with a likeable lot of very human persons. "Like us, they take themselves and their petty defeats so seriously that we are led to a philosophic awareness of how easily we get discouraged, of what small barriers keep us from happiness." In this way the audience is purged of its pettiness, and is prepared to face life on a grander scale.

Having seen an MAT production of *The Three Sisters,* Oliver Sayler in 1922 explained Chekhov's "spiritualized realism." By using deliberate restraint, Chekhov causes the spectator to complete the emotional circuit aroused by the characters. Disliking exaggeration, Chekhov decided to present life through its nuances. A cumulative effect gathers through this simple but subtle technique until, by the final act, it is overpowering. Sayler cited as examples the three love-duets between Masha and Vershinin.

John Shand, reviewing a Komisarjevsky production of *The Three Sisters* in 1926, said that Chekhov's only match in the theater was Shakespeare. "Something of divinity hedges round about Chekhov," said Shand, "as it also encircles Shakespeare. Chekhov shows us no mysteries, only the great mystery of life itself, and he mirrors every mood and passion of mankind in a crystal-clear vocabulary. His ineffable toleration is of the kind which passes understanding."

Reviewing a New York production of *The Three Sisters* in 1939, Grenville Vernon pointed out the difficulty of presenting the play properly. Chekhov's impressionism led him to introduce seeming irrelevancies into the action. "What is hinted at is often what is important. It is the color, the diapasonic undertow which is the secret of Chekhov's genius." Each line, each bit of business, must be fitted into the artful mosaic. Coarseness in acting or directing can easily disrupt this fragile art object.

Valency (1966) called *The Three Sisters* "the flower of impressionism in drama," a high point in the drama of character. The play's polyphonic structure captures poignantly the inner lives of the characters. Valency declared that no other play "has ever conveyed more subtly the sense of the transitory nature of human life, the sadness and beauty of the passing moment." Valency detected the influence of Maurice Maeterlinck in such matters as the atmosphere, lyricism, symbolism, and in the representation of everyday life. Valency found Chekhov to be more than an impressionist: "To understand him, it is important to add to the sense of episode, the sense of process, and after that, the all-enveloping doubt."

Joyce Carol Oates in 1971 said that Chekhov went beyond even the absurdists in drama, by discarding the climax. He gives us a birthday party that is elegiac rather than happy in tone. Instead of action, we get talk. The non sequiturs of disconnected dialogue provide additional absurdity. The meaningless plots in his plays are ignored, since they are not the subjects of the plays. In both Chekhov and Samuel Beckett, Oates says, "the less tangible the means of salvation, the greater the urgency for it." William Babula in 1975 adroitly observed that the continual reference to timepieces in this play gives one the impression that time really is in charge of the lives of the characters.

Stowell (1980) agreed with Oates that Chekhov laid the foundation for absurdist drama. In *The Three Sisters* Chekhov experimented with different senses of time. The characters have both clock time and their individual perceptions of subjective time. The audience is made aware of this distinction. The characters' moods are often determined by their senses of time. The interaction of these moods constitutes the play's structure. The proper effect requires an ensemble performance on the part of everyone—actor, director, stage designer, and audience. Chekhov's daring juxtapositions of comedy/tragedy, hero/villain, and action/stasis put a strain on the audience, but if they participate, they receive an impressionistic gestalt or effect that no other playwright gives.

Normand Berlin in 1981 agreed that Beckett is Chekhov's heir, and that his *Waiting for Godot* resembles the sisters' "waiting for Moscow." As in Beckett, the deterministic theme of death pervades *The Three Sisters*. Chekhov mingles the surface and the substructure, seeing both in the light of an ironic perspective. Since a balance of comedy and tragedy might confuse the audience, he tips the balance clearly in the direction of tragedy.

Eugene Bristow, in Barricelli (1981), discovered many triads used in this play. There are three sets, character groupings of three, love triangles, and even linguistic triads of subjects, verbs, and adverbial modifiers. Tusenbach's farewell to Irina has numerous triads forming a contrapuntal elaboration on the theme of unrequited love. Master (1982) notes that the characters react more than act: "Reactive sequences can encompass many activities—confessing, recollecting, complaining, speechifying."

Peace (1983) found many elements of classical drama in *The Three Sisters*. There is unity of place, a chorus, classical restraint, violent action offstage, and a sense of fate haunting the sisters. There is also the evoked presence of the dead and absent: Mrs. Prozorov, Mrs. Vershinin, Kulygin's headmaster, and Protopopov.

The MAT production of *The Cherry Orchard* in New York in 1924, even though acted in Russian, evoked great praise. Edmund Wilson confessed to experiencing a thrill seldom found in the theater: "the beauty and poignancy of an atmosphere, an idea, a person, are put before us with the highest art." The ineptitude of the charming but fading Russian gentry Wilson found "touched with the tragedy of all human failure." Stark Young found realism carried "to honest and spiritual depth and candor." Only in Shakespeare had Young seen such "tragic excitement, pathetic beauty, and baffling logic of emotion" as he found here. For Young, Chekhov somehow fused ordinary events "into a revelation of the very soul of that moment. As is true of Shakespeare's plays, the whole of *The Cherry Orchard* remains suspended in one's experience, an infectious mystery of human living."

John Mason Brown explained Chekhov's timelessness, as he reviewed a New York production of *The Cherry Orchard* in 1933. Knowing human nature well, Chekhov respected and loved his characters far too much to remove their complexities, contradictions, and absurdities. Actors are challenged, for the characters have "secrets they reveal only to those with the courage, intellect, gifts, and persistence to ferret them out." But actors never tire of the roles, for they continually find new elements of depth that have not previously been explored. Thus, "Chekhov has occupied a place in the contemporary theater that no other dramatist has filled."

In 1943 Francis Fergusson pointed out how Chekhov's dramatic technique resembled the fictional technique of Henry James. Both use little story but much theme. Both employ a sequence of social occasions, each of which throws light upon the central theme. In *The Cherry Orchard*, said Fergusson, "the completing of the total perspective of vision constitutes the play."

In 1949 Fergusson found that the play, "a theater-poem of the suffering of change," had a classical structure: Act I was the prologue, Act II the agon (or conflict), Act III the suffering and the reversal, and Act IV the epiphany. We know the world of *The Cherry Orchard,* he said. "We may recognize its main elements in a cocktail party in Connecticut or Westchester. Chekhov reduced dramatic art to its ancient root, from which new growths are possible."

Jean-Louis Barrault in 1961 noted the universality of the play's theme, since everyone is subject to time's corrosive influence. The play uses a musical structure, he said, with themes being stated, fading, and then returning. Full of action, the play has little plot. French actors, accustomed to enacting a plot, have trouble staging an action.

Robert W. Corrigan, in Goldstone (1965), provided a Jungian analysis of the characters of *The Cherry Orchard.* Chekhov, in his surrealism, showed that the mask (or persona) that people wear is not real, but just a posture. The mask helps provide esthetic distance, lest we identify too closely with the suffering characters, who are more concerned with context than with substance. Epikhodov (of all people) tells Varya, "I beg you to express yourself with delicacy."

Gilles explained the paradox of a play with little action being filled with suspense. Each action peak hits a new impediment, and one wonders what impediment will be next. Finally, as we come to identify with the actors, we earnestly desire impediments, because we know that action will only lead to the sale of the orchard. J.L. Styan in 1968 called Chekhov the first writer of "dark comedy," one who depicted the tragedy underlying everyday life. Beneath the surface gaiety lurks a profound *Weltschmerz*. In Act IV Styan found the structure of change and decay welded into a unity, made possible because by then "the sympathies of the audience are under careful restraint and control."

Styan (1971) spoke further on the structure of *The Cherry Orchard*. He called it "a plotless play with too many plots." In the play Chekhov uses "undercutting," the technique of reversing a feeling, muting a climax, or contradicting one statement by another. The end effect is to demonstrate that truth is relative. Here Chekhov employs comic ambivalence and assimilates some of the techniques of the symbolists in "his own gentle, anti-didactic symbolism." Like the Elizabethans, Chekhov used a double-stage set, providing an excellent vehicle for his contrapuntal technique of showing life's tragicomedy. Life's cycle is seen when the set in Act IV returns to the set of Act I.

Pitcher (1973) noted how in Act IV Chekhov unobtrusively dismantled the emotional network he had created. The characters leave in inverse order of their love of the estate (and thus Firs never leaves). By now, "Chekhov's technique of emotional shorthand is so highly developed that it is necessary for him to only touch the right emotional nerve in the audience very briefly to trigger a deep response." The sound of the breaking string completes the emotional distancing, giving a cosmic perspective on the pettiness of human affairs.

Hahn (1977) sees the play as the modern equivalent of a classical pastoral comedy. In this view the real protagonist is the cherry orchard, and the setting is the plot. Act II is pure pastoral: as Charlotta lists her sorrows, she imparts classical restraint to this portrait of cultural decay.

Nicholas Moravcevich, in Bristow (1977), said that Chekhov's great contribution to modern drama was impressionism. As examples of this technique in *The Cherry Orchard* he cites the outdoor sounds, the outdoor scenes even in interiors, and the centrifugal plot, in which characters are unconcerned about their fate. Impressionism helped Chekhov avoid didacticism: "Only the impressionistic technique could have provided his drama with that structural quality in which the microcosm of apparently haphazard detail could successfully suggest the macrocosm of the larger reality of life."

Stowell (1980) agrees with Moravcevich, giving as examples of impressionism Liubov's reverie about her lost childhood, and the many references to change in the play. Chekhov makes space suggest time, and time suggest space. He juxtaposes movement and stasis—the characters' world changes, but they remain static: "Lost in a directionless present, the characters search for the unreachable past and future."

Barricelli (1981) says that since Chekhov viewed life as paradoxical, he fittingly employed counterpoint to depict life's ambiguity. The breaking string is Atropos cutting life's final thread. The sound is more emphatic than a pistol shot, since it reaches even into the realms of the spirit. In folklore the sound unites the light and the dark of creation, and that is its meaning here, Barricelli believes.

In summary, many critics name Chekhov as the greatest playwright since Shakespeare. His one-act plays showed Chekhov's sense of humor and of satire, and indicated that he had insight into human beings and their problems. His mature drama has been controversial, because of his many innovations in dramatic technique. He by no means agreed with Aristotle's dictum that plot is the "soul" of drama. His centrifugal plots contain more action than traditional incident, handled with classical restraint and decorum. Since life was his esthetic norm, he continually mirrors life in its tragicomedy.

Chekhov's characters are his greatest achievement. Since he knew universal human nature, he creates living beings in a compassionate yet searching frame. As in life, there are few heroes or villains. His technique of characterization is subtle. One must guess, as in life, from a hummed tune or the color of a belt what interrelationships exist among the characters. Characters are often associated with a leitmotif; the play's structure is musical, using counterpoint based on the interweaving of the themes of the leitmotifs, as the characters clash, interrelate, or make love. These vivid personages live in the playgoer's imagination long after the performance is over.

Chekhov avoided blatant didacticism, so those seeking tendential drama need to look elsewhere. But he preaches his own subtle sermons, abhorring man's inhumanity to man, and asserting the dignity of the human personality. His many pictures of boredom strike one continuous chord: Time is a precious commodity, so do not waste it. Often his diffuse and reticent message is conveyed through symbolism. Recent critics find in him a forerunner of absurdist drama, for he found much absurdity in modern life. Other critics mention his impressionism, in which he blends a myriad of seemingly irrelevant details into a beautiful and meaningful whole, once the spectator achieves the proper esthetic distance. His catharsis is philosophical—when the spectators see the price paid for ubiquitous human pettiness, they are raised to the plane at which their own pettiness can be more easily handled or avoided.

Chekhov's outstanding contribution to dramatic language is his use of disconnected dialogue. Once he made this discovery, it is hard to realize that playwrights before him never really rendered the way people speak in life. The pauses, disconnections, and misunderstandings are typical of normal human speech, and give his plays humor, characterization, realism, irony, and many other dramatic qualities.

In the area of setting, Chekhov creates many memorable stage pictures and employs sound effects to reinforce emotions and moods. Sometimes his setting is so intense as to create an atmospheric effect, which is generally based upon group emotions. Chekhov observed that people behave differently in each group of which they are members. When his characters are accused of being inconsistent, the explanation may be found in the contrast between individual and group emotions.

If Chekhov is no Shakespeare, lacking the great poetry that puts the Elizabethan in a class by himself, he at least has been seen by many critics to have uncovered more distinctive dramatic devices than perhaps any other playwright in history. Actors, directors, dramatists, and audiences unfamiliar with his unique contributions to dramatic art cannot begin to fathom the untapped resources of the modern theater.

Critical Highlights: Chekhov as a Humanitarian

In a world tottering on the brink of nuclear destruction, Chekhov's humane values point a way out of a possible holocaust. Few Americans, for example, would cavil at the moral standards and ideals espoused in his stories and plays. His purity and high-mindedness stand as a cultural bridge across chasms of political suspicion, misunderstanding, and xenophobia. Wherever freedom, dignity, respect, and creativitiy are at home in human society, Chekhov's writings will be read and cherished.

The humor in Chekhov's early stories often consists of satire against bureaucracy and bullying. Critics noted that "Fat and Thin" (1883), for example, satirizes the nearly universal human trait of obsequiousness towards persons ranking above oneself in a power structure. "Sergeant Prishibeev" (1885) captured the officiousness of a tinhorn policeman who continually abuses people's rights in an unjust society.

As early as 1908 Kornei Chukovsky found Christian virtues at work in *The Three Sisters*, which "not only evokes sympathy for the downtrodden and suffering but makes them an image of beauty." Chukovsky stated that Chekhov's ability to find beauty in commonplace events brought his readers closer to God than do most religious tracts. Act IV of that play led Maurice Baring in 1910 to assert that Chekhov had "invincible trust in the coming day." Like many others, Baring quoted Olga's final words: "Happiness and peace will come on earth."

Persky (1913) found a cathartic element penetrating the gloom of "In the Ravine." Despite their suffering, Lipa and her mother give alms to the poor, retaining their dignity through faith in God. The calm night reminds them that "justice will be beautiful on God's earth." In 1915 Henry Seidel Canby found Chekhov portraying universal human nature in "Easter Eve," a story in which the monk Nikolai is a model of ideal conduct, creativity, and religious devotion.

Robert Lynd in 1916 noted Chekhov's attack upon egotism in "The House with the Mezzanine," stating that he knew of "no other writer who leaves one with the same vision of the human race as the lost sheep of the house of Israel." In 1920 Maxim Gorky remarked, "How abominable is the well-fed squire's mockery of a person who is lonely and strange" in "A Daughter of Albion." "In each of his humorous stories," said Gorky, "I hear the hopeless sigh of sympathy for men who do not know how to respect human dignity."

Many critics found Chekhov's characters to be grounded in universal human nature, as if he were writing for each locality on the globe. Conrad Aiken, for instance, in 1921 said that "Chekhov's sympathy, pity, and tenderness were inexhaustible. He lived, and thus permitted us to live, everywhere." Edward Garnett (1921) identified in "The Bishop" "an element of tenderness and sweetness of understanding that forms the spiritual background, and which dominates invisibly the coarse web of human struggle and the petty network of human egoism." Gerhardi (1923) believed that simple Olga in "The Darling" is so rich in kindness and love that she could be the beginning of a cultural tradition which, through the centuries, would develop in mankind the spirit we call God.

Commenting on Chekhov's letters, J. Middleton Murry in 1923 said that they revealed a new attitude, a simplicity that would undercut "all the complexities with which the modern consciousness is laden." Chekhov's intuitive perception placed him far ahead of James Joyce and Marcel Proust—by his side they are "curious antiquarian survivals of a superseded past."

Koteliansky (1925) revealed how Chekhov defended his trip to Sakhalin. He wrote to Suvorin that "the glorified sixties did nothing for the sick and the prisoners, and thus violated the chief commandment of Christian civilization." When his friend Jean Shcheglov asked him about his "morality," Chekhov replied that there was "only one morality, that which in olden times gave us Jesus Christ, and now prevents us from stealing, insulting, and lying."

M. Robinson in 1927 called Chekhov a prophet. She explained why he used "weak" people like Olga of "The Darling" as heroines. They demonstrated "courage the greater because it is hopeless, selflessness the purest because it is unconscious." One then realizes that in this kind of character alone "is success possible, because it alone is worthy of humanity on its divine side."

In the famous Jed Harris production of *Uncle Vanya* in 1930 Robert Littell discovered, beneath the strange names and fleeting moods of these Russian people, "something so human and true as to pass all boundaries, leap over prejudices, and recognize that as an artist and a creator of human characters, Chekhov is the first of all modern dramatists." Jed Harris modestly attributed the success of his production to the fact that the characters in the play reveal fundamental aspects of universal human nature.

Discussing "The House with the Mezzanine" in 1932, George Z. Patrick felt that the artist was Chekhov's mouthpiece when he said that "the highest vocation of man is spiritual activity. When science and art are real, they seek for eternal truth, for God, for the soul." At a London production of *Uncle Vanya* in 1937, Henry Adler said that "these people are as typical of Reading as of Russia," and Derek Verschoyle added that "one could transfer the setting almost without change to anywhere in County Cork or Galway."

An outstanding production of *The Cherry Orchard* in New York in 1944 led to a remarkable epistolary exchange. Actress-director Margaret Webster, in "an open letter to Chekhov," said that the play continued to be popular "because there has been no play since it was written in which man's faith in man is so ringingly pro-claimed." She predicted that it would hold audiences until that future day when modern hopes become realized. Olga Knipper-Chekhov replied that Chekhov's plays expressed confidence "in the better future which will dawn for mankind no matter what sufferings some generations have to endure on their way to happiness for all." She looked forward to seeing her husband's plays serve as a bridge of cultural understanding among all of the democratic countries of the world. Thus did two great ladies of the theater achieve an instant camaraderie, built upon Chekhov's drama, which powerful politicians and statesmen were stumbling in a vain effort to construct.

Hingley (1950) admired Chekhov's art in "Ward No. 6" in having the positive goals of a healthy society described by an alleged lunatic in a sick society. Gromov is incarcerated for saying such things as that people should find something more productive to do than play cards out of boredom; that the town needs better schools, an honest newspaper policy, and a public lecture series; that crooks are well fed while honest men have crumbs; and that violence tramples justice. Magarshack (*Life*, 1952) heard the voice of Chekhov speaking through Ivan in "Gooseberries," saying that someone should "knock on the door of the conscience of mankind," reminding smug and selfish people that there are poor persons in need of help.

Reviewing a New York production of *The Sea Gull* in 1954, Brooks Atkinson found Chekhov to be "the writer with the most profound insight. He is for all times and all places because he goes to the roots of life." In "The Student" Gunnar Jacob-son in 1960 saw the protagonist as voicing Chekhov's own beliefs, that one can eradicate pessimism through religious faith, and that perceiving the permanence of truth and beauty can give human life meaning and significance.

Simmons (1962) noted that Chekhov's letters to Suvorin from 1897 to 1899, dealing with student unrest and the Dreyfus affair, are fervent statements defending freedom of conscience and freedom of the press, and attacking anti–Semitism. Sim-mons quotes what Chekhov wrote upon his return from Sakhalin: "God's world is good. It is only we who are bad. We must work, and we must be just, and all the rest will come as a matter of course."

Howard Taubman, reviewing *The Sea Gull* in 1962, said that the cast, in modern dress, "looks like a troubled house party of middle-class Americans. By an obstinate paradox, the more Russian Chekhov's characters remain, the more readily other people can see themselves mirrored in them."

In his analysis of "The Betrothed," Payne (1963) stated that although Chekhov loathed the thought of a Russian revolution, this arch-conservative was in a way a most subversive writer, for "his stories are hosannas in praise of freedom, of the wanderings of the human heart in search of its own peace. And so, with the in-sidious power of genius, he prepares us for the revolution of the future." In 1966 Joseph L. Conrad found "The Man in a Case" expressing two of Chekhov's favorite themes: concern for personal freedom, and concern for moral responsibility.

Valency (1966) saw a universal theme in *The Cherry Orchard*—those who cannot adapt to change are lost. The sound of the breaking string captured modern man's tragic alienations: The chord connecting man with man and man with God has been snapped. The mournful overtone of the string reminds contemporary mankind of its eternal loneliness, until the alienation is overcome. Winner (1966) recalls Ivan in "Gooseberries" stating that rural withdrawal is selfish monasticism—a person should identify not with his own patch of land but with the whole earth.

Chudakov (1971), recounting the plot of "The Head Gardener's Story," describes the reaction when the judge frees the murderer of the exemplary Swedish doctor, saying, "It is impossible to imagine that any human could sink so low." The gardener's grandmother applauded the decision, stating that for such faith in humanity, God would forgive the town's sins: "He rejoices when we believe we are in His image, and grieves when we forget human dignity." Laffitte (1971) praised the lyricism of "The Betrothed," especially when Chekhov spoke of "a mysterious, beautiful, rich and holy life, beyond weak sinful man's understanding, burgeoning under the vault of the sky."

Styan (1971) identifies "the real enemy" in *The Three Sisters* as "a self-induced delusion about life." Chekhov was not so naïve, in Styan's opinion, as to think that any new society would not have supersensitive people, rejected lovers, or broken marriages. Chekhov showed the sisters "searching for answers they will never have because they are asking the wrong questions."

Pitcher (1973), speaking of *Uncle Vanya*, said that "Chekhov, like Telegin, harbored a stubborn underlying belief that men could ultimately live in peace and harmony." In his discussion of *The Three Sisters*, Pitcher noted that today's world has the same problems as those faced by the Prozorovs. "The main difference between our world and Chekhov's," he said, "is that these problems have acquired a far more agonizing relevance today." He found catharsis in the final scene of *The Cherry Orchard*. "Individual human lives may end," he declared, "but the emotional interrelatedness of human beings remains constant."

On this he would find agreement from M.H. Shotton, in Fennell (1973). "The Lady with a Dog" illustrates how man finds relevance in nature, Shotton said: "Man is mortal, mankind immortal. The life of the individual has meaning only when he sees his mortal span as one link in an unending chain." Chekhov's drama helps us understand ourselves, Shotton said while analyzing *The Cherry Orchard*. Chekhov's unusual blend of "ironic skepticism and dogged idealism" made him especially relevant in a world needing both qualities, Shotton felt.

Introducing his translation of Chekhov's letters, Yarmolinsky (1973) summarized Chekhov's personal traits. He had irrepressible humor, strong family feeling, and a great gusto for life, said Yarmolinsky. Although an agnostic, he seldom closed a letter without asking a heavenly blessing upon the addressee. Inwardly Chekhov was a free man, and "his honesty was equal to his humanity," in Yarmolinsky's opinion.

Rayfield (1975) said that "The Steppe" disclosed an immense world in which all people fit into a hierarchy, and thus the world of people is as unified as is the natural world. Treplev's playlet in *The Sea Gull* revealed Chekhov's lyrical and mystical feeling for nature, Rayfield believed. The playlet was a serious attempt to find new forms of art. Here Chekhov may have been influenced by Russian symbolists, "for the neo–Platonic idea of all creation reverting to the spiritual state of the World Soul and then fighting the spirit of evil is one of the main themes of Russian symbolism."

In "Ward No. 6" Elena Chervinskene in 1976 found universal values that could be used as a standard for humanity, "a civilized and humane attitude which reveals itself in respect for others, sensitivity, intelligence, talent, a capacity for work, and a love of beauty."

Robert Brustein, in Bristow (1977), found a spirit of revolt in *The Three Sisters*. Although at times he seems to have a gloomy outlook, Brustein said, "Chekhov possesses a deeper humanity than any other modern dramatist. No one has been able to write of him without the most profound love. Coupling sweetness of temper with toughness of mind, Chekhov makes his work an extraordinary compound of morality and reality, rebellion and acceptance, irony and sympathy. There are more powerful modern playwrights, but none more warm and generous, and none who brings the drama to a higher realization of its human role."

Describing the characters in *The Three Sisters*, Thomas R. Whitaker in 1977 quoted the philosopher Josiah Royce, who said that most human problems grow out of people's neglect of their relationship to God and to other people. Hingley (1978) said that "The Student" seemed to be a fictional sermon by a fervent Christian, although Chekhov actually was an agnostic. "Still, to reject the dogmas of the various Christian denominations is not necessarily to be wholly unsympathetic to the spirit of Christianity. No believer, Chekhov nevertheless respected religious faith in others, provided they were not given to excessive proselytizing." Chekhov considered this to be his best story, and cited it as an example of his optimism. It does an effective job, says Hingley, of depicting the essential unity of all peoples in all ages.

Simon Karlinsky, in Barricelli (1981), credits Chekhov with having an early understanding of ecology, in creating the shepherd Luka in "Panpipes." Luka crusades against deforestation, which leads to declining water levels in rivers and corresponding decline in biota. Along with nature's spoilation comes the degeneration of the people inhabiting the land, Luka feels. Kirk (1981) notes Chekhov's ability in *The Cherry Orchard* to show the comic side of what seem to be tragic events. "Only a great artist could succeed in portraying the comic aspects of metaphysical questions which have been plaguing man for centuries," Kirk said.

Kovitz, in Barricelli (1981), finds a philosophic depth in *The Three Sisters*. By constantly forcing the spectators to question the characters' moral and spiritual integrity, Chekhov thrusts them into what Kierkegaard called "the cleansing baptism of irony," which enables persons to retain their balance while facing life's frustrations. Kovitz adds that when Trofimov in *The Cherry Orchard* says that "all Russia is our garden," Simone Weil would agree, for she believed that "we all have to be catholic, that is, not bound to any created things, unless it be to creation in its totality."

Valency, in Barricelli (1981), says that in "On Official Business" it may have been the symbolist influence on Chekhov that led him to describe Lyzhin's sudden flash of insight: "Everything is filled with a universal idea, everything has one soul, one aim." Perhaps Hegel was the source of Chekhov's periodic intuition of a world soul. "It was a concept that sorted badly with his generally skeptical and scientific materialism," said Valency, "but it served to rationalize the idealistic strain that was at the core of his feeling of kinship with humanity, and the real concern for the suffering of others that eventually sent him to Sakhalin."

Barbara Heldt in 1982 said that each page of Chekhov's letters disclosed some aspect of Chekhov's "searching, compassionate genius," such as his practicality, his spiritual insight, or his utter truthfulness. Bitsilli (1983) observed how Vasiliev in "A Nervous Breakdown" finds his sympathy for prostitutes as exploited persons expanding until he empathizes with all victims of exploitation. In the symbolic ending, says Bitsilli, Vasiliev's breakdown is brought on by his realization of the enormity and the insurmountability of evil.

Reviewing *Uncle Vanya* in 1983, Benedict Nightingale stated that Chekhov realistically showed women as the product of what men wanted them to be, but incorporated a veiled protest into his fabric. For "the one badge he might have worn with pride," Nightingale observed, "was that of feminism—not of course the hard, narrow variety, but the sort that seeks to release and expand." Peace (1983) notes that in that play Elena voices Chekhov's own view that what destroys the world is not cataclysmic events but petty everyday hatred on the part of all of us. Discussing *The Cherry Orchard*, Peace states that Chekhov, though very Russian, creates plays for a world audience, "to whom they speak of problems, relationships, and values which are eternal, and thus his appeal is universal."

McConkey (1984) felt that "Gusev," more than any other Chekhov story, reveals Chekhov's spiritual essence, "the degree of his insight into the goal of that desire for freedom which for him underlies all of our values." Analyzing *Sakhalin Island*, McConkey noted that the final four chapters embody Chekhov's values as applied to the penal colony. The first of these chapters demonstrates that even the free population were all caught up in a web of human indignity. Next, exploring the morality of both convicts and settlers, Chekhov finds them in a state of spiritual paralysis. He then notices how they all thirst so deeply for freedom that everyone tries to escape from that environment. Finally, Chekhov gives specific recommendations for prison reform, such as eliminating beating and solitary confinement, providing education for the children, and raising the standard of dignity for everyone involved, but especially for the women.

Ralph Lindheim, in Clyman (1985), finds great catharsis in "Gusev." He says that the cause of Pavel will always speak out against exploitation of the weak by the strong, the cause of Gusev will always stand for strong family values, and the will and spirit of both men will not be broken. The final beautiful sunset scene symbolizes to Lindheim the need for persons to forever dedicate themselves to work for the coming of a more just society.

Senelick (1985) recalled that in *The Wood Demon* Chekhov postulated Tolstoy's doctrine of universal love as the solution to mankind's problems. Although Chekhov's dramatic technique advanced far beyond this play, Senelick believed that he retained its ideology throughout his life: honesty in human relations will cure far more social ills than will any doctrinaire political or economic reform program.

Summarizing the values of this gentle Russian physician gifted with enormous literary talent, one can postulate the kind of world he sought. First of all, what would be absent in Chekhovia?

Selfishness and egotism would be banned, not by fiat, but by the evolution of good taste. There would be no officious bureaucracy, since officials would care for individuals and respect their human dignity. There could be no bullying of the weak by the strong, and no exploitation of one person by another. This would automatically eliminate such things as prostitution, anti–Semitism, and male and female chauvinism. Above all, violence would be unthinkable, out of respect for the human body and human personality. War, or organized violence of any kind, would be the "Satan" in this scale of values.

Unlike most of us, Chekhov practiced what he preached. His personal traits, admired by many critics, were also noted in many of his protagonists. His more positive characters are tender and compassionate, and act out of naturalness and simplicity. Sometimes they reflect Chekhov's own strong set of family values. He had a sense of humor and a gusto for living that made him a fun-loving companion. His courage in the face of a terminal illness was heroic, and his strength of character in standing up for the principles he believed in was remarked upon by many critics.

Chekhov was more than a good citizen—he was an exemplary one. Wherever he lived there were good schools, clinics, libraries, roads, bridges, and an effective court system. Famine and epidemics found an implacable foe in this man. He strove constantly for good universities, humane prisons, and honest politicians. He crusaded on behalf of freedom of conscience and a free but responsible press. Like Johnny Appleseed, he planted trees wherever he went, for he wanted all of Russia to resemble a garden. He was an early ecologist, warning of the price paid for the rape of our ecosystem. Above all, he insisted upon the individual's moral responsibility for his conduct, which would automatically take care of many of these concerns.

Paradoxically, this non-churchgoer has many tender religious stories. He knew that faith in God strengthens people, and that most human problems grow out of alienation, the separation of the person from God and of the person from other persons. He recognized Christ's moral code as the only viable one, and he adhered to it with a remarkable consistency. Like Old Testament prophets, he asked what good religious ritual is when people show no sympathy for the downtrodden and the suffering. His pilgrimage to Sakhalin was his expiation of the debt that Russia owed suffering mankind for a penal system that violated standards of common human decency. He revered the spiritual search for God as mankind's highest aspiration.

Critics constantly referred to his characters as being grounded in universal human nature, thus recognizing that all human beings have certain fundamental similarities. Chekhov believed in the family of mankind, the oneness of the human race, the global village. He saw an unbroken chain linking all generations of mankind. Undergirding this world community was a neo–Platonic World Soul (or God), which would one day extinguish the effects of sin and evil in the world and usher in a society guided by peace, intelligence, and love.

The highest values in the world hastily sketched by Vershinin and Trofimov would be freedom of every conceivable sort, but unified with a responsible use of that freedom. There would be respect for every single human being, for the fact that we are made in God's image gives us not only human dignity but also a spark of the divine soul.

Other qualities prominent in Chekhovia will be beauty, creativity, happiness, intelligence, justice, peace, and hard work—all values espoused in Chekhov's stories and plays. It seems incredible that early critics, unaccustomed to his novel literary style, accused him of being amoral, indifferent, and lacking in humanity. All three manifestations of love—eros, philia, and agape—characterize human interrelationships in Chekhovia, with Christ-like agape providing the fundamental underlying tone of the society.

Above all, what would characterize Chekhovia would be the quality of faith—faith in a better future, faith in improved men and women, and faith in a more clearly discerned God. As a physician, Chekhov accepted a philosophy of change, and thus he saw life as a flux. In this view it is the striving towards these goals, rather than their achievement, that constitutes mankind's highest challenge and richest goal.

Persons interested in actualizing Chekhovia can do two things: Return to his stories and plays for continual insight, pleasure, and inspiration, and adopt Chekhov's own sturdy code of inner honesty—honesty towards oneself, honesty towards other people, and honesty towards God.

References

1. Chekhov in World Literature

1 Constance Garnett, tr., *Letters of Anton Chekhov to His Family and Friends* (Macmillan, 1920), p. 127.
2 Quoted in Ann Dunnigan, tr., *Anton Chekhov: Selected Stories* (Signet, 1960), p. vii. Hereinafter Leo Tolstoy will be called Tolstoy.
3 Vladimir Nabokov, *Lectures on Russian Literature* (Harcourt Brace Jovanovich, 1981), pp. 254–5.
4 Marc Slonim, *Modern Russian Literature from Chekhov to the Present* (Oxford Univ Pr, 1953), p. 61.
5 Ibid., p. 77.
6 Clarence Gohdes, *South Atlantic Quarterly* (April 1944) 43:209.
7 James T. Farrell, *The League of Frightened Philistines* (Vanguard, 1942), pp. 61, 71, 80–1.
8 George Calderon, tr., *Two Plays by Tchekhof* (Grant Richards, 1912), intro., pp. 7–22.
9 Stark Young, *North American Review* (March 1923) 217:351.
10 Daniel Gilles, *Chekhov: Observer Without Illusion* (Funk & Wagnalls, 1967), p. 350.
11 Henry Urbanski, *Chekhov As Viewed by His Russian Literary Contemporaries* (Ph.D. dissertation, New York Univ, 1973), pp. 25–6.
12 Ibid., p. 35.
13 Ibid., pp. 46–7.
14 Dates following a person's name indicate that this entry is found in the bibliography.
15 Urbanski, p. 52.
16 Ibid., p. 84.
17 Ibid., pp. 53, 112.
18 Ibid., pp. 87, 93.
19 Slonim, pp. 60, 78.
20 E.J. Dillon, *Review of Reviews* (July 1891) 4: 79–83.
21 R.E.C. Long, *Fortnightly Review* (1 July 1902) n.s. 62:103–18.
22 Arnold Bennett, *New Age* (8 June 1911) n.s. 9:132.
23 E.M. Forster, *New Statesman* (24 July 1915) 5:373–4.
24 Robert Lynd, *New Statesman* (18 Nov 1916) 8:159–60.
25 J. Middleton Murry, *Times Literary Supplement*, (6 Dec 1923), p. 841b.
26 Abraham Cahan, *Forum* (Sep 1899) 28:119–28.
27 Christian Brinton, *Critic* (Oct 1904) 45:318–20.
28 Leo Wiener, *Anthology of Russian Literature* (Putnam, 1903), vol. 2, pp. 459–60.
29 Moissaye Olgin, *Bookman* (New York) (Nov 1918) 48:356–64.
30 *Current Literature* (April 1906) 40:407–8.

31 Gertrude Besse King, *New Republic* (8 July 1916) 7:256–8.
32 Robert W. Corrigan & James L. Rosenberg, eds., *The Context and Craft of Drama* (Chandler, 1964), p. 153.
33 *New York Times Book Review*, 28 Dec 1986, p. 12.
34 Kenneth A. Lantz, *Anton Chekhov: A Reference Guide to Literature* (Hall, 1985), pp. 165, 199. Unless otherwise specified, "Lantz" refers to this work.
35 *Soviet Literature*, no. 1 (1980), p. 92.
36 Ibid., p. 99.
37 Many of the above references can be found in Charles W. Meister, *Chekhov Bibliography* (McFarland, 1985), passim.

Chapter 2. Stories: 1880–1883

1 Robert Louis Jackson, *Slavica Hierosolymitana* (1978) 4:70–8; ibid., *Revue de Littérature Comparée* (1981) 45:331–41.
2 Beverly Hahn, *Chekhov: A Study of the Major Stories and Plays* (Cambridge Univ Pr, 1977), p. 43.
3 Harvey Pitcher, in Toby W. Clyman, *A Chekhov Companion* (Greenwood Pr, 1985), p. 94. Unless otherwise specified, "Clyman" refers to this work.
4 Ronald Hingley, *A New Life of Anton Chekhov* (Oxford Univ Pr, 1976), p. 45.
5 H. Peter Stowell, *Literary Impressionism, James and Chekhov* (Univ of Georgia Pr, 1980), p. 69.
6 Robert Payne, tr., *The Image of Chekhov* (Knopf, 1963), p. xxii.
7 Irina Kirk, *Anton Chekhov* (Hall, 1981), pp. 33–4.
8 Clyman, pp. 55, 240.
9 A.P. Chudakov, *Chekhov's Poetics* (Ardis, 1983), p. 16. Orig. ed. 1971.

Chapter 3. Stories: 1884–1885

1 Walter H. Bruford, *Anton Chekhov* (Bowes & Bowes, 1957), p. 17.
2 Donald Rayfield, *Chekhov: The Evolution of His Art* (Elek Books, 1975), p. 42.
3 Clyman, p. 97.
4 Stowell, pp. 74–5.
5 Dorothy Brewster & Angus Burrell, *Dead Reckonings in Fiction* (Longmans, Green, 1924), p. 62.
6 *Current Literature* (Jan 1907) 42:112.
7 Thomas G. Winner, *Chekhov and His Prose* (Holt, Rinehart & Winston, 1966), p. 15.
8 Rayfield, p. 47.

Chapter 4. Stories: 1886

1 Sophie Laffitte, *Chekhov: 1860–1904* (Scribner, 1973), p. 83.
2 Forster, pp. 373–4.
3 Hahn, p. 217.
4 Renato Poggioli, *The Phoenix and the Spider* (Harvard Univ Pr, 1957), pp. 122–4.
5 Alan Lelchuk, *Studies in Short Fiction* (1968) 6:609–18.
6 Clyman, p. 151.
7 *Athenaeum* (13 Feb 1904), p. 205.
8 Ronald Hingley, *The Oxford Chekhov* (Oxford Univ Pr, 1978), vol. 7, p. 8.
9 Clyman, p. 128.

10 *Letters of James Gibbons Huneker* (Scribner, 1922), p. 49.
11 *New York Times Book Review,* 27 June 1920, p. 22.
12 Alexander Werth, *Slavonic Review* (March 1925) 3:633–4.
13 Serge Persky, *Contemporary Russian Novelists* (Books for Libraries Pr, 1968), p. 50. Orig. ed. 1913.
14 Henry Seidel Canby, *Atlantic Monthly* (July 1915) 116:60–8.
15 Francis Hackett, *New Republic* (21 April 1920) 22:254–5.
16 H. Hamburger, *Russian Literature* (1972) 3:5–15.
17 S.P. Mais, *Why We Should Read—* (Dodd, Mead, 1921), p. 308.
18 Joan D. Winslow, *RE: Artes Liberales* (1978) no. 2, pp. 1–7.
19 Walter Allen, *The Short Story in English* (Clarendon Pr, 1981), p. 168.
20 Kirk, p. 41.
21 *Nation* (London) (27 Nov 1915) 18:334.
22 Hahn, pp. 212, 220–1.
23 Clyman, p. 126.
24 Sean O'Faolain, *Life and Letters Today* (Autumn 1937) 17:60–9.
25 Anne Friis, *Katherine Mansfield: Life and Stories* (Copenhagen: Einar Munksgard, 1946), pp. 32, 158.
26 Ernest J. Simmons, *Chekhov: A Biography* (Little, Brown, 1962), p. 117.
27 Long, pp. 115–7.
28 *Review of Reviews* (London) (Nov 1903) 28:515.
29 *Daily Telegraph* (London), 30 May 1911, p. 14.
30 Lantz, p. 236.
31 M.P. Willcocks, *English Review* (March 1922) 34:207–16.
32 F.M. Perry, *Story Writing: Lessons from the Masters* (Holt, 1926), p. 95.
33 Constance Garnett, pp. 45–6.
34 Paul Selver, *New Age* (4 Feb 1915) n.s. 16:376.

Chapter 5. Stories: 1887–1888

1 N. Bryllion Fagin, *Poet Lore* (Autumn 1921) 32:416–24.
2 Werth, p. 634.
3 Peter Quennell, *New Statesman* (14 May 1927) 29:152–3.
4 William Lyon Phelps, *Yale Review* (Oct 1917) n.s. 7:189–91.
5 Dillon, p. 82.
6 Urbanski, p. 41.
7 Edward Garnett, *Quarterly Review* (Oct 1921) 236:268. Unless otherwise specified, "Edward Garnett" refers to this source.
8 *Review of Reviews* (London) (Nov 1903) 28:515.
9 *Athenaeum,* 13 Feb 1904, p. 205.
10 Lionel Trilling, *The Experience of Literature* (Doubleday, 1967), p. 559.
11 Lantz, p. 158.
12 Ann Frydam, *Ulbandus Review* (Fall 1979) 2:103–19,
13 Leo Hulanicki & David Savignac, eds. & trs., *Anton Cexov as a Master of Story Writing* (The Hague: Mouton, 1976), pp. 180–4. Unless otherwise specified, "Hulanicki" refers to this source.
14 Felix Grendon, *New York Times Book Review,* 12 Jan 1913, p. 14.
15 Nathan Rosen, *Ulbandus Review* (1979) no. 1, pp. 175–85.
16 Constance Garnett, pp. 82–3, 102.
17 Lillian Hellman, ed., *The Selected Letters of Anton Chekhov* (Farrar & Straus, 1955), p. 54.

18 Robert Littell, *New Republic* (25 March 1925) 42:131–3.
19 M.H. Shotton, in John Fennell, ed., *Nineteenth-Century Russian Literature* (Univ of Calif Pr, 1973), pp. 315–6.
20 Chudakov, p. 180.
21 Victor Torres, in Clyman, p. 174.
22 Lantz, pp. 168–9.
23 Constance Garnett, pp. 100–01.
24 Avrahm Yarmolinsky, ed., *Letters of Anton Chekhov* (Viking, 1973), pp. 82–3.
25 *New York Times Book Review*, 23 Dec 1917, p. 570.
26 J. Middleton Murry, ed., *The Letters of Katherine Mansfield* (Knopf, 1936), p. 480.
27 Edward Garnett, pp. 257–69.
28 Werth, p. 637.
29 *Harper's Monthly Magazine* (Feb 1926), vol. 152, n.p.
30 Ronald Hingley, *The Oxford Chekhov* (Oxford Univ Pr, 1980), vol. 4, pp. 263–5.
31 Constance Garnett, p. 107.
32 David Magarshack, *Chekhov: A Life* (Faber, 1952), p. 165.
33 Simmons, p. 166.
34 *Nation* (London) (27 Nov 1915) 18:334.
35 Joseph L. Conrad, *Slavic & East European Journal* (1969) 13:429–43.
36 Sonia Gotman, ibid. (1972) 16:297–306.
37 Urbanski, pp. 41–2.
38 F.M. Perry, p. 95.
39 *Times Literary Supplement*, 19 Nov 1920, p. 756c.
40 Urbanski, p. 42.
41 *Cosmopolitan Magazine* (June 1906) 41:151–6.
42 Elisabeth Schneider, *Modern Language Notes* (June 1935) 50:394–7.
43 Joseph L. Conrad, *Slavic & East European Journal* (Spring 1972) 16:60.
44 H. Peter Stowell, *Russian Literature Triquarterly* (1975) 11:435–42.
45 Kornei Chukovsky, *Chekhov the Man* (Hutchinson, 1945), p. 35.
46 Winner, p. 47.
47 Peter Kropotkin, *Athenaeum*, 7 July 1888, p. 26.
48 Kazimierz Waliszewski, *A History of Russian Literature* (Appleton, 1900), pp. 427–8.
49 Long, p. 117.
50 Brinton, p. 319.
51 *Athenaeum*, 5 June 1915, p. 505.
52 Forster, p. 374.
53 J. Middleton Murry, *Athenaeum*, 22 Aug 1919, p. 777.
54 Mansfield, p. 215.
55 *Nation* (New York) (6 March 1920) 110:306.
56 Edward Garnett, p. 267.
57 Brewster & Burrell, pp. 64, 85, 99.
58 Werth, p. 639.
59 John Cournos, *Dial* (Sep 1928) 85:261–4.
60 D.E. Maxwell, *Slavic & East European Journal* (Summer 1973) 17:146–54.
61 Rufus W. Mathewson, Jr., *Ulbandus Review* (1977) no. 1, pp. 28–40.
62 Jerome H. Katsell, *Slavic & East European Journal* (Fall 1978) 22:313–23.
63 Evgeny Evtushenko, *Soviet Literature* (1979) no. 1, pp. 182–4.
64 Leonard Polakiewicz, *Russian Language Journal* (1979) 116:96–111.
65 Paul Debreczeny & Thomas Eekman, eds., *Chekhov's Art of Writing* (Slavica, 1977), p. 98. Unless otherwise specified, "Debreczeny" refers to this source.
66 *Nation* (New York) (10 July 1920) 111:48.

67 O'Faolain, pp. 60–9.
68 Joseph L. Conrad, *Slavic & East European Journal* (Winter 1970) 14:465–74.
69 *Nation* (New York) (19 July 1917) 105:70.

Chapter 6. Stories: 1889–1892

1 J. Rives Child, *South Atlantic Quarterly* (Oct 1941) 40:397–400.
2 Ibid.
3 *Nation* (London) (27 Nov 1915) 18:334.
4 Leslie O'Bell, *Slavic & East European Journal* (Winter 1981) 26:33–46.
5 Henri Troyat, *Chekhov* (Dutton, 1986), p. 109. Orig. French ed. 1984.
6 Ibid., p. 111.
7 Chudakov, pp. 142–3.
8 Paul Milyukov, *Athenaeum*, 5 July 1890, p. 26.
9 Dillon, p. 79.
10 Phillip A. Duncan, in Debreczeny, pp. 114–5.
11 Lantz, p. 10.
12 Gerald Gould, *New Statesman* (27 Nov 1915) 6:186.
13 *New York Times Book Review*, 3 Sep 1916, p. 342.
14 *Nation* (New York) (24 Aug 1918) 107:208.
15 Mais, pp. 309–11.
16 Lantz, p. 37.
17 *The Journals of Arnold Bennett, 1896–1928* (Viking, 1933), pp. 660–1.
18 Robert Louis Jackson, ed., *Chekhov: A Collection of Critical Essays* (Prentice-Hall, 1967), pp. 186, 193. Unless otherwise specified, "Jackson" refers to this source.
19 Ilya Ehrenburg, *Chekhov, Stendhal and Other Essays* (Macgibbon & Kee, 1962), pp. 39, 48–9.
20 Sankar Basu, *Chekhov and Tagore* (New Delhi: Sterling, 1985), p. 22.
21 Logan Speirs, *Oxford Review* (1968) no. 8, pp. 81–93.
22 Peter Hodgson, *Pacific Coast Philology* (1972) 7:36–42.
23 Paul Milyukov, *Athenaeum*, 2 July 1892, p. 26.
24 Lantz, p. 5.
25 *North American Review* (Jan 1917) 205:152–3.
26 *New York Times Book Review*, 29 April 1917, p. 171.
27 Edward Garnett, pp. 262–3.
28 J. Middleton Murry, *Discoveries* (Collins, 1924), pp. 91–2.
29 D.S. Mirsky, *A History of Russian Literature* (Knopf, 1949), p. 366. Orig. ed. 1927.
30 William Gerhardi, *Memoirs of a Polyglot* (Knopf, 1931), p. 288.
31 Lantz, p. 168.
32 Troyat, p. 150.
33 Don W. Kleine, *Philological Quarterly* (1963) 42:284–8.
34 Lantz, p. 185.
35 Roger Freling, *Studies in Short Fiction* (Summer 1979) 16:183–7.
36 S. Hoare, *Golden Hind* (Oct. 1923) 2:9–14.
37 Henry B. Fuller, *New Republic* (26 March 1924) 38:129–30.
38 Lantz, p. 151.
39 Ibid., pp. 189–90.
40 Lantz, *Studies in Short Fiction* (Winter 1978) 15:55–61.
41 Milton Ehre, *Ulbandus Review* (Fall 1979) 2:76–85.

42 G.K. Das & J. Beer, eds., *E.M. Forster: A Human Exploration* (New York Univ Pr, 1979), pp. 231–44.

43 J. Berg Esenwein, *Lippincott's Monthly Magazine* (Sep 1912) 90:363–78.

44 Mansfield, p. 355.

45 Edward Garnett, *Manchester Guardian*, 21 June 1927, p. 9.

46 *Athenaeum*, June 1918, p. 285.

47 William Mills Todd III, *Literature and Society in Imperial Russia, 1800–1914* (Stanford Univ Pr, 1978), p. 142.

48 L.S.K. LeFleming, *Slavonic & East European Review* (July 1970) 48:323–40.

49 Berenice C. Skidelsky, *Book News Monthly* (Nov 1917) 36:89.

50 Lantz, p. 189.

51 Albert Leong, *Journal of Russian Studies* (1974) 27:15–20.

52 Lantz, p. 209.

53 Gleb Struve, in Barbara Makanowitzky, ed., *Anton Chekhov: Seven Short Novels* (Norton, 1971), p. 107.

54 Paul Milyukov, *Athenaeum*, 1 July 1893, pp. 28–9.

55 *Literature* (6 Nov 1897) 1:87.

56 *Review of Reviews* (London) (Nov 1903) 28:515.

57 Bennett, *Journals*, p. 320.

58 Fagin, pp. 416–24.

59 *New York Times Book Review*, 14 Aug 1921, p. 24.

60 Bennett, *Journals*, p. 729.

61 Chudakov, p. 63.

62 Montgomery Belgion, *Criterion* (Oct 1936) 16:14–32.

63 Lantz, p. 76.

64 Ibid., p. 93.

65 Thomas G. Winner, *Slavic & East European Journal* (Winter 1959) 17:321–34.

66 Randall Jarrell, *Third Book of Criticism* (Farrar, Straus, & Giroux, 1969), pp. 267–75.

67 Lantz, pp. 186–7.

68 Angus Calder, *Russia Discovered* (Barnes & Noble, 1976), pp. 238–63.

69 Lantz, p. 198.

70 Damir Mirkovic, *Canadian Slavonic Papers* (March 1976) 18:66–72.

71 Lantz, pp. 229–30.

72 Andrew R. Durkin, *Slavic Review* (Spring 1981) 40:49–59.

Chapter 7. Stories: 1893–1897

1 Paul Milyukov, *Athenaeum*, 1 July 1893, p. 29.

2 Lantz, pp. 5–6.

3 Phelps, *Yale Review* (Oct 1917) n.s. 7:190.

4 Robert Lynd, *New Statesman* (18 Nov 1916) 8:159–60.

5 Lantz, p. 236.

6 Ibid., pp. 254–5.

7 Yarmolinsky, *Letters*, p. 241.

8 Zygmunt Rukalski, *Canadian Slavonic Papers* (Fall 1969) 11:346–58.

9 Toby W. Clyman, *Russian Language* (Spring 1974) 28:26–31.

10 Constance Garnett, p. 323.

11 Simmons, p. 314.

12 *Review of Reviews* (London) (Nov 1903) 28:515.

13 Leonard Woolf, *New Statesman* (11 Aug 1917) 9:447.

14 *Athenaeum*, Aug 1917, p. 416.
15 George Sampson, *Bookman* (London) (Oct 1917) 53:8–14.
16 Edward J. O'Brien, *Forum* (June 1928) 79:913.
17 George Z. Patrick, *Slavic & East European Review* (April 1932) 10:665.
18 Peter Rossbacher, *Slavic & East European Journal* (1969) 13:191–9.
19 Lantz, pp. 164, 177.
20 Ibid., p. 187.
21 Ibid., pp. 201, 208.
22 David Matual, *International Fiction Review* (Jan 1978) 5:46–51.
23 Lantz, pp. 245, 252.
24 Ibid., p. 262.
25 Maxim Gorky, *Reminiscences of Tolstoy, Chekhov, and Andreyev* (Viking, 1959), p. 82. Orig. ed. 1920.
26 Lantz, p. 186.
27 Ibid., p. 261.
28 Vladimir Ermilov, *Anton Pavlovich Chekhov, 1860–1904* (Moscow: Foreign Languages Publishing House, 1956), pp. 259, 263.
29 Lynd, p. 160.
30 Patrick, p. 662.
31 Lantz, p. 127.
32 Ibid., p. 178.
33 Ibid., p. 135.
34 Ibid., p. 165.
35 O'Faolain, p. 68.
36 Lantz, p. 212.
37 Constance Garnett, p. 377.
38 Constantine Balmont, *Athenaeum*, 2 July 1898, pp. 24–5.
39 *Nation* (New York) (10 July 1920) 111:48.
40 Hackett, pp. 254–5.
41 Conrad Aiken, *Freeman* (6 April 1921) 3:91.
42 Mirsky, p. 298.
43 V.S. Pritchett, *New Statesman and Nation* (27 March 1943) 25:209.
44 Orlo Williams, *National Review* (June 1943) 120:504.
45 Lantz, pp. 190–2.
46 L.A. de Bogdanovich, *Athenaeum*, 3 July 1897, pp. 27–8.
47 *Literature* (6 Nov 1897) 1:87.
48 *Athenaeum*, 20 Feb 1909, p. 224.
49 *Spectator* (2 Jan 1915) 114:10.
50 *Nation* (New York) (16 Nov 1918) 107:589.
51 J. Middleton Murry, *Adelphi* (Oct 1937) 14:19–23.
52 John W. Harrison, *Modern Fiction Studies* (Winter 1961) 7:371–2.
53 Todd, p. 142.
54 L.M. O'Toole, *Structure, Style, and Interpretation in the Russian Short Story* (Yale Univ Pr, 1982), pp. 203–20.
55 Hackett, pp. 254–5.
56 Robert Louis Jackson, *Slavica Hierosolymitana* (1978) 3:55–67.
57 *Review of Reviews* (London) (July 1902) 26:64.
58 Lantz, pp. 57, 77, 106.
59 Ibid., p. 130.
60 L.M. O'Toole, *Slavonic & East European Review* (Jan 1971) 49:45–67.
61 John Glad, *Canadian Slavonic Papers* (1974) 16:99–103.

62 David Martin, *Canadian-American Slavonic Studies* (1978) 12:266–73.
63 Jefferson Hunter, *Hudson Review* (Spring 1980) 33:39–57.
64 Struve, pp. 196–7.
65 Troyat, p. 176.
66 Chudakov, p. 174.
67 Paul Milyukov, *Athenaeum*, 7 July 1894, p. 23.
68 Farrell, p. 81.
69 Lantz, pp. 256–7.

Chapter 8. Stories: 1898–1904

1 *Nation* (London) (25 May 1918) 23:193.
2 Richard Wear, *Revue Belge de Philologie et d'Histoire* (1977) 55:897–906.
3 L. Lieber, *Studia Slavica Academiae Scientiarum Hungaricae* (1982) 28:199–312.
4 Maria P. Chekhov, *The Chekhov Museum in Yalta* (Moscow: Foreign Languages Publishing House, 1958), p. 28.
5 Valery Bryusov, *Athenaeum*, 3 Sep 1904, pp. 312–4.
6 Chudakov, p. 97.
7 Lantz, pp. 106, 118.
8 Thomas G. Winner, *Indiana Slavic Studies* (1963) 3:163–72.
9 Toby W. Clyman, *Russian Language Journal* (Spring 1974) 28:26–31.
10 David Maxwell, *Russian Literature* (1974) no. 6, pp. 91–100.
11 Lantz, p. 209.
12 Yarmolinsky, *Letters*, p. 417.
13 *New York Times Book Review*, 26 Dec 1915, p. 527.
14 *Nation* (New York) (6 March 1920) 110:306.
15 Edward Garnett, p. 267.
16 W. Somerset Maugham, *East and West* (Garden City Publ. Co., 1934), pp. x–xiv.
17 Lantz, p. 201.
18 H. Peter Stowell, *Studies in Short Fiction* (Spring 1975) 12:117–26. Also, Bonamy Dobrée, *Nation & Athenaeum* (13 March 1926) 38:814.
19 Lantz, p. 201.
20 *Times Literary Supplement*, 9 Nov 1916, p. 537a.
21 Robert Lynd, *New Statesman*, 18 Nov 1916, pp. 159–60.
22 Mansfield, p. 480.
23 M. Robinson, *Adelphi* (May 1927) 4:683–7.
24 N. Elizabeth Monroe, *The Novel and Society* (Univ of No Car Pr, 1941), pp. 198–9.
25 Zygmunt Rukalski, *Canadian Slavonic Papers* (Fall 1969) 11:357.
26 Michael A. Sperber, *Psychological Review* (1971) 58:14–21.
27 Padmaharsha Kuranage, *Soviet Literature* (1980), no. 2, pp. 146–9.
28 Lantz, p. 238.
29 Barbara Heldt, *Ulbandus Review* (1982), no. 2, pp. 166–74.
30 Patrick, pp. 665–6.
31 Mark Schorer, *The Story: A Critical Anthology* (Prentice-Hall, 1950), pp. 61–5.
32 Lantz, p. 128.
33 Ibid., p. 176.
34 Ann E. Berthoff, *Sewanee Review* (Winter 1981) 89:57–82.
35 Lantz, pp. 254, 257.
36 Gilles, pp. 347, 380.
37 Lantz, pp. 8, 19.
38 *Nation* (New York) (16 July 1914) 99:75.

39 *Spectator* (2 Jan 1915) 114:10.
40 Aiken, p. 92.
41 Harrison, pp. 369–72.
42 Hugh McLean, in *American Contributions to the 6th International Congress of Slavists* (The Hague: Mouton, 1968), pp. 285–305.
43 Paul Debreczeny, in ibid., *8th Congress* (Columbus, OH: Slavica Pr, 1978), pp. 125–45.
44 Lantz, p. 230.
45 Zygmunt Rukalski, *Canadian Slavonic Papers* (Fall 1969) 11:346–58.
46 Woolf, p. 448.
47 Mais, p. 304.
48 Peter Quennell, *New Statesman* (14 May 1927) 29:152.
49 Lantz, pp. 78, 84, 96, 114.
50 Ibid., pp. 150–1.
51 Ibid., pp. 171, 173.
52 Ibid., pp. 197, 200.
53 Ibid., p. 224.
54 Urbanski, pp. 48, 85.
55 M.V. Trofimov, *Modern Language Teaching* (1916) 12:176–86.
56 Lantz, p. 51.
57 Ibid., pp. 95, 119.
58 Joseph L. Conrad, *Slavic & East European Journal* (1966) 10:400–10.
59 Lantz, pp. 208, 216.
60 Jerome H. Katsell, *Slavic & East European Review* (Winter 1974) 18:377–83.
61 Toby W. Clyman, *Melbourne Slavonic Studies* (1978), no. 13, pp. 63–70.

Chapter 9. Letters; Sakhalin Island; The Shooting Party

1 Lantz, pp. 26–7.
2 Robert Birkmyre, *Fortnightly Review* (1 March 1919) n.s. 105:434–5.
3 *London Mercury* (May 1920) 2:94.
4 *Spectator* (31 July 1920) 125:150.
5 *Times Literary Supplement*, 13 Feb 1920, p. 103a.
6 Maurice Baring, *New Statesman* (21 Feb 1920) 14:586.
7 Edmund Gosse, *Books on the Table* (London: Heinemann, 1921), p. 71.
8 Robert Lynd, *Nation* (London) (28 Feb 1920) 26:742–4.
9 J. Middleton Murry, *Athenaeum*, 5 March 1920, p. 299.
10 George Sampson, *Bookman* (London) (March 1920) 57:206.
11 *Bookman* (New York) (May 1920) 51:327. Also, ibid. (Oct 1921) 54:155.
12 John Mason Brown, *Theatre Arts Monthly* (Jan 1925) 9:67.
13 Francis Hackett, *New Republic* (14 April 1920) 22:226–7.
14 Robert Morss Lovett, *Dial* (May 1920) 68:628–30.
15 William Lyon Phelps, *Forum* (Dec 1923) 70:2239–40.
16 J. Middleton Murry, *Discoveries* (London: Collins, 1924), p. 91.
17 Mansfield, p. 505.
18 *Bookman* (New York) (Dec. 1924) 60:506.
19 *New York Times Book Review*, 2 Nov 1924, p. 2.
20 Johan Smertenko, *Nation* (New York) (10 Dec 1924) 119:652–4.
21 Leo Wiener, *Saturday Review of Literature* (4 April 1925) 1:646.
22 D.S. Mirsky, *London Mercury* (July 1925) 12:324.
23 *Saturday Review* (London) (14 March 1925) 139:274.

24 *Spectator* (14 Feb 1925) 134:241.
25 Iris Barry, *Spectator* (21 March 1925) 134:460.
26 John Freeman, *Bookman* (London) (April 1925) 68:36.
27 J.B. Priestley, *Saturday Review* (London) (17 Oct 1925) 140:446.
28 Leonard Woolf, *Nation and Athenaeum* (21 Feb 1925) 36:717.
29 *Times Literary Supplement*, 12 March 1925, p. 169c.
30 Rosamond Gilder, *Theatre Arts Monthly* (April 1926) 20:277–8.
31 Robert Littell, *New Republic* (25 March 1925) 42:131–3.
32 Robert Morss Lovett, *New Republic* (4 Nov 1925) 44:286–7.
33 Stuart Sherman, *New York Herald Tribune Books*, 15 Nov 1925, pp. 1–3.
34 Pitirim Sorokin, *Saturday Review of Literature* (24 Sep 1927) 4:133–4.
35 Jacob Zeitlin, *Bookman* (New York) (Jan 1926) 62:607–8.
36 D.S. Mirsky, *London Mercury* (Sep 1926) 14:542.
37 John Cournos, *Dial* (Sep 1928) 85:261–4.
38 Alexander Nazaroff, *New York Times Book Review*, 18 Jan 1931, p. 2.
39 Lantz, pp. 151–2.
40 Gleb Struve, *Slavonic & East European Review* (June 1955) 33:327–41.
41 Lantz, pp. 187, 192.
42 Ibid., pp. xiii, 261.
43 Ibid., p. 97.
44 Ibid., p. 147.
45 Ibid., pp. 189, 203.
46 Ibid., pp. 212, 219, 223.
47. Joanne Trautman, ed., *Healing Arts in Dialogue* (So Ill Univ Pr, 1981), pp. 125–37.
48 *Times Literary Supplement*, 16 Dec 1926, p. 932c.
49 *Nation and Athenaeum* (29 Jan 1927) 40:602.
50 *Spectator* (27 Nov 1926) 137:976.
51 John Hagan, *Slavic & East European Journal* (1965) 9:123–40.

Chapter 10. One-Act Plays

1 C.E. Bechhofer, *Five Russian Plays* (Dutton, 1916), pp. xiii–xiv.
2 *Nation* (London) (11 Nov 1916) 20:232.
3 S.S. Koteliansky & Philip Tomlinson, eds. & trs., *The Life and Letters of Anton Chekhov* (London: Cassell, 1925), p. 155. Hereinafter called Koteliansky.
4 *New York Times*, 29 March 1914, 4:6.
5 Hiram K. Moderwell, *The Theatre of Today* (Lane, 1914), p. 193.
6 *New York World*, 25 May 1915.
7 *Boston Transcript*, 9 Feb 1915.
8 *Nation* (New York) (7 Sep 1916) 103:225.
9 S.R. Littlewood, *Pall Mall Gazette*, 26 Jan 1920, p. 3.
10 M. Lykiardopolous, *New Statesman* (31 Jan 1920) 14:496.
11 Francis Birrell, *Nation and Athenaeum* (5 June 1926) 39:248.
12 Wolcott Gibbs, *New Yorker* (14 Feb 1948) 23:44.
13 Lantz, pp. 222–3.
14 *Spectator* (19 Feb 1916) 116:264.
15 J. Ranken Towse, *Nation* (New York) (13 April 1916) 102:419.
16 S.R. Littlewood, *Pall Mall Gazette*, 26 Jan 1920, p. 3.
17 M. Lykiardopolous, *New Statesman* (31 Jan 1920) 14:496.
18 *Times* (London), 26 Jan 1920, p. 10b.

19 *Nation* (New York) (30 Jan 1929) 128:142.
20 Brooks Atkinson, *New York Times*, 15 Jan 1929, p. 22.
21 B. Roland Lewis, *The Technique of the One-Act Play* (Luce, 1918), p. 15.
22 Hallie Flanagan, *Theatre Arts Monthly* (Jan 1928) 12:70–1.
23 *Era*, 9 Dec 1931, p. 10.
24 Nick Worrall, *File on Chekhov* (London: Methuen, 1986), p. 18.
25 Jerome Mellquist, *One-Act Play Magazine* (March 1939) 2:841–8.
26 *Nation* (New York) (21 Nov 1912) 95:492.
27 Henry T. Perry, *Masters of Dramatic Comedy and Their Social Themes* (Harvard Univ Pr, 1939), p. 340.
28 Mel Gussow, *New York Times*, 26 March 1972, drama section.
29 Lantz, p. 36.
30 Henry T. Perry, p. 339.
31 J. Redmond, ed., *Themes in Drama: 5* (Cambridge Univ Pr, 1983).
32 Percival Wilde, *The Craftsmanship of the One-Act Play* (Little, Brown, 1923), p. 203.
33 Gibbs, p. 44.
34 *London Star*, 15 May 1917.
35 Littlewood, p. 3.
36 *Times* (London), 26 Jan 1921, p. 10b.
37 M. Lykiardopolous, p. 496.
38 Lantz, p. 112.
39 William Whitebait, *New Statesman & Nation* (22 Dec 1945) n.s. 30:424.
40 Gibbs, p. 44.
41 Mel Gussow, *New York Times*, 26 March 1972, drama section.

Chapter 11. Platonov; Ivanov; The Wood Demon

1 Lantz, pp. 45–6.
2 Grace Anshutz, *Yale Review* (June 1930) n.s. 19:860–1.
3 Lyle Donaghy, *Nation and Athenaeum* (10 May 1930) 47:192–3.
4 Walter Prichard Eaton, *New York Herald Tribune Books*, 9 March 1930, p. 13.
5 O.W. Firkins, *Saturday Review of Literature* (7 June 1930) 6:1104.
6 Arthur Hood, *Poetry Review* (1930) 31:196–200.
7 T.S. Matthews, *New Republic* (2 April 1930) 62:198–9.
8 Alexander Nazaroff, *New York Times Book Review*, 2 Feb 1930, p. 1.
9 *Spectator* (12 April 1930) 144:627.
10 *Time* (20 Jan 1930) 15:64.
11 David Magarshack, *Chekhov the Dramatist* (London: Lehmann, 1952), p. 68.
12 *Saturday Review* (New York), 30 May 1953, pp. 35–6.
13 Lantz, pp. 75, 84, 86.
14 Brooks Atkinson, *New York Times*, 15 May 1960, 2:1.
15 Lantz, p. 136.
16 Worrall, p. 26.
17 Lantz, p. 169.
18 Ibid., p. 217.
19 Frank Rich, *New York Times*, 5 Aug 1984, 2:7.
20 Benedict Nightingale, ibid., 14 Dec 1986, 2:1, 4.
21 Mel Gussow, ibid., 28 Dec 1986, 2:4.
22 Brendan Gill, *New Yorker* (29 Dec 1986) 62:76.
23 Paul Milyukov, *Athenaeum*, 6 July 1889, p. 27.

24 Lantz, pp. 10, 19.
25 *Nation* (New York) (21 Nov 1912) 95:492.
26 *English Review* (London) (Feb 1913) 13:502.
27 Neith Boyce, *Harper's Weekly* (27 Dec 1913) 58:22–3.
28 Trofimov, pp. 176–86.
29 Mansfield, pp. 80–2.
30 *New York Times*, 27 Nov 1923, p. 23.
31 *New York Tribune*, 27 Nov 1923, p. 13.
32 *New York World*, 28 Nov 1923, p. 12.
33 Frederick Donaghey, *Chicago Tribune*, 7 April 1924, p. 21.
34 Amy Leslie, *Chicago Daily News*, 7 April 1924, p. 20.
35 Kenneth Macgowan, *Theatre Arts Monthly* (April 1924) 8:215–28.
36 Leo Wiener, *The Contemporary Drama of Russia* (Little, Brown, 1924), p. 96.
37 E.A. Baughan, *Daily News* (London), 8 Dec. 1925, p. 9.
38 Ivor Brown, *Saturday Review* (London) (12 Dec 1925) 140:698–9.
39 J.T. Grein, *Illustrated London News*, 16 Jan 1926, p. 104.
40 *Morning Post* (London), 8 Dec 1925, p. 9.
41 *Stage* (London), 10 Dec 1925, p. 31.
42 *Times* (London), 8 Dec 1925, p. 14b.
43 Desmond MacCarthy, *New Statesman* (19 Dec 1925) 26:301.
44 Lantz, p. 39.
45 Ibid., pp. 75, 83.
46 Elisaveta Fen, *New York Times*, 5 Oct 1958, 2:3.
47 Lantz, pp. 93, 97.
48 Ibid., pp. 108, 109, 117, 119, 131.
49 John Gielgud, *New York Times*, 1 May 1966, 2:1, 3.
50 Stanley Kauffmann, ibid., 3 May 1966, 2:1.
51 Wilfred Sheen, *Commonweal* (27 May 1966) 84:283.
52 *Variety*, 23 Feb 1966.
53 Joseph S.M. Lau, *Contemporary Literature* (1969) 10:85–102.
54 Lantz, pp. 184, 193.
55 Benedict Nightingale, *New York Times*, 26 Sep 1976, 2:5.
56 Lantz, pp. 215, 217–8.
57 Marianna Stroyeva, *Soviet Literature* (1980), no. 2, pp. 138–46.
58 D.S. Mirsky, *Nation and Athenaeum* (4 Dec 1926) 40:340; *Observer* (London), 15 May 1927, p. 6.
59 *Times Literary Supplement* (11 Nov 1926) 25:790c.
60 *New Statesman* (21 May 1927) 29:190.
61 Lantz, pp. 39–40.
62 A.V. Cookman, *New York Times*, 7 Aug 1938, 9:1.
63 Eric Bentley, *Kenyon Review* (1949) 11:226–50.
64 Thomas G. Winner, *Slavic & East European Journal* (1961) 5:255–62.
65 Ian Matley, *Russian Review* (Oct 1972) 31:376–82.
66 Lantz, p. 239.

Chapter 12. The Sea Gull (1896)

1 Wiener, *Anthology of Russian Literature*, p. 459.
2 Homer Saint-Gaudens, *Critic* (April 1906) 48:318–23.
3 Christian Brinton, *Cosmopolitan* (April 1906) 40:616–7.

4 *Chicago Daily Journal,* 22 Feb 1906, p. 9.
5 James O'Donnell Bennett, *Chicago Record-Herald,* 22 Feb 1906, p. 8.
6 *Glasgow Evening Times,* 3 Nov 1909.
7 *Glasgow Herald,* 3 Nov 1909, p. 9.
8 Maurice Baring, *Landmarks in Russian Literature* (Macmillan, 1910), p. 273.
9 P. Kropotkin, *Athenaeum,* 24 Feb 1912, pp. 234–5.
10 *New York Times Book Review,* 5 May 1912, p. 272.
11 *Daily Telegraph* (London), 1 April 1912, p. 13; *Times* (London), 1 April, p. 12d; John Palmer, *Saturday Review* (London) (13 April) 113:653–4.
12 *Academy* (London), 13 April 1912, p. 471.
13 Huntly Carter, *New Age* (25 April 1912) n.s. 10:619.
14 Ashley Dukes, *Modern Dramatists* (Chicago: Sergel, 1913), pp. 190–210.
15 Barrett Clark, *The Continental Drama of Today* (Holt, 1914), pp. 62–5.
16 Emma Goldman, *The Social Significance of the Modern Drama* (Boston: Badger, 1914), pp. 283–93.
17 *New York Herald,* 23 May 1916, p. 9; *New York Times,* 23 May, p. 9; *New York World,* 23 May, p. 9; *Theatre* (July 1916) 24:10–1; Walter Prichard Eaton, *Plays and Players* (Cincinnati: Stewart & Kidd, 1916), pp. 408–9.
18 H.D. Fuller, *Nation* (New York) (1 June 1916) 102:603.
19 *New York Tribune,* 24 May 1916, p. 11.
20 Philip Littell, *New Republic* (17 June 1916) 7:175.
21 *Athenaeum,* 13 June 1919, pp. 469–70.
22 Gilbert Cannan, *Nation* (London) (7 June 1919) 25:293.
23 M. Lykiardopolous, *New Statesman* (7 June 1919) 13:238–9.
24 Storm Jameson, *Modern Drama in Europe* (London: Collins, 1920), pp. 245–53.
25 Quoted in Dorothy C. Bennett, *Arnold Bennett* (Kendall & Sharp, 1935), p. 184.
26 Wiener, *The Contemporary Drama of Russia,* pp. 101, 113–4.
27 *Spectator,* 31 Oct 1925, pp. 753–4; *Times* (London), 20 Oct, p. 12b; Ivor Brown, *Saturday Review* (London) (24 Oct) 140:472–3; Horace Shipp, *English Review* (Dec) 41:879–80.
28 *Stage,* 22 Oct 1925, p. 18; J.C. Squire, *London Mercury* (Dec) 13:200–1.
29 Francis Birrell, *Nation and Athenaeum* (31 Oct 1925) 38:180.
30 Desmond MacCarthy, *New Statesman* (14 Nov 1925) 26:143.
31 W.A. Darlington, *Daily Telegraph* (London), 17 Jan 1929, p.7.
32 *Era,* 23 Jan 1929, p. 1; *London Observer,* 20 Jan, p. 13; *Times* (London), 17 Jan, p. 10c.
33 *Nation and Athenaeum* (26 Jan 1929) 44:584.
34 *New Statesman* (26 Jan 1929) 32:497.
35 *Nation and Athenaeum* (5 Oct 1929) 46:15; *Times* (London), 26 Sep, p. 10c; Hannen Swaffer, *Sunday Express* (London), 29 Sep, p. 5.
36 Ivor Brown, *Saturday Review* (London) (5 Oct 1929) 148:378–9; St. John Ervine, *London Observer,* 29 Sep, p. 15; J.T. Grein, *Illustrated London News,* 5 Oct, p. 580.
37 Herbert Farjeon, *Graphic* (London) (5 Oct 1929) 126:23.
38 Richard Dana Skinner, *Commonweal* (8 May 1929) 10:21.
39 Brooks Atkinson, *New York Times,* 10 April 1929, p. 32; Howard Barnes, *New York Tribune,* 10 April, p. 24.
40 Joseph Wood Krutch, *Nation* (New York) (22 May 1929) 128:626–7.
41 Robert Benchley, *New Yorker* (28 Sep 1929) 5:41; Elizabeth Jordan, *America* (26 Oct) 42:68; Richard Dana Skinner, *Commonweal* (2 Oct) 10:564.
42 *Catholic World* (Dec 1929) 130:330–1; J. W. Krutch, *Nation* (N. Y.) (2 Oct) 129:366–7.
43 Brooks Atkinson, *New York Times,* 17 Sep 1929, p. 34; Francis Bellamy, *Outlook and Independent* (25 Dec) 153:672.

44 Stark Young, *New Republic* (9 Oct 1929) 60:205.

45 E.H. Carr, *Spectator* (20 July 1929) 143:72–3.

46 *Evening News* (London), 21 May 1936, p. 7; Charles Morgan, *New York Times*, 4 June, 9:1; Stephen Williams, *Evening Standard* (London), 21 May, p. 9.

47 *New English Weekly* (18 June 1936) 9:194–5.

48 Ashley Dukes, *Theatre Arts Monthly* (Sep 1936) 20:665–70.

49 *Times* (London), 21 May 1936, p. 14b; Ivor Brown, *London Observer*, 24 May; H.K Fisher, *Life & Letters Today* (Autumn) 15:162–3; Derek Verschoyle, *Spectator* (29 May) 156:978.

50 Desmond MacCarthy, *New Statesman & Nation* (30 May 1936) n.s. 11:858–60.

51 Lantz, pp. 53–4.

52 Stark Young, *New Republic* (13 April 1938) 94:305–6; ibid. (20 April) 94:332–3; *Theatre Arts Monthly* (Oct) 22:737–42.

53 Brooks Atkinson, *New York Times*, 29 March 1938, p. 19; George Jean Nathan, *Newsweek* 11:22; Euphemia Wyatt, *Catholic World* (May) 147:214–5.

54 *Variety* (30 March 1938) 130:56.

55 *New York Herald Tribune*, 27 March 1938, 6:2; John Mason Brown, *Evening Post* (New York), 29 March & 2 April; Grenville Vernon, *Commonweal* (15 April) 27:692.

56 *Time* (11 April 1938) 31:36–8; Brooks Atkinson, *New York Times*, 3 April, 9:1; Edith Isaacs, *Theatre Arts Monthly* (May) 22:326–8; Joseph Wood Krutch, *Nation* (New York) (9 April) 146:422–3.

57 Richard Watts Jr., *New York Herald Tribune*, 29 March 1938, p. 10.

58 C.J. Bulliet, *Chicago Daily News*, 10 Jan 1939, p. 17.

59 Cecil Smith, *Chicago Tribune*, 10 Jan 1939, p. 11.

60 Henry T. Perry, p. 345.

61 Cleanth Brooks & Robert B. Heilman, *Understanding Drama* (Holt, Rinehart & Winston, 1945), pp. 490–502.

62 Lantz, p. 63.

63 Brooks Atkinson, New York Times, 13 Sep 1953, p. 6.

64 Ibid., 23 May 1954, 2:1.

65 John Beaufort, *Christian Science Monitor*, 15 May 1954.

66 John Gassner, *Masters of the Drama*, 3rd ed. (Dover, 1954), pp. 508–20.

67 Thomas G. Winner, *American Slavic & East European Review* (Feb 1956) 15:103–11.

68 Lantz, pp. 91, 94, 97, 108, 114.

69 Howard Taubman, *New York Times*, 1 April 1962, 2:1.

70 Jim W. Miller, *Georgia Review* (1964) 18:98–115.

71 Lantz, pp. 130, 132, 133, 135.

72 Dorothy Seyler, *Modern Drama* (Sep 1965) 8:167–73.

73 Lantz, pp. 142, 145.

74 Ibid., pp. 159, 160, 164, 167.

75 Jacob Adler, *Journal of Modern Literature* (1970) 1:226–48.

76 Burton Kendle, *Modern Drama* (May 1970) 13:63–6.

77 James M. Curtis, *Canadian American Slavic Studies* (1972) 6:13–37.

78 Lantz, pp. 178, 187, 189, 190, 191, 193.

79 John Gruen, *New York Times*, 5 Jan 1975, 2:5.

80 Lantz, pp. 196, 201, 203.

81 Ibid., pp. 215, 223, 224.

82 Walter Kerr, *New York Times*, 23 Nov 1980, 2:3, 9.

83 Henry Popkin, *New York Times*, 7 Sep 1980, 2:3.

84 Lantz, pp. 232, 235, 239, 242, 248.

85 Carol Strongin, *Comparative Drama* (Winter 1981–82) 15:366–80.

86 Michael Manheim, *Eugene O'Neill Newsletter* (1982) 6:24.
87 George Stade, *New York Times Book Review*, 21 Nov 1982, p. 12.
88 Lantz, pp. 259–60.
89 Edith Oliver, *New Yorker*, 5 Dec 1983, p. 183.

Chapter 13. Uncle Vanya (1897)

1 *Independent* (5 Dec 1912) 73:1318.
2 *Nation* (New York) (21 Nov 1912) 95:492.
3 Ibid. (18 July 1912) 95:65.
4 *Daily Telegraph* (London), 12 May 1914, p. 6; E.A. Baughan, *Daily News & Leader* (London), 12 May, p. 3; Egan Mew, *Academy* (London), 23 May, pp. 662–3.
5 *Athenaeum*, 16 May 1914, p. 700; S.R. Littlewood, *Daily Chronicle* (London), 12 May, p. 4.
6 H.W. Massingham, *Nation* (London) (16 May 1914) 15:265–6.
7 *Times* (London), 12 May 1914, p. 11d.
8 Desmond MacCarthy, *New Statesman* (16 May 1914) 111:180–1.
9 *New Republic* (11 Dec 1915) 5:149.
10 James Agate, *Saturday Review* (London) (10 Dec 1921) 132:658–9.
11 *Sunday Times* (London), 4 Dec. 1921, p. 6; *Times* (London), 29 Nov, p. 8d; H.W. Massingham, *Nation and Athenaeum* (3 Dec) 30:390–2; W.J. Turner, *London Mercury* (Jan 1922) 5:311.
12 *Referee* (London), 4 Dec 1921, p. 7.
13 E. Graham Sutton, *Bookman* (London) (Dec 1921) 61:169–70.
14 Desmond MacCarthy, *New Statesman* (3 Dec 1921) 18:254–5.
15 *Spectator* (3 Dec 1921) 127:743–4.
16 W.J. Turner, *New Statesman* (11 Aug 1923) 21:521–2.
17 C. Nabokoff, *Contemporary Review* (March 1924) 125:338–46.
18 *New York World*, 29 Jan 1924, p. 13.
19 *New York Tribune*, 29 Jan 1924, p. 8.
20 *New York Times*, 29 Jan 1924, p. 16; Amy Leslie, *Chicago Daily News*, 12 April, p. 14.
21 Frederick Donaghey, *Chicago Tribune*, 11 April 1924, p. 21.
22 Konstantin Stanislavsky, *My Life in Art* (Little, Brown, 1924), pp. 361–6.
23 *Daily Herald* (London), 18 Feb 1926, p. 4; *Daily Telegraph* (London), 18 Jan, p. 13; *Spectator* (23 Jan) 136:124–5; *Times* (London), 18 Jan, p. 12c.
24 Francis Birrell, *Nation and Athenaeum* (23 Jan 1926) 38:583–4.
25 *Morning Post* (London), 18 Jan 1926, p. 7.
26 John Shand, *Adelphi* (March 1926) 3:691–3.
27 Horace Shipp, *English Review* (April 1926) 42:563–5.
28 *Daily Telegraph* (London), 1 May 1928, p. 8.
29 *London Observer*, 6 May 1928, p. 15.
30 *Times* (London), 1 May 1928, p. 14c.
31 Alison Smith, *New York World*, 25 May 1929, p. 13.
32 Brooks Atkinson, *New York Times*, 25 May 1929, p. 17.
33 Robert Littell, *New York World*, 16 April 1930, p. 15.
34 Ibid., *Theatre Magazine* (June 1930) 51:18–9.
35 Brooks Atkinson, *New York Times*, 16 April 1930, p. 26; R. Manieff, *New York World*, 20 April, metro section, p. 3.
36 Joseph Wood Krutch, *Nation* (New York) (7 May 1930) 130:554–6.
37 *Outlook & Independent* (30 April 1930) 154:711.

38 Stark Young, *New Republic* (30 April 1930) 62:299–300.
39 *Time* (28 April 1930) 15:68; William Lyon Phelps, *Scribner's Magazine* (Sep) 88:328; Euphemia Wyatt, *Catholic World* (June) 131:338–9.
40 Richard Dana Skinner, *Commonweal* (30 April 1930) 11:742–3.
41 John Hutchens, *Theatre Arts Monthly* (June 1930) 14:460–2.
42 George Jean Nathan, *New Freeman* (26 April 1930) 1:157.
43 Lloyd Lewis, *Chicago Daily News*, 21 Oct 1930, p. 15; Charles Collins, *Chicago Tribune*, 21 Oct, p. 29.
44 Jed Harris, *New York Times*, 23 July 1972, 2:1, 3, 23.
45 Walter Prichard Eaton, *New York Herald Tribune Books*, 6 July 1930, p. 11.
46 Henry Adler, *New English Weekly* (18 Feb 1937) 10:375.
47 Derek Verschoyle, *Spectator* (12 Feb 1937) 158:267.
48 *Times* (London), 6 Feb 1937, p. 10d; Ivor Brown, *London Observer*, 7 Feb, p. 15.
49 *Time & Tide* (13 Feb 1937) 18:192.
50 Desmond MacCarthy, *New Statesman and Nation* (13 Feb 1937) n.s. 13:241–2.
51 Dorothy L. Sayers, ibid. (27 Feb 1937) n.s. 13:324.
52 Henry T. Perry, pp. 346–7.
53 *Manchester Guardian*, 4 Sep 1943, p. 7.
54 *London News Chronicle*, 3 Sep 1943, p. 3; Desmond MacCarthy, *New Statesman and Nation* (11 Sep) 26:167–8; James Redfern, *Spectator* (10 Sep) 171:239.
55 Herbert Farjeon, *Time & Tide* (11 Sep 1943) 24:742.
56 Ashley Dukes, *Theatre Arts* (Dec 1943) 27:721-2.
57 *Times* (London), 17 Jan 1945, p. 6; Beverly Baxter, *Evening Standard*, 29 Jan, p. 6; Ivor Brown, *London Observer*, 21 Jan, p. 2; Desmond MacCarthy, *New Statesman and Nation* (27 Jan) 29:55–6; Philip Page, *Sphere* (27 Jan) 180:122.
58 Dido Milroy, *New English Weekly* (15 Feb 1945) 26:139.
59 Herbert Farjeon, *Sunday Graphic* (London), 21 Jan 1945, p. 12.
60 James Redfern, *Spectator* (26 Jan 1945) 174:79.
61 *Newsweek* (27 May 1946) 27:84; *Time* (27 May) 47:66; John Gassner, *Forum* (July) 106:79–80; Kappo Phelan, *Commonweal* (31 May) 44:166; Stark Young, *New Republic* (3 June) 114:805.
62 Wolcott Gibbs, *New Yorker* (25 May 1946) 22:44–6.
63 Euphemia Wyatt, *Catholic World* (July 1946) 163:357–8.
64 John Mason Brown, *Saturday Review of Literature* (1 June 1946) 29:32–4.
65 Joseph Wood Krutch, *Nation* (New York) (1 June 1946) 162:671.
66 Eric Bentley, *Kenyon Review* (Spring 1949) 11:226–50.
67 Louis Kronenberger, *The Republic of Letters* (Knopf, 1955) pp. 184–5.
68 Walter Kerr, *New York Herald Tribune*, 1 Feb 1956.
69 Brooks Atkinson, *New York Times*, 12 Feb 1956, 2:1.
70 Stark Young, ibid., 29 Jan 1956, 2:3.
71 Milton Esterow, ibid., 24 June 1956, 2:5.
72 Lantz, pp. 88, 91, 108.
73 Ibid., pp. 123, 127.
74 Matley, pp. 376–82.
75 Edgar L. Frost, *Russian Language Journal* (Winter 1977) 31:11–20.
76 Lantz, pp. 210, 224.
77 Clayton A. Hubbs, *Modern Drama* (June 1979) 22:115–24.
78 Worrall, pp. 52–3.
79 Benedict Nightingale, *New York Times*, 18 Sep 1983, 2:1.
80 Edith Oliver, *New Yorker*, 26 Sep 1983, pp. 126–7.
81 Lantz, p. 262.

Chapter 14. The Three Sisters (1901)

1 Chudakov, pp. 152, 161–2.
2 Simmons, pp. 542–3.
3 Valery Bryusov, *Athenaeum*, 20 July 1901, p. 86.
4 Urbanski, p. 101.
5 Yarmolinsky, *Letters*, p. 398.
6 Lantz, pp. 9, 14, 20.
7 Baring, *Landmarks in Russian Literature*, pp. 297–8.
8 Dukes, *Modern Dramatists*, pp. 190–210.
9 Gertrude Besse King, *New Republic* (8 July 1916) 7:256–8.
10 J. Ranken Towse, *Nation* (New York) (13 April 1916) 102:419.
11 Hamilton Fyfe, *English Review* (May 1917) 24:408–14.
12 Harley Granville Barker, *Seven Arts*, Sept 1917, pp. 659–61.
13 Arthur Ruhl, *Collier's* (28 July 1917) 59:18–22.
14 N. Teleshov, *A Writer Remembers* (London: Hutchinson, n.d.), p. 63.
15 *Morning Post* (London), 9 March 1920, p. 5.
16 *Times* (London), 9 March 1920, p. 14b; Ralph Wright, *Everyman* (20 March) 15:513–4.
17 May Bateman, *Fortnightly Review* (1 May 1920) n.s. 107:808–16.
18 Frank Swinnerton, *Nation* (London) (13 March 1920) 26:806.
19 *Athenaeum*, 19 March 1920, p. 378.
20 Desmond MacCarthy, *New Statesman* (13 March 1920) 14:676–7.
21 W.J. Turner, *London Mercury* (6 April 1920) 1:755–6.
22 Oliver Sayler, *The Russian Theatre* (Brentano's, 1922), pp. 45–63.
23 S. Hoare, *Golden Hind* (Oct 1923) 2:9–14.
24 Heywood Broun, *New York World*, 30 Jan 1923; Percy Hammond, *New York Tribune*, 30 Jan, p. 6; Alexander Woolcott, *New York Herald*, 31 Jan, p. 10.
25 John Corbin, *New York Times*, 30 Jan 1923, p. 12; ibid., 31 Jan, p. 14.
26 Sheppard Butler, *Chicago Tribune*, 18 April 1923, p. 21; Mollie Morris, *Chicago Daily News*, 17 April, p. 28.
27 *New York Times*, 4 June 1923, p. 13.
28 E.A. Baughan, *Daily News* (London), 17 Feb 1926, p. 5.
29 *Star* (London), 17 Feb 1926, p. 3; *Times* (London), 17 Feb, p. 12c; J.T. Grein, *Illustrated London News*, 27 Feb, p. 366; Desmond MacCarthy, *New Statesman* (6 March) 26:645–6; Milton Waldman, *London Mercury* (April) 13:648–9.
30 *Spectator* (27 Feb 1926) 136: 363–4.
31 *Nation and Athenaeum* (27 Feb 1926) 38:745; ibid. (30 Oct) 40:146.
32 Ivor Brown, *Saturday Review* (London) (27 Feb 1926) 141:257–8.
33 John Shand, *Adelphi* (Dec 1926) 4:379–82.
34 *Drama Calendar* (New York) (1 Nov 1926) 9:3–4; *New York Herald Tribune*, 27 Oct, p. 21.
35 Arthur Hornblow, *Theatre Magazine* (Jan 1927) 45:18; Joseph Wood Krutch, *Nation* (New York) (10 Nov 1926) 123:488; Gilbert Seldes, *Dial* (Jan 1927) 82:79.
36 Brooks Atkinson, *New York Times*, 27 Oct 1926, p. 24.
37 John Mason Brown, *Theatre Arts Monthly* (Jan 1927) 11:9–22.
38 Walter Prichard Eaton, *McNaught's Monthly* (Dec 1926) 6:187.
39 Stark Young, *The Theater* (Doran, 1927), p. 54.
40 *Nation and Athenaeum* (2 Nov 1929) 46:171; E.A. Baughan, *Daily News* (London), 24 Oct, p. 10.
41 *London Observer*, 27 Oct 1929, p. 15; *Times* (London), 24 Oct, p. 14c; Harris Deans, *Illustrated Sporting & Dramatic News* (London), 2 Nov., p. 294.

42 Ivor Brown, *Saturday Review* (London) (2 Nov 1929) 148:508.

43 Herbert Farjeon, *Graphic* (London) (9 Nov 1929) 126:275.

44 Desmond MacCarthy, *New Statesman* (30 Nov 1929) 34:263–4.

45 Burns Mantle, *American Playwrights of Today* (Dodd, Mead, 1929), p. 29.

46 *New York Herald Tribune*, 9 Jan 1930, p. 20; *New York Times*, 9 Jan, p. 22; *Time*, 20 Jan, p. 34; John Hutchens, *Theatre Arts Monthly* (March) 14:190–200.

47 Theodore Komisarjevsky, *Myself and the Theatre* (Dutton, 1930), pp. 135–41, 172.

48 *Manchester Guardian*, 13 Nov 1935, p. 6; *Times* (London), 13 Nov, p. 10b; James Agate, *Sunday Times* (London), 17 Nov, p. 6; Michael Sayers, *New English Weekly*, 21 Nov, p. 113; Derek Verschoyle, *Spectator* (15 Nov) 155:814.

49 Ivor Brown, *London Observer*, 17 Nov 1935, p. 17.

50 *New English Weekly* (10 Feb 1938) 12:354–5.

51 *Stage* (London), 3 Feb 1938, p. 10; Ivor Brown, *Illustrated London News* (12 Feb) 102:242; ibid., *London Observer*, 30 Jan; A.V. Cookman, *London Mercury* (March) 37:533–4; Rosamond Gilder, *Theatre Arts Monthly* (May) 22:373–4; John Grime, *Daily Express* (London), 29 Jan, p. 15; Rupert Hart-Davis, *Spectator* (4 Feb) 160:179; Desmond MacCarthy, *New Statesman & Nation* (5 Feb) n.s. 15:205–7.

52 *Time & Tide* (5 Feb 1938) 19:186.

53 Henry Adler, *London Mercury* (Nov 1938) 39:47–55.

54 Ashley Dukes, *Theatre Arts Monthly* (June 1938) 22:407–11.

55 Lionel Hale, *News Chronicle* (London), 1 Feb 1938, p. 9.

56 Paul Shishkoff, *Listener* (3 Nov 1938) 20:927–9.

57 Anita Block, *The Changing World in Plays and Theatre* (Little, Brown, 1939), pp. 68–75.

58 Henry T. Perry, p. 352.

59 *Variety* (18 Oct 1939) 136:50; Brooks Atkinson, *New York Times*, 16 Oct, p. 23; John Mason Brown, *New York Post*, 16 Oct; Rosamond Gilder, *Theatre Arts Monthly* (Dec) 23:851–64; Richard Watts Jr., *New York Herald Tribune*, 16 Oct, p. 11; Stark Young, *New Republic* (1 Nov) 199:368–9.

60 Grenville Vernon, *Commonweal* (27 Oct 1939) 31:14.

61 Gabriel Fallon, *Irish Monthly* (July 1940) 68:286–90.

62 Stark Young, tr., *The Three Sisters* (French, 1941), p. xix.

63 George Jean Nathan, *American Mercury* (Aug 1943) 57:236.

64 *New York Critics' Theatre Reviews, 1942*, vol. 3, pp. 135–8.

65 *Newsweek* (4 Jan 1943) 21:64; *Variety* (23 Dec 1942) 149:50; Wolcott Gibbs, *New Yorker* (2 Jan 1943) 18:32.

66 Mary McCarthy, *Partisan Review* (March–April 1943) 10:184–6.

67 Elizabeth Jordan, *America* (9 Jan 1943) 68:388; George Jean Nathan, *American Mercury* (March) 56:361 & (June) 56:749; James Vaughan, *Commonweal* (15 Jan) 37:326; Euphemia Wyatt, *Catholic World* (Feb) 156:597–8; Stark Young, *New Republic* (28 Dec 1942) 107:857.

68 Rosamond Gilder, *Theatre Arts Monthly* (Feb 1943) 27:73–6.

69 Joseph Wood Krutch, *Nation* (New York) (2 Jan 1943) 156:31–2.

70 Guthrie McClintic, *Theatre Arts Monthly* (April 1943) 27:212–5.

71 "Danchenko Directs," *Theatre Arts Monthly* (Oct 1943) 27:603–6.

72 Nina Toumanova, *America* (23 Sep 1944) 71:597.

73 *New York Times*, 15 July 1944, p. 12.

74 Lantz, p. 61.

75 Helen Muchnic, *An Introduction to Russian Literature* (Doubleday, 1947), p. 233.

76 Lantz, pp. 76, 79, 80, 82–3.

77 Brooks Atkinson, *New York Times*, 20 March 1955, 2:1.

78　Judith Crist, *New York Herald Tribune*, 28 Feb 1955.
79　Maurice Zolotow, *Theatre Arts* (May 1955) 39:87–8.
80　Brooks Atkinson, *New York Times*, 4 Oct. 1959, 2:1.
81　Lantz, pp. 101, 115.
82　Judith Crist, *New York Herald Tribune*, 23 June 1964.
83　Howard Taubman, *New York Times*, 5 July 1964, 2:1.
84　Robert Lewis, *Slings and Arrows* (Stein & Day, 1984).
85　Howard Taubman, *New York Times*, 21 Feb 1965, 2:1.
86　Lantz, pp. 133–4, 137–8.
87　Ibid., pp. 151–5.
88　Stanley Kauffmann, *New Republic* (1 Nov 1969) 161:33.
89　Lantz, pp. 163, 167, 169.
90　Ibid., pp. 174–6.
91　William Babula, *Modern Drama* (Dec 1975) 18:365–9.
92　Anna Quindlen, *New York Times*, 1 May 1977, 2:1.
93　Lantz, pp. 206, 212, 216, 222.
94　Ibid., pp. 240, 243.
95　Ibid., pp. 249, 255, 257, 260.
96　Mel Gussow, *New York Times*, 19 Feb 1984, p. 44.
97　Ibid., 5 Jan 1986, 2:3.
98　Vincent Canby, *New York Times*, 28 Dec 1986, 2:22.

Chapter 15.　The Cherry Orchard (1904)

1　Valery Brysuov, *Athenaeum*, 3 Sep 1904, p. 313.
2　Lantz, pp. 10, 11.
3　*Literary Digest* (30 April 1904) 28:619–20.
4　Lantz, p. 15.
5　Max Mandell, tr., *The Cherry Garden* (Yale Courant, 1908), pp. 7–10.
6　Lantz, p. 19.
7　Baring, pp. 288–99.
8　*Academy & Literature* (3 June 1911) 80:684; *Daily Telegraph* (London), 30 May, p. 14; *Nation* (London) (22 June) 92:633; *Times* (London), 30 May, p. 13d.
9　J.T. Grein, *Sunday Times* (London), 4 June 1911, p. 6.
10　*Morning Post* (London), 30 May 1911, p. 6: H.W. Massingham, *Nation* (London) (3 June) 92:359–60.
11　Arnold Bennett, *Books and Persons* (Doran, 1917), pp. 323–4.
12　John Palmer, *Saturday Review* (London) (3 June 1911) 111:677–8.
13　George Calderon, *Quarterly Review* (July 1912) 217:27–9.
14　*Nation* (London) (18 July 1912) 95:65; *Times Literary Supplement*, 1 Feb, p. 45a; Richard Burton, *Dial* (16 June) 52:470.
15　W.L. Courtney, *Quarterly Review* (July 1913) 219:80–103.
16　Storm Jameson, *Egoist* (16 March 1914) 1:116–7.
17　*Dramatist* (New York) (July 1915) 6:590–1.
18　Gertrude Besse King, *New Republic* (26 June 1915) 3:207.
19　*Spectator* (2 Jan 1915) 114:10–1.
20　Homer Woodbridge, *Dial* (8 Feb 1917) 62:100.
21　Brander Matthews, *North American Review* (Nov. 1917) 206:758.
22　J. Middleton Murry, *New Republic* (8 Sep 1920) 24:41–3.
23　*Morning Post* (London), 13 July 1920, p. 10; E.A. Baughan, *Daily News* (London), 13

July, p. 3; Sydney Carroll, *Sunday Times* (London), 18 July, p. 6; St. John Ervine, *London Observer*, 18 July, p. 11.

24 W.J. Turner, *London Mercury* (Aug 1920) 2:480.

25 Katherine Mansfield, *Athenaeum*, 16 July 1920, p. 91.

26 Frank Swinnerton, *Nation* (London) (17 July 1920) 27:498–9.

27 Virginia Woolf, *New Statesman* (24 July 1920) 15:446–7.

28 Harley Granville Barker, *The Exemplary Theatre* (London: Chatto & Windus, 1922), pp. 229, 246–7.

29 Kenneth Macgowan, *Freeman* (18 Oct 1922) 6:136–8.

30 Sheppard Butler, *Chicago Tribune*, 11 April 1923, p. 21; Percy Hammond, *New York Tribune*, 23 Jan, p. 8; Mollie Morris, *Chicago Daily News*, 11 April, p. 20; Robert A. Parker, *Independent* (3 Feb) 110:97–8 & (17 Feb) 110:140–1; Arthur Hobson Quinn, *Scribner's* (July) 74:63–71.

31 Heywood Broun, *New York World*, 23 Jan 1923.

32 John Corbin, *New York Times*, 23 Jan 1923, p. 18 & 28 Jan, 7:10.

33 Stark Young, *New Republic* (28 Feb 1923) 34:19–20 & *North American Review* (March) 217:343–52.

34 Edmund Wilson, *Dial* (March 1923) 74:319.

35 Ivor Brown, *Saturday Review* (London) (30 May 1925) 139:582–3.

36 A.E. Wilson, *London Star*, 26 May 1925, p. 6.

37 *Illustrated London News* (6 June 1925) 76:1136; *Spectator* (6 June) 134:924–5; *Times* (London), 26 May, p. 14c; E.A. Baughan, *Daily News* (London), 26 May, p. 8; Francis Birrell, *Nation and Athenaeum* (30 May) 37:267–8; Arnold Gibbons, *Adelphi* (July) 3:129–30; Desmond MacCarthy, *New Statesman* (13 June) 25:253–4; Graham Sutton, *Bookman* (London) (July) 68:231–2.

38 James Agate, *Sunday Times* (London), 25 May 1925, p. 4.

39 Ashley Dukes, *Illustrated Sporting & Dramatic News*, 6 June 1925, p. 632.

40 *Times* (London), 29 Sep 1926, p. 10c.

41 *Nation and Athenaeum* (9 Oct 1926) 40:21; Desmond MacCarthy, *New Statesman* (2 Oct) 27:706.

42 Brooks Atkinson, *New York Times*, 6 March 1928, p. 20 & 11 March, 8:1.

43 *New Statesman* (28 April 1928) 31:81–2; *Times* (London), 12 April, p. 10b; James Agate, *Sunday Times* (London), 15 April, p. 6.

44 Ivor Brown, *Manchester Guardian*, 12 April 1928, p. 10; ibid., *Saturday Review* (London) (21 April) 145:491–2.

45 Brooks Atkinson, *New York Times*, 18 Nov 1928, 9:1; V.F. Calverton, *Modern Quarterly* (Spring 1929) 5:267; Francis Fergusson, *Hound & Horn* (April–June 1930) 3:416; Robert Littell, *Theatre Arts Monthly* (Dec 1928) 12: 858–70; Richard Watts Jr., *New York Tribune*, 16 Oct 1928, p. 26; Euphemia Wyatt, *Catholic World* (April 1929) 129:78–80.

46 Joseph Wood Krutch, *Nation* (New York) (31 Oct 1928) 127:461.

47 Brooks Atkinson, *New York Times*, 8 Nov 1928, p. 26 & 2 June 1929, 8:1.

48 Harley Granville Barker, *On Dramatic Method* (London: Sidgwick & Jackson, 1931), pp. 186–7.

49 J.B. Priestley, *Theatre Arts Monthly* (Aug 1930) 14:655–9.

50 Anna Miller, *The Independent Theatre in Europe* (Long & Smith, 1931), p. 339.

51 Francis Fergusson, *Bookman* (New York) (Nov 1931) 74:298–9.

52 Brooks Atkinson, *New York Times*, 7 March 1933, p. 20; Lucius Beebe, *New York Herald Tribune*, 7 March, p. 10; Richard Dana Skinner, *Commonweal* (19 April) 17:693.

53 Cy Caldwell, *New Outlook* (April 1933) 161:47.

54 John Mason Brown, *New York Evening Post*, 18 & 20 March, 1933.
55 W.A. Darlington, *Daily Telegraph* (London), 10 Oct 1933, p. 10; Ashley Dukes, *Theatre Arts Monthly* (Dec) 17:922–8; Leslie Rees, *Era*, 11 Oct, p. 8.
56 *Times* (London), 10 Oct 1933, p. 12c; Derek Verschoyle, *Spectator* (20 Oct) 151:522.
57 *Time & Tide* (21 Oct 1933) 14:1267.
58 Desmond MacCarthy, *New Statesman & Nation* (21 Oct 1933) n.s. 6:481–2.
59 Elizabeth Drew, *Discovering Drama* (Norton, 1937), p. 164.
60 Stark Young, *New Republic* (8 June 1938) 95:130–1.
61 Henry T. Perry, pp. 353–7.
62 *London Observer*, 31 Aug 1941; *Times* (London), 29 Aug, p. 6c; Graham Greene, *Spectator* (5 Sep) 167:235.
63 Alan Dent, *Time & Tide* (6 Sep 1941) 22:752–3.
64 Francis Fergusson, *Kenyon Review* (1943) 5:495–507.
65 Ivar Spector, *The Golden Age of Russian Literature*, rev. ed. (Caldwell, ID: Caxton, 1943), pp. 209–210.
66 *New York Theatre Critics' Reviews, 1944*, vol. 5, pp. 276–9.
67 Rosamond Gilder, *Theatre Arts* (April 1944) 28:197–208; Margaret Marshall, *Nation* (New York) (5 Feb 1944) 158:167; George Jean Nathan, *American Mercury* (March 1945) 60:318; Kappo Phelan, *Commonweal* (11 Feb 1944) 39:420.
68 *Time* (7 Feb 1944) 43:94.
69 *Variety* (12 Jan 1944) 153:58 (no. 5) & (2 Feb) 153:44 (no. 8).
70 Elizabeth Jordan, *America* (12 Feb 1944) 70:529; Stark Young, *New Republic* (7 Feb) 110:180–1 & (14 Feb) 110:211.
71 Euphemia Wyatt, *Catholic World* (March 1944) 158:584–5.
72 Margaret Webster, *New York Times*, 23 Jan 1944, 2:1.
73 Olga Knipper-Chekhov, ibid., 19 March 1944, 2:1.
74 Francis Fergusson, *The Idea of a Theater* (Doubleday, 1953), pp. 175–9, 185, 190. Orig. ed. 1949.
75 Charles W. Meister, *Poet Lore* (Autumn 1950) 55:249–57.
76 Ibid., *American Slavic & East European Review* (Feb 1953) 12:109–21.
77 Lantz, pp. 73–4, 82.
78 Ibid., pp. 89–93, 97.
79 Ibid., pp. 102, 111, 115.
80 Jean-Louis Barrault, *The Theatre of Jean-Louis Barrault* (Hill & Wang, 1961), pp. 104–11.
81 Walter Kerr, *New York Herald Tribune*, 15 Nov 1962.
82 Michael Smith, *Village Voice*, 22 Nov 1962.
83 Robert Brustein, *The Theatre of Revolt* (Little, Brown, 1962), pp. 137–79.
84 Lantz, pp. 122, 127.
85 Howard Taubman, *New York Times*, 21 Feb 1965, 2:1.
86 Karl S. Guthke, *Modern Tragicomedy* (Random House, 1966), pp. 22, 66, 79, 140.
87 Lantz, p. 138.
88 J.L. Styan, *Dark Comedy*, 2nd ed. (Cambridge Univ Pr, 1968), pp. 74–8.
89 Clive Barnes, *New York Times*, 20 March 1968, p. 41.
90 Martin Gottfried, *Women's Wear Daily*, 20 March 1968.
91 Lantz, pp. 154–6, 159, 165.
92 Ibid., pp. 174, 177.
93 Edward Mabley, *Dramatic Construction* (Chilton, 1972), pp. 151–2.
94 Lantz, p. 181.
95 Laurence Senelick, *Prologue* (Tufts Univ Theater) (Nov 1973) 29:1.
96 Lantz, pp. 198, 200, 203, 213.

97 Edgar L. Frost, *Russian Language Journal* (Winter 1977) 31:111–20.
98 Richard Eder, *New York Times Magazine*, 13 Feb 1977, p. 42.
99 Walter Kerr, *New York Times*, 27 Feb 1977, 2:1.
100 Jack Kroll, *Newsweek* (28 Feb 1977) 89:78.
101 Lally Weymouth, *New York Times*, 6 March 1977, 2:5.
102 Lantz, pp. 221–2, 225, 229.
103 Mel Gussow, *New York Times*, 9 Aug 1981, 2:3.
104 Lantz, pp. 246, 256.
105 Jane Kramer, *New Yorker*, 31 Oct. 1983, pp. 132–3.

Chapter 16. High Points in Chekhov Criticism

See the bibliography for sources referred to in this chapter.

Bibliography

Albright, Evelyn May. Introduction to Anton Chekhov, *Short Stories*. Tr. by Constance Garnett. New York: Macmillan, 1928.

Avilov, Lydia. *Chekhov in My Life*. Tr. by David Magarshack. London: Lehmann, 1950.

Baring, Maurice. *Landmarks in Russian Literature*. New York: Macmillan, 1910.

Barricelli, Jean-Pierre, ed. *Chekhov's Great Plays: A Critical Anthology*. New York: New York University Press, 1981.

Basu, Sankar. *Chekhov and Tagore*. New Delhi: Sterling, 1985.

Berlin, Normand. *The Secret Cause*. Amherst: University of Massachusetts Press, 1981.

Bitsilli, Peter M. *Chekhov's Art: A Stylistic Analysis*. Tr. by Toby W. Clyman and Edwina Cruise. Ann Arbor: Ardis, 1983.

Brahms, Caryl. *Reflections in a Lake: A Study of Chekhov's Four Greatest Plays*. London: Weidenfeld & Nicholson, 1976.

Brewster, Dorothy and Angus Burrell. *Dead Reckonings in Fiction*. New York: Longmans, Green, 1924.

Bristow, Eugene K., ed. & tr. *Anton Chekhov's Plays*. New York: Norton, 1977.

Bruford, Walter H. *Anton Chekhov*. London: Bowes & Bowes, 1957.

_____. *Chekhov and His Russia: A Sociological Study*. London: Paul, Trench & Trubner, 1948.

Calderon, George, tr. *Two Plays by Tchekhof*. London: Richards, 1912.

Chudakov, A.P. *Chekhov's Poetics*. Tr. by Edwina Cruise and Donald Dragt. Ann Arbor: Ardis, 1983. Orig. ed. 1971.

Chukovsky, Kornei. *Chekhov the Man*. Tr. by Pauline Rose. London: Hutchinson, 1945.

Clardy, Jess V. and Betty S. Clardy. *The Superfluous Man in Russian Letters*. Wash, DC: University Press of America, 1980.

Clyman, Toby W. *A Chekhov Companion*. Westport, CT: Greenwood, 1985.

Corrigan, Robert W., tr. *Six Plays of Chekhov*. New York: Holt, Rinehart & Winston, 1962.

Debreczeny, Paul and Thomas Eekman, eds. *Chekhov's Art of Writing: A Collection of Critical Essays*. Columbus, OH: Slavica, 1977.

Dillon, E.J. *Review of Reviews* (London) (July 1891) 4:79–83.

Dunnigan, Ann, tr. *Anton Chekhov: Selected Stories*. New York: Signet, 1960.

Eekman, Thomas, ed. *Anton Chekhov, 1860–1904. Some Essays*. Leiden: Brill, 1960.

Egri, Peter. *Chekhov and O'Neill: The Uses of the Short Story in Chekhov's and O'Neill's Plays*. Budapest: Akademiai Kiado, 1986.

Ehrenburg, Ilya. *Chekhov, Stendhal and Other Essays*. London: Macgibbon & Kee, 1962.

Eisen, Donald G. *The Art of Anton Chekhov: Principles of Technique in His Drama and Fiction*. Ph.D. dissertation. University of Pittsburgh, 1982.

Elton, Oliver. *Chekhov*. Oxford: Clarendon Press, 1929.

Emeljanow, Victor, ed. *Chekhov: The Critical Heritage*. London: Routledge & Kegan, 1981.

Ermilov, Vladimir. *Anton Pavlovich Chekhov, 1860–1904.* Tr. by Ivy Litvinov. Moscow: Foreign Languages Publishing House, 1956.

Esenwein, J. Berg. *Lippincott's Monthly* (Sep 1912) 90:363–78.

Fen, Elisaveta. *Anton Chekhov: Three Plays.* London: Penguin, 1951.

————. *Plays: Anton Chekhov.* London: Penguin, 1959.

Fennell, John, ed. *Nineteenth-Century Russian Literature.* Berkeley: University of California Press, 1973.

Fernald, John. *Sense of Direction.* New York: Stein & Day, 1968.

Friedland, Louis S., ed. & tr. *Letters on the Short Story, the Drama, and Other Literary Topics, by Anton Chekhov.* New York: Minto Balch, 1924.

Garnett, Constance, tr. *Letters of Anton Tchehov to His Family and Friends.* London: Chatto & Windus, 1920.

Garnett, Edward. *Quarterly Review* (Oct 1921) 236:257–69.

Gerhardi, William. *Anton Chehov: A Critical Study.* London: Cobden-Sanderson, 1923.

Gilles, Daniel. *Chekhov: Observer Without Illusion.* Tr. by Charles L. Markman. New York: Funk & Wagnalls, 1967.

Goldstone, Herbert, ed. *Chekhov's The Cherry Orchard.* Boston: Allyn & Bacon, 1965.

Gorky, Maxim. *Reminiscences of Tolstoy, Chekhov, and Andreyev.* New York: Viking, 1959. Orig. ed. 1920.

Gottlieb, Vera. *Chekhov and the Vaudeville: A Study of Chekhov's One-Act Plays.* Cambridge: Cambridge University Press, 1982.

Guthrie, Tyrone and Leonid Kipnis, trs. *The Cherry Orchard.* Minneapolis: University of Minnesota Press, 1965.

Hahn, Beverly. *Chekhov: A Study of the Major Stories and Plays.* Cambridge: Cambridge University Press, 1977.

Heim, Michael H. and Simon Karlinsky, trs. *Anton Chekhov's Life and Thought: Selected Letters and Commentary.* Berkeley: University of Calif Press, 1973.

Hellman, Lillian, ed. *The Selected Letters of Anton Chekhov.* Tr. by Sidonie Lederer. New York: Farrar & Straus, 1955.

Hingley, Ronald. *Chekhov: A Biographical and Critical Study.* London: Allen & Unwin, 1950.

————, ed. & tr. *Chekhov: Five Major Plays.* London: Oxford University Press, 1977.

————. *A New Life of Anton Chekhov.* London: Oxford University Press, 1976.

————, ed. & tr. *The Oxford Chekhov.* 9 vols. London: Oxford University Press:
    Vol. 1. *Short Plays* (1968)
    Vol. 2. *Platonov; Ivanov; The Sea Gull* (1967)
    Vol. 3. *Uncle Vanya; The Three Sisters; The Cherry Orchard; The Wood Demon (1964)*
    Vol. 4. *Stories, 1880–88* (1980)
    Vol. 5. *Stories, 1889–91* (1970)
    Vol. 6. *Stories, 1892–93* (1971)
    Vol. 7. *Stories, 1893–95* (1978)
    Vol. 8. *Stories, 1895–97* (1965)
    Vol. 9. *Stories, 1898–1904* (1975)

Hulanicki, Leo and David Savignac, eds. & trs. *Anton Cexov as a Master of Story-Writing.* The Hague: Mouton, 1976.

Jackson, Robert Louis, ed. *Chekhov: A Collection of Critical Essays.* Englewood Cliffs, NJ: Prentice-Hall, 1967.

Jones, Frances H., tr. *St. Peter's Day and Other Tales.* New York: Capricorn, 1949.

Josephson, Matthew, ed. *The Personal Papers of Anton Chekhov.* New York: Lear, 1948.

Kirk, Irina. *Anton Chekhov.* Boston: Hall, 1981.

Koteliansky, S.S. and Philip Tomlinson, eds. & trs. *The Life and Letters of Anton Tchekhov.* London: Cassell, 1925.

Kramer, Karl D. *The Chameleon and the Dream: The Image of Reality in Cexov's Stories.* The Hague: Mouton, 1970.

Laffitte, Sophie. *Chekhov: 1860–1904.* Tr. by Moura Budberg and Gordon Latta. New York: Scribner, 1973. Orig. ed. 1971.

Lantz, Kenneth A. *Anton Chekhov: A Reference Guide to Literature.* Boston: Hall, 1985.

Long, R.E.C. *Fortnightly Review* (1 July 1902) n.s. 72:103–18.

Lucas, Frank L. *The Drama of Chekhov, Synge, Yeats and Pirandello.* London: Cassell, 1963.

McConkey, James. *To a Distant Island.* New York: Dutton, 1984.

McMillin, Arnold B. *Chekhov Plays.* London: Heron, 1969.

Magarshack, David. *Chekhov the Dramatist.* London: Lehmann, 1952.

_____. *Chekhov: A Life.* London: Faber, 1952.

_____. *The Real Chekhov: An Introduction to Chekhov's Last Plays.* London: Allen & Unwin, 1972.

Mais, S.P.B. *Why We Should Read–.* New York: Dodd, Mead, 1921.

Makanowitzsky, Barbara, tr. *Anton Chekhov: Seven Short Novels.* New York: Norton, 1971.

Master, Carol Tendler. *The Development of the Chekhovian Scene: A Study in Dramatic Technique.* Ph.D. dissertation. Columbia University, 1982.

Meister, Charles W. *Chekhov Bibliography.* Jefferson, NC: McFarland, 1985.

_____. *English and American Criticism of Chekhov.* Ph.D. dissertation. University of Chicago, 1948.

Melchinger, Siegfried. *Anton Chekhov.* Tr. by Edith Tarcov. New York: Ungar, 1972.

Mirsky, D.S. *A History of Russian Literature.* New York: Knopf, 1949. Orig. ed. 1927.

Nabokov, Vladimir. *Lectures on Russian Literature.* New York: Harcourt Brace Jovanovich, 1981.

Nemirovsky, Irene. *A Life of Chekhov.* Tr. by Erik de Mauny. London: Grey Walls Press, 1950.

Nilsson, Nils Ake. *Studies in Chekhov's Narrative Technique.* Stockholm: Almqvist & Wiksell, 1968.

Ober, William B. *Boswell's Clap and Other Essays.* Carbondale: Southern Illinois University Press, 1979.

O'Toole, L. Michael. *Structure, Style, and Interpretation in the Russian Short Story.* New Haven: Yale University Press, 1982.

Payne, Robert, tr. *The Image of Chekhov.* New York: Knopf, 1963.

Peace, Richard A. *Chekhov: A Study of the Four Major Plays.* New Haven: Yale University Press, 1983.

Perry, F.M. *Story Writing: Lessons from the Masters.* New York: Holt, 1926.

Perry, Henry T. *Masters of Dramatic Comedy and Their Social Themes.* Cambridge: Harvard University Press, 1939.

Persky, Serge. *Contemporary Russian Novelists.* Freeport, NY: Books for Libraries Press, 1968. Orig. ed. 1913.

Pitcher, Harvey. *The Chekhov Play: A New Interpretation.* London: Chatto & Windus, 1973.

Poggioli, Renato. *The Phoenix and the Spider.* Cambridge: Harvard Univ. Press, 1957.

Popkin, Henry, ed. *The Cherry Orchard.* Tr. by Avrahm Yarmolinsky. New York: Avon, 1965.

Priestley, J.B. *Anton Chekhov.* London: International Profiles, 1970.

Rayfield, Donald. *Chekhov: The Evolution of His Art.* London: Elek Books, 1975.

Redmond, James, ed. *Drama and Symbolism.* Cambridge: Cambridge University Press, 1982.

Reeve, Franklin D. *The Russian Novel.* London: Muller, 1966.

Saunders, Beatrice. *Tchehov the Man*. London: Centaur, 1960.

Senelick, Laurence. *Anton Chekhov*. London: Macmillan, 1985.

Simmons, Ernest J. *Chekhov: A Biography*. Boston: Little, Brown, 1962.

Slonim, Marc. *Modern Russian Literature from Chekhov to the Present*. London: Oxford University Press, 1953.

Smith, Virginia Llewellyn. *Anton Chekhov and the Lady with a Dog*. London: Oxford University Press, 1973.

Speirs, Logan. *Tolstoy and Chekhov*. Cambridge: Cambridge University Press, 1971.

Stowell, H. Peter. *Literary Impressionism, James and Chekhov*. Athens: University of Georgia Press, 1980.

Styan, J.L. *Chekhov in Performance: A Commentary on the Major Plays*. Cambridge: Cambridge University Press, 1971.

Toumanova, Nina A. *Anton Chekhov: The Voice of Twilight Russia*. New York: Columbia University Press, 1937.

Troyat, Henri. *Chekhov*. Tr. by Michael H. Heim. New York: Dutton, 1986. Orig. French ed. 1984.

Tulloch, John. *Chekhov: A Structuralist Study*. London: Macmillan, 1980.

Urbanski, Henry. *Chekhov as Viewed by His Russian Literary Contemporaries*. Wroclaw, Poland: Wroclaw University Press, 1979.

Valency, Maurice. *The Breaking String: The Plays of Anton Chekhov*. London: Oxford University Press, 1966.

Waliszewski, Kazimierz. *A History of Russian Literature*. New York: Appleton, 1900.

Wellek, René and Nonna D. Wellek, eds. *Chekhov: New Perspectives*. Englewood Cliffs, NJ: Prentice-Hall, 1984.

Werth, Alexander. *Slavonic Review* (London) (March 1925) 3:622–41.

West, Julius, tr. *Plays by Anton Tchekoff: Second Series*. London: Duckworth, 1915.

Wilks, Ronald, tr. *The Kiss and Other Stories*. Harmondsworth: Penguin, 1982.

Williams, Raymond. *Drama in Performance*. New York: Basic Books, 1968.

Winner, Anthony. *Characters in the Twilight: Hardy, Zola, and Chekhov*. Charlottesville: University Press of Virginia, 1981.

Winner, Thomas G. *Chekhov and His Prose*. New York: Holt, Rinehart & Winston, 1966.

Worrall, Nick. *File on Chekhov*. London: Methuen, 1986.

Yarmolinsky, Avrahm, ed. & tr. *Letters of Anton Chekhov*. New York: Viking, 1973.

_____, ed. & tr. *The Portable Chekhov*. New York: Viking, 1947.

_____, ed. & tr. *The Unknown Chekhov*. New York: Noonday Press, 1954.

Index